THE GREAT BLACK SPIDER
ON ITS KNOCK-KNEED TRIPOD

Reflections of Cinema in Early
Twentieth-Century Italy

MICHAEL SYRIMIS

The Great Black Spider on Its Knock-Kneed Tripod

Reflections of Cinema in Early Twentieth-Century Italy

UNIVERSITY OF TORONTO PRESS
Toronto Buffalo London

Printed on acid-free, 100% post-consumer recycled paper
with vegetable-based inks.

Toronto Italian Studies

Library and Archives Canada Cataloguing in Publication

Syrimis, Michael, 1962–
The great black spider on its knock-kneed tripod: reflections of cinema in
early twentieth-century Italy / Michael Syrimis.

(Toronto Italian studies)
Includes bibliographical references and index.
ISBN 978-1-4426-4401-4

1. Motion pictures – Italy – History – 20th century.   2. Motion pictures and
literature – Italy – History – 20th century.   3. Marinetti, Filippo Tommaso,
1876–1944 – Criticism and interpretation.   4. D'Annunzio, Gabriele,
1863–1938 – Criticism and interpretation.   5. Pirandello, Luigi, 1867–1936 –
Criticism and interpretation.   I. Title.   II. Series: Toronto Italian studies

PN1993.5.188S97 2012   791.430945'09041   C2012-902654-9

This book has been published with the assistance of a grant from Tulane
University, School of Liberal Arts Dean's Office.

University of Toronto Press acknowledges the financial assistance
to its publishing program of the Canada Council for the Arts
and the Ontario Arts Council.

 Canada Council   Conseil des Arts
for the Arts   du Canada
 ONTARIO ARTS COUNCIL
CONSEIL DES ARTS DE L'ONTARIO

University of Toronto Press acknowledges the financial
support of the Government of Canada through the Canada Book
Fund for its publishing activities.

To Barbara and George Syrimis

Contents

Contents

Acknowledgments

I owe this book to the support of many individuals and institutions. I express my deepest gratitude to my friend Armando Maggi, professor at the University of Chicago, for his continued mentorship throughout my academic career in general and the completion of this project in particular. My deepest gratitude also goes to Matthew Howard, whose friendship and extensive background in the academic publishing industry have benefitted me in important ways.

My mentors at the University of Chicago helped me to shape this work conceptually at its earliest stages. Many thanks to Professors Yuri Tsivian, Rebecca West, and especially Miriam Hansen, who, prior to her arrival at Chicago, was the first to inspire my dedication to the study of film during my undergraduate studies at Rutgers University.

Friends and colleagues expressed their devotion in many ways, by discussing parts of the manuscript, helping me to translate text, making suggestions on planning, and more. Thank you very much my friends, Beatrice Arduini, George Bernstein, Laura Ferretti, John Garganigo, Ora Gelley, Akis Ioannides, Suzanne Magnanini, Giorgio Mobili, Kyriakos Papadopoulos, Raffaella Sforza, Tom Strider, and Michele White. I thank especially Kevin Greer, who proofread an early draft of the entire manuscript.

The publication of my manuscript was made possible through a generous grant from Tulane University, School of Liberal Arts Dean's Office. I am grateful to Dean Carole Haber for her support. The dean as well as my colleagues in the Department of French and Italian all provided a motivating and stimulating environment that made this project feasible and enjoyable. I thank Jean-Godefroy Bidima, Fayçal Falaky, Hope Glidden, Erec Koch, Elizabeth Poe, Vaheed Ramazani, and Jeanny Keck. I am especially grateful to Linda Carroll for sharing her rich knowledge in Italian language, literature, and history. Special thanks go also to Felicia McCarren for our many enlightening discussions on film studies and early twentieth-century modernity. Thomas Klingler followed my progress and offered invaluable advice about the publishing process.

I owe parts of the manuscript to a Tulane University Committee on Research Summer Fellowship and a Tulane University Research Enhancement Fund Phase II grant, which allowed me to conduct library and archival research in the United States and Italy in 2006, 2007, and 2008. I thank George Bernstein and Anne McCall of the School of Liberal Arts, who at the time were dean and associate dean, respectively, and assisted me greatly in applying for the above grants.

The generosity and warm hospitality of the following individuals made my research in Italy efficient and fruitful: Valentina Abbatecola, Alberto Blasetti, Laura Ceccarelli, Debora Demontis, Enrico Di Addario, Marco Giovannini, Antonella Montaldi, Laura Pompei, Stefania Tuveri, and above all Americo Bazzoffia, of the Centro Sperimentale di Cinematografia in Rome; Alfredo Barbina, Dina Saponaro, and Lucia Torsello, of the Studio di Pirandello in Rome; the staff of the Biblioteca Universitaria Alessandrina and the Biblioteca Nazionale Centrale in Rome in May 2007; the staff of the Sala Periodici at the Biblioteca Nazionale Centrale in Florence in June 2007; Stefania Carta, Stella Dagna, Claudia Gianetto, and especially Anna Sperone, of the Cineteca del Museo Nazionale del Cinema in Turin.

I was honoured to present a chapter of the manuscript to the Tulane University Seminar on Historical Change and Social Theory. I thank the coordinators, Michele White and Justin Wolfe, for this opportunity, Michael Wood for his insightful comments as the respondent, and the participants on 8 March 2010 for the stimulating discussion and valuable feedback.

I extend my gratitude to Ron Schoeffel, acquisitions editor at the University of Toronto Press, for his faith in my project and tireless dedication to its completion. I also had two highly supportive readers of the manuscript, whom I thank deeply for their insightful comments and constructive criticism.

The following individuals kindly granted me permission to reuse my copyrighted work or assisted me with this process: Anthony Julian Tamburri of Bordighera Press; Jana O'Keefe Bazzoni and Susan Tenneriello of *The Journal of the Pirandello Society of America*; Konrad

Eisenbichler and Gabriele Scardellato of *Quaderni d'italianistica*; and Monica Rector and Grant Gearhart of *Romance Notes*.

I extend my thanks to the persons and organizations who granted me permission to reproduce images and/or assisted me with the reproductions: Mallory Jacobs of Kino Lorber Incorporated; Jeffrey Wechsler and Kiki Michael of the Jane Voorhees Zimmerli Art Museum; Annika Keller of Art Resource; the Artists Rights Society; Mario Militello of *Bianco e Nero*, Centro Sperimentale di Cinematografia; Brooke Sansosti of the Newcomb Art Department, Tulane University; and especially John C. O'Day of the Language Learning Center, Tulane University. In spite of my efforts, I have not been able to identify the owners of the copyright for the still images from the 1916 film *Vita futurista*.

Finally, I could not have completed this work without the support of my mother and father and the rest of my family. I thank my sister-in-law Lefkí for our frequent and pleasant conversations about the progress of my work. I also thank Marfé for sharing my enthusiasm.

Illustrations

Abbreviations

'Del cinema'	Gabriele D'Annunzio, 'Del cinematografo considerato come strumento di liberazione e come arte di trasfigurazione'
Humor	Luigi Pirandello, *On Humor*
Pleasure	Gabriele D'Annunzio, *Il piacere (The Pleasure)*
PRI	Gabriele D'Annunzio, *Prose di romanzi*, vol. 1
PRII	Gabriele D'Annunzio, *Prose di romanzi*, vol. 2
Shoot!	Luigi Pirandello, *Shoot!: The Notebooks of Serafino Gubbio, Cinematograph Operator*
Sp	Filippo Tommaso Marinetti, 'Speed'
SPSV	Luigi Pirandello, *Saggi, poesie, scritti varii*
TIF	Filippo Tommaso Marinetti et al., *Teoria e invenzione futurista*
TR	Luigi Pirandello, *Tutti i romanzi*
TSM	Gabriele D'Annunzio, *Tragedie, sogni e misteri*
Vel	Filippo Tommaso Marinetti, 'Velocità'

THE GREAT BLACK SPIDER
ON ITS KNOCK-KNEED TRIPOD

Reflections of Cinema in Early
Twentieth-Century Italy

Introduction

Reflections of Cinema and Technology in Marinetti, D'Annunzio, and Pirandello

The modernization of technology at the end of the nineteenth and beginning of the twentieth centuries met with an active cultural climate in Italy, characterized by diverse and conflicting attitudes towards aesthetic production – a climate that we may define with respect to the *-ismi* of the period, *futurismo*, *decadentismo*, and *umorismo* being among the most influential and the three on which the present study concentrates. Cinema was one of modernity's scientific 'miracles.' Its association with a new, technologically constructed experience of movement, and the radical notions of spatial and temporal relations that it implemented, allows us to list cinema next to inventions such as the airplane and the automobile, while its development into a predominant form of mass entertainment made it an important factor of a growing consumer culture, comparable to large-scale industry and its processes of mass production. The thing that distinguished cinema from its parallel historical phenomena was its function as a primarily *aesthetic* medium. As a revolutionary apparatus that combined modern technology with aesthetics, it entered Italy's cultural scene with force. Not only did it provide a form of distraction of extraordinary mass appeal, it also fulfilled the technical prerequisites for the development of a radically new art. Its popularity spread across class and educational boundaries, its novelty attracting intellectuals and laymen alike, challenging the traditional dichotomy between high and low culture. It thus made it necessary for intellectuals to rethink their definitions of art in industrial modernity and the very criteria by which they critiqued culture.

The present study traces the encounter of technology, and cinema in particular, with three of Italy's most influential men of letters: Filippo Tommaso Marinetti (1876–1944), founder of the Futurist movement

and often described as the father of the European avant-garde; Gabriele
D'Annunzio (1863–1938), representative of the Italian decadent movement and the most internationally acclaimed Italian cultural figure at
the turn of the century; and Luigi Pirandello (1867–1936), a father of
the modern European theatre and winner of the 1934 Nobel Prize in
Literature for the play *Sei personaggi in cerca d'autore* (Six Characters
in Search of an Author, 1921), also known for his theory of *umorismo*
(humour), a seminal concept developed in the context of his complex
poetics. The question that I will raise regarding the encounters of these
figures with industrial modernity is threefold, each of its three facets
emphasized to a greater or lesser extent as pertinent to the specific work
under discussion. First, how does technology, and cinema in particular,
influence each author's aesthetic, ideological, or philosophical outlook?
Second, to what extent and through which discursive forms – essays,
films, manifestos, novels, screenplays – does each author reconcile the
theories and new aesthetic horizons inspired by technology with his
known position on aesthetics, be it Futurism, Decadentism, or humour?
Third, how did the encounter affect the areas of discord among three
distinct approaches to aesthetics? To what extent did the pervasive cultural impact of technology and cinema enforce or neutralize their differences? This third question allows us to scrutinize the very boundaries
between established critical categories, such as Futurism, Decadentism,
and humour, promoting a view of modernity that recognizes its complex cultural dimension, a view of it as less a constellation of exclusive categories than the product of fluid intersections between diverse
strains of thought.

At first glance, cinema inspires a distinct concept of temporality in
each author. For Marinetti, it constitutes the promise of a radical future,
liberated from any pre-existing notions of creativity. The Futurists'
fervent claims about cinema, first articulated in 1916, are driven by
a violent impulse to eradicate traditional culture, the same impulse
that marked the earliest years of the movement, known as its 'heroic
period.'[1] Advocate of the tradition that the Futurists claimed to eradicate was D'Annunzio, who spoke of cinema as the modern incarnation of sublime primordial forces, the kind of spectacle that the nude
wall of the theatre of Dionysus at the Athenian Acropolis awaited for
millennia. In contrast to his peers' flamboyant claims, Pirandello finds
in cinema neither the harbinger of a radical future nor modernity's
re-articulation of a sublime past. In his somewhat surreal universe, the
value of the medium lies in its ability to display, in ways more concrete

than those furnished by any aesthetic medium that preceded it, the existential dilemma that humans have confronted all along and that they will always confront – namely, the unending struggle to define truth and identity and the multiple illusions created in its course.

The three authors' diverse concepts of temporality parallel the relations that they propose between aesthetics and politics. One thing that unites the three is their overt nationalism, articulated especially with respect to the First World War and the advent of Fascism. Before the war, Italy was part of the Triple Alliance with Germany and Austria-Hungary. Following the outbreak of war in 1914, Italy declared neutrality, while public opinion was divided between neutralists and interventionists. The latter, aspiring to liberate the north-eastern territories of Trento and Trieste from Austria, advocated Italy's defiance of its previous allies and siding instead with the Entente of Britain, France, and Russia. Italy declared war on Austria in May 1915. In this climate, Marinetti, D'Annunzio, and Pirandello were overt interventionists. Furthermore, with Fascism's ascent to power in the 1920s, all three became strong supporters of the regime, although their encounters with it displayed some ups and downs. As regards cinema, Marinetti is the only one who articulates a direct connection between aesthetics and contemporary politics. The anti-traditional aesthetic that he prescribes for cinema is a significant step towards Italy's cultural world hegemony, beginning gloriously at present with its intervention in the First World War. The brief political discourse in which D'Annunzio enshrouds cinema makes no reference to the day's politics. Nonetheless, through his allusions to Ancient Rome and the medium's ability to bring past glory before the public's eye, D'Annunzio promotes the ideal of the nation's regeneration in the image of the old. Despite their conceptual particularities, a strong bellicose spirit, supported by the philosophy of *arditismo*, which cultivates action, boldness, bravery, and courage, defines the sensibilities of both writers. Pirandello is the one who, despite his overt political convictions, does not politicize cinema. He maintains the neutrality that marks his attitude towards the question of temporality. To be exact, he does not politicize cinema explicitly. The link that he allows us to draw between cinema and humour, a theory about the infinite ways in which reality may be interpreted, may inspire one to think of his concept of cinema as politically subversive.

As we study the three authors' attitudes towards cinema, we realize that all three, each in a different way, demand that we articulate two distinct notions of 'cinema.' One is an abstract notion that refers to the medium's essence, its status as a technological apparatus in its pure form, available to a diverse range of practical applications. The other is a historically and culturally specific notion that refers to cinema as an institution, and in this particular case, to the application of the apparatus by the Italian film industry of the 1910s. This distinction is crucial. Depending on which of the two notions we address, a writer's encounter with *it* – either the apparatus or the institution – may enforce or neutralize his differences from another writer. At first glance, as in the case of politics, the three authors' diverse concepts of temporality extend to their attitudes towards cinema as an institution and a vital component of 1910s mass culture. Whereas Marinetti promotes an alternative and abstract aesthetic for filmmaking, D'Annunzio subscribes to the institution of narrative cinema as developed in the 1910s. That is to say, he subscribes to the kind of cinema that Marinetti attacks as the suppression of the medium's revolutionary potential, its downgrading to a copy of traditional theatre, a symptom of the regressive tendency that plagues contemporary culture, hence the urgent need for Futurism's 'great hygienic war' to combat and cure it. Pirandello sets himself apart. His neutrality with respect to temporality and politics pervades also his attitude towards the institution of cinema.

If Marinetti's and D'Annunzio's positions on narrative cinema as addressed above represent their assertions at the most explicit level, further analysis of their theoretical formulations and practical experimentation with the medium suggests that their encounters with *it* – either the institution or the apparatus in its pure form – to some extent neutralize the differences between them. Inasmuch as Marinetti boasts the emancipation of the apparatus, what suggests the restoration of its pure form, his work also betrays a level of collaboration with the practice of narrative cinema. Conversely, inasmuch as D'Annunzio subscribes to the institution of narrative cinema, the inspiration that he receives from the novelty of film technology – which is to say, from the notion of the apparatus in its pure form – inlays his film projects, theoretical or practical, with an avant-garde dimension. Pirandello, by contrast, seems to maintain his philosophical neutrality also with respect to the institution of narrative cinema. No doubt, he will fool us at times, leading us to believe that, like Marinetti, he condemns the institution, and that an alternative use of film technology, emancipated and restored to its pure form, grants access to the most authentic layers of the psyche. We soon realize, however, that all forms of cinematic practice, institutional or alternative, merge in Pirandello. The very notion of narrativity, which Marinetti claims to deprecate and D'Annunzio to validate, is here dismantled. In Pirandello's work, the narrative is exposed to be a fragment in the first place, one that lies in wait of its own completion through the arrival of the next narrative-fragment. The theoretical significance with which he invests the medium neither rejects nor praises the new mass culture. He gazes at the institution of cinema with an air of neutrality, because he accepts it as a historical fact, one that reinforces, as well as shapes to some extent, his construction of reality through the lens of humour.

Futurism, Cinema, and the 'Renewed Sensibility'

Il Futurismo si fonda sul completo rinnovamento della sensibilità umana avvenuto per effetto delle grandi scoperte scientifiche. Coloro che usano oggi del telegrafo, del telefono e del grammofono, del treno, della bicicletta, della motocicletta, dell'automobile, del transatlantico, del dirigibile, dell'aeroplano, del cinematografo, del grande quotidiano (sintesi di una giornata del mondo) non pensano che queste diverse forme di comunicazione, di trasporto e d'informazione esercitano sulla loro psiche una decisiva influenza. (*TIF* 65–6)

[Futurism is founded on the complete renewal of human sensibility that took place because of the great discoveries of science. Those who today use the telegraph, the telephone and the phonograph, the train, the bicycle, the motorcycle, the automobile, the transatlantic liner, the dirigible, the airplane, the cinema, the great daily news (a synthesis of a day of the world) do not think that these different forms of communication, transportation, and information exert a decisive influence on their psyche.][2]

Marinetti here attributes a historically and socially significant role to Futurism as a movement that is founded on a new reality and undertakes the project of articulating this reality's effects on humanity. The numerous manifestos published in various periodicals between 1909 and the early 1940s, many written by Marinetti alone, others signed collectively by several Futurists, present a multifaceted study of the aforementioned 'renewal.'[3] What unifies them at heart is the notion that a new sensibility derives from the contact with revolutionary technological products that radically restructure daily life. *Movement* and *speed* become life's ontological principles and efface the most conventional notions of the divine.[4] The manifestos address many forms of cultural production – architecture, cinema, dance, music, painting, photography, poetry, sculpture, theatre, and more – and prescribe a set of radical aesthetics to reflect modernity's new sensibility, while they urge the indiscriminate extinction of traditional art, uncompromisingly labelling it as passéist. A fundamental principle of Futurist aesthetics is the 'perception by analogy,' introduced by Marinetti in his definition of Futurist literature. New means of transportation allow the perception of similarities among things that otherwise seem dissimilar. This perceptual discovery is indispensable to a liberated artistic production, the essence of which Marinetti expresses in the motto *immaginazione senza fili*, or imagination without strings. Literature is to break the logical strings that hitherto ensured the understanding of reality and by means of intuition to unravel the 'illogical connections' among objects. By abandoning traditional syntax, punctuation, and the primacy of the 'I' as the basis of discourse, poets are to attain the celebrated *parole in libertà*, or words-in-freedom.[5]

Futurism's rejection of tradition, in its ideological and aesthetic manifestations, corresponds roughly to the canonical definitions of the avant-garde. Renato Poggioli sees in Futurism the four aspects that he considers fundamental in every avant-garde movement: *activism, antagonism, nihilism*, and *agonism*.[6] The aspect that prevails in Futurism, or the 'down-with-the-past' movement, as he calls it, is *antagonism*, which is manifest in the movement's anti-traditionalism.[7] Peter Bürger's own definition may be applied to Futurism with more apprehension. The avant-garde project, according to Bürger, involves the dismantling of the institution of art as established in bourgeois society, defined by art's autonomy and isolation from life praxis. It attacks not merely a school within the institution but the institution as a whole, aiming to integrate art with life praxis.[8] Claudia Salaris finds this integration in Marinetti's career, noting the exchange between art and advertising. While the words-in-freedom use lettering derived from advertising, advertising draws upon designs pioneered by Futurism. Thus, art leaves the museum and extends into streets and public spaces.[9] Bürger, however, whose references to Italian Futurism are sparse, claims that the movement fits within his model only in part.[10] While he does not specify its limitations, politics is clearly the area in which Futurism deviates from his model: its exaltation of war and zealous interventionism during the First World War; its affiliation with Fascism; and its uncritical attitude towards the capitalist system. For Bürger, art's autonomy in bourgeois society is rooted in the division of labour. The praxis of life into which the avant-garde aims to transfer art is unrelated to 'the means-ends rationality of the bourgeois everyday.' Rather, the aim is 'to organize a new life praxis from a basis in art ... Only an art ... wholly distinct from the (bad) praxis of the existing society can be the center that can be the starting point for the organization of a new life praxis.'[11] Contrary to this view, in deifying modernity's technological inventions, Marinetti not only leaves unquestioned the economic structure that regulates them; his exaltation of war also praises modern weapons as divine bearers of the new predicament of speed.[12]

The radical aesthetic that Futurism advocates exhibits an ideological contradiction. It neither annuls the movement's indirect affirmation of capitalism or adherence to Fascist politics nor surrenders entirely its subversive potential to those structures. Challenging Theodor Adorno's view that the use of montage for an aesthetics of fragmentation is essentially anti-capitalist, Bürger finds contrary evidence in Futurism: 'That montage was used both by the Italian futurists, of whom it can hardly be said that they wanted to abolish capitalism, and by Russian avant-gardistes after the October revolution, who were working in a developing socialist society, is not the only fact that militates against [Adorno's] formulation.'[13] According to Poggioli, 'That aesthetic radicalism and social radicalism, revolutionaries in art and revolutionaries in politics, are allied, which empirically seems valid, is theoretically and historically erroneous. This is further demonstrated, to some extent at least, by the relation between futurism and fascism.'[14] According to Emilio Gentile, the two ideologies converge at the deepest level in 'modernist nationalism,' a 'state of mind' at the root of Fascist rhetoric combining the myth of the nation with the explosive energies of modernity. Both Marinetti and Mussolini articulated some of the myths and ideals of 'modernist nationalism' (youth, war, to 'conquer modernity,' to form a 'new Italy') at least a decade before Fascism rose to power.[15] This is not to say that the relationship between Futurism and Fascism was strictly harmonious. Futurist anti-traditionalism countered the regime's classicism, which was part of its methodical invocation of Imperial Rome as a model nation to be reincarnated under Mussolini's leadership.[16] Furthermore, the principle of 'imagination without strings' aspires to an aesthetic defined by fragmentation, which despite the Futurists' political intentions does not relinquish its potential to sabotage the formation of any discourse that relies on coherence, unity, and closure in order to articulate a stable identity for the nation.

A similar contradiction characterizes Marinetti's attitude towards cinema. In several ways, cinema is the ideal form to express Futurist sensibility. Its newness alone makes it anti-traditional, while its existence constitutes a technological discovery, hence, a part of that milieu that incites the conception of the Futurist outlook. Furthermore, its technical specificity may have been instrumental in Futurism's philosophical and aesthetic principles. It inaugurated a mode of representation based on *movement* and *montage*, bearing affinities to *speed* and *analogy*. Mario Verdone sees movement and montage as the engineering forces of every avant-garde endeavour, describing the literary analogy as the 'montage of words.'[17] Moreover, film technology allows the realization of radical aesthetics – through camera movement, montage, multiple exposure, and animation, to name a few techniques – that satisfy Futurist inquiries and decisively surpass the technical constraints of any older form of spectacle. In their 1916 manifesto on film, the Futurists praise the technical merits of the medium, describing it as 'eminently Futurist' (*TIF* 138–44). At the same time, they politicize this aesthetic, not by claiming that it is inherently political, but through the rhetorical structure of the manifesto as a whole. Its opening and closing are both marked by a nationalistic language that alludes to Italy's state of war. Through film, Futurism will multiply 'la potenza del genio creatore italiano e il suo predominio assoluto nel mondo' [the power of the creative Italian genius and its absolute supremacy in the world] (*TIF* 144). Thus, the avant-garde style is in a sense framed by a political discourse in support of Italy's cultural hegemony. To be sure, the union of aesthetics with politics is undermined by the fact that the two levels of discourse are not well integrated. The political opening and closing strike the reader as alien to the strictly aesthetic issues that occupy the manifesto's main body. Nonetheless, the alliance between aesthetics and politics is dramatized in the reception of *Vita futurista* (Futurist Life, 1916), the only film that the Futurists produced as a movement. As we will see, the film's reception lacked that belligerent spirit that Marinetti aspired to arouse among his spectators. This 'unheroic' reception was a result of once again injecting political discourse into an avant-garde aesthetic.

Inasmuch as Marinetti advocated a radical film aesthetic, he displayed ambivalence, rather than outright rejection, with respect to the institution of narrative cinema. In praising cinema's technical capabilities, the Futurists knew that cinema did not exist in a vacuum. What they idealized was the medium's essence as a technological apparatus, but they were also facing the appropriation of the apparatus by the Italian film industry of the 1910s, largely consisting of the production of feature-length narratives. Things had been different during the first years of cinema, from its inception in the mid-1890s and for about a decade thereafter, when the standard modes of exhibition were much in line with the kind of spectacle that Marinetti valued. Around the turn of the century, in Italy's main urban centres, films were usually shown in the *caffè-concerto*, a derivative of the French *Café chantant*. In this venue, the main activity consisted of eating and drinking, while enjoying a variety show. Rather than being systematically included in the program, the 'animated projections' appeared as occasional variety numbers, or 'attractions.'[18] By 1916, however, as in other European countries and the United States, in Italy cinema underwent significant stages of transformation in both its aesthetic form and its mode of exhibition. Since the mid-1900s, the gradual expansion of the film auditorium proper began to threaten the existence of the earliest modes of exhibition, reaching a peak in 1908 with Milan as the film auditorium capital.[19] It was not long before conservatives condemned cinema as dangerous and immoral, a school of pornography and corruption lacking in cultural dignity.[20] In the aim of cultural legitimization, major producers started making films of 'noble' subjects, to qualify as both artistic works and instruments of information and education.[21] The need for respectability prompted the adaptations of famous works of literature (in 1909 Milano Films made *Inferno*, from Dante's *Divine Comedy*), and the hiring of notable literary figures for the supply of screenplays.[22]

Another strategy for gaining cultural legitimacy was the strong diversification of subject matter and marketing of films according to genre.[23] Particularly widespread was the *film storico* or *in costume*, a narrative genre stylistically influenced by nineteenth-century theatre and opera, and set in various stages of world history, such as the Greco-Roman era, the Renaissance, the French Revolution, and the Risorgimento. Furthermore, as early as 1910, preceded by its Danish counterpart, and anticipating its American and French counterparts, Italian cinema made a decisive move towards the feature-length narrative.[24] As a result, shows became less frequent and exhibition required larger spaces. Small auditoriums gave way to larger and elegant ones, aiming at providing comfort to both an elite audience and the masses.[25] Allowing the prolonged presence of individual actors on screen, the feature film stirred the public's curiosity about them, thus preparing the ground for *divismo*, or stardom. This phenomenon exploded in 1913 with the appearance of Lyda Borelli in Mario Caserini's *Ma l'amor mio non muore*, the film that also marked the beginning of the *cinema in frak*, which was to become one of the most popular genres of the 1910s. Typically about a destructive love affair involving a morally complex heroine, these melodramas were set in a decadent upper-class milieu marked by a lavish mise-en-scène.[26] The phenomenon of *divismo* is also found in the film *verista*, a form of melodramatic realism typically seen in competition with the *frak*, in that it focuses on the Neapolitan underclass. Exemplary of the film *verista* is *Assunta Spina* (1915), based on a play by Salvatore Di Giacomo and starring the diva Francesca Bertini.[27] Beyond the *frak* and the *verista*, however, the dominating presence of a fascinating heroine in numerous films that dealt with difficult love affairs, the exploitation of women by men, and the examination of gender roles, allows us to consider the *diva film* as a genre in its own right, one at least as important as any genre of the silent era.[28] Italian divas also had their male counterparts, not only in the delicate heroes of the *frak* but also in the muscular and morally intact men of the *forzuto*, or strongman – another popular genre that arose after the sensational appearance of Bartolomeo Pagano as Maciste in Giovanni Pastrone's 1914 historical epic *Cabiria*, set in the Second Punic War.[29]

For Marinetti, such developments in Italy's film culture signified a regression to tradition. While the manifesto praises the medium's Futuristic potential, it scorns the industry for turning cinema into the semblance of respectable theatre by adopting old-fashioned narrative forms. It thus presupposes the distinction between the medium's essence as an apparatus open to a diverse range of applications and its historically specific appropriation by the film industry. Hence, cinema presented itself to the Futurists in two conflicting faces: strictly as an apparatus, it was an ally; as an institution, it was a villain against which the manifesto proposed its aesthetic alternative. It seems, however, that Marinetti's enchantment with narrative cinema was deeper than what the manifesto suggests. For one, with its popular genres, which secured for it a large international audience, the Italian cinema had achieved, in a sense, that cultural world hegemony that the film manifesto was craving and towards which it was summoning its avant-garde aesthetics.[30]

What strikes me as more important, however, is the use of the term *cinema* in the passage quoted earlier, where Marinetti enumerates the technologies responsible for the 'renewal of human sensibility.' The position of cinema in this constellation is unique. Compared to the other phenomena that Marinetti enumerates, its role in daily life has little to do with practical functionality. Its inclusion here exposes its distinct status as a primarily aesthetic medium. There is a reason of course that cinema belongs here in the first place. As an aesthetic practice that required specialized technologies, high capital investment, and complex systems of production and distribution, it shook the boundaries between industry and art. In fact, by listing *only* this aesthetic medium next to the phenomena responsible for the 'renewal' of sensibility, Marinetti recognizes its unique status also in relation to the other arts. If cinema differs from other industrial products because it is also an art, it is also unique in relation to the other arts because it is an industrial product. Undeniably, the notion of cinema as both an aesthetic and an industrial product refers to the cinematic institution, to the aesthetic forms established by the mid-1910s with the development of the film industry. It is this kind of cinema – of the narrative genres, of wide mass appeal, available to the public on a daily basis, next to the telegraph, the telephone, the train, and the daily news – that partakes of the historical constellation responsible for the formation of modernity's 'renewed' sensibility, hence the formation of Futurism's own conceptual foundations. Ironically, the Futurist film aesthetic, like all of Futurist art, evokes a sensibility that is being created, if in part, by cinema as institutional practice, by the very cinema that this avant-garde aesthetic aims to abolish. The ambition to attack the institution of cinema takes place in the name of paying tribute to this institution's social effects.

The Aesthete and Technology

In a 1925 manifesto on new Futurist poets, Marinetti lists D'Annunzio in a group of writers, next to Carducci, Pascoli, and Verga, whom he criticizes as passéist. The Futurists are eager to uncover new poetic genius, whereas 'questi illustri letterati si sono sempre infischiati dei giovani' [these illustrious men of letters never gave a damn about the young] (*TIF* 185). Their indifference is of course only a side-effect of passéism. Above all, it is their literary style that Marinetti rejects. The words-in-freedom, which abandon narrative sequence in order to attain 'la poliespressione simultanea del mondo' [the world's simultaneous multi-expression], set the Futurists apart from Homer, whereas before Futurism, men always sang *like* Homer. Marinetti asserts: 'Fra i versi di Omero e quelli di Gabriele D'Annunzio non esiste differenza sostanziale' [No substantial difference exists between Homer's verses and those of Gabriele D'Annunzio] (187).

Two decades before Marinetti's Futurist debut, D'Annunzio defined Italian Decadentism with his first novel, *Il piacere* (1889).[31] Against a dominating positivist outlook, Decadentism adopts an irrational vision that sees all aspects of being as unified by arcane analogies and correspondences. It seeks a union between ego and world, realized in the unconscious.[32] Held as the ideal means to attain such knowledge, art acquires a religious dimension. Aestheticism ignores common definitions of good and evil and designates the beautiful as the main criterion for judgment. Always in search of rare and exquisite sensations, the aesthete is aloof to social problems. His is *art for art's sake*. Writing is esoteric, has aura, and resists the new mass culture, exemplified in photography's infinite reproductions. Not technology but nature is its inspiration. Music is the supreme form, as the lack of rational links between sounds and world allows the subject's loss into oneness. Literature is musical, as the word's phonetic value takes special importance. Aestheticism and musicality are essential in D'Annunzio's style, while his novels operate on themes typical of Decadentism. The hero aims to transform life into art. His search for beauty and scorn for common morality are tied up with lasciviousness. Illness, mental or physical, is a nobleman's privilege. It extends to an attraction towards death, a delight in the thought of annihilation – but not without its counterforce, the exaltation of life and vitality. In D'Annunzio's variation of the Nietzschean Superman, vitality is the flip side of illness. It serves to exorcise the magnetism of death and conceal the hero's self-destructive impulses. It is these impulses that draw him to the threat of his powerful antagonist, lascivious and perverse, seductive and evasive – *la Nemica* (the Enemy), as Giorgio Aurispa of *Trionfo della morte* (1894) describes Ippolita Sanzio.[33]

In the same manifesto in which Marinetti attacks D'Annunzio as passéist, he also recognizes the latter's adoption of a radical style – not to praise his originality but to claim the influence of Futurism on the traditionalists themselves.

Le parole in libertà hanno conquistato i nostri maggiori scrittori: fra i quali Gabriele D'Annunzio, che nel suo *Notturno* ... ha saputo trovare questi effetti simili al notissimo *Vampe vampe vampe* della mia *Battaglia di Adrianopoli*.

'Volti, volti, volti, tutte le passioni di tutti i volti scorrono attraverso il mio occhio piagato, innumerabilmente, come la sabbia calda attraverso il pugno. Ma li riconosco.

'Mi volto. Discendo. La guerra! La Guerra! Volti. Volti. Volti. Tutte le passioni di tutti i volti. Ceneri. E un acquazzone di marzo. Bora. Pioggia. Origlio lo scroscio.' (*TIF* 189–90)

[The words-in-freedom conquered our major writers: among whom Gabriele D'Annunzio who, in his *Nocturne* ... , learnt how to find these effects similar to the well-known *Flashes flashes flashes* of my *Battle of Adrianople*.

'Faces, faces, faces, all the passions of all the faces, flow through my wounded eye, innumerably, like hot sand flows through a clenched fist. But I recognize them.

  'I turn. I go down. The war! The War! Faces. Faces. Faces. All the passions of all the faces. Ashes. And a downpour of March. Bora. Rain. I listen to the thunder.']³⁴

In the *Notturno* D'Annunzio uses a fragmentary prose to express his lyrical thoughts on the perils of war. While the style may evoke the words-in-freedom, it may or may not represent a direct influence. Although it was published in 1921, D'Annunzio wrote it in 1916 after a traumatic war experience. In the midst of a combat flight, the plane in which he was an observer made an emergency landing, causing his loss of vision in the right eye. He then spent several months putting on paper his impressions of shadows, memories, and dreams.³⁵ The incoherent facts of war may have played the most decisive role in the work's style, while the repetition of the plural noun was not exclusive to author but was a topos for describing large quantities.³⁶ Whether or not D'Annunzio was inspired by Futurism, with the *Notturno* he was found, according to Raymond Rosenthal, 'with one foot in the camp of modernism.'³⁷

The 'prince' of Italian Decadentism, in fact, displayed his enchantment with modernity long before the *Notturno*.³⁸ *Forse che sì forse che no* (Perhaps Yes Perhaps No, 1910) glorifies the discovery of aviation as the realization of man's primordial wish to surpass the prohibitions of nature, 'a lottar contro il vento e contro l'emulo nell'aria' [to fight against the wind and against the rival in the air], and to witness 'un'assunzione della sua specie' [an Assumption of his species].³⁹ The novel marks the amalgamation of two sensibilities. Its point of departure is the nineteenth-century decadent temperament, which adapts to modernity's 'renewed sensibility.' While Marinetti celebrates speed and derides slowness, *Forse che sì* oscillates between, so to speak, a slow and a more-or-less fast style. Technology is not merely a component of narrative action. It conditions the writing style itself, the figurative use of language and the pace of the descriptions. If *Il piacere* lingers ceaselessly in its meticulous descriptions of aristocratic parlours and the tortuous explorations of the hero's psychosexual dilemmas, *Forse che sì* marks a balance between that 'slow' style and the 'synthetic' (to use a Marinettian term) descriptions of landscapes as they appear from the perspective of automobiles and airplanes, or the unsettling construction of the heroine as a fleeting entity whose objective correlatives are those very machines, while it remedies the hero's unfulfilled desire through his vertiginous flying adventures.[40] The amalgamation, however, is not limited to writing style, to its sometimes slow, sometimes fast pace of narration. It is also a result of the thematic frame within which the novel celebrates modernity, specifically, the lyrical evocation of man's aspirations to fly since the myth of Daedalus and Icarus. Unlike Marinetti, D'Annunzio exalts not rupture but continuity. The modern acquires its glory from its genealogical affirmation of and by the ancient. That is why *Forse che sì* becomes vital in a study of D'Annunzio's relationship with cinema, since several years before the author's involvement with the medium, *Forse che sì* vigorously launched the union of the old with the new – what also defines his film-related projects, and which he reasserts, as we will see, in his allusion to film as that modern apparition that the sublime nude wall of the Acropolis awaited throughout the ages.

Like Marinetti, D'Annunzio praised cinema for its radical aesthetic potential. Unlike Marinetti, who saw narrative film as the medium's seizure by passéism, he allowed his prestige to be exploited – and reaffirmed – through his direct dealings with the film industry. Not only did he consent to the adaptations of his works, he also wrote intertitles and original *soggetti*.[41] He was the most esteemed of the many writers through whose contributions the industry sought its cultural legitimacy. His influence is also believed to have played a role in the aesthetic configuration of some of the most successful genres of the 1910s, the *film storico* and the *cinema in frak*, often labelled as 'Dannunzian.' From a Marinettian standpoint, his condoning of narrative cinema is further testimony to his passéism. The two authors share, however, the nationalistic appropriation of the medium. D'Annunzio's work with cinema is largely identified with his intertitles for Pastrone's *Cabiria*, the peak of the *storico*'s technical achievement and international appeal. The text was sold at the theatre in the form of a libretto, *Cabiria: Visione storica del terzo secolo a.C.*, and opens with a hymn to *romanità* (Roman-ness). *Cabiria*, we learn, is a film about *fire*: 'Il soffio della guerra converte i popoli in una specie di materia infiammata, che Roma si sforza di foggiare a sua simiglianza' [The breath of war converts peoples into a sort of blazing matter, which Rome strives to mould in its likeness].[42] Gian Piero Brunetta finds a precursor to *Cabiria* in D'Annunzio's *La nave* (1905). The play exalts sixth-century Venice as the 'first authentic ideal place from which D'Annunzio imagines that the spark of the spirit of conquest and domination, which seems asleep in the men of the newborn Italian nation, may rekindle.' 'National palingenesis' requires blood and sacrifice. These are also the motifs of *La nave*, which D'Annunzio will 'recover and decant, almost without solution of continuity, into his work for Pastrone.'[43] Although Marinetti and D'Annunzio share a national ideal, their temporal visions are diametrically opposed. If Marinetti envisions Italy's world hegemony in cinema's flight into an unknown future, D'Annunzio's 'cinema,' anticipating Fascism, aspires to revive the glory of ancient worlds. In this particular sense, D'Annunzio may qualify as a passéist.

If nationalism links D'Annunzio to the *storico* and complicates his relationship with Marinetti, the *frak* is 'Dannunzian' for reasons unrelated to nation or Futurism. It has to do with the portrayal of a decadent class reminiscent of his prose, and with the phenomenon of *divismo*, which is essential to this genre. It is mainly through the *frak* that the divas of the 1910s, such as Lyda Borelli, Francesca Bertini, and Pina Menichelli, conquered the screen. Aristocratic, mysterious, and seductive, the diva recalls the Dannunzian heroine – Elena Muti of *Il piacere*, Isabella Inghirami of *Forse che sì*, and Basiliola of *La nave*, to name a few.[44] Not only her actions but also her acting style and overall disposition are seen as Dannunzian. When at a young age she aspired at a career in theatre, Bertini read D'Annunzio in order to internalize the sensibility that, as she was told, would make her a better actress.[45] Furthermore, *divismo* is associated with things extraneous to literature: 'The true star of the era,' Verdone claims, 'was above all D'Annunzio himself, with his appearances at the horse races, at the opera, in society.'[46] According to this view, to construct its stars, the industry followed not only the models found in D'Annunzio's literature but also that of his public persona, so mesmerizing and popular that it sometimes eclipsed that of Mussolini.[47]

However, labelling this luminous aspect of the 1910s Italian cinema as Dannunzian – that is, in terms of a most luminous aspect of turn-of-the-century Italian literature – is to some extent misleading. First, it suggests that one may gain familiarity with D'Annunzio's literature by viewing 'Dannunzian' films.[48] Second, applying Dannunzianism as a critical tool to the study of Italian cinema overlooks crucial aspects of this cinema that are unrelated to the author's work or life, such as the medium's technical specificity or the influence of other national cinemas. Arguing that Italian *divismo* originates in D'Annunzio, Verdone emphasizes the extra-cinematic origins of the phenomenon as a whole: 'There is a *divismo* of life and a literary *divismo* . . . , in painting (the paintings of Boldini), in photography (the photos of Nunes Veis), and in the liberty posters. It is not cinema that creates it: if anything it imitates it.'[49] Studying the precedents of *divismo* in areas other than cinema is important, but not adequate. One must address technical specificity, examples of which are the framing and lighting of the diva and the impact of such techniques on narrative themes.[50] Third and most important for the purposes of this study, Dannunzianism barely addresses the writer's own views on cinema. His engagement with the medium as found in texts not as religiously mentioned as the intertitles of *Cabiria* exposes an aspect of the author that is addressed neither by Dannunzianism, nor by literary Decadentism, nor by the contrast with Marinetti. Surely, Marinetti finds in technology the means to free art from tradition, whereas D'Annunzio aims to integrate the aesthetic possibilities of film with his decadent style. Nonetheless, technology inspires D'Annunzio to address critical questions about the role of art in modernity, and to envision the medium's application in ways that bring him closer to the avant-garde than his obvious differences from it allow us to imagine.

A Humoristic Lens

Unlike Futurism and Decadentism, Pirandello's humour refers not to a historically specific literary or art movement but to a disposition the aesthetic concretization of which Pirandello traces in literary works of different historical periods – yet one that serves as the ideal model of the modern subject's versatile and conflicted psyche. It is a disposition that informs Pirandello's world view as articulated in his seminal 1908 essay *L'umorismo*, which serves as a blueprint of his poetics. Thus, it provides an interpretative tool for much of Pirandello's work, a tool that is applicable to both the thematic and the structural dimensions of any given work. By selecting the term *umorismo*, Pirandello perplexes his reader. Not only does the term not signify strictly the comic, but the condition to which it refers, the experiencing of multiple moods all at once, what Pirandello calls *sentimento del contrario*, or feeling of the opposite, may not even include the comic. As either a disposition or its aesthetic concretization, humour leads to the unsettling process of articulating multiple and competing responses to any observable phenomenon, what Pirandello calls *riflessione*, or reflection. Certainly, the comic may be, and often is, one of the components of humour, when the urge to laugh informs one of the humorist's competing moods or responses. The comic is not, however, given free rein, as it is accompanied by a counterforce, a feeling of sadness or moral ambivalence with respect to the phenomenon under question, which inhibits laughter while it informs another of the multiple moods that humour entails. Hence, with the term *umorismo* Pirandello perplexes his reader, perhaps intentionally so. On the one hand, as the Italian word for *humour*, the term evokes laughter. On the other hand, as a derivative of *umore*, which translates as 'mood,' *umorismo* may be understood as the theory, or play, of moods. In fact, as the term leads in different conceptual directions all at once, we may characterize Pirandello's use of it as humoristic, in the Pirandellian sense of the word.[51]

Not speed, beauty, technology, nature, future, or past, but contradiction, ambivalence, and irresoluteness are the things that Pirandello postulates as life's ontological principles – and as my study of his portrayal of cinema and technology will propose, of modern life in particular. Thus, with respect to Marinetti and D'Annunzio, at least as regards the attitude towards cinema, we may say that Pirandello is on safe ground. If Marinetti is drawn to the institution of cinema in ways that his criticism of it conceals, and if D'Annunzio's work with film brings him closer to the avant-garde than his overt support of the institution of cinema suggests, an inherently conflicted state of mind is for Pirandello fundamental, inevitable, and triumphant. It is in this light that we must study his rigorous and multifaceted commentary on cinema, found in the 1915 novel *Si gira* (Shoot!), launched in 1925 under the new title *Quaderni di Serafino Gubbio operatore* (Notebooks of Serafino Gubbio, Cameraman). The novel's portrayal of industrial film production, in its verisimilar dimension, exposes the nexus of the various implications of the young institution: aesthetic, cultural, economic, historical, moral, psychological, and social. It is not, however, the verisimilar portrayal alone that promotes a view of cinema along the lines of humour but also the essayistic factor that pervades this portrayal, as achieved by the investigative, multilayered, and enigmatic discursive frame articulated by Pirandello's exemplary narrator, Serafino Gubbio. The cameraman suffers from an existential crisis because he sees his profession as the embodiment of the alienation that plagues modern industrial society. His description of the camera as a monstrous beast that devours life only to convert it to stupid fictions summarizes his view of cinema as a corrupt, capitalist industry indifferent to basic human values and true artistic expression. His contempt finds relief in his few allusions to the film image as able to reveal human truths that otherwise remain unrecognized, if only the camera were rescued from its industrial exploitation and put to different use. Hence, like Marinetti and D'Annunzio, Pirandello seems to grapple with two notions of cinema: an institution that is culturally specific and an apparatus in its pure form that is employable in alternative ways.

If Pirandello, however, hints at the capability of an emancipated apparatus to collaborate in the search for essential truth, that is only to allow humour to expose any such truth as an impossibility, as an illusion that is no less fictional than the narrative films that are sold daily by the industry. Undeniably, the idea of unveiling primordial truths is tempting, especially as suggested by the religiously cited passage about a diva who enters a state of shock every time she sees her own image on the screen (usually in footage that the studio deems unfit and discards), because there she confronts, as it were, a possessed woman whom she has always carried within and with whom she fails to cope. There is a good reason that critics find in this passage a precursor to Walter Benjamin's 'optical unconscious,' the ability of the camera, through the use of special techniques, such as extreme close-ups or slow motion, to reveal spaces unseen by the naked eye. 'A space informed by human consciousness,' states Benjamin, 'gives way to a space informed by the unconscious.' Thus, the camera may perform a function analogous to that of psychoanalysis.[52] It is tempting, in fact, to draw comparisons between Pirandello and Freud, even if Freudian terminology is foreign to Pirandello's vocabulary. His essay on humour at times strikes us as an attempt to articulate something analogous to the Freudian unconscious. The humorist's aim is to expose the illusory constructs that one adopts in conforming to socially imposed ideals, a notion that evokes the repression of inadmissible wishes, hence the negotiation between id and superego. What I hope to achieve, however, is to differentiate Pirandello's model from that of Benjamin and its Freudian implications, and to articulate the specificity of his humoristic view of cinema. *Si gira*'s multilevelled discourse – comprising the narration of diegetic episodes, descriptions of visual renderings of the diva, and the cameraman's musings – produces a novel-essay about cinema's relation to humour. According to this novel-essay, despite the cameraman's contempt for the industry and his search for authenticity in alternative images, any film product is a fiction, be it an institutional product or an alternative attempt, a narrative film or a single image. Every such fiction partakes of a uniquely modern constellation of fictions that promotes a humoristic view of the world, that is, a view of the world as an infinite articulation of illusory constructs, the diverse interpretations of experience and the multiple moods that those entail. Pirandello delights in observing the clash between such constructs as it unfolds *here and now*. He aspires neither to a glorious future nor to the unveiling of a primordial past. The humorist, he tells us, amuses himself in the act of *unmasking* – yet beneath each mask he finds another mask.

What further distinguishes Pirandello from Marinetti and D'Annunzio is his relation to politics. Like his peers, in facing the prospect of Italy's entrance in the First World War, Pirandello was an interventionist. As we learn from Gaspare Giudice, in spite of Pirandello's overt disdain for Dannunzian rhetoric, specific elements of prose from an interventionist speech that D'Annunzio delivered in Rome in May 1915, that is, a few days before Italy declared war on Austria, found their way into Pirandello's *Berecche e la guerra*, a novella that he wrote shortly thereafter. Though reworked in a more bizarre style, D'Annunzio's expressions reappear in the patriotic letter that a soldier writes to his father while departing for the front. Pirandello's, however, was a milder and rather subjective form of interventionism, seen as an extension of the ideals of the Risorgimento that an idealized maternal bond had inspired in him during childhood, and expressed in sharper terms in August 1915 after his son Stefano enlisted and started fighting at the Austrian front.[53] Rather dubious was his seemingly passionate affiliation with Fascism and exaltation of Mussolini, ideals that the content of his creative work kept at a distance, while his politically active persona barely outlasted the first few years of the regime's life.[54] The declarations that he made in the course of a 1924 interview following his return from America add up to a self-negating, 'humoristic' if I may, discourse: 'Sono apolitico: mi sento soltanto uomo sulla terra ... L'errore fondamentale su cui riposa tutta la vita americana è quello stesso che, secondo me, informa la concezione democratica della vita. Sono antidemocratico per eccellenza. La massa per se stessa ha bisogno di chi la formi' [I am apolitical: I feel just like a man on earth ... The basic error on which all of American life is based is the same one that, in my opinion, informs the democratic conception of life. I am antidemocratic *par excellence*. The masses need someone to form them].[55]

If Pirandello's stance on Fascism compares with the other two authors' rather irregular encounters with it, what sharply distinguishes Pirandello from Marinetti and D'Annunzio is the discourse on cinema, which in his case is devoid of patriotic effusions or national politics of any kind. Arguably, his work even suggests an implicit wish to dismantle nationalism's ideological foundations, if only because Pirandellian humour tends to dismantle the rational foundations of any given discourse. In Giudice's words, 'the self-proclaiming *antidemocrat* is, on the contrary, the most democratic of the known playwrights ... In Pirandello there is no feeling and taste for organized society; but certainly there is pleasure in the anarchic extremes inherent in a democratic structure.'[56] While he makes no explicit attempt to politicize the medium, the link that his fiction allows us to draw between cinema and humour derails any tendency to articulate a stable identity, national or other. More so than Marinetti's fragmentary aesthetics, the notion of cinema as a medium capable of unravelling the conflicting layers of the psyche renders problematic Pirandello's affiliation with Fascism. If Fascist rhetoric relies on coherence, unity, and closure to repress any elements that disrupt the imaginary articulation of identity, as a constellation of fictions that promotes a humoristic view of the world, an infinite articulation of diverse interpretations of experience, cinema stirs up the incongruity between the imaginary ideal and the versatility of the psyche. One is inspired not to identify with a prescriptive type of discourse but to embark on a journey of introspection leading to the recognition and explosion of the conflicting forces within.

The concept of identity as fluid and constantly changing, what I would describe as the product of an ongoing negotiation between multiple and diverse constructs, of which any essential or stable layer is unavailable to consciousness, is fundamental in Pirandello's humoristic outlook. As my discussion of the diva character in *Si gira* will argue, the medium of cinema plays a significant role in such a process. In Italy, the new prospects that cinema created for the conceptualization of identity in this way triumphed early on in the medium's life, in the hilarious shorts with which Leopoldo Fregoli amazed Italian entertainment seekers as early as 1899. Enjoying an international popularity as a *trasformista*, a live performer staging a series of rapid identity transformations, Fregoli went to Paris where he learned the craft of filmmaking from the Lumière brothers. Following the French pioneers' Cinématographe, he developed his own apparatus, the Fregoligraph, bringing to the Italian screens the *meraviglioso*, or marvellous, films of tricks that privileged the shows of the *trasformista*.[57] Exemplary of this type of spectacle is *Maestri di musica*, which shows Fregoli behind a wall that covers him up to the waist. He quickly bends down so as to hide entirely, and immediately stands up again. He repeats this gesture four times, each time appearing in the guise of a different composer – Rossini, Wagner, Verdi, Mascagni – displaying striking variations with respect to age, hair colour, and facial hair. After the Mascagni flash, he takes off his wig and bows.[58] The Fregoligraph met an enthusiastic reception in Italy, starting in Rome, where Pirandello lived at the time.[59] I am not claiming that Pirandello attended the Fregoligraph or that there was a direct exchange between the two men. If anything, Futurist dynamism is what one may readily associate with Fregoli.[60] Marinetti's manifesto on the variety theatre mentions Fregoli in a positive light, while the Fregoligraph belongs to the era of the early attractions the effacement of which by narrative cinema Marinetti scorned.[61] We may nonetheless view Pirandello's humour and the Fregoligraph as diverse expressions of a sensibility developing along with the multiple options that cinema introduced in the sphere of culture. Filmed or live, Fregoli's quick transformations celebrate an era in which the notion of the psyche as versatile and multilayered, expressed in diverse intellectual and cultural forms, thrives indeed. The dynamism and hilarity of modernity Pirandello reworks as humour.

The Structure of This Work

This book is not a descriptive study of each author's comprehensive work with cinema. Rather, it posits as crucial the historical moment in which cinema in Italy developed as an institution, one that privileged the feature-length narrative, became an extraordinary form of mass entertainment, and incited the curiosity of intellectuals – that is, the early 1910s. I therefore focus on those projects that reflect each author's contemporary response to this developing cultural phenomenon. I also focus on works that are not about cinema, which nonetheless I deem instrumental in this study, such as D'Annunzio's *Forse che sì* and Pirandello's *L'umorismo*. The projects that undergo substantial analysis in my book are from the years 1908 to 1920, beginning with Pirandello's *L'umorismo* in 1908, and ending with that essay's revised version and with D'Annunzio's screenplay *L'uomo che rubò la 'Gioconda'* (The Man Who Stole the 'Gioconda'), both from 1920. This chronology does not include other works on which I comment at a variable length for the sake of contrast or comparison, such as D'Annunzio's nineteenth-century novels. The title of the book borrows Pirandello's metaphor of the film camera as a 'grosso ragno nero sul treppiedi a gambe rientranti,' translated by C.K. Scott Moncrieff as a 'great black spider on its knock-kneed tripod.'[62] The metaphor alludes, among other things, to cinema as a man-made apparatus able to occupy contemporary thought with the authority of a spider that captures its prey in its web. The second part of the title, 'reflections of cinema,' refers to the book's wide scope in addressing reflections of various forms: theoretical views on the medium as presented in essays and manifestos; elements of cinematic representation as described in written works, such as novels and screenplays; cinematic reflections in a literal sense, as in visual elements found in actual films; and the influence of the institution of cinema on cultural products in general, which is to say, the ways in which such products *reflect* that influence.

I devote the first section to Marinetti, whose manifestos, despite their indisputable literary and polemical qualities, provide a theoretical basis for defining the cultural climate with which D'Annunzio and Pirandello also grapple. Chapters 1 and 2 are complementary in addressing the inconsistency that marks the Futurist cinematic project. Despite the Futurists' praise of film technology, *Vita futurista* represents both the beginning and the end of their film practice. After I address their enthusiastic claims and application of those to their single film, I perform a close study of the film's 1917 exhibition in Florence and Rome. Underlining the film's political dimension with respect to the First World War, I examine the impact of politics on the Futurists' willingness to exploit the medium further. Chapter 3 addresses a further inconsistency in Futurism, which concerns Marinetti's own position on the institution of cinema. His screenplay *Velocità* (Speed), probably written in the late 1910s, yet never realized as a film, is marked by an overarching narrative structure of an epic quality, as well as complex images that require means of production characteristic of the practice of cinema as industry. Furthermore, in this chapter I

trace the influence of the institution in the manifesto writing itself, in
the effervescent language that articulates the movement's fundamental philosophical principles, such as the notion of 'speed' as modernity's 'new divine.'

Chapter 4 concentrates on a text that makes no reference to cinema, a
text that provides, however, a conceptual framework most suitable for
the study of the author's work on cinema that followed. As I previously
suggested, *Forse che sì* is the first major work in which D'Annunzio
unites his decadent sensibility, largely informed by an admiration for
the glorious moments of past cultures, and his new passion for modern technology, the experience of speed, and the diverse perspectives
on reality that technology allows. The shift in temperament becomes
evident in a comparison between this 1910 novel and his earlier prose,
which exposes the transition of specific themes from their nineteenth-
century rendering to their twentieth-century reformulation in face
of the new era's technological inventions. The union of the old with
the new, launched forcefully in this 1910 novel, is found at the core
of D'Annunzio's work on film, now inspired not by airplanes but by
film technology. Following a route other than 'Dannunzianism,' which
overlooks the author's own inspiration by cinema, chapter 5 traces the
medium's influence on his thought in two important works: his single
theoretical piece on cinema, written in 1914 in the context of his contribution to *Cabiria*, and his 1920 screenplay on the *Gioconda*. Whether in
theory or practice, D'Annunzio viewed cinema both as a medium of
unique technical possibilities and as a historical phenomenon that chal-
lenged the traditional notions of art and thus the barrier between high
art and mass culture.

The last two chapters together articulate a concept of cinema based
on Pirandello's *Si gira* with respect to his theory of humour. Focusing
primarily, though not exclusively, on the character of the diva, chapter 6
discusses the humoristic function of the single image, the multiple
ways in which it may be interpreted, and the versions of identity to
which such readings correspond. The novel reinforces the notion of a
stable identity as inaccessible – in place of which it gives what I call
the product of a negotiation between diverse identity constructs – by
supplying a number of visual renderings of the diva. Insofar as she is
a diva, the role of cinema in the construction of her multiplied image is
fundamental. Chapter 7 extends the role of the institution in supplying
diverse versions of reality beyond the construction of the single image,
to encompass the film narrative, which like the image is exposed as

lacking, as infinitely requiring its complement. The dilemma of Serafino Gubbio, whose degree of identification with Pirandello is analysed extensively in this chapter, hinges on this dubious function of cinema as industrial practice. His contempt for the industry's 'idiotic fictions' is at odds with his persona as a humorist. The latter is the one that brings him closer to the author, while it allows us to think of cinema as modernity's specific tool for a view of reality through the lens of humour. The infinite process of defining reality through cinematic representation is perhaps what is represented by Pirandello's use of suspension points in the novel's original title (*Si gira* …). For practical purposes, in the body of this text I will use a shortened form of the novel's title (*Si gira*).

1

Film Aesthetics of a 'Heroic' Futurism

On 1 June 1916, in introducing the first issue of the Florentine biweekly *L'Italia Futurista*, Emilio Settimelli declared as one of its main objectives the rebirth of Italian spectacle in accordance with the ideals of Futurism: 'Il giornale avrà una grande parte consacrata al Teatro e al Cinematografo. Il Teatro è in preda agli stranieri il Cinematografo a gente che non sa trarre vantaggio dalla sua modernissima, complicatissima capacità espressiva. Questo è il momento di piantare anche sul palcoscenico il nostro tricolore trionfante' [The newspaper will have a large part dedicated to Theatre and Cinema. The Theatre is prey to foreigners, Cinema to people who do not know how to profit from its very modern and complicated expressive ability. This is the time to plant our triumphant tricolour also on the stage]. If Settimelli conflated the two media under the category of 'stage' for reasons that he left unexplained (and that I will address below), it was not long before *L'Italia Futurista* dedicated a large part of its front page to a manifesto exclusively on cinema. 'La cinematografia futurista' (Futurist Cinema), appearing on the 15 November 1916 issue, and signed by Marinetti, Corra, Settimelli, Ginna, Balla, and Chiti, celebrates its discovery of a new medium: 'Il cinematografo, nato da pochi anni, può sembrare già futurista, cioè privo di passato e libero di tradizioni . . . [N]oi vediamo in esso la possibilità di un'arte eminentemente futurista e *il mezzo di espressione più adatto alla plurisensibilità di un artista futurista*' [Cinema, born only a few years ago, may already seem Futurist, that is, lacking a past and free of traditions . . . We see in it the possibility of an art that is eminently Futurist and *the medium of expression most suited to the multifaceted sensibility of a Futurist artist*] (*TIF* 139–40).

Inasmuch as the Futurists recognized cinema's affinity to the conceptual foundations of their movement, and although they proposed its application with enthusiasm, the development of a Futurist film theory or practice, compared to Futurist work in other fields, never surpassed the stage of infancy. Settimelli's promise remained unrealized, as the periodical's references to film were sporadic at best, while the Futurists wrote only one other manifesto on film, published more than two decades after its antecedent.[1] In addition, they left us the records of no more than two cinematic projects that qualify as official works of the movement. *Vita futurista* was the only film that the Futurists produced collaboratively as a movement, while *Velocità*, a *soggetto*, or film scenario, written by Marinetti, was never realized as a film.[2] The numbers are minute in comparison to the movement's volume of work, both theoretical and practical, in other artistic areas, such as literature, theatre, and painting. One wonders why the Futurists abandoned this 'eminently Futurist' medium soon after they discovered it.

This contradiction has not escaped the attention of critics. The most comprehensive studies thus far on Futurist cinema agree that in the realm of spectacle the Futurists preferred live performance to the mechanically recorded image. According to Mario Verdone, after briefly experimenting with cinema, Marinetti remained faithful to theatre, while he continued to value cinema not as an art in itself but for its *compenetrazione*, or interpenetration, with the other arts, its ability as a technological invention to inspire the conception of new expressive devices in other fields.[3] In a similar vein, Giovanni Lista discusses Futurist dynamism with respect to Henri Bergson's concept of *durée*, which had a strong influence on Boccioni, Futurism's predominant theoretician in the early 1910s. According to Lista, the Futurists saw in cinema the possibility of a new expressive model, one that poets, painters, and sculptors could apply towards their dynamic readings of reality, yet they denied cinema the status of an aesthetic medium in its own right. Inasmuch as it portrays movement, the film image 'destroys the invigorating dimension of action, it surrenders the vital occurrence to the immutable fixity of that which was.' This is why, Lista argues, the Futurists invented 'performance,' an expressive form that requires that the artist is physically present and thus free of any mediation. In performance, 'it is the subjectivity of the artist that creates the work, while the work is a living act, inscribed in the most immediate present.'[4] Wanda Strauven also addresses Bergson's influence on Boccioni and the ensuing rejection of cinema. She notes that the 1916 film manifesto was published exactly three months after the death of 'the great cine-sceptic Boccioni, who undoubtedly would not have approved of such an act.'[5]

While the above observations suggest that Boccioni's influence delayed the Futurists' experimentation with cinema, they do not explain why the experimentation did not carry on once it began. Strauven discusses further conditions that explain Futurism's (specifically Marinetti's) preference for live performance and failure to develop a substantial body of cinematic work. Most important is the role of the spectator in the Futurist notion of spectacle.[6] In their auditoriums the Futurists attempted to create a revolutionary field of aesthetic experience, to break with the conventions that had traditionally shaped the reception of theatre. The theatrical performances that prevailed in Italy at the turn of the century displayed those formal traits that Futurism rejected by definition. They relied on the spectator's acceptance of the play as a self-contained work, hence his/her passive role vis-à-vis the performance, and the phenomena of illusionism and voyeurism as enforced by the 'fourth wall,' that is, the imaginary spatial division between stage and auditorium.[7] Instead, the Futurists wished to establish such conditions of reception as to make possible the conception of a new form of spectacle, one that was experienced not as something evolving only on stage but as the product of the spectators' participation and direct interaction with the performers. It was to implement layers of experience that trespassed both the spatial and the temporal boundaries of the pre-organized performance, thus entering life at large. As a means towards such an experience, cinema was clearly at a disadvantage because of its very nature. Its live counterpart offered a more tangible opportunity to disrupt the illusion through the direct interaction between spectators and performers, thus allowing for a 'spectacle' that we may accurately describe as a *physical encounter*.[8]

It is precisely from this angle, with respect to the role of the audience and the necessity to engage it in a physical encounter, that I will approach the question of Futurism's abandonment of cinema. However, I will reach beyond the evident obstacle posed by the medium's nature, to take into account a set of historical factors, comprising aspects of both national and film history, and study their interference with the kind of encounter that the Futurists sought. *Vita futurista* is testimony to such a phenomenon. The film premiered in early 1917 when Italy was at war with Austria. The notion of war, in both its literal and symbolic dimensions, was crucial to the realization of such an encounter. We may describe this type of encounter as the implementation of an *aesthetics of war*: not only did it involve an antagonistic interaction between the participants but the spirit that defined it was fuelled by the Futurists' exaltation of war, which typically set the atmosphere of their performances. Despite cinema's restrictive nature, the film should not have hindered this aesthetic, as the Futurists added the film to a series of diverse live performances. Yet the best-documented cases of its exhibition suggest that the film appeased the spectators' aggressive impulses and the belligerent spirit that the Futurists envisioned. This failure was not only a result of the medium's limitations but also a reflection of the country's state of war. The film's nationalism aroused a patriotic sentiment that provoked the audience's identification with the spectacle rather than its collision with it.

A crucial factor of this ironic outcome was Futurism's ambivalent relation to popular narrative cinema, which constituted a venue in its own right for the celebration of patriotism. Next to its abstract aesthetics, *Vita futurista* used some representational strategies originating in the domain of narrative cinema. The conjunction between the film's patriotic highlights and its allusion to narrative cinematic tropes activated a mode of reception that was specific to cinema as mass entertainment, thus reinforcing the audience's collusion (rather than collision) with the on-screen presentation. In this chapter I will examine the prominent claims made by the Futurists about the virtues of the new medium and the extent to which these claims found a concrete application in the content and style of *Vita futurista*. I will thus identify the cinematic framework, both conceptual and applied, within which the Futurists aspired to engage their audience in what I have called an aesthetics of war. The next chapter will follow with a close study of the exhibition of *Vita futurista*, underlining the nexus of historical factors, both cinematic and political, that shaped the experience of film exhibition for the audience. This will allow me to formulate a hypothesis about the effects of history upon the Futurists' ability to exploit the cinematic medium in the manner that they envisioned, hence, their desire or lack thereof to further pursue the practice of filmmaking.[9]

Virtues and Quandaries of a New Art

'La cinematografia futurista' describes film as a uniquely promising art form, called upon to collaborate with the rest of the arts in society's Futurist renewal, through the rejection, mockery, and replacement of respectable literature, theatre, and art in general.[10] The manifesto opens with an attack on the book, which it describes as an entirely passéist means of preserving and communicating thought, destined to disappear with all the other antiquated symbols of passéism, such as cathedrals, towers, and museums. Its place is to be occupied by Futurist cinema, which will constitute a school of joy, speed, force, courage, and heroism: 'Il cinematografo futurista acutizzerà, svilupperà la sensibilità, velocizzerà l'immaginazione creatrice, . . . collaborerà così al rinnovamento generale, . . . uccidendo il libro (sempre tedioso e opprimente)' [Futurist cinema will sharpen and develop sensibility, will accelerate creative imagination, . . . will thus collaborate in the general renewal, . . . by killing the (always tedious and oppressive) book] (*TIF* 138–9). Not the book alone but also traditional theatre, itself an obsolete form that exemplified the unwarranted prolongation of a sluggish culture that had run its course, was to be replaced by the spontaneous and forceful utterances of Futurist spectacle. Yet to the Futurists' discontent, the cinematic medium, having adopted the feature-length narrative form that by now dominated public cinema experience, chose instead to imitate theatre.

> A prima vista il cinematografo, nato da pochi anni, può sembrare già futurista, cioè privo di passato e libero di tradizioni: in realtà, esso, sorgendo come *teatro senza parole*, ha ereditate tutte le più tradizionali spazzature del teatro letterario . . . [I]l cinematografo sino ad oggi *è stato, e tende a rimanere profondamente passatista*, mentre noi vediamo in esso la possibilità di un'arte eminentemente futurista. (*TIF* 139–40)

> [At first glance cinema, born only a few years ago, may already seem Futurist, that is, lacking a past and free of traditions: in reality, rising as *theatre without words*, it has inherited all the most traditional sweepings of the literary theatre . . . Cinema until this moment *has been and tends to remain deeply passéist*, whereas we see in it the possibility of an eminently Futurist art.]

Hence, traditional theatre was not only problematic in its own right but also invaded cinema and prevented it from actualizing its Futuristic potential. It succeeded thanks to the advocates of traditionalism, who aspired to cinema's cultural legitimacy in accordance with older notions of artistic efficacy, aiming at things such as the development of historical themes and the adaptations of canonical works of literature.

The manifesto advises to think of cinema as an independent medium. It does so in a series of statements that may at first seem contradictory.

The Futurists describe cinema as 'un'altra zona del teatro' [another zone of the theatre],[11] shortly before claiming the following:

> Il cinematografo è un'arte a sé. Il cinematografo non deve dunque mai copiare il palcoscenico. Il cinematografo, essendo essenzialmente visivo, deve compiere anzitutto l'evoluzione della pittura: distaccarsi dalla realtà, dalla fotografia, dal grazioso e dal solenne. (*TIF* 140)

> [Cinema is an art in itself. Cinema must therefore never copy the stage. Cinema, being essentially a visual medium, must complete above all the evolution of painting: it must detach itself from reality, from photography, from the graceful and the solemn.]

The 'stage' that cinema 'must never copy' refers to traditional theatre, whereas the theatre of which cinema is 'another zone' is clearly the Futurist kind. The latter, in 1916 consisting of the 'synthetic theatre,' was surely an acceptable venue for the promotion of Futurist cinema, while its structural peculiarities, which the Futurists had outlined in a 1915 manifesto, are to some extent emulated by the aesthetic propositions of the film manifesto itself. A similar discourse is at work with respect to painting. Can cinema be an 'art in itself' if it must 'complete the evolution of painting'? The villain in this scenario is photographic verisimilitude, the dominance of which suppresses cinema's creative potential and facilitates its denigration to 'theatre without words.' As the tendency of traditional art towards verisimilitude culminates with photography, cinema is to abstain from this process and, like painting, remain abstract. However, as in the case of the stage, we are speaking not of just any form of painting but of the Futurist. Whereas all painting, even the realist, is worlds away from the mechanical operation that grants photography its verisimilitude, it would be misleading to suggest that Futurist cinema is to fulfil the evolution of any form of painting, including the realist. By 'evolution of painting,' the writers evoke the recent achievements of artists like Balla, Boccioni, Carrà, Russolo, and Severini.

Therefore, in speaking of cinema as an 'art in itself,' the Futurists are articulating a relative concept, not the emancipation of cinema *as a whole* vis-à-vis any other art *as a whole* but the medium's liberation from traditionalism and the actualization of its Futurist potential, in line with the pre-established principles of Futurist theatre, painting, and Futurist art in general. It is in this manner that cinema will become a true collaborator in the 'general renewal,' as the manifesto declares in its opening statements. Furthermore, cinema's cultivation of its affinities with other Futurist forms does not necessarily endanger its structural specificity: '**Occorre liberare il cinematografo come mezzo di espressione** per farne lo strumento ideale *di una nuova arte* immensamente più vasta e più agile di tute quelle esistenti' [**It is necessary to liberate cinema as a means of expression** in order to make of it the ideal instrument *of a new art*, immensely broader and more versatile than all the existing arts] (*TIF* 140).[12] It is none but cinema's technological specificity that accounts for its superiority. It is the only medium able to express the essentially multifaceted nature of Futurist sensibility, envisioned in the creation of a *sinfonia poli-espressiva*, a polyexpressive symphony, which consists in the amalgamation of all the arts, including the most diverse elements: fragments of real life, streaks of colour, words-in-freedom, chromatic and plastic music, painting, architecture, sculpture, and others (140).[13]

The manifesto describes a variety of techniques to be deployed by Futurist filmmaking. Most prominent is the concept of 'analogy,' which Marinetti introduced in his 1912 'Manifesto tecnico della letteratura futurista' (Technical Manifesto of Futurist Literature). It is here reintroduced in a film context, where it seems to be an effect of montage, namely, a succession of images the relations among which are not explicit. For instance, a man's state of anguish may be expressed through the depiction of a jagged and cavernous mountain. Or, 'rappresentando un uomo che dirà alla sua donna: Sei bella come una gazzella, daremo la gazzella' [representing a man who will say to his woman, 'You are beautiful like a gazelle,' we will show the gazelle] (*TIF* 141). There follows a technique the purpose of which is to directly mock the canon. The literal translation of highly esteemed poems into violent and exhilarating filmic images will provide relief to a public that is fed up with what the manifesto calls the monotonous, nostalgic, and whimpering tone of traditional poetry. A filmic transcription of Carducci's line 'il cor mi fuggì su 'l Tirreno' [my heart fled to the Tyrrhenian Sea] would portray Carducci himself as his heart literally 'gli sbotta fuori dalla giacca e vola come un enorme pallone rosso sul golfo di Rapallo' [pops out of his jacket and flies like a huge red balloon over the Gulf of Rapallo] (142–3). The use of film to literalize the metaphor not only ridicules the poem, but also suggests that film technology provides updated forms of aesthetic representation. In an era in which the visualization of any idea is possible with film, the conventional figurative uses of language, if not entirely obsolete, face an urgent need for revision. The manifesto proposes many more techniques, all of which depend on the medium's specific technology, among these: simultaneity and interpenetration of different times and places; musical researches, such as the dissonances, harmonies, and symphonies of gestures, facts, colours, and lines; dramas of objects; unrealistic reconstructions of the human body; dramas of disproportions, such as a man drinking up an entire lake with a giant straw; words-in-freedom represented in movement, including dramas of humanized or animated letters, or orthographic, typographic, and geometrical dramas (143–4).

Though adamant in its support of abstract aesthetics and contempt for realism, the manifesto endorses a specific type of film that relies largely on photographic verisimilitude: 'Salvo i films interessanti di viaggi, caccie, guerre, ecc., non hanno saputo infliggerci che drammi, drammoni e drammetti passatistissimi' [Except for interesting films about travel, hunting, wars, etc., they have done no more than inflict on us the most old-fashioned dramas] (*TIF* 140). Strauven sees this as a reference to the documentaries made in the first decade of the century by filmmakers such as Calcina, Comerio, Omegna, and Vitrotti, which focused on different sorts of current events, such as sports competitions, the hunting of wild animals, and natural or man-made disasters. She reconciles the films' documentary aspect with the aesthetic principles of Futurism. The films' main objective, she explains, was not narrative linearity or a well-constructed plot, but a new 'synthetic' vision of the world.[14] As described by Brunetta, they were not documentaries told 'in the third person' (mere registrations of events for journalistic purposes), but expressions of the filmmaker's subjective experience 'in the first person.'[15] Isabella Innamorati, by contrast, reads the manifesto's approval of documentaries with respect to Marinetti's praise of film's ability to *communicate* facts. She highlights a 1918 remark from Marinetti's notebooks, where reflecting upon a visit to the movies Marinetti concludes that the public's obsession with cinema indicates its growing passion for facts: 'Il *Teatro muto* senza tiritere psicologiche senza esitazioni meditative soddisfa il desiderio universale di avere dei fatti delle azioni veloci. Fatto o fattaccio violento, il pubblico odia le chiacchiere vuole veder *agire velocemente*' [The *mute Theatre*, without psychological rigmaroles or meditative hesitations, fulfils the universal desire to have facts, fast actions. Be it a mere fact or an ugly violent fact, the public hates chatter, it wants to see *fast action*].[16] Strauven's and Innamorati's remarks are complementary. If the Futurists approve of the documentaries because they are non-narrative, Marinetti's praise of film's ability to communicate fast actions without chatter is itself an attack on traditional theatre's reliance on dialogue and the analytical narrative that typically ensues. Yet narrative and verisimilitude, albeit their frequent co-presence, are distinct categories. The manifesto is consistently aloof towards narrative, yet its censure of verisimilitude in claiming cinema's need to 'detach itself from reality, from photography' remains at odds with its approval of documentaries, which Innamorati instructively aligns with Marinetti's praise of cinema's communicability, itself largely a result of verisimilitude.

The question of communicability is critical because it concerns the relationship between the on-screen presentation and the audience's response. In the film manifesto, it not only lurks under the endorsement of the documentaries, but also enters the discourse on analogy, an aesthetic device found at the core of the manifesto's pursuit of abstract representation. When he defines analogy in the 1912 literature manifesto, Marinetti presumes that abstraction and communicability are incompatible. What is 'analogy'? 'L'analogia non è altro che l'amore profondo che collega le cose distanti, apparentemente diverse ed ostili' [Analogy is nothing more than the deep love that connects distant, seemingly different and hostile things] (*TIF* 48).[17] Technically, it is built as follows:

Ogni sostantivo deve avere il suo doppio, cioè il sostantivo deve essere seguito, senza congiunzione, dal sostantivo a cui è legato per analogia. Esempio: uomo-torpediniera, donna-golfo, folla-risacca, piazza-imbuto, porta-rubinetto.

Siccome la velocità aerea ha moltiplicato la nostra conoscenza del mondo, la percezione per analogia diventa sempre più naturale per l'uomo. Bisogna dunque sopprimere il *come*, il *quale*, il *così*, il *simile a*. (*TIF* 47)

[**Every noun must have its double**, that is, the noun must be followed, with no conjunction, by the noun to which it is bound by analogy. Example: man-torpedo boat, woman-gulf, crowd-backwash, piazza-funnel, door-faucet.

Since aerial speed has multiplied our knowledge of the world, perception by analogy becomes ever more natural for man. It is therefore necessary to suppress the *like*, the *which*, the *thus*, the *similar to*.]

If Marinetti's examples do little more than echo conventional metaphorical associations, the concept becomes rather perplexing once he proposes the elimination of one of the two elements: 'Meglio ancora, bisogna fondere direttamente l'oggetto coll'immagine che esso evoca, dando l'immagine in iscorcio mediante una sola parola essenziale' [Better still, one needs to fuse the object directly with the image that it evokes, foreshortening the image to a single, essential word] (*TIF* 47). This is what Strauven aptly names 'analogy *in absentia*,' to be distinguished from 'analogy *in praesentia*' where both nouns appear side by side.[18] The unbroken sequence of such unipartite analogies will signal a radical expansion of the capabilities of the mind: 'Noi inventeremo insieme ciò che io chiamo **l'immaginazione senza fili**. Giungeremo un giorno ad un'arte ancor più essenziale, quando oseremo sopprimere tutti i primi termini delle nostre analogie per non dare più altro che il seguito ininterrotto dei secondi termini' [Together we will invent what I call **imagination without strings**. One day we will reach an even more essential art, when we dare to suppress all the first terms of our analogies in order to give but the uninterrupted series of the second terms]. That this type of discourse will be incomprehensible to the reader is stated categorically and does not trouble Marinetti a bit: 'Bisognerà, per questo, rinunciare ad essere compresi. Esser compresi, non è necessario' [For that, we will have to renounce being understood. Being understood is not necessary] (*TIF* 53).

The re-articulation of analogy for film is more evasive than its initial instance in the literature manifesto. At first glance, the cinematic equivalent is defined as analogy *in absentia*. Futurist cinema is to include '**analogie cinematografiche** usando la realtà direttamente come uno dei due elementi dell'analogia' [**filmed analogies** using reality directly as one of the two elements of the analogy] (*TIF* 141). It therefore seems determined to seek that expansion of the mind, that 'imagination without strings' that the literature manifesto had promised, now realizable quite vividly through the montage of tangible images.[19] Yet the example that follows relapses into a rather familiar structure: 'Se vorremo esprimere lo stato angoscioso di un nostro protagonista invece di descriverlo nelle sue varie fasi di dolore daremo un'equivalente impressione con lo spettacolo di una montagna frastagliata e cavernosa' [If we want to express the state of anguish of one of our protagonists, instead of describing it in its various phases of pain, we will give an equivalent impression by showing a jagged and cavernous mountain] (*TIF* 141). If this is to constitute an analogy *in absentia*, under no circumstances should the anguished face of the protagonist appear in the shot preceding the one of the mountain, as that would constitute instead an analogy *in praesentia*. In the absence of his face as first term, however, why would a 'jagged and cavernous mountain' convey his suffering rather than, let us say, an uplifting encounter with divine mystery, a sexual orgasm, or a geographical exploration? Will the anguished protagonist have appeared earlier in the film? If so, would that not constitute a mere variation of the analogy *in praesentia*, one that is simply amplified by a few intermediary shots separating the anguished face from the mountain? Furthermore, what would the content of those intermediary shots be? Would they or would they not relate to anguish? Moreover, what is the meaning of having a 'protagonist' whose feelings the film wants to express? Will the film be a narrative? Will it have a well-defined diegesis? Clearly, if the filmmaker's goal is to convey the protagonist's anguish, the filmmaker must reach a compromise between his wish to maintain an abstract aesthetic born out of an 'imagination without strings' and the necessity to succumb to the demands of narrative structure.

After a few relatively unambiguous suggestions of analogies *in absentia*, the manifesto resumes its discourse on the 'cervelli dei personaggi' [minds of the characters]. Evidently, analogy will be able to convey ideas that conventionally relied on dialogues:

> Coloriremo il dialogo dando velocemente e simultaneamente ogni immagine che attraversi i cervelli dei personaggi. Esempio: rappresentando un uomo che dirà alla sua donna: Sei bella come una gazzella, daremo la gazzella. – Esempio: se un personaggio dice: Contemplo il tuo sorriso fresco e luminoso come un viaggiatore contempla dopo lunghe fatiche il mare dall'alto di una montagna, daremo viaggiatore, mare, montagna.
>
> In tal modo i nostri personaggi saranno perfettamente comprensibili come *se parlassero*. (*TIF* 141–2)

[We will colourize the dialogue by swiftly and simultaneously showing every image that crosses the minds of the characters. Example: representing a man who will say to his woman, 'You are beautiful like a gazelle,' we will show the gazelle. – Example: if a character says, 'I contemplate your fresh and bright smile like a traveller after a long struggle contemplates the sea from high up on a mountain,' we will show traveller, sea, mountain.

In this way, our characters will be perfectly comprehensible *as if they spoke*.]

Which type of analogy do the above examples deploy and what are its implications for the film's communicability vis-à-vis the audience? In

the first example, it is indeed suggested that the line 'You are beautiful like a gazelle' is not enunciated. The use of the future tense ('dirà')
suggests that when the man is about to speak the line, we instead see
the gazelle.[20] The problem, however, concerns the presence/absence of
the woman. If she is present, we have an analogy *in praesentia*, one that
certainly revises a conventional metaphor (the one based on the gazelle
as an especially beautiful animal) with any connotations its filmic rendition may create – perhaps a mocking effect like the one intended
through the literal rendition of Carducci's metaphors. If the woman
is absent, however, we have the much-desired analogy *in absentia*, yet
the meaning of the relationship between the image of the man and the
subsequent image of the gazelle bears infinite possibilities and is by no
means restricted to a lover's compliment. The second example is even
more challenging. Unless the line 'I contemplate your fresh and bright
smile' appears in intertitles, even an analogy *in praesentia* (showing the
woman's smile followed by 'traveller, sea, mountain') would permit
numerous meanings other than the one sought by the writers.

The writers clearly oscillate between the wish to convey certain ideas
to the viewer (anguish, beauty, love) and the need to sacrifice communicability for a truly radical form of discourse, one that derives from
that 'imagination without strings' that the human mind is only now
about to discover. What is especially striking is that this incompatibility
between abstraction and communicability, which the literature manifesto boasted quite unapologetically ('Being understood is not necessary'), is now negated by an evidently incongruous statement that
asserts the lucidity of analogical discourse. In what sense will the characters be 'perfectly comprehensible *as if they spoke*'? On the one hand,
this may be an ironic statement with a polemical intention, namely, to
portray film as an art the silence of which does not render it at all inad-
equate compared to the verbose theatre. Perhaps what must be sacrificed is communicability *in its present state*, while the new imagination
will cultivate ways of communicating that are still unknown. In this
view, being 'perfectly comprehensible' does not imply the recognition
of a single idea as intended by the filmmaker (anguish, beauty, love),
but in line with the aim to 'accelerate creative imagination' it validates
the diverse and subjective ways in which images may be understood
by countless spectators.[21] On the other hand, the statement may simply
reflect the writers' sincere concern for the spectator's ability to comprehend, *here and now*. This would signify the writers' denial (conscious or
not) of the essential ambiguity that defines the unipartite analogy. Such
denial, of course, is the symptom of a deep indecisiveness, between

plunging into an enticing ideal the functionality of which remains to be seen and utilizing any conventional method that would guarantee communicability *in its present state*. Regardless of how we interpret the statement, 'being understood' is a larger concern here than in the literature manifesto. Why was communicability in poetry so effortlessly dismissed while it is more at stake when it regards the film spectator? Who is the film spectator and what is *his/her present state*?

The Futurist Spectator

The role of the spectator is a crucial aspect of Futurist performance. Yet the film manifesto does not address it directly, thus differing noticeably from the Futurist writings on theatre, which tell us vividly how the writers envision the audience. In 'Il Teatro di Varietà' (The Variety Theatre, 1913) Marinetti emphasizes above all the atmosphere that defines this form of diversion, describing the activities that unfold both on stage and in the auditorium. He claims that the variety theatre exemplifies the spirit of that new sensibility that informs the conception of Futurism itself. Like Futurism, it is born from electricity, free of traditions, masters, and dogma, and fed by swift actuality (*TIF* 81). Comic, erotic, astonishing; based on instinct, laughter, and muscular agility; averse of grief, anti-academic, intent upon destroying 'il Sublime dell'Arte coll'A maiuscolo' [the Sublime of Art with a capital A], the variety theatre generates the *meraviglioso futurista*, or Futurist marvellous, and replaces the theatre's traditional reliance on *psicologia*, or psychology, with the exhilarating *fisicofollia*, or body madness (86–7). By pushing some of its most crucial elements to their limits, Futurism will turn the variety theatre into a proper Futurist spectacle.[22] By removing any trace of logic, eliminating its tendency to establish any kind of tradition, 'prostituting' every respectable artwork represented, and introducing a strong element of surprise among the spectators, Futurism will transform the variety theatre into a theatre of amazement, record-setting, and body madness (*TIF* 88–9).

The phenomenon of 'body madness,' which is the primary aim of the experience, does not only refer to the eccentric activity of the stage performers (actors, singers, dancers, comedians, jugglers, gymnasts, among others) but rests upon the audience's active participation:

Il Teatro di Varietà è il solo che utilizzi la collaborazione del pubblico. Questo non vi rimane statico come uno stupido *voyeur*, ma partecipa rumorosamente all'azione, cantando anch'esso, accompagnando l'orchestra, comunicando con motti imprevisti e dialoghi bizzarri cogli attori. Questi polemizzano buffonescamente coi musicanti. (*TIF* 83)

[The Variety Theatre is the only one that makes use of the audience's collaboration. The audience does not remain static like a stupid *voyeur*, but participates noisily in the action, singing along, accompanying the orchestra, communicating with the actors in unforeseen witticisms and bizarre dialogues. The actors argue clownishly with the musicians.]

Singing and verbal exchange are not the only means of audience participation. The very definition of 'performance' is under question as the traditional conception of its space and time parameters is radically revised. Its actualization is limited neither by the physical space of the stage nor by the time frame for which the show is officially scheduled:

Il Teatro di Varietà utilizza il fumo dei sigari e delle sigarette per fondere l'atmosfera del pubblico con quella del palcoscenico. E poiché il pubblico collabora così colla fantasia degli attori, l'azione si svolge ad un tempo sul palcoscenico, nei palchi e nella platea. Continua poi alla fine dello spettacolo, fra i battaglioni di ammiratori, smockings caramellati che si assiepano all'uscita per disputarsi la *stella*; doppia vittoria finale: cena *chic* e letto. (*TIF* 83–4)

[The Variety Theatre uses the smoke of cigars and cigarettes to fuse the atmosphere of the auditorium with that of the stage. And since the audience in this way collaborates with the actors' imagination, the action unfolds simultaneously on the stage, in the boxes, and in the orchestra. It then continues after the end of the show, among the battalions of admirers, sybaritic dandies who crowd around the exit to fight over the *star*; double final victory: *chic* dinner and bed.]

As the action carries on beyond the 'end' of the show, and the erotic tension between spectator and performer begun during the performance is extended indefinitely, the thing that disintegrates is not only the fourth wall, but also the very distinction between aesthetic experience and life at large. Furthermore, aiming to expand the prospects of body madness, Marinetti proposes the introduction of *surprise* in the auditorium, as a result of which the spectators would make a spectacle out of themselves. He suggests various things to this end, such as putting glue on some of the seats so that the 'victims' cause laughter, selling the same seat to many persons so as to create an amusing traffic jam, offering free admission to persons notoriously eccentric, irritable, and obscene, or sprinkling the seats with itching and sneezing powder (*TIF* 88–9).

'Il teatro futurista sintetico' (The Futurist Synthetic Theatre), a manifesto written in 1915 by Marinetti, Settimelli, and Corra, appropriates the variety theatre's parodying of respectable art and rejection of logic, and proceeds to define the parameters of the 'synthetic theatre,' a Futurist trademark. The notion of 'synthesis' stands against the 'analytic,' or detailed (therefore slow and tedious), mode of representation that defines traditional theatre. It refers to condensed and very brief acts, which, 'in perfetta armonia colla velocissima e laconica nostra sensibilità futurista ... potranno anche essere *attimi*, e cioè durare pochi secondi' [in perfect harmony with our very fast and laconic Futurist sensibility ... can also be *moments*, and thus last a few seconds] (*TIF* 115). The concept of 'synthesis,' although not emphasized as such, was already implicit in the variety theatre manifesto. Marinetti praised the variety theatre for explaining 'in an incisive and rapid manner the most sentimental and abstruse problems.' He also suggested things such as representing in a single evening all the Greek, French, and Italian tragedies comically mixed up, or all of Shakespeare in a single act.[23] The participation of the audience in the event is likewise extended from the variety to the synthetic theatre:

> *sinfonizzare la sensibilità del pubblico esplorandone, risvegliandone con ogni mezzo le propaggini più pigre; eliminare il preconcetto della ribalta lanciando delle reti di sensazioni tra palcoscenico e pubblico; l'azione scenica invaderà platea e spettatori;* (TIF 121)

> [*to symphonize the audience's sensibility by exploring, by reawakening its laziest layers by every possible means; eliminate the preconception of the footlights by casting nets of sensations between stage and auditorium; the stage action will invade orchestra and spectators;*]

The metaphor of 'casting nets of sensations' suggests the elimination of the fourth wall while it also privileges a sensual experience over the analytical/intellectual prerequisite of traditional theatre. Furthermore,

> *creare tra di noi e la folla, mediante un contatto continuato, una corrente di confidenza senza rispetto, così da trasfondere nei nostri pubblici la vivacità dinamica di una nuova teatralità futurista.* (TIF 121)

[to create between us and the crowd, through a continuous contact, a current of confidence without respect, so as to instil in our audiences the dynamic liveliness of a new Futurist theatricality.]

In place of the conventional 'respect,' which rendered the audience's attitude towards the stage one of awe and passive surrender, a relation of 'confidence without respect' between the spectators and the producers of the 'synthesis' implies the active participation of the former in the implementation of the spectacle, or the event.

The role of the Futurist *film* spectator, if not explicitly addressed in the film manifesto, must be inferred from its theatrical counterpart. Marinetti's exaltation of the variety theatre provides raw material for Tom Gunning's articulation of the 'cinema of attractions':

> Writing on the variety theatre, Marinetti not only praised its aesthetics of astonishment and stimulation, but particularly its creation of a new spectator who contrasts with the 'static,' 'stupid voyeur' of traditional theatre. The spectator at the variety theatre feels directly addressed by the spectacle and joins in, singing along, heckling the comedians.[24]

Aiming to complicate a prejudice of previous scholarship that viewed early cinema as a 'primitive' stage of development towards classicism, Gunning elucidates the specificity of early cinema in terms of both style of representation and modes of exhibition. Founded on 'exhibitionism' rather than voyeurism and narrative absorption, early cinema flaunted 'its ability to *show* something.' By means of visual display, through things such as tricks and the actor's look at the camera, its purpose was to shock, surprise, assault, incite visual curiosity, create pleasure through spectacle, and establish direct contact with the spectator, always at the expense of the story and the diegesis. The mode of exhibition contributed greatly to the stimulation of the spectator through direct address. Until about 1905, unlike the later modes that developed along with cinema's adoption of the feature-length narrative, exhibition consisted primarily of the inclusion of films as one part of a larger and diverse vaudeville program, as one 'attraction' within a non-narrative and illogical succession of distinct acts and performances. In his 1913/14 manifesto, Marinetti himself praised the variety theatre for including the projection of films, 'che lo arricchisce d'un numero incalcolabile di visioni e di spettacoli irrealizzabili' [which enriches it with an incalculable number of unrealizable visions and shows] (*TIF* 81).[25] Evidently, at least for the purposes of Futurism, Marinetti held film and theatre audiences as indistinguishable.

By 1916, however, when the film manifesto was written, the exhibition of feature-length narratives in the film auditorium proper had been established as the prevalent form of cinematic experience. Exemplary 'Dannunzian' genres such as the *storico* and the *cinema in frak*, which had mesmerized Italian audiences with their operatic re-enactments of milestones of world history and lavish adaptations of romantic nineteenth-century novels, epitomized what the film manifesto attacked as a passéist appropriation of the new medium. One wonders which role the writers of the film manifesto envisioned for the spectator while they abstained from articulating it directly. Were they still aiming for an active, unruly audience like that of the variety theatre, or were they surrendering to the newly formed 'static,' 'stupid voyeur' of the fashionable 'theatre without words'? One would assume that Marinetti had every reason to detach his film audience from the 'fate' that had befallen the average moviegoer. Indeed, if the manifesto does not directly address the question, *Vita futurista* provides a practical answer. Entirely outside the prevailing modes of film distribution and exhibition, it was shown for the first time at a Florentine theatre as the last part of a longer spectacle, following the performance of four Futurist 'syntheses' and the reading of Futurist poetry.[26]

This type of 'variety' performance, in both its formal organization and mode of address, exemplifies a later phase of the infamous *serate futuriste*, or Futurist evenings. As early as 1910, moving from city to city, the *serate* were public gatherings that consisted of a series of extremely provocative performances, including things such as the declamation of poetry, the reading of manifestos, and the presentation of paintings. Typically, the audience was provoked to such a degree that it responded quite violently, turning the event into a 'miniature war' between themselves and the performers.[27] The type of performance that Marinetti praised in the variety theatre manifesto described also, if implicitly, the project of the *serata* as an encounter that stirred a high degree of hyperactivity.[28] The *serata* represented the Futurists' own means of creating a spirit similar to that of variety, of which the close affinity to Futurist sensibility Marinetti cherished. It is important to note, however, that although the term 'serata' sometimes refers to any Futurist performance from the 1910s or early 1920s, the Futurist *serata* in the strict sense displayed a set of distinct qualities that prevailed only in the first four or five years of the movement's life.[29] It consisted of a loose structure and open format, allowing for improvisation and last-minute additions not included in the advertised program. Marinetti himself differentiated the *serata* from those types of performances that were fully rehearsed and based on dramatic texts.[30] Although audience participation was very much an aspiration of the 1915 synthetic theatre manifesto, the systematic incorporation of 'syntheses' into the *serata*, in that they constituted orchestrated acts often acted by professional actors, contributed to its modification and to a certain degree of 'taming' of the audience.[31] Nonetheless, despite any modification that the *serata* may have undergone, the 1916 exhibition of *Vita futurista* still speaks to the Futurists' desire to practise cinema in the context of a peculiar form of variety. By premiering their film in an evening of diverse performances, the Futurists refuted the contemporaneous structure of cinema as mass entertainment, which boasted the feature-length film, narrative genre, and the large film auditorium proper, and for which the 'spectator' was a specifically cinematic concept radically distinguishable from the original (active) audience of the cinema of attractions and the variety theatre.[32]

Hence, Futurist theatre and cinema do not constitute two distinct media, as the culture of traditional theatre and the narrativization of film would have it, but two complementary parts of one single experience, produced by a formal organization and mode of address the origin of which is the *serata futurista*. As Marinetti aspired to a form of spectacle that would liberate film from overpowering traditionalist influences, through this type of venue he was driving film back towards its origins.[33] He was refuelling that very energy that had formed the spirit of the *caffè-concerto* or the French *Café chantant*. In citing Marinetti, besides illuminating a specific aspect of early cinema, Gunning also demonstrates the enthusiasm that the early avant-garde exhibited for the cinema of attractions. He selects the term 'attractions' from Eisenstein's writings on theatre, to highlight the concern that the avant-garde shared with early cinema as regards the relation of the spectator to the spectacle, namely, 'that of exhibitionist confrontation rather than diegetic absorption.' According to Gunning, what attracted the avant-garde towards early cinema's exhibitionism was the sense of 'liberation' that it offered to mass audiences not acculturated to the traditional arts.[34] In designating the *serata* (though in its later form) as the space of exhibition of Futurist film, Marinetti attempted to offer his audiences that feeling of 'liberation' that early cinema had offered.[35]

Yet to re-enact in the mid-1910s the 'liberation' brought about with early cinema meant something quite different from the initial experience. The thing that early cinema had offered to a non-acculturated public was the opportunity for a social and aesthetic experience that traditional culture had denied it. In the mid-1910s, however, the Futurists were operating in a different setting. 'The enormous development of the entertainment industry since the 1910s,' says Gunning, 'and its growing acceptance by middle-class culture . . . have made it difficult to understand the liberation popular entertainment offered at the beginning of the century.'[36] Whether or not the public that the Futurists addressed in the mid-1910s was one acculturated to the traditional arts, it was certainly one acculturated to narrative cinema. Thus, for such a public, experiencing a 'liberation' would signify, rather, experiencing a feeling of *oscillation*: between its wish to reach the fulfilment that the new mass culture was promising it and the prevention of this fulfilment imposed by the aesthetics of Futurist spectacle. Undoubtedly, the project of challenging the position of this new mass public defines the conception of Futurist film as an oppositional practice and is therefore one of the factors that grant Futurism its status as an avant-garde movement.

Vita futurista

The single film that the Futurists produced as a movement was a collaborative project, written and acted by a group of Futurists with Ginna as producer and director. As the film is not extant, our knowledge of its content relies on secondary sources, such as testimonies by Futurists involved in its making, advertisements of its premiere, newspaper reviews following its exhibition, a treatment submitted to the authorities for censorship clearance (the Nulla Osta), and several surviving stills previously published in various scholarly works.[37] More recently, Lista contributed the description of six surviving brief fragments from the film.[38] Four documents in particular include what seems to be a summary of the entire film: a 1965 article by Ginna; a recurrent advertisement in *L'Italia Futurista*; a poster of Florence's Teatro Niccolini advertising the film's premiere; and the version submitted for the Nulla Osta. These documents differ substantially from each other, especially regarding the film's length, the total number of episodes, the order in which the episodes were placed, and the exact titles of some of the episodes.[39] The Nulla Osta submission, discovered in the 1980s by Innamorati, offers the most comprehensive of the four versions.[40] According to this document, the film's original length was 990 metres. However, after the censorship of the last episode, 'Perché Francesco Giuseppe non moriva' (Why Francesco Giuseppe Wouldn't Die), and the Futurists' decision to reintegrate 'Colazione futurista' (Futurist Meal), the final product was probably 800 metres in length, corresponding to the duration of approximately 40 minutes.[41] It is possible that the film was edited differently on different occasions, which would explain the varying reports on its content and length.[42] The episodes were diegetically autonomous and marked by a diverse range of narrative situations and film techniques, while sharing the overarching and more-or-less explicit themes of anti-traditionalism and political anti-neutralism. Michael Kirby frames his analysis of *Vita futurista* within the question of the film's avant-garde status. That is confirmed, he concludes, both on sociological and stylistic grounds. The film was produced independently by a group of artists for their own aesthetic purposes, aiming to be innovative and break with the traditions of filmmaking.[43] Strauven also confirms the film's avant-gardism, highlighting its improvisational approach, technical experimentation, and anti-narrative mission. Specifically, she notes, the film lacks an overall narrative progression, despite a degree of storytelling within the individual episodes.[44]

Some of the episodes clearly correspond to the abstract aesthetics proposed in the film manifesto. 'Uccidiamo il chiaro di luna' (Let's Murder the Moonlight) is described in the Nulla Osta document as the story of a young Futurist who falls in love and wastes his virile energy in 'vani romanticismi platonici' [vain platonic romanticism].[45] According to Ginna's essay, where the episode is titled 'Il futurista sentimentale' (The Sentimental Futurist), the young man 'si lascia sopraffare da sentimentalismo amoroso, vinto dall'addensarsi su di lui di forze psichiche passatiste' [allows himself to be overwhelmed by amorous sentimentality, defeated by passéist psychic forces that gather upon him].[46] The Nulla Osta states that the man's troubled state of mind is represented by spluttering dots in the air around him. As we learn from Ginna and Venna, the Futurist who assisted Ginna in the filmmaking, during development the film was exposed to dust, sprinkling the image with white dots. Ginna reacted creatively by hand colouring the dots so as to portray the man's disturbed state of mind.[47] Another example of abstract style is the multipartite segment 'Deformazioni' (Deformations), which includes the love story between Balla and a chair and the resulting birth of a footstool. The surviving stills suggest the distortion of the human figure through the use of special mirrors and the practice of double exposure in only part of the image. One still shows Balla in the left of the frame extending his arm towards the chair in the right. His figure is stretched laterally and his arm is elongated, while the background seems to consist of wallpaper the vertical stripes of which are also distorted (figure 1.1). (Although the wallpaper stripes seem to have faded in the copy of the image that I have had at my disposal, they appear more clearly in other reproductions of the same image.)[48] Another set of stills, evidently from the same episode, portrays a dancing female in a white dress. The ethereal dancer appears in the left of the frame and is superimposed, undistorted, on the persistently distorted wall stripes, while Balla's figure, also still distorted, is now in the right and visible only in part (figure 1.2). Critics interpret the female dancer as the soul of the chair with which Balla falls in love.[49]

Moreover, the segment 'Ricerche d'ispirazione – Dramma d'oggetti' (Researches of Inspiration – Drama of Objects) depicts things as

Figure 1.1 Balla's distorted figure in the 1916 film *Vita futurista*. (Reprinted from Mario Verdone, *Cinema e letteratura del futurismo* [Rome: Centro Sperimentale di Cinematografia, Edizioni di Bianco e Nero, 1968])

Figure 1.2 An ethereal dancer in *Vita futurista*. (Reprinted from Mario
Verdone, *Cinema e letteratura del futurismo* [Rome: Centro Sperimentale di
Cinematografia, Edizioni di Bianco e Nero, 1968])

imaginative as the exploration of herrings, carrots, and eggplants, the scene of a ball that falls on the head of a statue and stays still, and the 'discussion' between a foot, a hammer, and an umbrella. The artists aimed to position various objects strangely and outside their habitual ambience so as to view them from a new perspective (*TIF* cxxx), achieving something of a defamiliarization effect.[50] Surely, the abstract qualities of the above episodes constitute a filmic equivalent of the 'Futurist marvellous,' which Marinetti defined in 'Il Teatro di Varietà' as a product of *meccanismo moderno*, or modern mechanics, and includes things such as the deep analogies between humanity, the animal world, the plant world, and the mechanical world, or 'tutte le nuove significazioni della luce, del suono, del rumore e della parola, coi loro prolungamenti misteriosi e inesplicabili nella parte più inesplorata della nostra sensibilità' [all the new meanings of light, sound, noise and language, with their mysterious and inexplicable extensions into the least-explored part of our sensibility] (*TIF* 82). Let us note that inasmuch as the film's 'marvellous' exemplifies the techniques that the manifesto launches as innovations in search of a utopian future, it also represents the revival of a recent past. As in later (and specifically American) avant-garde movements, it evokes that 'marvellous,' the exploration of the absurd and nonsensical, that characterized the cinema of Méliès at the turn of the century.[51]

A tribute to the cinema of attractions is also suggested in 'Danza dello splendore geometrico' (Dance of Geometric Splendour), which Ginna describes as a group of young women engaged in a dynamic-rhythmic dance, dressed in variously shaped costumes made of tinfoil. Bright reflectors shining against the moving tinfoil created the peculiar effect of luminous flashes intersecting each other so as to destroy the ponderability of the bodies.[52] Lista endorses Ginna's account, adding that the scene was a revival of the 'Dance of Steel' that Loïe Fuller had presented in 1914 in Paris. Fuller's dancers were covered with pieces of fabric bearing metal spangles and, being violently illuminated, wriggled about to a rigid and incisive music by Florent Schmitt. According to Lista, the film medium enhanced the intensity of the light effects.[53] Whether the episode is a tribute to the variety theatre's ballerinas, whom Marinetti included in a list of diverse performers responsible for variety's 'dinamismo di forma e di colore' [dynamism of form and colour], achieved by the simultaneous movements of jugglers, gymnasts, and spiral cyclones of dancers spinning on the points of their feet (*TIF* 83), or to the figure of Loïe Fuller, whose 'serpentine dance' provided the subject matter of some of the earliest examples of moving pictures by both Edison and Lumière, it stages the alliance between Futurism and attractions.[54] The metallic effect achieved between the costumes and the lighting adds a significant dimension to the conventional variety dance. In a Futuristic manner, it flaunts the film's metonymic relation to an era defined by steel and electricity.

The examples of the 'Futurist marvellous,' which shared something with the cinema of Méliès, were interspersed with episodes shot in a more verisimilar style. These 'realistic' ones did not intend to imitate the now popular feature-length narrative, but, like their more abstract counterparts, evoked earlier modes of representation now being over-shadowed by its institutionalization. In 'Colazione futurista,' which Ginna calls 'Scena al ristorante di Piazzale Michelangelo' (Scene at the Restaurant of Michelangelo Square), an outdoors restaurant scene in Florence depicts a white-bearded old man as a symbol of traditionalism (played by Venna in disguise) whose eating style is mocked by a group of young Futurists. During the shooting, an Englishman misunderstood the fiction for reality and reproached Marinetti for insulting the elderly. The combination of the on-location shooting with the fortuitous incident allowed some scholars to view the episode as a precursor of the French *cinéma vérité* or the unplanned sequences of Dziga Vertov, among others.[55] The episode, however, also invokes an earlier moment of cinema, the Italian actualities filmed around 1900 under the influence of Lumière, as well as the early Lumière actualities themselves. A surviving still portrays roughly eight men sitting at the tables of a restaurant (as suggested by the white table cloths), against a background of trees and what seem to be the columns of an arcade. The white-bearded Venna is visible in the centre and towards the background (figure 1.3).[56] The on-location shooting at an outdoors Florentine restaurant recalls the work of some Italian pioneers, the most prominent being Filoteo Alberini and Rodolfo Remondini, who had adopted the Lumière stratagem of shooting in populated streets and piazzas as a way of recruiting those potential clients who craved to catch a glimpse of themselves on screen.[57]

Actualities often portrayed special outdoors events many of which involved a mass audience and the public appearances of influential figures, such as politicians, royalty, and prominent clergy. Others focused on the common activities of individuals, especially during the very first years of cinema when the apparatus's ability to portray movement was itself a crucial aspect of the film's appeal. Films such as *Card Party* (1895), *The Baby's Meal* (1895), and *Boat Leaving the Port* (1895) are

Figure 1.3 The scene of a Futurist meal from *Vita futurista*. (Reprinted from Mario Verdone, *Cinema e letteratura del futurismo* [Rome: Centro Sperimentale di Cinematografia, Edizioni di Bianco e Nero, 1968])

only a small sample of the Lumière filmography in this area. There is a thematic affinity between 'Colazione futurista' and *Card Party*, which shows three men playing cards, drinking, and smoking at an outdoors café, while the server displays his fascination with the mechanics of the game. Each film seems to rejoice about its own assembly of jovial men eager to exhibit their astuteness in public. The affinities with *The Baby's Meal* are also evident. This film portrays one of its makers, Auguste Lumière, during the family's daily activity of feeding the baby. Similarly, 'Colazione futurista' shows Marinetti (also one of the film's makers) involved in the equally common activity of eating with his fellow Futurists. If the Futurist episode appears to lack realism as compared to the Lumière short, that is because it aspires not simply to capture a random moment of daily life but to stage Futurism's rejection of passéism. The Lumière short, however, is not wholly transparent either. Not only does it rely on a given degree of staging, it aspires to display its own negation of the past, as represented, if implicitly, by the very invention of the Cinématographe.

The intrusion of reality into the staged event, which in 'Colazione futurista' occurs with the Englishman's reaction, does not only anticipate

later traditions (*cinéma vérité*, Vertov) but also constitutes the appropriation of an element that had already existed in Lumière. In his reading
of *Boat Leaving the Port*, Dai Vaughan sees in the unpredicted 'invasion
of the spontaneous into the human arts' an early indication of cinema's
unique potentialities. Three men take off on a rowboat in seemingly
calm waters, before they are forced to struggle against a threatening
wave that they had not foreseen. The boat ride, like the Futurist meal,
is what the filmmaker intended, while the wave, like the Englishman,
is an intrusion that forces the performers to react spontaneously and
beyond the filmmaker's initial intention. In Vaughan's words, we have
a 'veritable doubling-back of the world into its own imagery, a denial
of the order of a coded system: an escape of the represented from the
representational act.' This is a specifically cinematic trait, Vaughan indicates.[58] Indeed, differently from theatre, where an intrusion of this sort
would signify failure, in each of these cases the unplanned element
stays and becomes part of the final product. This distinction, however,
does not apply to Futurism. For one, it is traditional theatre that perceived such intrusions as failures, whereas Futurist theatre welcomed
unanticipated intrusions joyously. Let us also recall that Futurist film
and theatre are complementary, more so than distinct, forms of spectacle. Furthermore, it is fitting that Marinetti, who contested traditional
theatre by crafting his *serata* and synthesis upon the foundation of the
variety theatre, now offers an alternative to cinema's own degradation
into 'theatre without words' by paying tribute to the cinema of attractions, which was, in a sense, variety's adopted child.

A verisimilar visual style, albeit the awkward action, also prevails
in those episodes that celebrate the superior physical prowess of the
Futurists over the traditionalists or neutralists. A still from 'Come dorme
un futurista' (How a Futurist Sleeps) shows a neutralist immersed
in sleep on a normal (that is, horizontal) bed, next to a Futurist who
sleeps vertically, thus staying always alert (figure 1.4). Furthermore,
'Passeggiata futurista' (Futurist Walk) is most likely the episode that
theatre critic and director Corrado Pavolini, in a 1926 article in which
he recalls his viewing of *Vita futurista*, described as follows: 'At a certain
moment my scene at the Cascine reappeared. It was the *neutralist step*,
hesitant, fearful, Hamletian, in contrast with the *interventionist step* that
Marinetti achieved heatedly, running like a bayonet.'[59] Four additional
episodes of a related theme appear in some of the sources as a unit and
in this order: 'Ginnastica mattutina' (Morning Gymnastics), 'Scherma,
boxe' (Fencing, Boxing), 'Assalto futurista alla spada fra Marinetti e

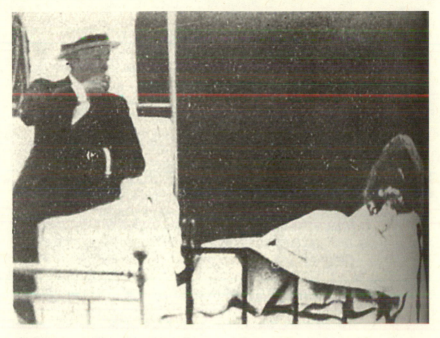

Figure 1.4 A Futurist sleeps vertically in *Vita futurista*. (Reprinted from Mario Verdone, *Cinema e letteratura del futurismo* [Rome: Centro Sperimentale di Cinematografia, Edizioni di Bianco e Nero, 1968])

Remo Chiti' (Futurist Attack with Swords between Marinetti and Remo Chiti), and 'Discussione coi guantoni fra Marinetti e Ungari' (Discussion with Boxing Gloves between Marinetti and Ungari).[60] As the descriptions and titles indicate, most of the episodes portray a Futurist (often Marinetti) engaged in some form of a 'duel' and exhibiting his superior flexibility and dexterity against his non-Futurist opponent.

A significant stylistic element that these episodes share is that of slapstick. They all seem to rely on a depiction of the body as particularly elastic and in unlikely and caricatural positions, which the descriptions and titles invite us to interpret as comical, especially in its combination with the accentuated bravado and other histrionics with which the Futurists exhibit their pre-eminence. The film's slapstick constitutes an additional form of tribute to the variety theatre and to the cinema of attractions. According to Innamorati, these episodes represent the 'implementation of *fisicofollia*, of caricature, of the crafts of the variety theatre, the spirit of which animates a large part of *Vita futurista*.'[61] According to Lista, the Futurist film is, among other things, a parody of early ethnographic documentaries. It functions as a manual of sorts that demonstrates satirically how the Futurists live vis-à-vis ordinary people: how they eat, sleep, run, attack, fence, and box. In addition, Lista sees the film as the 'heir of the most authentic genre of Italian cinema,' namely, Fregoli's *commedia improvvisa*, or impromptu comedy, which enjoyed great popularity in Italy near the turn of the century, and the spirit of which revived that of the Commedia dell'Arte.[62]

The film's slapstick, however, also evokes a much more recent genre. A still that is presumably from 'Discussione coi guantoni' depicts an outdoors field where two men are engaged in a boxing match. Both are fully clothed in what seem to be evening tails. Shown in long-shot and centre-frame, Marinetti faces the camera while Ungari, facing the background, falls on the grass, evidently after a blow he received from Marinetti's left arm (figure 1.5). The combination of slapstick with elegant attire during boxing evokes the *comica*, a popular genre of the early 1910s that consisted of the production of short comedies in a series. All films within any given series portrayed the adventures and blunders of a steady protagonist played by the same actor. The genre's origins are to be found in its French equivalent, developed by Pathé Frères in the previous decade. Its expansion in Italy began in 1908–9, after Pastrone of Itala Film succeeded in hiring away André Deed, Pathé's most popular comic actor at the time, to play the role of a shrewd troublemaker by the name of Cretinetti. Other Italian producers followed suit with the invention of numerous lovable 'cretins,' such as Fricot, Jouliceur, Kri Kri, Polidor, Ravioli, Robinet, and Tontolini, among others.[63]

As regards the affinity between the *comica* and Marinetti's boxing match, let us note that the amusing portrayals of faulty duels and boxing matches must have been quite popular at the time as they provided the subject matter of the *comica* with remarkable frequency.[64] In addition, the *comica* was often set in a bourgeois milieu, aiming to parody its code of gestures and rituals, especially as incarnated in the figure of the dandy.[65] The collapse of such a code and of the physical world that nurtured it was often the *comica*'s main cause of laughter and was achieved to a large extent via the effects of slapstick.[66] Marinetti's and Ungari's formal garments are of course signifiers of that code, while their incongruous blend with a ritualized sport and the slapstick effect that follows, much in the style of the *comica*, disrupt the code's inherent stability.

Figure 1.5 Marinetti beats Ungari in boxing, in *Vita futurista*. (Reprinted from Mario Verdone, *Cinema e letteratura del futurismo* [Rome: Centro Sperimentale di Cinematografia, Edizioni di Bianco e Nero, 1968])

Having enjoyed an immense popularity in the first half of the decade, in 1915 the *comica* faced a rapid decline. It was the victim of an economic crisis, which resulted in part from the competition with American cinema, now claiming its space on Italian screens more decisively, and to which the Italian film industry responded with increased investments in feature-length narratives and the further development of stardom.[67] Even in the genre's most glorious days in the early 1910s, it was typical to exhibit a *comica* only at the very end of the show, following a feature-length historical film or melodrama, the reason for which the genre is also known as that of the *comiche finali*. Although it ostensibly constituted a minor part of the evening, its inclusion functioned, according to Brunetta, as a 'healthy antidote' against the danger of '*galvanization* produced by the exaltation of virtue, the cult of heroes, the representation of edifying deeds, bathed in a rich aura of cultural echoes and reflections.'[68] Aldo Bernardini calls the genre a 'free trade zone,' in that it remained uncontaminated by the moralism, cult of patriotism, fine sentiments, and respectability that dominated the dramatic and historical films of those years.[69] With its various athletic competitions – running, fencing, attacking with a sword, boxing – all presumably performed in tails, *Vita futurista* perhaps hoped to share some of the *comica*'s antidotal properties; and with its Méliès-like marvellous and Lumière-like realism, to commemorate any form of cinema that had been effaced by the medium's theatricalization.

A further invocation of early cinema is perhaps found in the episode described by Ginna as the declamation of poetry with the simultaneous accompaniment of arm movements. 'Certainly,' says Kirby, 'the arm movements would have been very important because this was a silent film.'[70] In the absence of further evidence, Kirby may be correct in seeing this as a strictly visual rather than verbal presentation. Yet considering the context of the film's projection, preceded by syntheses and poetry readings, it is possible that the episode was accompanied by live reading. This would have resembled the presence of the lecturer in early attractions, whose goal was less to facilitate the audience's comprehension of the narrative than to enhance the intensity of the spectacle and the auditorium's lively atmosphere. Furthermore, besides the distinct elements from this or that episode, *Vita futurista* as a whole also displays affinities with earlier cinemas. For instance, with the exception of one surviving still that shows a close-up of Remo Chiti, the remaining stills suggest an overall prevalence of tableauesque compositions. In addition, there is the question of montage. The secondary sources do not indicate the extent to which any episode relied on montage to tell its story. Presuming the narrative simplicity of most episodes and the privileged place of the 'synthesis' in Futurist aesthetics, it is possible that the film's montage, even if practised within individual episodes (and arguably with the exception of a seemingly intricate episode portraying a *serata futurista* in Naples, to be discussed in the next chapter), avoided any complex techniques aiming at narrative continuity. Nonetheless, one thing that we may posit with certainty is that the montage of the film as a whole, comprising scenes that were narratively and diegetically autonomous, simulated the mode of presentation typical of a variety show and therefore of this very *serata*.

The notion that the film's formal organization mirrors that of the *serata* in which it is exhibited invites a discussion of self-referentiality, an aspect of the film that also comprises its essayistic dimension. The film aims not only to entertain but also to explore Futurism's position vis-à-vis popular cinema and culture, and society in general. Self-referentiality and essayism are tendencies that distinguish *Vita futurista* from the cinema of attractions, not because these tendencies were absent from attractions, but because the thematic concerns with which they are associated are specific to Futurism. We have noted a parallel between 'Colazione futurista' and *The Baby's Meal*, both of which portray their own creators and assert, explicitly or implicitly, the will to transcend the old and worship the new. Self-referentiality finds its least camouflaged form in Lumière's *Leaving the Factory* (1895), where the action focuses on the crowd of Lumière workers while exiting the factory after a day's work. Also, later attractions abound in examples that draw on the very act of film viewing, commenting on its social and psychological repercussions. This is the case with Robert Paul's *The Countryman and the Cinematograph* (1901), and its remake, Edwin S. Porter's *Uncle Josh at the Moving Picture Show* (1902), both of which represent a naive spectator whose first encounter with cinema leads him to mistake the action on the screen for reality. This is also the case with D.W. Griffith's *Those Awful Hats* (1909), where the lofty feathered hats of the bourgeois ladies in the audience infuriate those spectators whose view they block, thus raising questions of spectatorship regarding cinema as social practice. Next to the Lumière shorts, these films display a more complex form of self-referentiality, or what we may call metacinema. Comparing *Leaving the Factory* to *Uncle Josh* illustrates the difference between an apparatus that exhibits itself and one that both exhibits and critiques itself. During his first experience as a moviegoer, Uncle Josh, a country rube, watches three films, *Parisian Dancer*, *The Black Diamond Express*, and *The Country Couple*, all of which are clips from earlier Edison films. Upon seeing the dancer, he jumps onto the stage and tries to dance with her, when the onrushing train makes him run back to his seat in terror. Yet when he witnesses the man's flirting with the woman in the third film, his morals compel him again to interfere, only to break down the screen and expose the projectionist behind it.[71]

Vita futurista is to a great extent a film about film. Its metacinematic aspect, however, differs notably from the metacinematic concerns of the films mentioned above. If those explore the challenges confronting the average spectator in grappling with a technological novelty, *Vita futurista*, a decade or two later, aims to launch a mode of viewing that contradicts the one cultivated in recent years by a now familiar and well-founded institution. According to the advertisement 'Alcune parti del film "Vita Futurista"' (Some Parts of the Film 'Futurist Life'), which appeared in all issues of *L'Italia Futurista* from 15 October to 1 December 1916, the film's opening included the projection of written text addressing the Futurists' intention to realize their radical theoretical propositions for cinema:

ALCUNE PARTI DEL FILM 'VITA FUTURISTA'
I.

Proiezione delle principali affermazioni novatrici del manifesto sulla cinematografia futurista scritto e lanciato in molte migliaia di copie da Marinetti, Settimelli, Bruno Corra, A. Ginna, G. Balla.[72]

'Abolizione della tecnica finita, lisciata, antimpressionistica, *FOTOGRAFICA* che toglie alle luci e alle masse la suggestione delle loro vibrazioni – ' 'L'ambiente *deve* esprimere anch'esso lo stato d'animo del personaggio che naviga in lui.'

'Liberiamo il cinematografo dalla sua schiavitù di semplice riproduttore della realtà dai confini di una fotografia movimentata, e innalziamolo ad arte, cioè a mezzo d'espressione: pittura, scultura, architettura, letteratura ecc.'

'Noi principiamo a creare una nuova arte, la *Poliespressività*, fusione di tutte le arti, arte che nasce con noi, assolutamente italiana – .'

'Ricordiamo a scanso di facili ironie i successi concretati dal futurismo nella lirica violentemente rinnovata in appena sei anni, nella pittura fortemente influenzata e incanalata verso nuove ricerche. Ricordiamo che i futuristi furono i primi a propugnare la fatalità della guerra e Marinetti, fra lo stupore e le risa di tutti, sette anni or sono in pieno pacifismo triplicista gridò in pubblico (al teatro Lirico di Milano) *Guerra all'Austria*!'

II.

Presentazione dei futuristi: Marinetti, Settimelli, B. Corra, Remo Chiti, G. Balla, Arnaldo Ginna. (*TIF* cxxix)

[SOME PARTS OF THE FILM 'FUTURIST LIFE'
I.

Projection of the main innovative affirmations of the manifesto on Futurist cinema, written and distributed in many thousands of copies by Marinetti, Settimelli, Bruno Corra, A. Ginna, G. Balla.

'Abolition of the finite, polished, anti-impressionistic, *PHOTOGRAPHIC* technique that takes away from the lights and the masses the suggestiveness of their vibrations –' 'The environment itself *must* express the state of mind of the character that navigates in it.'

'Let us free cinema from its servitude as a simple reproducer of reality, from the limits of animated photography, and let us raise it to an art, that is, to a means of expression: painting, sculpture, architecture, literature etc.'

'We are beginning to create a new art, *Polyexpressiveness*, a fusion of all the arts, an art that is born with us, absolutely Italian –.'

'To avoid facile ironies, let us remember the achievements realized by Futurism in poetry, which was violently renewed in just six years, and in painting, which was strongly influenced and channelled towards new pursuits. Let us remember that the Futurists were the first to support the inevitability of war and Marinetti, to the astonishment and derision of all, seven years ago, in the midst of the complete pacifism of the Triple Alliance shouted in public (in Milan's Teatro Lirico), *War on Austria!'*

II.

Presentation of the Futurists: Marinetti, Settimelli, B. Corra, Remo Chiti, G. Balla, Arnaldo Ginna.]

The announcement suggests that the parts presented in quotation marks are excerpts from the aforementioned manifesto as well as text projected on screen.[73] Whether this theoretical overture was indeed part of the film, it reveals that the film was initially conceived as a polemic against contemporary narrative cinema. The function of early cinema as an inspiration thus led to a both diachronic and synchronic project. The revival of aspects of early attractions was not mere nostalgia. The Lumière- and Méliès-like portrayals were meant to challenge the assumptions of an audience conditioned by a cinematic experience that the Futurists saw as the proliferation of traditional theatrical forms. That the film was intended to attract a mass audience is clear in the above document. The reference to a manifesto as having been distributed 'in many thousands of copies' reveals the wish to deliver also *this* 'manifesto' to many thousands of viewers – hence, not an intellectual minority educated in current debates on aesthetics, but a majority whose involvement in cinema as a social and aesthetic experience was shaped by something quite different from 'Futurist cinema.'

Furthermore, while this polemic is quite explicit in the discourse on film style that appears in part I of the above document, it is also suggested in the 'Presentation of the Futurists' in part II, some of who appear as characters in the film. Whether such a presentation involved a photographic reproduction of the participants or a listing of their names on screen, it mimics narrative cinema's practice of listing the names of the stars in the opening titles. Certainly, the Futurist actors' notoriety as the leaders of a radical movement is proposed as an aesthetic and institutional alternative to the *divismo* of narrative cinema. In addition, some of the Futurists appearing in the film were also present in the theatre during projection. As Lista notes, the spectator's special chance to see on screen the men whom s/he saw a moment ago in flesh and blood was characteristic of the shows of Fregoli and Max Linder, while it also short-circuited the distance between the myth of the star and the real person.[74] By frustrating the expectations for things such as verisimilitude, continuity, narrative coherence, closure, and star image, and by providing its alternative stimuli, Futurist film was to awaken the audience's suppressed psychical forces, the inscriptions that formed its renewed sensibility in the mechanical age.

Although for the above reasons we may label the film as metacinematic, we would best consider it as metadiscursive in a general, rather than strictly cinematic, sense. Cinema may be the explicit subject matter of the film's theoretical opening, but that is not true for its individual episodes, which focus on the Futurists' physical activities, romantic dilemmas, and the life of matter, among others. The film mirrors less itself as cinema than the larger discursive structure within which it is placed, namely, the *serata*. It is self-referential not as a film but as a Futurist product, one that mirrors another Futurist product. In replicating that other product on screen, it reaffirms it from another angle. It thus functions as Futurist self-advertisement. It differs from films such as Paul's *Countryman* or Porter's *Uncle Josh*, the main function of which is to draw the viewer's attention to the traps of film viewing. It has a stronger affinity with a film like Lumière's *Leaving the Factory*, since it advertises Futurism, just as the Lumière short advertised Lumière. It also differs from the latter, however, in that it addresses the wide range of discourses that concern Futurism in the mid-1910s. In exhibiting the Lumière workers, the Lumière short advertises the invention of an apparatus. To be sure, this invention promised to broaden dramatically the horizons of many aspects of life, first and foremost aesthetic representation and its social implications, but also scientific investigation, ethnographic documentation, and others. Despite the crucial questions of the turn of the century with which we may associate the invention, the thing that the film itself promotes remains a single apparatus. *Vita futurista*, by contrast, makes explicit references to the various facets that constitute the 'apparatus' of Futurism at this particular historical moment. As Innamorati states, the film is 'a further proclamation or manifesto in images of Futurism's mission of renewal.'[75] Generally speaking, its thematic preoccupations as developed in its individual brief narratives are part and parcel of Futurism's all-encompassing rejection of the old and launching of the new as an absolute value. At the same time, it addresses distinct aspects of the Futurist outlook. It promotes the movement's political position on the war; it mocks romantic notions of love that it holds responsible for man's flawed judgment and wounded virility; it attacks traditional art and the popular cinema of the mid-1910s. Hence, its self-referentiality, which involves the mirroring of the *serata*, renders it a form of metadiscourse in a general sense, one that functions as a treatise on the state of Futurism.

2

An Aesthetics of War: The (Un)Problematic Screening of *Vita futurista*

What we may deem as the most direct historical evidence regarding the reception of the Futurists' single film is quite scarce, provided by no more than three, evidently impartial, newspaper reviews of the period. Its scarcity, however, must not allow free rein to the Futurists' own, equally scarce, reports and recollections. In sharp contrast to the event's contemporary reviews, the Futurists' own reports suggest that *Vita futurista*, thanks to its provocative compilation of audacious themes and unconventional styles, was able to elicit a violent response worthy of the auditorium 'wars' that had been the trademark of the *serate* in the 'heroic' years, now with the newly discovered (if belatedly so) 'eminently Futurist' medium of cinema. The Futurist film's ability to re-enact the sought-after 'aesthetics of war' has congealed into a myth, one that not only was created by Futurist self-representation, which is to say, self-idealization, but is also reaffirmed time and again by scholarship on Futurism – perhaps because as readers of Futurism we hesitate to relinquish the exuberance that the movement's 'heroic' formulations and accomplishments tend to arouse, or because the historical and cultural aura that surrounds the key figures of Futurism incites little desire to pit their assertions against more viable historical evidence. The latter in fact encompasses more than what I characterize above as its most direct form. It involves the convergence of a variety of factors, including the Futurists' political views in the context of the Great War as expressed in the Futurist film itself, the larger political framework that determined the very organization and conceptualization of the *serata* in which the film was incorporated, as well as the aesthetic and ideological intersections between the Futurist film and Italy's likewise politicized cinematic culture of that time.

The premiere of *Vita futurista* took place at Florence's Teatro Niccolini on 28 January 1917. On the following day, at least two reviews appeared in Florentine newspapers, both of which were anonymous and described the atmosphere of this *serata* as rather agreeable, in that it lacked the violent response typically aroused during such events.[1] According to *La Nazione*, after the four syntheses and poetry readings were well applauded, the film 'interessò e suscitò una ilarità rumorosa: e in alcune sue parti . . . è di una comicità esilarante' [interested and stirred up a noisy hilarity: and in some of its parts . . . it displays an exhilarating comic spirit].[2] This is how the writer of *Il Nuovo Giornale* perceived the audience:

> Questo aveva oggi l'aria di pensare: 'Su da bravi futuristi! Non siamo in vena di rissa, né di pugilati! La guerra ahimè altrove e le patate costano un po' care! Siate voi artisti o guastamestieri, non siamo qui per combattere una battaglia letteraria, ma per ridere, sia alle vostre spalle, sia alle nostre!'

> [This one today seemed to think: 'Good boys, Futurists! We're not in the mood for brawls or pugilism! The war, alas, is somewhere else and potatoes are a little expensive! Whether you're artists or bunglers, we're not here to fight a literary battle, but to laugh, be it at your expense, or at ours!']

According to this writer, the event was relatively peaceful: 'Pochi sibili, poche risate ironiche e niente commestibili . . . Il futurismo progredisce forse perché il pubblico si è un po' più avvicinato a lui' [Little hissing, few ironic laughs, and no foodstuffs . . . Futurism is perhaps improving because the public has come a little closer to it] (ellipsis in original).[3]

It is not difficult to detect an ironic tone in this review. Based on the history of Futurist theatre in Italy, it is questionable whether, in the Futurists' own terms, the audience's mere amusement and peaceful approval of the show meant that the public was 'coming closer' to Futurism. In introducing his historical account of Futurist spectacle in Italy, Giovanni Antonucci states that theatre, for Marinetti, was mainly 'an unprejudiced and antagonistic rapport with the audience.'[4] With the performance of *La donna è mobile* at Turin's Teatro Alfieri on 15 January 1909 – their very first stage performance in Italy – the Futurists initiated a tradition of clamorous encounters that lasted at least half a decade. According to the reviews of the time, in the midst of being booed by an audience expressing its disapproval of the play, Marinetti appeared on stage and announced: 'Ringrazio gli organizzatori di questa fischiata, che altamente mi onora' [I thank the organizers of this booing, which highly honours me].[5] One wonders why anyone would 'organize' a booing. As this show preceded both the publication of any manifestos and the inauguration of the *serate*, the Futurists were not yet notorious as a radical movement.[6] The press also described the audience's reaction as spontaneous. According to Turin's *Gazzetta del Popolo*, the first act, rather traditional in its form, was applauded with approval. The second act, extremely unconventional, was the one that was booed. By the time the third act began, the audience was so agitated that the performance could be neither watched nor heard. This was anything but a failure for Marinetti. The play succeeded in upsetting an audience who, according to Milan's *La Scena di Prosa*, was generally proper and patient towards all novelties.[7] By referring to this spontaneous response as an organized action, Marinetti betrayed his own wish to implement from the start this type of stage–audience interaction in his theatres. In fact, his relation to the booing may have been more substantial than a mere wish. Gigi Livio demonstrates that the manner in which some reviewers of the time discussed this event, as well as the statements that Marinetti himself made shortly thereafter, allow us to speculate that the booing was indeed an organized action, the organizer perhaps having been none other than Marinetti.[8]

Body Madness, or Lack Thereof

'La voluttà di essere fischiati' (The Pleasure of Being Booed) proclaims the disinterest of Futurist theatre in a traditional kind of success.[9] According to this manifesto, the goal of Futurism is to teach authors how to *despise* the audience. Immersed in a set of established practices that surrounds traditional theatregoing – from fashion and other vanity rivalries, to the auditorium's hierarchical socio-economic layout, to the desire to digest pleasurably at the theatre – the audience is incapable of evaluating a work of art. Such an audience's immediate acceptance of a dramatic work indicates none but the author's lack of creative intelligence. Authors should have no other concern than to attain absolute innovative originality and cultivate a feeling of *horror of immediate success*. Being booed, on the other hand, confirms the work's ability to astonish and thus participate in the great shudders that agitate the crowds, speaking directly to their transformed sensibilities in a machine-dominated age (*TIF* 310–12). Finally:

> Tutto ciò che viene fischiato non è necessariamente bello o nuovo. Ma tutto ciò che viene immediatamente applaudito, certo non è superiore alla

media delle intelligenze ed è quindi *cosa mediocre, banale, rivomitata o troppo ben digerita.* (*TIF* 313)

[Everything that is booed is not necessarily either beautiful or new. But everything that is immediately applauded is certainly not superior to the average intelligence and is therefore *something mediocre, banal, regurgitated, or too well digested.*]

Indeed, it was not long before audiences went to the *serate* with the intention of entering a battle, by either fighting against the performers or defending the Futurists.[10] This rapport with the public was largely a result of Marinetti's personality and exceptional ability to animate the spectators. Though Futurism claimed to oppose any tendency towards the development of a tradition, some conventions were soon established in the interaction between performers and spectators. Audiences often arrived equipped with bags of fruits and vegetables to serve as projectiles. As the actors were running away or hiding behind stage props to escape the flying oranges, Marinetti, who felt responsible for their well-being, would make futile appeals to the spectators, explaining that the actors were not Futurists. On one occasion, a broom was also given to the Futurists, for the cleaning of the auditorium after the event.[11]

Such uproar was typical of the *serata* in the strict sense, which only lasted until 1914. As noted earlier, with the introduction of the synthetic theatre in 1914, which consisted of rehearsed acts performed by professional actors, the *serata* developed into a relatively tempered event. The Futurists' turn towards the synthetic theatre determined the context in which *Vita futurista* was exhibited. For this reason alone, it should not surprise us that the reviews spoke of a relatively peaceful event throughout this 1917 evening. We must also examine, however, the validity of such anonymous reviews. In his analysis of the 1910–14 *serate*, Günter Berghaus cautions that 'even printed reports in major national newspapers can be unreliable as "documents," since they were often written by Marinetti himself and hence "messaged" to present an image of Futurism as designed by its leader.' He notes that the writing style itself may raise suspicion: 'when five newspaper reports contain more or less the same wording and phrases, we have good reason to assume that they were not written by independent eye-witnesses either.' He distinguishes, however, the critics in major national newspapers from those in local ones, indicating that the latter were more independent and thus provide a more valid historical source.[12] Let us speculate on the

Futurists' direct involvement in the reviews of their cinematic debut. Both *La Nazione* and *Il Nuovo Giornale* are local newspapers, the kind that Berghaus might consider impartial. Importantly, the 1910–14 *serate*, which Berghaus studies through the local press, involved continuous travel across Italy. Berghaus alone discusses the *serate* of Trieste, Milan, Turin, Naples, Venice, Padua, Rome, Modena, and Florence, while additional *serate* took place in Ferrara, Mantua, Como, Treviso, Palermo, Pisa, Bologna, Forlì, Perugia, and Genoa, not to mention Paris, London, Berlin, and Moscow.[13] In sharp contrast to those, however, the 1917 premiere of *Vita futurista* was a single event that took place in a city where the Futurists had established a solid nucleus, at least since 1913 with the founding of the journal *Lacerba*, and later under the auspices of *L'Italia Futurista*. It is therefore fitting to inquire into the Futurists' possible role in Florence's local press at the time.

Anonymous reports aiming to incite excitement about the upcoming Futurist film, written in a worshipful tone that is hardly impartial, appear as early as eight months before the film's premiere. The 15 May 1916 issue of *La Nazione*, includes the following announcement:

> Marinetti, Settimelli, Corra e tutti gli altri futuristi hanno finito proprio in questi giorni il soggetto di una gigantesca *film*, alla quale han collaborato un po' tutti, mettendovi ciascuno le più strabilianti bizzarrie. Sarà certamente una *film* di interesse eccezionale, e una novità … senza paragoni. Non sappiamo ancora quale casa metterà in iscena il grandioso lavoro dei futuristi, ma già ne sappiamo il titolo 'Vita futurista' e sappiamo che tra non molto la *film* 'piramidale' avrà un'attuazione pratica. (ellipsis in original)[14]

> [Marinetti, Settimelli, Corra and all the other Futurists just finished the treatment of a gigantic film, on which everyone collaborated a little, each one contributing the most astonishing oddities. It will certainly be a film of exceptional interest, and something new … without comparisons. We don't know yet which company will produce the great work of the Futurists, but we already know the title 'Futurist Life' and we know that soon the 'pyramidal' film will have a practical implementation.]

Equally enthusiastic is the article 'Cinematografia futurista al Niccolini pro famiglie richiamati' (Futurist Cinema at the Niccolini for Families of Recalled Servicemen), appearing in *La Nazione*, on 27 January 1917, that is, the day preceding the film's premiere. Besides boasting the honourable gesture of donating the proceeds to the families of recalled servicemen, a wartime institution to which I will return, the article attempts to excite the reader with expressions such as 'domani domenica avremo *finalmente* al nostro "Niccolini" le due *grandi* rappresentazioni del "1° Film Futurista"' [tomorrow Sunday we will have *at last*, at our 'Niccolini,' the two *great* shows of the '1st Futurist Film'] (emphasis added). The show is described as very original and having 'tutto il pregio della novità, poiché rispecchia i nuovi tentativi che l'audacia dei futuristi ha creato in questi ultimi tempi' [the full merit of the new, as it reflects the new attempts that the Futurists' boldness created recently]; remarks, in other words, that betray the writer's sharp familiarity with the yet-to-be-seen product. Furthermore, the article's unconventional closing with an unfinished sentence suggests the craftsmanship of a partial announcer: 'Le richieste dei biglietti al botteghino del Teatro sono grandi, ed il pubblico è avvertito ... ' [The requests for tickets at the theatre's box office are large, and the public is warned ...] (ellipsis in original).[15]

Articles anticipating the film's premiere also appeared in *Il Nuovo Giornale* on 22, 23, 25, 26, and 27 January. They share the writing style and specific points of emphasis, not only with each other but also with the 27 January article from *La Nazione* as discussed above. The patriotic and philanthropic cause and the film's originality and bizarre nature are systematically praised. Some specify that the evening is sponsored by students: 'Il Comitato studentesco fiorentino col nobile intento di giovare alle famiglie dei richiamati è riuscito ad ottenere di rappresentare per la prima volta le più originali proiezioni cinematografiche' [The Florentine Student Committee, with the noble intention of benefiting the families of recalled servicemen, was able to obtain permission to show the most original film projections for the first time].[16] The writer sometimes teases the reader by revealing excessive knowledge of the upcoming show, thus strongly suggesting a direct affiliation with the Futurists, all the while posing as an impartial reporter.

> In grazia dell'indiscrezione di qualche studente facente parte del Comitato, possiamo dare i titoli delle 'films' che saranno proiettate: 'Come dorme un futurista' – 'Esposizione di carote, aringhe e melanzane' ...
> ... Ci sarà poi ... il 'clou' della serata che, però, non ci è stato dato sapere in che consisterà.

> [Thanks to the indiscretion of some students who are part of the Committee, we may give the titles of the 'films' that will be projected: 'How a Futurist sleeps' – 'Exposition of carrots, herrings and eggplants' ...

... Then there will be ... the 'climax' of the evening, but we were not
told in what it will consist.]

Some of the articles craft an image of Florence as a place already
immersed in anxious anticipation: 'Dato lo scopo patriottico ed umani-
tario delle due rappresentazioni che si daranno, una, alle 16 ed una, alle
20,45, è lecito ritenere che il pubblico, accorrerà in folla a giudicare del
valore intrinseco della nuova conquista futurista' [Given the patriotic
and humanitarian goal of the two shows that will be given, one at 16:00
and one at 20:45, it is fair to think that the public will rush in crowds
to judge the intrinsic value of the new Futurist conquest].[17] As the premiere approaches, impatience grows and the city takes on the appearance of a Futurist stage:

> Ormai un solo giorno ci separa da quel bizzarro avvenimento che più
> volte abbiamo annunziato: il nuovo tentativo del futurismo nella cine-
> matografia. E poiché tutta Firenze è oggi tappezzata di manifesti multicol-
> ori, programma della serata, sarebbe inutile ripetere qui dettagliatamente
> tutti i numeri attraentissimi dello spettacolo che ha attirato la curiosità del
> pubblico fiorentino.

> [By now a single day separates us from that bizarre event that we
> announced several times: Futurism's new attempt in cinema. And since all
> of Florence is today covered in multicoloured posters, that is, the evening's
> program, it would be useless to repeat here in detail all the very attractive
> numbers of the show that caught the curiosity of the Florentine public.]

In resonance with its counterpart from *La Nazione* of that same day, the
article closes with the same technique of suspense: 'Grande è l'attesa e la
richiesta dei biglietti al botteghino del teatro conferma le nostre passate
previsioni. Chi desidera dunque divertirsi e fare anche un po' di bene
è avvertito ... ' [The expectation is great and the demand for tickets at
the box office confirms our past predictions. So whoever wants to have
a good time and do some good is warned ...] (ellipsis in original).[18]

Despite the likelihood of the Futurists' direct involvement in the
Florentine press, the two 29 January reviews following the film's premiere display a neutral stance as compared to the announcements
discussed above. Their appraisal of the *serata* is even-handed, based
on an investigative approach free of hostility, indifference, or enthusiasm. Both acknowledge that the audience was large in spite of the

'Siberian' weather. They critique the individual performances rather positively, yet in a measured tone and exhibiting no more familiarity with Futurism than one would expect of a reasonably informed critic. According to *La Nazione*, the four syntheses by Settimelli and Corra, under the single title *Il dramma del futurista* (The Futurist's Drama), had 'un relativo sapore futurista: appaiono come brevi scene passatiste, un po' primitive e scheletriche, ma assai efficaci' [a relative Futurist flavour: they appear like brief passéist scenes, primitive and skeletal, yet very effective]. The actors who performed the syntheses are described as praiseworthy, while Ines Masi and Giulio Ricci in particular are described as precise and brave. The lyrics written by Maria Ginanni, Mario Carli, and Bruno Corra, and recited by Settimelli and Remo Chiti after the syntheses, displayed flashes of vivacious wit.[19]

Compared to *La Nazione*, *Il Nuovo Giornale* displays a more apprehensive, as well as ironic, tone that is perceptible from the start: 'In uno spettacolo futurista tutto è interessante, anche il pubblico' [In a Futurist show, everything is interesting, even the audience]. The opening is followed by the audience's impersonation as noted above ('Good boys, Futurists! We're not in the mood for brawls or pugilism!'). As for *Il dramma del futurista*, the four episodes are described as acted with good will and 'accettati dal pubblico con una certa simpatia: attraverso una recitazione alquanto stentata dei barlumi di verità sono apparsi agli ascoltatori e son bastati a far accettare le pillole più ingrate' [accepted by the audience with a certain liking: through a rather laboured acting, some gleams of reality appeared to the listeners and were enough to make one accept the more unpleasant parts]. The writer acknowledges that Ginanni's lyrics received the honours of applause, yet he conveys doubt about the success, saying that it was probably 'per la vivezza delle immagini felicemente rappresentative' [for the liveliness of the happily representative images]. This ambiguous remark may be referring to an unproblematic equivalence between the 'images' and what they represent of reality, a hint at verisimilitude implying that Futurism was not, or was no longer, as radical as it claimed to be. The remark also agrees with this writer's conclusion that Futurism was 'improving because the public has come a little closer to it,' as previously noted. The other writer is not devoid of irony, at least as regards the question of 'coming closer': *Il dramma del futurista* 'si tratta di un nuovo tentativo di teatro futurista, più accessibile alle menti ed ai gusti degli spettatori che si ostinano a rimaner passatisti' [represents a new effort of Futurist theatre, more accessible to the minds and tastes of the spectators who insist on remaining passéist].[20] If Futurism pleases a public that 'insists on remaining passéist,' then Futurism itself must have become passéist. Perhaps what initiated this 'coming closer' was not just the introduction of the synthetic theatre – a rehearsed element – into the *serata*, but that the *serata* as a whole acquired a traditional dimension.

Whether the above remarks were made by shrewd Futurists in disguise or by objective critics, some form of 'coming closer' evidently did occur, one that *Vita futurista*, despite its oddity, did not prevent. Perhaps the Futurists, wishing to boast a newly sprung popularity, disguised themselves so as to make the reviews appear objective. It is unlikely, however, that they would allow us to conclude that the peril of such popularity was Futurism's own move towards passéism. It is more likely that the Futurists, if no longer scorning popularity altogether, would have liked to uphold the idea that Futurism never lost its revolutionary impetus, the ability to shock and agitate that had been its defining characteristic during its 'heroic' years. Such an idealized view of Futurism is exemplified by Ginna who, reminiscing about the movement's experimentation with cinema in his 1965 article 'Note sul film d'avanguardia "*Vita futurista*"' (Notes on the Avant-Garde Film *Futurist Life*), offers an account of the film's reception that sharply contradicts the 1917 reviews. In his view, the film generated that auditorium battle that characterized the early *serate*. His report received serious consideration from scholars engaged in the study of Futurism and film, thus complicating our comprehension of the film's reception.[21]

Several factors, however, cast doubt on Ginna's report, which he wrote from memory five decades after the events. As regards the place of exhibition, Ginna does not mention the Teatro Niccolini, the only venue confirmed by more reliable sources, such as the newspaper announcements and reviews discussed above. Instead, he claims that the film was shown for the first time at the cinema Marconi in Florence, which belonged to Mr Castellani. He adds:

Aneddoto: durante la proiezione del film: mentre Settimelli cercava di convincere il Sig. Castellani di acquistare il film un certo Trilluci, strano tipo di originale, criticò il film: *al buio si udì il rumore* di uno schiaffo dato da Settimelli al disturbatore. Questo episodio contribuì ad eccitare maggiormente *il pubblico già rumoreggiante*. (emphasis added)[22]

[Anecdote: during the projection of the film: while Settimelli was trying to convince Mr Castellani to purchase the film, a certain Trilluci, a strange, peculiar type, criticized the film: the noise of a smack given by Settimelli to the troublemaker was *heard in the dark*. This episode helped to further excite the *already noisy audience*.]

Surely, this Trilluci may have been a nuisance, and Settimelli, with the audacity and unruly energy that marked the Futurists' daily behaviour – Cangiullo's autobiographical novel allows us to imagine it – may indeed have smacked him. Of course, the anecdote implies that *Vita futurista* caused clamorous reactions, as Ginna states more explicitly later in the report, when addressing the film's exhibition in Rome. The anecdote, however, is problematic. That a smack was 'heard in the dark' pre-supposes a correlation of darkness and silence, which may be true in venues of film exhibition other than the *serata*, while the claim that the audience was 'already noisy' reduces the odds that silence prevailed; and yet, if the sound of a smack stood out, the auditorium must have been sufficiently quiet.

In his late 1960s seminal work on Futurist cinema, besides including a reprint of Ginna's article, Verdone reinforces the myth of the audience's violent reaction, by paraphrasing Ginna's report on the Marconi with more flavoursome images: 'At the screenings of *Vita futurista*, which in Florence took place at the cinema Marconi, those who liked brawls and clamorous displays were glad to join in. There were even some who threw tomatoes and shoes at the white sheet, enough to knock down the screen.'[23] More recently, Verdone and Berghaus's collaborative essay '"Vita futurista" and Early Futurist Cinema' (2000) served to broaden the lacuna in our understanding of the film's reception. Not only do the authors take Ginna's recollections at face value, they build upon those rather subjectively. Failing to acknowledge the contradiction between the Florentine press and Ginna's account, they seek to reconcile the two by contriving a narrative that lacks substantiating evidence. After stating, in line with the newspaper reviews, that the film premiered at the Teatro Niccolini on 28 January, they claim that it provoked no violent response on this particular day because 'the audience was composed in their majority of philo-Futurists, i.e. friends of the artists and other enlightened art lovers.' They add that such information 'transpires from the reports in the Florentine newspapers,' citing the same two reviews that we have examined above.[24] The latter, however, give no hint as to the audience's intellectual or ideological orientation, much less that it was 'philo-Futurist.' In their dispassionate tone, the anonymous writers observe not what the audience *was* but what it *did*: that it applauded the performances, became noisily cheerful with *Vita futurista*, and refrained from fighting. I fail to see how, based on the information provided by the reviews, one may conclude that the audience was 'philo-Futurist.' On the contrary, in impersonating the audience ('Good boys, Futurists! We're not in the mood for brawls or pugilism!'), the writer of *Il Nuovo Giornale* conveys a tension between the audience and Futurism, one in which the audience is the winner. In thanking the Futurists for a peaceful evening, the audience is being ironic, since the Futurists, through their live acts and radical cinematic debut, may have hoped to enact a battle, as in the old days. Yet the praise implies a defeat, namely, that the Futurists made a step towards passéism, if unwittingly so. Hence, quite subtly, the audience seems to mock the Futurists.

Yet 'when the film was shown at the Teatro Marconi,' continue Verdone and Berghaus, now citing Ginna, 'there was less of an art audience in the hall. The reaction was therefore more as one would expect at a Futurist event. A particularly noisy spectator was slapped in the face by Settimelli, which caused an even more riotous response from the audience.'[25] The claim is problematic. Ginna's article, from which the authors gather their information regarding the screening at the Marconi, does not address the audience's intellectual nature. Like the Florentine reviewers, Ginna observes what the audience *did* and not what it *was*, namely, that it became more excited even though it was already noisy. Furthermore, by first acknowledging that the film premiered at the Niccolini and then discussing the screening at the Marconi as a subsequent one, the authors ignore Ginna's claim that the Marconi event was the film's first screening. Certainly, if the reaction at the Marconi had been 'as one would expect at a Futurist event' – they seem to allude to the *serate* of the early years, with their showers of potatoes and oranges – the 'smack' would not have been quite as notorious, since in the midst of the pandemonium it would have drawn very little attention to itself.

Ginna's comment on the film's exhibition in Rome greatly reinforced the myth of the public's violent response:

> Il film fu dato in altri cinema a Roma, ma fu necessario sospendere le proiezioni, perché il pubblico gettava oggetti, sassi ecc. contro lo schermo, che si rivelava troppo vulnerabile per questo genere di combattutissime rappresentazioni.[26]

> [The film was shown in other cinemas in Rome, but it was necessary to suspend the projections, because the audience threw objects, rocks etc.

against the screen, which proved too vulnerable for such hard-fought
performances.]

He does not mention when or in which Roman cinemas the film was
screened. Other sources certainly provide such information. Ginanni's
article 'La prima a Roma della Cinematografia futurista' (The Premiere
of Futurist Cinema in Rome), appearing in *L'Italia Futurista* on 17 June
1917, states: 'Ci telefonano da Roma ... Siamo felici di annunziare la
prima a Roma della Cinematografia futurista. Lo spettacolo è dato al
grande cinematografo Costanzi giovedì 14 e venerdì 15 giugno' [They
are telephoning us from Rome ... We are happy to announce the premiere of Futurist Cinema in Rome. The show is presented at the great
cinema Costanzi on Thursday 14 and Friday 15 June].[27] Also, the inau-
gural 16 June issue of the Roman weekly *Il Cinema Illustrato*, while it
does not provide a specific date and time schedule, includes a column
of anonymous, brief, and subtly humorous remarks about films cur-
rently shown in Rome: 'Al CINEMA SALA COSTANZI grande spettacolo futurista *Per uccidere il chiaro di luna*. Non aggiungiamo altro'
[At the CINEMA SALA COSTANZI the great Futurist show *To Murder
the Moonlight*. We add no more].[28] Yet none of the above sources helps
our inquiry into the film's reception. Ginanni focuses on praising the
campaign launched by Futurist cinema against those films that corrupt
'l'intelligenza del nostro grande pubblico italiano' [the intelligence of
our great Italian public]. She also portrays Rome as a city overtaken
by a Futurist spirit: 'Sono stati lanciati 5000 manifesti e tutta la città è
elettrizzata dai nostri colori!' [5000 manifestos were launched and the
whole city is electrified by our colours!]. She does not mention reception, however, as she evidently wrote the article before the Roman
premiere.[29]

A vivid impression of the Roman audience's reaction is given by
E.C.O., identified by Lista as the painter Cipriano Efisio Oppo, in the
relatively detailed review 'La prima della film futurista "Uccidiamo il
chiaro di luna"' (The Premiere of the Futurist Film 'Let's Murder the
Moonlight'), which appeared in the second issue of *Il Cinema Illustrato*,
on 23 June.[30] While the review does not state that the show took place
at the Costanzi, its temporal proximity to the two sources mentioned
above allows us to presume so. Much like the Florentine reviewers,
E.C.O. allows us to put Ginna to the test. Opening by vehemently
declaring his disappointment, he underlines the audience's reaction.
Apparently, not only did it stay calm, it was not even amused:

Dopo tante strombazzature, tante bizzarrie cartellonistiche, m'aspettavo davvero da questa prima *film* futurista, qualche grossa rivoluzione nell'arte cinematografica.

Invece non ho mai visto nel campo del fantastico e dello strano cosa più meschina e bambinesca di questa. Nessun nuovo motivo, nessuna trovata, nessuna arditezza. Banalità e piattume. Il pubblico, infatti, non s'inquietava nemmeno, non rideva, per quanto l'ilarità era stata promessa a caratteri cubitali nei manifesti.

[After so much razzmatazz, so many advertising oddities, I really expected from this first Futurist film some major revolution in the cinematographic art.

Instead I have never seen in the area of the fantastic and the strange anything more pitiable and infantile than this. No new motifs, no discoveries, no boldness. Banality and dullness. The audience, in fact, didn't even get disturbed, it didn't laugh, however much hilarity had been promised in block capitals in the advertisements.]

After a few brief descriptions of episodes from the film, made in a belittling and often sarcastic tone that suggests the film's conceptual simplicity and lack of originality, E.C.O. closes with a return to his impressions of the audience:

Il pubblico, già ho detto, era assente (anche perché ce n'era pochissimo) da ogni intenzione di plauso e di riprovazione: sopportò s'immalinconì e pensò tutto il tempo dello spettacolo ai molti denari che aveva speso.

[The audience, I already said, was absent (also because there was very little of it) from any intention of approval or reprehension: it endured, grew melancholy and thought, the entire time of the show, about all the money that it had spent.]

Making no reference to E.C.O.'s testimony (which I believe is the only one discovered thus far that is contemporary with the Roman show), Verdone and Berghaus endorse Ginna's scenario with respect to Rome and through the use of an exceptionally strong image: 'In Rome projections had to be suspended because spectators *demolished the cinema* by throwing stones and similar objects at the screen' (emphasis added).[31]

The Teatro Costanzi, where *Vita futurista* was allegedly shown, was Rome's large and elegant opera house, built in 1880 by the impresario

Domenico Costanzi and renamed Teatro Reale dell'Opera in 1928, after the city acquired and renovated it.[32] It is not surprising that the Futurists chose it for their film screening. Two *serate* had taken place there previously, in February and March 1913,[33] the first of which was particularly infamous – not so much for the uproar that it caused as for the irritation and boredom with which an elite Roman audience received Giovanni Papini's unimpressive declamation of the particularly insulting 'Speech Against Rome.'[34] Also, Stravinsky's *Feu d'artifice*, directed by the composer himself, accompanying a show of lights designed by Balla and produced by Diaghilev, was performed in April 1917.[35] Yet in his chronology of the Costanzi official programing, Vittorio Frajese does not include the June 1917 screenings of *Vita futurista*. Instead, he lists Verdi's *La forza del destino* for 14 June and no show at all for 15 June.[36] Also, the theatre listings in Roman newspapers and magazines are in agreement with Frajese.[37] Given that the 14 June opera performance began at nine o' clock in the evening,[38] it is possible that the screening of *Vita futurista* was a matinee, as well as an extraordinary show not included in the theatre's official programing.[39] In fact, it is unclear whether the programing included any film, in spite of Frajese's claim that 'the chronology lists all shows, of any type, that took place at the Teatro Costanzi, the Teatro Reale dell'Opera and the Teatro dell'Opera [as the venue was renamed after the end of the monarchy] from 1880 to 1960.' He specifically lists 'lyric operas, ballets, operettas and zarzuelas, variety shows, pantomimes, comedies, farces and dramas, and the announcements of any event taking place in the Teatro.' He adds that 'only the "Concerts" are omitted,' as they appear in a separate volume.[40] Evidently, cinema is also omitted from the otherwise comprehensive list.

It is also likely that the Teatro Costanzi and the Sala Cinema Costanzi were separate auditoriums, as indicated by this announcement: 'Mentre al COSTANZI *La battaglia da Plava al Mare* desta il maggiore entusiasmo, alla SALA CINEMA COSTANZI l'interpretazione sempre magnifica della Bertini trionfa in *Sangue Bleu*' [While at the COSTANZI *La battaglia da Plava al Mare* awakes the greatest enthusiasm, in the SALA CINEMA COSTANZI, Bertini's always magnificent acting triumphs in *Sangue Bleu*].[41] In fact, they may have been two separate establishments; but even if they shared the roof of the opera house, it is possible that Frajese's chronology only represents the official programing of the Teatro Costanzi proper, that is, the events that took place in the opera auditorium and not in the adjacent film auditorium. It is also possible that film screenings sometimes took place in the opera auditorium without entering the theatre's official programing. Such may be the case of *La battaglia da Plava al Mare*, a documentary on the ongoing war, which according to the above announcement was shown in the 'Costanzi' rather than the 'Sala Cinema Costanzi,' as well as the case of *Vita futurista*. At any rate, regardless of where *Vita futurista* was shown, it is doubtful that the 'demolition' of any Costanzi venue took place. If the film played in the opera auditorium on 14 June as a matinee, *La forza del destino* peacefully followed that same evening with no evidence to the contrary. If it played instead in Sala Cinema Costanzi, that *sala* resumed its regular business, as we may infer from an announcement that appeared only a few days later in *Il Cinema Illustrato*: 'Alla SALA COSTANZI Maria Jacobini richiama sempre gran pubblico con *Come le foglie*' [At the SALA COSTANZI Maria Jacobini continues to attract a mass audience with *Come le foglie*].[42]

In her rigorous study of *Vita futurista*, Strauven reaffirms the myth nonetheless. Like Verdone and Berghaus, she overlooks E.C.O., who emphasizes the film's failure to elicit a strong response. What distinguishes her argument is that she assumes – for reasons that she leaves unaddressed – that the 'knocked down screens' were not those of the Costanzi but those of other Roman theatres. Though imaginable, this scenario is not supported by historical evidence to date and may be the result of a hasty reading of Ginna. After Strauven affirms that in Florence the film was applauded and that in Rome it premiered at the Costanzi, she adds:

> Nonetheless the screens on which *Vita futurista* is projected will continue to be *knocked down*, at least according to Ginna's memories. He tells how, *after the shows at the Teatro Costanzi*, the film was *also* shown in other cinemas of the capital and how it was necessary to suspend these last projections because 'the audience threw objects rocks etc. against the screen.' (emphasis added)[43]

The truth is that Ginna does not say that the film was shown in Rome 'after the shows at the Teatro Costanzi.' Following the anecdote about the Trilluci smack at Florence's Marconi, Ginna briefly describes the film's structure, before closing with the remark that 'the film was shown in other cinemas in Rome, but it was necessary to suspend the projections.'[44] By 'other cinemas in Rome,' Ginna refers to cinemas other than the Marconi in Florence. Neither Costanzi nor any other Roman theatre is mentioned in his article. Of course, to presume that Ginna intended that in Rome the film played in theatres other than the Costanzi allows one to accommodate the unlikelihood of the prestigious Costanzi's involvement in any such uproar and still endorse Ginna's remark on the damaging of Roman theatres. It is based on such a reading, I think, that Strauven proceeds to draw conclusions on the film's ability to elicit a violent response and thus the medium's ability to reawaken Futurism's heroic impetus: 'After the experience of the synthetic theatre we return, with the appearance of *Vita futurista*, to the origins of Futurist spectacle, that is, to the ritual of scandal and transgression.' By failing to question the empirical weight of Ginna's memoir, Strauven disregards the real possibility that Futurism made a step towards traditionalism. As concerns the Futurist desire for a spectator who is physically engaged in the creation of the spectacle, she resolves the problem of cinema's technical limitations vis-à-vis live performance by calling it a paradox: 'Paradoxically, it is thanks to the film medium that the Futurists were able to recreate the violent and chaotic climate of the first *serate*, which the practice of the synthetic theatre had in some way made disappear.'[45]

To be sure, the claims that the theatre was 'demolished' or that the screens were 'knocked down' may be rhetorical tropes, while any theatre might have been able to adequately recuperate for its next show, even after having incurred light damage. What is crucial, however, is not to determine beyond any doubt whether, or the extent to which, any Roman theatre was physically damaged by *Vita futurista*, but to acknowledge that the Futurists' reputation as troublemakers, capable of causing riots and uproars, much as in the case of Florence five months earlier, was not justified in the Rome of June 1917. Except for the one announcement and E.C.O.'s review as discussed above, found respectively in the 16 and 23 June issues of *Il Cinema Illustrato*, major Roman newspapers, such as *Il Giornale d'Italia, Il Messaggero*, and *La Tribuna*, as well as culture and film magazines, such as *L'Asino, Il Travaso delle Idee, Cine-gazzetta, Contropelo,* and *La Rassegna del Cinema*, at least for the month of June, do not mention any Futurist film screening in Rome, much less any physical damage incurred by a theatre as a result. If anything, two months after the alleged 'demolition,' a writer signing as Gio:livo, who kept a column in *Cine-gazzetta*, after quoting extensively the 1916 Futurist film manifesto and noting grudgingly that it is almost a year old, expresses much disappointment in still waiting for the Futurists to demonstrate in actions, not mere words, their impressive promises: 'Questo ritardo nell'attuazione delle azzardate – per quanto, qua e là geniali – teorie di Marinetti e compagni sembra a me alquanto passatista o, per lo meno, presentista!' [This delay in the realization of the risky – though brilliant here and there – theories of Marinetti and company seems to me rather passéist, or at least presentist!], which is to say, of the present, or, non-Futurist.[46] Evidently, contrary to what Ginanni would have liked her readers to believe, despite the launching of 5000 manifestos, the entire city of Rome was not after all 'electrified by [the Futurists'] colours.'

The hesitation to question the empirical verifiability of Ginna's recollections probably has less to do with any scholar's personal wish to preserve an idealized image of Futurism as a movement that firmly adhered to its revolutionary principles, than with the stamp of authority with which the claims of any figure surrounded by a halo of cultural aura reach the reader. This may be the reason that a specific document, one that should have been an indispensable accompaniment to any reading of Ginna's 1965 article, has received little attention as compared to Ginna's own article. Lucio Venna, the artist who assisted Ginna in the filming of *Vita futurista* and played the role of the white-bearded passéist in the episode known as 'Colazione futurista' (see chapter 1), is certainly less prestigious than Ginna, who not only is recognized as the film's producer and director, but also was a painter, collaborated in the writing of many manifestos, and accomplished an extensive amount of independent writing, in addition to having experimented with abstract cinematography, along with his brother Bruno Corra, long before they became members of the Futurist movement. Yet some crucial points that Ginna makes in his widely cited article are found in a letter that Venna had written to him just previously. As we learn from Verdone, Ginna submitted his article to the Centro Studi Bragaglia on 10 May 1965.[47] Venna's letter was quite recent, as it bears the date of 27 April 1965, and was clearly a reply to an earlier letter from Ginna, in which Ginna was asking Venna's help in gathering information on the events surrounding *Vita futurista*.[48]

Venna's letter strikes us as familiar, as it refers to things that we have already learned from Ginna: the offended Englishman during a meal at Piazzale Michelangelo; the white dots on the film after its exposure to dust and their hand colouring; the 'geometric dance' in a costume made of tinfoil; the Futurist who sleeps vertically. What immediately distinguishes the letter is Venna's warning that its content is based strictly on memory – understandably so, if on such short notice he was asked to report on events that occurred fifty years earlier: 'Carissimo Arnaldo, ho la tua graditissima e ti rispondo intanto su quanto ho immediatamente nel ricordo senza nessuna ricerca' [Dearest Arnaldo, I have your most kind letter and for the time being I respond to you with as much as I remember off the top of my head]. His sincerity sharply contradicts the certainty with which Ginna will reiterate those recollections, to the source of which he will make no allusion. In Venna, a pragmatic view of the past and disinterest in creating a myth are confirmed time and again by an almost obsessive deference to memory. Differently from Ginna's article, where the mediation of memory is definitively repressed, here the past involves not the unveiling of facts but a series of more-or-less feasible evocations:

Come ricordi, mi ero appiccicato un barbone lungo un metro e i futuristi, mangiando *non ricordo* che spregi mi facessero ... *Penso* riguardo la data che deve essere stato fra la fine del 1916 e i primi del 1917 ... *Ricordi* quando si trovò lo specchio convesso ... ? ... *Ricordi* la danza geometrica? I tubi di stagnola coi quali si vestì quella bionda amica di Nerino e *ricordi* come eravamo tutti d'accordo quando si doveva illuminarla ... [E] come dormisse Ungari in quella posizione *non lo ricordo*. (emphasis added)

[*As you remember*, I had glued a metre-long beard on myself, and the Futurists, while eating, *I don't remember* what scornful things they were doing to me ... *I think*, regarding the date, it had to be between the end of 1916 and the beginning of 1917 ... *Do you remember* when we found the convex mirror ... ? ... *Do you remember* the geometric dance? The tinfoil tubes with which that blond friend of Nerino's got dressed and *you remember* how we all agreed when we had to illuminate her ... And *I don't remember* how Ungari slept in that position.]

Furthermore, the abrupt manner in which he closes the letter betrays the urgency with which his recollections needed to reach Ginna: 'Per ora basta voglio spedirti questa lettera che attendi per espresso' [Enough for now, I want to send you this letter that you are expecting via express].

The following excerpt is particularly enlightening:

La prima del film, anzi l'anteprima, che io ricordi, fu al Cinema Marconi in Piazza Strozzi ... Ricordo che anche qui ci fu la scena tragi-comica perché mentre Emilio Settimelli cercava di convincere il proprietario all'acquisto della pellicola magnificandola in ogni modo, Trilluci (ricordi?) uscì con una frase eccessivamente critica, nel buio si sentì uno schiaffo ... povero Trilluci! (second ellipsis in original)

[The film's premiere, its preview rather, as I remember, was at the Cinema Marconi in Piazza Strozzi ... I remember that here also a tragi-comic scene took place because while Emilio Settimelli was trying to convince the owner to purchase the film by glorifying it in every way, Trilluci (do you remember?) came out with an expression that was excessively critical, a smack was heard in the dark ... poor Trilluci!]

We are finally inclined to believe that the film's first screening was held at the Marconi rather than the Niccolini, now that we are told that the Marconi screening was not a premiere but an *anteprima*, a form of sneak preview the main purpose of which was to market the film. It is doubtful that Settimelli would try to sell the film to the theatre owner during its premiere or any other public screening (as Verdone and Berghaus assume), since either of those implies that the film has already been sold. Again, given the promotional aims of such a screening, Verdone and Berghaus's suggestion that 'there was less of an art audience in the hall' is questionable. If any one show were to attract more 'philo-Futurists, i.e. friends of the artists and other enlightened art lovers,' the promotional would most likely be the one.[49] What makes Verdone and Berghaus envision a 'less of an art audience' at the Marconi is their faith in Ginna's remark that the audience was 'already noisy.' Importantly, Venna nowhere speaks of the audience. His observation that a 'smack was heard in the dark' supports what we have already suspected, namely, that the auditorium was rather quiet. That the 'episode helped to further excite the already noisy audience' is what Ginna added to Venna's recollection, a detail that, accurate or not, reinforces the fossilization of Futurism into a 'heroic' and audacious image. Preserving such an image was clearly not a priority for Venna. Besides his emphasis on the mediation of memory, which occurs three times in this excerpt alone, his modesty is unmistakable when he states that Settimelli tried to sell the film 'magnificandola in ogni modo,' that is, magnifying, aggrandizing, glorifying it, in every way possible – which casts some doubt on the film's aesthetic qualities, and which Ginna, though he added the noisy audience, carefully subtracted.

Hence, not only was Ginna's 1965 report susceptible to the deceptiveness of memory, it was also to a large extent a product of second-hand memory, which went unrecognized by Ginna and some of his readers. Yet the most revealing document concerning the validity of Ginna's account is a later article that he himself wrote, which appeared in Rome's *Il Secolo d'Italia* on 21 February 1969. To celebrate the sixtieth anniversary of the Futurists' exordium in Paris's *Le Figaro* (20 February 1909), the Roman paper dedicated its Terza Pagina to 'Sessanta anni dal primo manifesto futurista di F. T. Marinetti' (Sixty Years from F. T. Marinetti's First Futurist Manifesto). The project consisted of various interventions from figures with close ties to Futurism, including Ginna's 'Le vicende di un film' (The Vicissitudes of a Film), again relating his memories of the 1916 cinematic venture. After commenting on the production of *Vita futurista* and gratefully acknowledging that his fellow Futurists, despite their imperfections as actors and collaborators, inspired him with originality, Ginna definitely revises his earlier take on the film's reception:

> Nei teatri le serate futuriste potevano anche essere ironizzate e accompagnate dal lancio di 'proiettili' vegetali, verdure varie senza arrecare alcun danno. Nelle sale cinematografiche il lancio di simili 'proiettili vegetali' *avrebbe inevitabilmente deteriorato gli schermi, ragion per cui gli esercenti dei cinematografi si rifiutarono invariabilmente di correre codesti rischi.* (emphasis added)[50]

> [In the theatres, the *serate futuriste* could also be treated with irony and accompanied by the throwing of vegetable 'projectiles,' various greens, without causing any damage. In the film auditoriums the throwing of such 'vegetable projectiles' *would have inevitably damaged the screens, for which reason the film exhibitors invariably refused to run those risks.*]

In contrast to his earlier article, Ginna does not only refrain from claiming that the film provoked violence, but even suggests that it did not. The use of the past conditional ('avrebbe inevitabilmente deteriorato gli schermi'), suggesting that the action was never realized, is at odds with the earlier article's imperfect ('gettava oggetti'), which expresses a realized action.[51]

War, Futurism, and Cinema

If any such thing as a 'coming closer' between Futurism and the public occurred, which exactly were the conditions that sparked it in this particular historical moment? Innamorati makes a strong point when she claims that after the hubbub of the 'heroic' *serate* 'public and Futurism ended up coming closer to each other, if not in fact understanding each other completely,' adding that this was the result of several developments, the war being one of the most crucial. Over time, she argues, audiences became accustomed to the 'unwinding model' of the *serate*, which in the end 'no longer constituted a scandal but rather an occasion to repeat, on both sides of the proscenium, an amusing ritual that was tacitly agreed upon.' Then there was the synthetic theatre, the rehearsed structure of which imposed a sense of discipline on the *serata*. Yet the backdrop of this 'reciprocal approaching,' she continues, consisted of the 'unifying experience of the war and the patriotic sentiment,' evident not only in the Futurists' political ideology but also in their commitment as enlisted soldiers.[52] Following Italy's entrance into the war in May 1915, many Futurists enlisted. Some were wounded in battle, including Marinetti and Russolo, while Sant'Elia and Boccioni lost their lives, the former at the front and the latter in a war-related accident.[53]

The exaltation of war constitutes an essential aspect of Futurist discourse and functions both as an explicit ideology related to current political affairs and as an aesthetic principle. On the political front, Marinetti was a strong supporter of irredentism concerning the reclamation of Trento and Trieste from Austria, hence a passionate opponent of Italy's Triple Alliance with Germany and Austria. When the outbreak of war in 1914 set off the split in Italian public opinion between neutralists and interventionists, Marinetti's irredentism turned into an acute interventionism, favouring Italy's alliance with the Entente. As regards aesthetics, war represents a struggle against traditional culture and its replacement with aesthetic forms to reflect the present state of humanity. Modern war machinery, having introduced faster and more efficient – synthetic, if I may – weapons, was among the technologies that informed the Futurist aesthetics of speed. In the words of Luciano De Maria, Marinetti's polemology involves a theoretical conception of struggle and fighting as a 'natural' law of being, and a belief in finding in war, as a concrete state of affairs, an experience of 'vital exuberance, a playful discharge of energy, a hygiene not in the preventive but in the active and liberating sense' (*TIF* lxiii–lxv).[54] While a political spirit fuelled the Futurist *serate* from their inception, the 'battle' that the Futurists aspired to arouse in their theatres was itself a symbolic enactment of war, aiming for that 'vital exuberance,' the 'liberating hygiene,' that De Maria describes.[55] In Marinetti's own words, 'il Futurismo segnò appunto l'irrompere della guerra nell'arte, col creare quel fenomeno che è la Serata futurista (efficacissima propaganda di coraggio)' [Futurism marked the irruption of war into art, by creating that phenomenon that is the *Serata futurista* (a strong propaganda of courage)] (*TIF* 333).[56]

War provides an explicit ideological frame for much of the conceptualization of Futurist aesthetics. The synthetic theatre manifesto, written in early 1915, opens with an interventionist sermon that posits the synthetic theatre as a means to cultivate the Italian bellicose spirit. In late 1916, with Italy well into war, the film manifesto itself will offer abstract cinematography as the answer to the nation's pressing needs. At its opening, the film manifesto states:

Il libro, statico compagno dei sedentari, dei nostalgici e dei neutralisti, non può divertire né esaltare le nuove generazioni futuriste ebbre di dinamismo rivoluzionario e bellicoso.

La conflagrazione agilizza sempre più la sensibilità europea. La nostra grande guerra igienica, che dovrà soddisfare *tutte* le nostre aspirazioni nazionali, centuplica la forza novatrice della razza italiana. (*TIF* 138–9)

[The book, static companion of the sedentary, the nostalgic, and the neutralists, can neither entertain nor exalt the new Futurist generations intoxicated by revolutionary and bellicose dynamism.

The conflagration is making European sensibility ever more agile. Our great hygienic war, which must satisfy *all* our national aspirations, is increasing the revitalizing power of the Italian race a hundredfold.]

The opening anticipates the manifesto's own conclusion, thus placing this revolutionary conception of cinema within the frame of a distinctly nationalistic, if not proto-fascistic, discourse on cultural and political hegemony: '**Scomponiamo e ricomponiamo così l'Universo secondo i nostri meravigliosi capricci**, per centuplicare la potenza del genio creatore italiano e il suo predominio assoluto nel mondo' [**In this way we dismantle and reassemble the Universe according to our marvellous whims**, to increase a hundredfold the power of the creative Italian genius and its absolute supremacy in the world] (*TIF* 144).

War also determined the climate surrounding the premiere of *Vita futurista* at Florence's Niccolini. As we have seen, the film's advertising campaign in the press, most likely carried out by unidentified Futurists, emphasized the event's cause in support of the families of recalled servicemen.[57] This must have sent a clear message to the Florentine public that the event was going to be as much a patriotic experience as a cultural one. Moreover, the *serata* was not alone in its philanthropic aims, but entered an institution that was well established during the war years. Browsing through the January 1917 issues of *Il Nuovo Giornale*, we find countless announcements of war-related charity events taking place in local theatres, the families of recalled servicemen being among the most frequent causes. An article published just three weeks before the *serata* raises questions about Futurism's relationship to this institution. It is a review of what the title presents as 'the great benefit show at the Pergola,' which took place on 5 January and was sponsored by the regional Committee of Propaganda for the benefit of the Red Cross and the families of recalled servicemen.[58] The article opens by praising the frequency of such events: 'Dopo due anni di spettacoli di beneficenza a getto continuo è un po' difficile trovare degli aggettivi nuovi e delle espressioni adeguate per esaltare chi si presta gentilmente a divertire il pubblico a vantaggio delle istituzioni che la guerra ha reso necessarie' [After two years of non-stop benefit shows, it is a little difficult to find new adjectives and adequate expressions to exalt those who kindly offer to entertain the public for the advantage of the institutions that the war made necessary]. The *serata*'s unfolding within this framework surely reduces its status as a unique aesthetic endeavour, the goal of which might have been to challenge tradition, and highlights instead its patriotic dimension and collaboration with the collective.

The article notes this show's extraordinary success: 'Contrariamente al solito, dunque, si debbono ritenere per veritiere tutte le lodi che dovremo tributare agli artisti autentici ed improvvisati della bella serata' [So, contrary to what is usual, one must consider truthful all the praise that we will have to give to the professional and non-professional artists of the beautiful evening]. The writer commends the atypical attire of the evening's select audience: 'Le signore indossavano, salvo poche eccezioni, *toilettes* di un gusto sobrio, intonato giustamente al momento: gli *smokings* e i *fraks* erano, se dio vuole, in minoranza: avremmo preferito che non ve ne fossero affatto, perché questa non è ora di ostentazioni vane' [Besides a few exceptions, the ladies wore gowns of sober taste, rightly in tune with the occasion: the smoking jackets and tails were, God willing, a minority: we would have preferred that they hadn't been there at all, as this is no time for vain displays]. In its impressive roll call of the evening's attendees, including generals, prefects, *commendatori, cavalieri*, counts, countesses, dukes, duchesses, princesses, *marquis, marquises*, baronesses, colonels, lawyers, doctors, professors, and 'un'infinità di ufficiali, reduci dal fronte, nella gloriosa divisa grigio-verde' [an endless number of officers, survivors from the front, in the glorious grey-green uniform], the article notes the presence of the 'baldo bombardiere' [daring bomber]

Marinetti. An overview of the performance reveals its traditional character. Highlights included music from Rossini's *Guglielmo Tell*, Grieg's
Peer Gynt, and Mascagni's *Inno al Sole*.[59] Romances by contemporary
Italian composers were sung 'con l'arte finissima dell'illustre baritono
[Mario Ancona] e la signora Anna Kruscentski fu acclamata ... per il
vivo sentimento posto nell'esecuzione di due suggestive arie antiche e
della meravigliosa romanza della *Wally* [di Catalani]' [with the pure art
of the illustrious baritone Mario Ancona and Signora Anna Kruscentski
was acclaimed ... for the live emotion put in the execution of two suggestive old arias and the marvellous romance from Catalani's *La Wally*].
The finale was the *Allegoria delle nazioni*, an impersonation of various
nations by actresses dressed accordingly, of which the young *marquise*
playing Italy was *bellissima*, the writer notes.

Marinetti had every reason to attend a performance in honour of a
war to which he was committed. Yet his appearance at Florentine charity functions just before the *serata*'s own contribution to the cause surely
strengthens the link between Futurism and this institution. Furthermore,
one wonders whether the new necessities created by the war made
Marinetti revisit his contempt for traditional culture. Does his appearance at this event imply that he grew more tolerant of the things that he
had previously ridiculed? Given this event's type of performance and
audience, may we assume that he now endorses the proper execution
of great musical works, the bizarre and irreverent distortions of which
the variety theatre manifesto feverishly promoted (*TIF* 89); or that he no
longer scorns the audiences of theatrical premieres, similar to benefit
shows in their distinctiveness, where he previously saw little more than
'rivalità di cappelli e di *toilettes* femminili, ... vanità del posto pagato
caro, che si trasforma in orgoglio intellettuale, ... uomini maturi e ric-
chi ... dalla digestione laboriosissima, che rende impossibile qualsiasi
sforzo della mente' [women's rivalries about hats and gowns, ... vanity
of the expensive seat that turns into intellectual pride, ... older and
rich men ... with a very poor digestion, which makes any mental effort
impossible] (*TIF* 310)? One also wonders whether this show's audience
is indicative of who was to attend the premiere of *Vita futurista* three
weeks later – which was, after all, one more event held for the same
cause. If the audience of the *serata* was of the same socio-economic
stature as the one described above, and if one of its primary concerns
in attending the *serata* was to display its financial contribution to the
cause, we need not expect it to invest any more mental or physical effort
in the experience than was needed for a civilized applause, despite how

bizarre the film may have been. Certainly, in the absence of precise evidence concerning either Marinetti's views at the time or the audience of the *serata*, the above is mere speculation. Yet peripheral evidence offers a vivid picture of the political and socio-cultural climate in which the *serata* occurred and which it directly or indirectly espoused.

In assessing the political dimension of the January 1917 *serata*, we must also view it in relation to the synthetic theatre: while its program included four syntheses, the synthetic theatre was also the Futurists' main project at the time. The discipline that the orchestrated form of the synthesis imposed on the later *serate* does not alone explain the peaceful reception that those enjoyed vis-à-vis the earlier ones. In the interventionist spirit of the synthetic theatre manifesto, during war the Futurists produced several syntheses of a political subject matter that appealed to the public's patriotic sentiment, thus further securing the agreeable reception of the *serate*.[60] Indeed, two of the four syntheses preceding the screening of *Vita futurista* at the Niccolini exalt Futurist anti-neutralist action.[61] Their ideology finds a voice in the courageous Futurist poet Italo. In *Dichiarazione di guerra* (Declaration of War) we see his encounter with other artists upon Italy's declaration of war in May 1915. After he scornfully sends away the cynical and Germanophile Giulio, Italo convinces the apolitical Carlo to enlist. He praises Carlo as one of those men whose soul is strong and 'al momento opportuno sa liberarsi dallo stolido concetto passatista che l'arte sia estranea alla politica' [at the right moment knows how to free itself from the stupid passéist idea that art is foreign to politics]. He proceeds with a treatise on the intimate connection between Italian art and the Italian race, its blood, and its blessed land.[62] In *Attacco di aeroplani austriaci* (Attack of Austrian Airplanes), Italo's legs are bandaged, evidently after he is wounded in battle, his mother and sister looking after him. Once the bombardment begins, inspired by his sister's reading of Marinetti's manifesto on the 'uomo meccanico dalle parti smontabili' [mechanical man with dismountable parts], Italo rushes to the street and rejoins his regiment, thus disproving his doctor's advice that his legs may not make a single step. He defies the women's desperate pleas, and during a counterattack that brings down some Austrian planes he dies heroically, repeating the word 'Italy' with his last waning breaths.[63]

The content of *Vita futurista* was no less political than the rest of the program. In its initial form, the film had an even stronger political component than what Florentine and Roman audiences saw in January and June 1917. The film's treatment as it appears in the Nulla Osta document, submitted for censorship clearance on 2 December 1916, also includes 'Perché Francesco Giuseppe non moriva,' an episode written by Marinetti and Settimelli and intended as the film's finale, before it was removed by the censor.[64] The episode satirizes the recently deceased and notoriously bloodthirsty Franz Josef, Austrian emperor and king of Hungary, whose career lasted sixty-eight years. Following the outbreak of the Great War, the emperor signs a contract with Madame Death, agreeing that she will spare his life if he provides her with at least 100,000 deaths per week. When at one point the dead are only 60,000, the emperor's grief causes his health to deteriorate. Upon his doctor's recommendation, he intensifies the massacres across Europe, ordering the death of all living beings through all possible means, such as the spreading of disease and the bombing of sparrows by military aircraft. Meanwhile, Madame Death claims her contractual rights, yet she is so struck by the stench of the emperor's ailing body that she nearly faints and is urgently taken away for medical care.[65] According to Innamorati, as the satire was obviously at the expense of the nation's enemy, the censor may have acted out of incomprehension and uncertainty rather than a consistent selection plan. He must have been apprehensive, she notes, with respect to the satire's insistence on brutal images and a great number of deaths. As similar things were known to happen during the ongoing war, evoking them could have upset the audience and brought chaos in the auditorium.[66]

The episode's censorship, however, does not erase the film's politics. As found in the Nulla Osta, the screenplay is divided into two parts, the second of which begins with 'L'ora del the' (Tea Time), an episode about a meeting of a group of Germanophile pacifists followed by the Futurists' Italian intervention. Innamorati argues that the removal of the Francesco Giuseppe episode eliminated the structural equilibrium of the film's second part. Unlike the rest of the film, the beginning of the second part with 'L'ora del the' was explicit political discourse that was to be resumed at the end with the Francesco Giuseppe episode, thus placing the rest of the action in a political thematic frame.[67] Let us also recall the film's opening as described in 'Alcune parti del film "Vita futurista,"' the announcement appearing in the four issues of *L'Italia Futurista* from October to December 1916. As noted in chapter 1, the announcement exalts the film's anti-realist aesthetics, but also inserts a political statement: 'Let us remember that the Futurists were the first to support the inevitability of war and Marinetti, to the astonishment and derision of all, seven years ago, in the midst of the complete pacifism of the Triple Alliance, shouted in public (in Milan's Teatro Lirico), *War on Austria!*'

The latter is an evocation of the 15 February 1910 *serata* in Milan, known for the fierce controversy that it aroused. During this *serata*, poet Michelangelo Zimolo recited Paolo Buzzi's *Ode to General Vittorio Asinari di Bernezzo*, a general who had been forced into early retirement because of his anti-Austrian and irredentist speeches, now celebrated as a Futurist hero. Pandemonium followed, including fights between the irredentists and the internationalists in the audience, and diverse political shouts, from 'Long live Italy!' to 'Down with the Fatherland!' After Marinetti turned towards the box of Prince Joachim von Hohenzollern and exclaimed, 'Down with Austria,' he and Zimolo together shouted: 'Long live Asinari di Bernezzo! Glory to war, the sole hygiene of the world.' Both Marinetti and Zimolo were arrested.[68] Yet the 1917 evocation of the 1910 event – the latter having occurred *during* the Triple Alliance – would have had a different effect on the present audience, that is, years after the dissolution of the Alliance and with Italy already at war against Austria. If the initial gesture had been truly subversive in asking the public to reject the nation's official political allegiances, its later evocation, given the nation's radical turn in the interim, was little more than a self-congratulatory statement celebrating the now officially recognized righteousness of that early gesture. Hence, if the earlier gesture had stirred up the conflicting political views within the audience, the later one would have simply indulged the audience's patriotism.

Had we known beyond doubt that the evocation of the 1910 *serata* was part not only of the film's advertisement in *L'Italia Futurista* but also of its exhibition, we would have been able to discuss the audience's response to the film's politics with more certainty. We have noted that E.C.O.'s review of the film's exhibition in Rome suggests that some written text appeared on screen upon the film's opening (see chapter 1). However, in expressing his disdain for those 'absurd claims,' E.C.O. does not specify that any such claim addressed politics. Also, that such text was shown in Rome does not mean that the same cut of the film played in Florence. Moreover, the version of the film found in the Nulla Osta also opens with a series of statements, which may have served as a form of opening credits. That version differs, however, from the one in *L'Italia Futurista*, in that it is much briefer and includes no political statements. Let us note that the Futurists submitted the Nulla Osta application on 2 December 1916, while the last printing of 'Alcune parti del film "Vita futurista"' in *L'Italia Futurista* appeared only a day earlier, in the 1 December issue. The Futurists may have hastened to remove politics from the film's opening as a precaution in applying for censorship clearance. Perhaps they kept 'L'ora del the' and the Francesco Giuseppe episode because they considered them less risqué, as those constituted fiction and satire rather than raw political declarations. To be sure, exalting Marinetti's interventionism should not have countered contemporary national politics. Yet we also know that despite his patriotism Marinetti faced huge obstacles in trying to enlist as a volunteer, to the point that he hired a lawyer to support his case, only because the authorities had labelled him as one 'committed to brawls.'[69] Aiming to pass censorship, the Futurists may have thought it wise to remove any raw political statements, especially those evoking Marinetti's 'brawls,' despite their specific ideological content. Did they then reinstate such statements for the film's exhibition? Again, in the absence of evidence or a print of the film, the question persists. The distinct elements pointing to the film's political context and content are difficult to verify. Nonetheless, their sum allows us to conjecture that the film's conception and exhibition took place in a generally nationalistic climate that would have strongly influenced its reception.

The film's political impact may also be sought in its humorous portrayals of the Futurists' superior prowess over the passéists, as found in 'Come dorme un futurista' (How a Futurist Sleeps), 'Passeggiata futurista' (Futurist Walk), 'Scherma, boxe' (Fencing, Boxing), 'Assalto futurista alla spada fra Marinetti e Remo Chiti' (Futurist Attack with Swords between Marinetti and Remo Chiti), and 'Discussione coi guantoni fra Marinetti e Ungari' (Discussion with Boxing Gloves between Marinetti and Ungari). Whether the passéist figure is explicitly identified as a neutralist, the episodes may not be divorced from Futurist war ideology. Just as the meaning of war in Futurism is neither strictly literal nor strictly metaphorical, but its literal dimension regarding Italy's intervention and its metaphorical one as an attack on passéism are inextricably linked, the passéist antagonist derided in any given episode is equally identifiable as a neutralist. If the evocation of Marinetti's 1910 anti-Austrian declarations never found its way into the film, the comical 'duels' (along with 'L'ora del the') undoubtedly filled that void. Deriding neutralism in 1917, before an audience eager to display its support for the nation's heroes, was more likely to indulge the audience's patriotism than trigger an auditorium 'battle.' Yet what is peculiar about these 'duels,' which mixed prowess, nationalism, and humour, is that their patriotism clashed with the wish to enact yet another 'battle,' one that should have been ignited by a film that shattered the established viewing mechanisms of a public by now acculturated to narrative cinema.

Patriotism did not merely inhibit the possibility of such a battle. It even served as a locus of convergence, of a harmonious encounter, between two otherwise divergent notions of cinema. To be exact, inasmuch as *Vita futurista* attacked the conventions of the feature-length narrative, its delightful fights between active Futurists and passive neutralists evoked the likewise nationalistic scenarios of boldness and masculinity that were the trademark of the *forzuto* (strongman), a young genre the popularity of which was then rapidly on the rise.

The *forzuto* was founded on the exaltation of a hero who combined super-human muscular strength with an exceptional degree of moral integrity. Most exemplary in the mid-1910s was the figure of Maciste, initially conceived by Pastrone of Itala Film for his pivotal historical epic *Cabiria* (1914), set during the Second Punic War. Maciste was baptized as such by D'Annunzio, writer of the film's intertitles, and took shape in the person of Bartolomeo Pagano, not yet a professional actor but a muscular stevedore discovered by Pastrone at the port of Genoa. In *Cabiria*, Maciste is an African slave distinguished by his loyalty to

Figure 2.1 Maciste breaks his chains of bondage in Giovanni Pastrone's 1914 film *Cabiria*. (Image provided by Kino Lorber Incorporated)

Figure 2.2 Maciste effortlessly bends the iron bars of his prison cell in *Cabiria*. (Image provided by Kino Lorber Incorporated)

his Roman master, Fulvio Axilla, with whom he resides in Carthage on an espionage mission. The film's box office success, both in Italy and abroad, was not only a result of Pastrone's acclaimed technical innovations, D'Annunzio's prestigious signature, the opulent mise-en-scène, or the sensuous appearance of Italia Almirante Manzini as the Carthaginian princess. It was largely owed to Maciste's amiable and sprightly presence, especially in scenes demonstrating his strength in the service of good will, such as the cartoonist handling of physically inferior villains, the breaking of his chains of bondage after ten years of detention, or the effortless bending of the iron bars of his prison cell in trying to escape and rescue the innocent Cabiria (figures 2.1 and 2.2). Maciste's immense popularity sparked the formation of the *forzuto* as a genre in its own right, which included an extensive series of Maciste films played by Pagano.[70]

The two Maciste films that followed *Cabiria* operate on a metacinematic premise that aims to enhance the image of the film industry as the creator of positive role models. In *Maciste* (produced in 1915 by Itala Film, directed by Romano Luigi Borgnetto and Vincent Denizot),

a group of kidnappers pursue a young girl for the benefit of her vil-
lainous uncle, a certain 'duke Alexis' whose nationality is unspecified.
The girl seeks refuge in the darkness of a movie theatre where *Cabiria*
is playing. Inspired by Maciste's ability to save little Cabiria, she writes
him a letter seeking his assistance. Thus, the real Maciste (who as we
now learn exists outside *Cabiria*'s diegetic register) eagerly meets the
girl and begins tracing the villains. Furthermore, the war proved useful
for the industry's building of role models. In *Maciste alpino* (produced
by Itala Film in 1916, directed by Borgnetto and Luigi Maggi), Maciste
is an actor at Italia Film (note the allusion to Itala). In May 1915, an Italia
crew is shooting a film in an Austrian village near the Italian border.
When Italy declares war, a telegram arrives from Italia ordering them
to interrupt the project and return home. After a series of adventures
against the local authorities that try to prevent their departure, Maciste
joins the alpine troops and heroically saves his compatriots and fellow
soldiers. In the words of Alberto Farassino, the film's patriotic message
upon its release during war was that 'Italy's sons are all Macisti.'[71]

Patriotism constitutes a thread that links *Vita futurista* to the *forzuto*.
This thread is not only thematic but also structural: the point of convergence between the two discourses involves not only patriotism
as a referent but also the formal means through which patriotism is
represented. The most apparent formal link between the two types of
spectacle is photographic verisimilitude, by which the Marinetti shorts
deviate from the manifesto's radical proclamations for an abstract style,
endorsing instead narrative cinema's notion of the diegesis as a fictional
world that resembles the real one. Let us note that verisimilitude here is
strictly photographic, as it refers to how things look and not to the likelihood of the action. Engaging in a boxing match while wearing tails
(figure 1.5) is physically possible but improbable. At times the action is
so absurd that it verges on the impossible. A man's sleeping vertically
and holding a cigarette, as in 'Come dorme un futurista' (figure 1.4),
may be feasible for a second or two but not with the perfect composure
displayed by our Futurist. Physical ability that oscillates between the
highly improbable and the impossible abounds in the *forzuto*. In *Cabiria*,
after the Carthaginians chase Maciste to the roof of the temple, Maciste
effortlessly lifts them up and with the agility of a basketball champion
hurls them into the boiling pot nearby or into the air and out of the
frame. In *Maciste*, when the hero receives the girl's letter, he is in the
process of doing his daily exercises. The huge pair of barbells that he is
lifting is so light for him that he has a man hang on either side of the bar

to make the exercise worthwhile. What may astonish the viewer is to the hero an enjoyable routine, 'L'aperitivo di Maciste,' his aperitif, as the intertitles say.[72] Maciste's physical dominance over the national other, as seen in *Cabiria*, *Maciste*, and *Maciste alpino*, parallels the Futurists' derision of the neutralist, whom they label as a Germanophile, a traitor, and thus a national other of sorts, while the union of masculinity with righteousness in both cases unfolds in a realistic setting, yet through actions that challenge the limits of probability.[73]

The audience is untroubled by such negations of probability to the extent that it perceives them as slapstick. This means that in such moments the ongoing film, either *Vita futurista* or the *forzuto*, crosses another genre, that is, the *comica*, where slapstick prevails and is generically motivated. Slapstick is an essential part of the structural thread that links the two types of film. We have identified the Futurist film's evocation of the *comica* in things such as a boxing match in elegant attire (see chapter 1). Continuities also exist between the *comica* and the *forzuto*. Bernardini notes 'the attention to a popular audience, the taste for a simple diversion free of intellectual ambitions [and] the valorization of the physical talents of actors coming from the circus and the sports hall.'[74] Yet the manner in which *Vita futurista* accommodates slapstick differs from the analogous process in the *forzuto*, and we must examine this difference before we accurately define the formal link between them. The descriptions of *Vita futurista* suggest that the episodes under discussion, while they evoked the *comica*, did not merely imitate it. The comedies were short narratives usually shown after a feature-length film. Narrative form was rudimentary, as it often relied on a single and uncomplicated line of action that served as the background and motivating force of a series of gags. It seems that the Marinetti 'duels,' unlike the *comica* or the film's more developed episodes (such as 'Colazione futurista' or the Balla-chair love story), abandoned narrative structure altogether. They were brief scenes with a single action, aiming to swiftly and forcefully impress upon the viewer the Futurist's prowess in diverse settings, such as boxing, sleeping, running, and fencing. These quickies, despite photographic verisimilitude, reflected the declared attempt to challenge narrative cinema – if not through the nature of the diegesis, then through the pursuit of an earlier form of spectatorship, that of the cinema of attractions, also evoked by the film's simulation of a variety show. The manifestations of masculinity in a series of swift and causally unrelated numbers would have achieved the direct address that distinguished early attractions from narrative cinema. Hence, while

Vita futurista drew on the contemporary *comica* in order to exploit its antidotal properties, it also stripped it of its narrativity and applied it to the revival of an earlier cinematic configuration.[75]

The *forzuto*'s appropriation of the comedic element moves in the opposite direction. If Futurism strips slapstick of its rudimentary narrativity, the *forzuto* over-narrativizes it. It inserts it in a complex narrative, assigning a fixed and exclusive post to it, as in a large jigsaw puzzle. Yet these delightful manifestations of physical strength, even from their rigid posts, demand the audience's special attention. They stand out like brief numbers in a variety show, like inserts of excess, which suspend narrative progression while they appeal to our fascination with a hero or actor as an entity that exists outside the diegetic constraints of this or that narrative.[76] They constitute that dimension of the film that we may describe as *attractionist*; they are attractions narrativized. This marks a time when the boundaries between film exhibition and other types of show had already been rather solidified, yet narrative cinema did not efface attractions altogether, but sought a balance between storytelling and spectacle for spectacle's sake.[77] It is the relation to early attractions that puts *Vita futurista* on a par with the *forzuto* as regards the audience. Ironically, while the Futurists looked to an earlier form of spectatorship in order to undo their audience's by now standardized viewing patterns, this very gaze backward undid itself, as the 'synthetic' portrayals of masculinity in *Vita futurista* resonated with the distinct moments of pleasure given to us by the strongman, by this genre's attractionist moments.

That Maciste's heroic deeds were part of the mindset of audiences watching *Vita futurista* is irrefutable. *Cabiria* was re-released in Florence in the week before the Futurist film's premiere. Advertisements of both the Futurist cinematic debut at the Niccolini and the showing of *Cabiria* at the Pergola appeared daily and almost side-by-side in the 'Cronaca Fiorentina' section of *Il Nuovo Giornale*. Readers needed to decide how to make the best of that Sunday afternoon, either to discover Futurist cinema or delight once again in the familiar antics of their beloved Maciste.[78] On the day following *Cabiria*'s opening, of the many marvels that Pastrone's epic brought to the screen, Maciste was among the most highly praised by the reviewers:

> Fin dal suo primo apparire Maciste conquistò ieri le simpatie del pubblico del teatro Pergola che ne ammirò l'erculea corporatura, ne seguì con applausi le meravigliose avventure, ne disapprovò la cattura come

una sventura propria e ne salutò infine la liberazione come un trionfo del coraggio indomito e della magnanima generosità.

[From his first appearance Maciste yesterday conquered the affections of the Pergola audience, who admired his Herculean physique, followed his marvellous adventures with applause, disapproved of his capture as if it were its own misfortune, and finally greeted his liberation as a triumph of indomitable courage and noble generosity.]

The nationalistic implications were not lacking: 'Fulvio Axilla, sempre pronto a servire l'idea romana e a sacrificarsi per essa, condivise con Maciste le calorose simpatie degli spettatori' [Fulvio Axilla, always ready to serve the Roman ideal and sacrifice himself for it, shared with Maciste the warm affections of the spectators]. As to D'Annunzio, writer of the film's intertitles and guarantor of its cultural prestige, 'Il popolo nostro ... trovò anch'esso, ieri che Gabriele D'Annunzio impresse all'arte cinematografica un senso di sovrana originalità, ed applaudì calorosamente l'opera ed il grande Poeta Soldato' [Our people ... also found yesterday that Gabriele D'Annunzio impressed upon the cinematographic art a sense of supreme originality, and warmly applauded the work and the great Soldier Poet].[79]

Maciste alpino, marking the return of *Cabiria*'s Gigante Buono, or Good Giant (Maciste's nickname), evidently did not reach Florence until February, that is, a month after the exhibition of *Vita futurista*.[80] To be sure, *Cabiria* alone provided a popular equivalent to Marinetti's amusing accents on nationalism and masculinity. *Maciste alpino*, however, was to play a similar role in Rome, where it was shown in June at the same time as *Vita futurista*. Noteworthy is the manner in which Rome's *Il Cinema Illustrato* advertises the Maciste film, listed under the same rubric as the Futurist film (let us recall: 'At the CINEMA SALA COSTANZI the great Futurist show, *To Murder the Moonlight*. We add no more'). The paper announces that at the Manzoni 'si proiettano ora le gesta di *Maciste Alpino*' [the deeds of *Maciste Alpino* are now shown].[81] By thus isolating Maciste's deeds from their narrative context, the writer asserts their attractionist qualities, their function as distinct numbers to be enjoyed for their own sake.

To understand the core of this formal mechanism, we must consider its thematic factor. The similar audience response rests on the fact that both types of spectacle combine slapstick (the 'attraction') with as many as three precise thematic elements: nationalism, masculinity, and violence. In the still from 'Discussione coi guantoni,' Ungari is both a passéist and a neutralist, while the act of boxing comprises masculinity and a given degree of violence, as Ungari is shown falling down, probably when hit by Marinetti. Of the Maciste films discussed above, the one that most directly adheres to this model is *Maciste alpino*. In the genre overall, Maciste uses his strength only if necessary for the restitution of justice and the protection of the weak and righteous – a moral strategy that contradicts Futurism's aggressive tactics and unconditional worship of war. It is not so with *Maciste alpino*, which portrays the subjugation of the enemy in an abundance of disquieting images that amalgamate comedy with strong violence, the narrative indispensability of which is hardly evident.[82] When the film crew is arrested, Maciste launches his boot through the cell's barred window onto the Austrian officer's head, before he bursts into hearty laughter. His punishment is to receive fifty blows with the stick, yet he manages to debilitate all the soldiers in charge of confining him. After he lifts them up and throws them on the ground, he grabs one of them by the feet and uses his body as a weapon with which he beats the others. He then snatches the stick with which he was to receive his blows and beats them incessantly. He throws them on top of each other into a corner, when a close-up of their legs reveals little more than a pile of limp bodies. Throughout the film, we delight in seeing Austrian bodies being tossed about and flying into each other, kicked off over steep cliffs, caught and held up hanging by the hair, their faces used as Maciste's chair, their necks tied together and sliding down a snowy slope like a sleigh, all thanks to our hero's strength, swiftness, and bodily wit.[83]

The combination of humour with aggressiveness as found in Marinetti's 'duels' is not an aberration of Futurism. We find a humorous component in various projects, such as syntheses, manifestos, or the activity of the *serate*, often linked to the audacity with which the Futurists critique their cultural or political adversaries. However, what distinguishes the use of cinematic slapstick from other instances of humour is that cinema boasted a much larger audience than that of any other aesthetic medium, such as theatre or literature, and by using slapstick in 1917 the Futurists adopted a widespread model that likewise combined humour with aggressiveness and politics, as in *Cabiria* and *Maciste alpino*. Thus, Futurism moved a step closer to that mass culture that it set out to refute. One may run to Futurism's defence, to reaffirm its status as a radical movement the integrity and subversiveness of which were not hindered by any representational faux pas.

The Futurists did not intend, after all, to *quote* any of the 'analytical' genres, but were inspired by the *comica* precisely because of its function as an antidote. They even tried to free it from its simple narrative framework and revive the mode of reception of a previous era. The public, however, in order to comprehend and enjoy any film, relies on a set of expectations and preoccupations that have been shaped primarily by the most recent cinematic conventions, and much less so by those that prevailed decades earlier. Furthermore, despite its alleged marginality, the *comica* was part and parcel of what the institution of cinema represented at that time. Its popularity and frequency in theatrical programs may have begun to wane by 1917, but during the last phase of its glory, the genre undoubtedly participated in the amalgamation of comedy with politics that characterized Italian mass culture during war.

That the *comica* normally constituted the finale of a longer film program undermines any attempt to separate it ideologically from the institution as a whole. Throughout 1915 and 1916, both before and after Italy's entrance in the war, the *comica* may have provided a ritualized form of relief from the fears and uncertainties linked to the political climate. As regards the portrayal of war on screen, the inclusion of the *comica finale* involved different combinations of films. In Florence, for example, sometimes neither the *comica* nor the film(s) preceding it hinted at the war, while at other times at least one of the two parts addressed war directly. Often, a documentary about a special event, such as the preparations of a given sector of the military, or a recent battle, was included in the first part of the program, to be followed by a short comedy with no apparent thematic connection to it.[84] Ironically, in such cases we may indeed speak of an antidote, but not one that ideologically cured the viewer of the main feature's melodramatic or epic rehearsals of higher culture. Rather, its function was to appease the viewer after s/he had been exposed to unsettling images of the war, thus speaking to the industry's wish to ensure that viewers left the theatre with a smile, if that counted as a token of their future return.

If the *comica finale* alleviated the anxieties stirred up by the war film(s) just preceding it, many comedies dealt with war directly, integrating its menacing aspects with laughter.[85] Especially noteworthy is *Cretinetti e la paura degli aereomobili nemici* (Cretinetti and the Fear of Enemy Aircraft), starring André Deed and released by Itala Film in November 1915.[86] After the ceremony of Cretinetti's wedding to his beloved and robust

Dulcinea, couple and guests walk to the house for a banquet, when an announcement posted by the sidewalk grabs their attention:

> Per l'eventualità di voli sulla città di aeromobili nemici, visto l'articolo
> Nº 1234567890 della legge sulla paura pubblica,
> SI DECRETA:
> Segnale d'allarme – Occultamento della città – Misure di prevenzione
> contro gli incendi.

> [In the event of flights of enemy aircraft over the city, considering article
> No. 1234567890 of the law on public fear,
> THE FOLLOWING IS ORDERED:
> Alarm signal – Concealment of the city – Preventive measures against fires.]

The warning recommends specific measures, such as preparing a large supply of sand (known to soothe the effects of inflammatory substances) in containers easy to handle, and placing water containers anywhere in the house where fire is likely to occur. The bunch rushes away in a state of hysteria. Women in elegant gowns and feathered hats are fainting, when their male escorts, in hats and tails, drag them at full speed from one street corner to the next. Cretinetti observes the official recommendations closely and orders an extravagant amount of sand to be delivered to the house, while he furnishes every imaginable spot with a bucket of water. What follows is easy to imagine. Thanks to Cretinetti's clumsiness and faulty reasoning, the exquisite bourgeois dining room and the newlyweds' private quarters fall into total chaos, as if they had been bombarded indeed: buckets of water overturn and get spilled at every step, huge sacks full of sand split open and empty over the guests, bathtubs roll down staircases, floors collapse, water pipes break and the house floods, while bride and guests desperately try to stay afloat.[87]

That the film parodies bourgeois rituals and the image of the dandy is unquestionable, as it unfolds in the context of a refined wedding banquet. However, the collapse of this ambience as a result of the hero's excessive precautionary measures, in a film released just six months after Italy entered war, is also a satire of war-induced paranoia, providing relief from the anxieties haunting Italians at this time. It is a kind of exorcism that stirs up the anxieties only to laugh them away. Yet the film's ending merits special attention, as it allows for an alternative reading. While everyone is struggling against the flood inside the house, two officers of the state come and rescue Cretinetti, only to hand him a letter that orders his immediate departure for the anti-aircraft artillery. Though Cretinetti objects, the men force him into a garbage can and carry him away. At first glance, the ending is critical of the war. If those destined to protect Italy from the enemy are as crafty as Cretinetti, the prospects for a strong national defence are ludicrous. Yet the finale is also part of the film's satire, aiming to replace fear with laughter through every narrative device imaginable. Moreover, seeing how absurd it would be to rely on such a person for Italy's defence, the deeper implication is one of reassurance, namely, that this is only a comedy, whereas in reality the men who protect us are quite competent.

To be sure, this *comica* is ideologically more nuanced than *Vita futurista*, the passéist characters of which are decisively inferior to the Futurists. What the Futurist film deeply shares with the *comica*, however, is that it adapts to a cultural framework where political references in a comedic light operate as a form of exorcism. For all its aggressiveness, through its echoes of the *comica* or subtle affinities with the *forzuto*, Futurism partook of that operation with which popular culture neutralized war unease, yet without rejecting war. If the film failed to cause a collision between Futurists and audience, it is because it failed to collide sufficiently with the culture that shaped public response. Instead, there was collusion of sorts, as film and audience silently conspired in the concurrent exaltation and suppression of war. Hence the film's reception at this precise moment of (film) history was the outcome of an intersection of vital factors, some structural, some thematic. Its recourse to attractions through the re-elaboration of the *comica* met its popular equivalent in the attractionist elements of the *forzuto*, while its portrayal of patriotism in an amusing light evoked something familiar, what mass audiences had experienced in films such as *Cabiria, Maciste alpino*, and the farces of Cretinetti. The film's alignment of these specific political and formal elements instigated a mode of reception that had recently been cultivated by narrative cinema's own alignment of such elements. The 'immediate applause' that the Futurists dreaded in 'La voluttà di essere fischiati' was now assaulting Futurism itself. It was the reaction of an audience facing the ambiguities of war, an audience who latched onto a spectacle assuring it of the war's reason but also wanted to forget something, or, as one of the chroniclers perceived it, was not in the mood 'to fight a literary battle, but to laugh, be it at your expense, or at ours.' Such 'immediate applause' exposed nothing but a clash, one that existed from the start, between the exaltation of war as a literal discourse, as an explicit theme in the performance, and war as an aesthetics of spectacle, as a model for a specific mode of reception.

Vita futurista displayed a wide range of styles, most of which we have addressed: narratives that reject verisimilitude (such as the Balla-chair love story), narratives that resemble actualities ('Colazione futurista'), political satire (the Francesco Giuseppe episode), comical scenes based on a single action (the anti-passéist 'duels'), and spectacular celebrations of the era of electricity (such as 'Danza dello splendore geometrico'). The Nulla Osta, however, also includes a seemingly realist segment that re-enacts previous Futurist events, emphasizing their belligerent spirit. One of the events portrayed is the legendary *serata* at the Teatro Mercadante in Naples on 20 April 1910. Both the style and the themes of this episode merit a closer view:

- Pugni invettive lancio di verdure. Episodio di una celebre serata al Mercadante di Napoli.
- I futuristi non si scompongono e fumano tranquillamente.
- La folla attende l'uscita dei futuristi.
- Marinetti Settimelli Nannetti Spada ecc. affrontano il pubblico. Pugilato.[88]

[– Fists, invectives, throwing of vegetables. Episode of a famous evening at Naples's Mercadante.
- The Futurists do not become flustered and smoke calmly.
- The crowd waits for the Futurists' exit.
- Marinetti, Settimelli, Nannetti, Spada, etc. confront the public. Boxing.]

The episode also appears in the Niccolini poster as follows: 'Riproduzione della celebre serata al Mercadante di Napoli. / Marinetti parla in teatro – Declamazione futurista – Pugilato' [Reproduction of the famous evening at Naples's Mercadante / Marinetti speaks in the theatre – Futurist declamation – Boxing].[89] What does the episode tell us about the Futurists' attitude towards filmmaking and their perception of both their audience and the direction in which Futurism was headed?

Historically, the *serata* at the Mercadante stands at the core of the movement's 'heroic' phase and is exemplary of the clamour aroused during the early *serate*. Although it was only the fourth *serata* in the movement's history (the first three had been in Trieste, Milan, and Turin, all within three and a half months before this one), the public's aggressive impulses began seething several days before the event. Not only had Marinetti's notoriety been well established by then, but a series of unusual events leading to that evening also served as a form of publicity. Though the *serata* was scheduled for 15 April, the owner of that venue withdrew his concession. Marinetti then managed to reserve the Teatro Mercadante, yet for several days the police forbade the performance. Berghaus describes the arrival of the audience at the event quite vividly:

> A huge crowd had assembled in front of the theatre in the hope of finding a seat. 'The surroundings of the Mercadante looked like the ramparts of a citadel about to be attacked by the enemy,' wrote the journal *Roma*. A cohort of policemen marched into the theatre and tried (unsuccessfully) to keep the onslaught of the spectators under control . . . The theatre was filled to more than double its normal capacity, wrote *Roma* . . . ' . . . The plentiful array of *carabinieri*, security guards, constables and commissioners was forced to declare their impotence and inability to repress such unheard-of violence' (*Don Marzo*).

Despite the audience's aggressive behaviour, Marinetti was physically safe, as over a hundred policemen stood behind him on stage. Yet 'he was swamped by a rain of tomatoes, potatoes and chestnuts.' The uproar was such that the performers' declamations were hardly audible. Fights broke out in the stalls, accompanied by more showers of vegetables and witty repartees between audience and performers. Finally, Marinetti's witticism conquered some of the audience, who followed him into the streets well beyond the end of the scheduled event. The crowd was so large that 'not even the police could dam the flood that surged through Via Roma.'[90]

To represent such an event in the realist manner in which the Nulla Osta suggests, the Futurists would have had to rely on some narrative conventions, such as photographic verisimilitude, montage aiming at storytelling, and a high budget. Hence, they would have refuted their own campaign against cinema's 'finite, polished, anti-impressionistic, *PHOTOGRAPHIC* technique' and 'servitude as a simple reproducer ['riproduttore'] of reality,' which they launched, as we have seen, in *L'Italia Futurista*'s recurrent announcement. It is crucial that the Niccolini poster calls the episode a 'reproduction' ('riproduzione'). In echoing the newspaper's rejection of cinema as a 'riproduttore,' the poster's characterization of the episode as a 'riproduzione' in effect undermines the newspaper's attack on verisimilitude and exposes the Futurists' ambivalence about the medium's application. Besides the need for veri-similitude, the episode requires montage for storytelling. Even if its Nulla Osta version may be filmed in as few as two shots, one inside the theatre and one outdoors, montage serves a mode of narration based on chronological order. One of the film's surviving stills is a close-up of Chiti with an expression of pain and a seemingly bloodstained bandage on his head (figure 2.3). Critics believe that the still is from this episode, Chiti's wounded face representing a traditionalist who was defeated during the theatre battle.[91] Of course, a close-up would indicate an even more complex use of montage for narration. Also, like popular cinema, the episode requires a high budget. Who will compensate the crowd?[92] Who will reimburse the theatre owner for damages? Yet such factors are not unique to this episode. Narrativity and high budget also mark other complex parts of the script, such as the Francesco Giuseppe satire. To see what is unique about this episode, let us recall our discussion

Figure 2.3 A close-up of Remo Chiti from *Vita futurista*. (Reprinted from Mario Verdone, *Cinema e letteratura del futurismo* [Rome: Centro Sperimentale di Cinematografia, Edizioni di Bianco e Nero, 1968])

of the film's metadiscourse, its replication of the variety format of the *serata* in which it is shown, hence its function as Futurist self-advertisement (see chapter 1). This episode is unique in that its portrayal of a Futurist *serata* endows it with independent metadiscursive qualities. First, it is, in and of itself, a Futurist show that portrays a Futurist show. Second, the show that it portrays being a *serata*, it evokes the present *serata* directly, thus bypassing its reliance on the 'variety' film. Hence, it promotes a comparison between the *serata* on screen and the one off screen, offering the Mercadante's violent audience as a model for the present audience.

This redoubled self-referentiality dramatizes the Futurists' self-consciousness and invites us to speculate on the manner in which they envisioned both their audience and the direction in which Futurism was headed, insofar as the audience's response was indicative of it. If their attitude towards film style wavered between abstractness and realism, this ambivalence extended to their attitude towards the audience. On the one hand, they aspired to an innovative film capable of inciting a violent response. Surely, *Vita futurista* arrived after the *serata* had been modified because disciplined, as it were, by the rigid form of the synthesis. Marinetti, however, would still have seen the film's 'immediate applause' as a failure, or at least with suspicion. It is crucial that *Vita futurista* was the Futurists' first experiment with the medium and shared the revolutionary impetus of the film manifesto. Perhaps in facing the tempering virtues of the synthesis, the Futurists invested in cinema the hope of reviving the dynamism of a recent past that now seemed to fade away. The act of plunging into a hitherto unused medium, and a relatively young one to boot, may have offered a sense of new beginning and thus rendered tangible the possibility of rekindling a fading but unique splendour. On the other hand, for all their attempts, through a parade of filmic styles and the insistence on a variety mode of exhibition, to combat 'theatre without words' and revive an older cinema experience, the Futurists failed to escape the allure of popular narrative cinema, the powers of which swept through the sphere of culture like a cyclone. This process of seduction is not only visible in those segments of *Vita futurista* that display a realist style, or those elements that under the influence of politics shared something with the *forzuto* or replicated the *comica*'s complicity with the institution of cinema. It is also manifest in the Futurists' attempt to market the film through the established distribution circuit, for which Bragaglia organized its first screening in December 1916 strictly for distributors and critics.[93]

Perhaps the most seductive aspect of the institution of cinema for the Futurists was the prospect of reaching a mass audience, of making a radical film able to shock society at large.

To be sure, the failure to break into the film industry indicates that the film, although it borrowed aspects of mass culture, was not conventional enough for the industry's distribution criteria. Also, notwithstanding the Futurists' ambivalence vis-à-vis popular cinema, I hesitate to propose that they abandoned cinema simply because they failed to break into the industry and insert themselves in the very culture that they vigorously attacked. I do, however, suspect that the abandonment of cinema was linked to the Futurists' anxiety about the ontological crisis that the movement underwent at that moment, namely, the crisis that historically stands for the end of Futurism's 'heroic' phase. Such a crisis did not start with cinema. Its symptoms were already seen in the discipline that the synthetic theatre imposed onto the *serata* and were intensified by the politics of the time, which set the ideal conditions for collusion (not collision) between Futurism and the public. Cinema, in its turn, related to the crisis in a twofold manner. First, it reinforced it in that *Vita futurista*, in all its freshness, did not adequately do away with narrative cinema's representational strategies. Second, it alluded to it, exposed it, in that the film's 'immediate applause' was a profoundly ambivalent outcome and served as a warning. It taught that despite all attempts to combat popular culture, the Futurists unwittingly entered the complex territory of that culture, where responses were to an extent preconditioned. It was a territory out of bounds, or one that could be exploited only at a peril.

Consciously or not, the Futurists abandoned cinema in order to protect avant-gardism from the seductions of the new mass culture. The redoubled self-referentiality of the episode on the Mercadante expresses their inkling about this crisis, one that pre-existed this first cinematic venture. It reveals the wish to affirm anew an image of Futurism defined by vitality and belligerence, a 'heroic' Futurism that never ceased to hold war as the world's only hygiene. At the same time, the episode betrays the tendency to proliferate the crisis through cinema itself. For all its diegetic vigour, the episode arrested a precious past moment and froze it in order to cherish it. If the Futurists saw in cinema the hope to offset the disciplinary effects of the synthesis, to rekindle a recent splendour, the seductive mechanisms of the medium, a medium in history, allowed that rekindling to occur, not in the auditorium, not by engaging the spectators in an exuberant state of *fisicofollia*, but only vicariously, on screen. By thus turning that moment into a legend, the Futurists did not only acknowledge and lament its loss. Five decades before Ginna, they initiated the process of Futurism's fossilization into a heroic image. The scene of the Mercadante, allegedly filmed in 1916, was intended as a tangible document of Futurist heroism to persevere for ages to come.

3

Velocità: Between Avant-Garde and Narrativity

In addition to the creative possibilities that the film medium, strictly as a technological apparatus, made available to Futurist artistic practice, the more general philosophical formulations of Futurism were responding to a different concept of cinema, namely, to the specific application of the apparatus within the prevalent cinematic practice of the early and mid-1910s. I am referring to the Italian institution of cinema – with its opulent historical spectacles and melodramas, comedy shorts, *divismo*, strongmen – which was a vital part of the historical constellation that shaped our notion of modernity, or what Marinetti characterized as the 'complete renewal of human sensibility.' If the 1916 film manifesto's exaltation of the medium as 'eminently Futurist' did not result in an extensive film practice, it nevertheless betrayed, despite the writers' explicit intents in attacking narrative cinema as an updated version of passéist theatre, a theoretical investment in this very concept of cinema – as a universal historical phenomenon of a predominantly symbolic significance, one that surpassed the particularities of Futurist filmmaking. Hence, we are able to attain an understanding of the Futurist notion of 'avant-garde' in its specificity, through a study of the movement's ambivalent relation to the institution of cinema as part of the very culture against which the movement waged a war.

We may view Futurism as a movement that oscillated between its universal and particular dimensions. On the one hand, it celebrated the universal effects of high industrialization upon sensibility in its manifestos. On the other hand, it aimed to convey and regenerate those effects through the production of specific avant-garde works of various artistic forms – such as paintings, poems, sculpture, theatrical 'syntheses,' a film, the manifestos themselves – and their presentation in local theatres.[1] Yet it is likely that Marinetti had a higher aspiration than what this local or lower-scale dimension of the Futurist project was able to achieve.[2] If the works presented at the *serate*, with their revolutionary style, managed to articulate and to some extent proliferate modern sensibility, they lacked the ability to control the shape of that sensibility with the immediate, radical, and decisive force that was exercised by other phenomena, such as the new and highly industrialized methods of production and transportation. Only cinema among the artistic forms available would have seemed suitable for the realization of such an aspiration. In comparison with the other arts, cinema was unique in having established conditions of production that resembled large-scale industry. Therefore, as a technological apparatus that permitted the invention of revolutionary aesthetic techniques, it enabled the expression of modern sensibility on the local level. At the same time, as an institution that resembled large-scale industry, one with an international mass appeal emerging at a given historical moment, it claimed its place in the generation of that ambience that radically *shaped* – not merely expressed – sensibility. It appears that after having attempted to 'express locally' with *Vita futurista*, Marinetti perceived this alluring duplicity of cinema and aspired, by proposing a new cinematic project, to participate in that radical formation of sensibility at a universal scale that high industry had the means of achieving. To be sure, this higher ambition relied on the realization of a film that shared, if in part, the aesthetic project and methods of production and distribution of the contemporary film industry.

Marinetti's *Velocità*, a screenplay discovered in the 1990s by Lista, was never filmed.[3] As Lista explains, its discovery constitutes an important event, not only because the Futurist film products proper are extremely sparse, but also because as the single film script written by Marinetti himself it constitutes a unique document. Although the year of the script's writing is unknown, Lista places it between the end of 1917 and the middle of 1918, that is, after the exhibition of *Vita futurista*.[4] This was also a time at which Marinetti established contacts with Cines of Rome, one of Italy's largest production houses, aiming to launch a production line of Futurist films – a partnership that was never realized possibly because of the infamous reception of the previous film. According to Lista, *Velocità* 'applies in a canonical way the dynamic and analogical principles of cinematic Futurism.' Thus, it shares the structural and thematic concerns of *Vita futurista*. It follows a fragmentary structure in that it consists of eleven autonomous sequences. It was inspired by the early cinema of fairground attractions, which 'in its own turn resembled the fragmentary structure and the quantitative and serial editing of Variety theatre.' Furthermore, the script is a visual embodiment of Futurist ideology, illustrating in didactic fashion the movement's philosophy. In Lista's words, it 'presents "speed" as the only ontological value, as the mode of being that is typical of modern times.'[5]

It is my view that Lista overstates the script's formal resemblance to *Vita futurista*, as well as its compliance with the abstract aesthetics of the 1916 film manifesto. Undeniably, the eleven sequences are autonomous in that they constitute brief, self-enclosed narratives, some of which bear stylistic affinities to *Vita futurista*. However, I disagree with Lista's claim that the script is 'constructed through a juxtaposition of sketches following each other *without any narrative development or organic link between them*' (emphasis added).[6] The serial progression of the sequences, if read in the numerical order provided in the published text, conveys a sense of completion, which largely derives from the consistent presence of an overarching theme that informs each individual part. That theme is society's Futurist reconstruction according to the philosophical principle of 'speed.' The sense of completion is also a result of a perhaps subtle, yet unfailingly detectable, degree of narrative continuity. The script in its entirety surpasses any individual segment, or set of segments, in thematic development and narrative closure. It is certainly not written in the style of what we typically consider a screenplay. Lacking in any explicit specification of film technique – such as montage, camera movement, camera angle, or intertitles – it consists of extremely concise instances of narration and condensed descriptions of images, the technical dimension of which is generally left to the reader's imagination. It is very 'synthetic,' to use a Marinettian term. Yet in spite of its synthetic quality, in most cases the narration follows a linear and verisimilar pattern, which from a practical point of view would necessitate filming techniques typical of narrative (and not avant-garde) cinema. The subject matter involves the adventures of four Futurist brothers, who are named according to their specific areas of expertise: an Engineer and Minister; an Infantry Lieutenant; a Navy Captain; and a Painter and Volunteer Soldier. The story follows the struggle of the four brothers in their efforts to achieve a global revolution for society's Futurist resurgence. An unmistakable gradual progression marks the representation of the various levels of conflict that the men must face, moving steadily from small-scale to large-scale conflict. Specifically, conflict is enacted successively in the spheres of family, work, city, and nation. A climactic finale portrays the realization of a Futurist universe animated by technology and defined by an exuberant feeling of 'speed' as its dominant ontological value.

Towards a Psychological Narrative

Of the script's eleven sequences, 'Quadro 1°: Passatismo e futurismo' (Scene 1: Passéism and Futurism) is the one that most closely resembles the style of *Vita futurista* and faithfully deploys the abstract techniques proposed in the 1916 film manifesto. The scene opens in the house of the four brothers' Grandpa and Grandma, a house 'impregnato di vecchiezza, d'austerità, di moralismo e di noia' [pregnant with age, austerity, moralism, and boredom], crowded with old and decrepit furniture (*Vel* 15; *Sp* 143). The dark and frozen austerity is upset by the sudden arrival of the four brothers, who bring intense sunlight and energy into the room.[7] This abrupt change irritates the grandparents, whose disapproval frightens the young men. The brothers withdraw in a corner and occupy themselves with various creative activities until their attention is drawn to the arrival of the Cousin, a woman of twenty who provokes them by whipping their faces with a bouquet of flowers. The sexual tension between her and the men resolves into a parade of highly abstract images. Her flowers grow gigantic and form a tropical forest. Date palms and bananas swell rapidly to monstrous dimensions, in the shade of which the men sit down to rest. One of the brothers rushes to follow a setting sun in the background, another discovers the opening of a cave and descents towards the 'center of the earth,' while another jumps onto the back of an ostrich the feathers of which grow enormous in his hands. The surrounding huts become elegant ladies' hats, while the fruit becomes delicate women's faces.[8]

The formal resemblance that scene 1 bears to the abstract qualities of *Vita futurista* is neither randomly placed in the script nor devoid of a specific narrative function. To be sure, the scene is unique in its usage of abstract cinematography. Although fantastic imagery is also found in some of the other segments, abstraction including such a high level of visual transformation is not repeated anywhere in the script. Nevertheless, even though scene 1 is neither echoed by a later segment in terms of visual style nor followed by an explicit narrative succession of events, it carries a specific theme that performs an important narrative function: it sets the psychological premise that determines the four brothers' subsequent actions and achievements all the way to the script's finale. At the scolding of the old grandparents, the brothers passively and fearfully withdraw. The grandparents, who are sunk in their armchairs, inactive, and lacking in physical energy, along with the darkness and austerity of their house, represent a passéist sensibility and impose the first obstacle that the young men must surpass. Thus, the first stage of conflict takes place in the sphere of the family, to be concluded with the success of the brothers in liberating themselves from its pressures. The scene bears psychological narrative significance, as it implies that only after overcoming a constricting family tradition, thus achieving emotional independence, may one realize a revolution, be it artistic, social, or political.[9]

The role of the Cousin in the men's initial step towards maturity is both ambiguous and of central importance. On the one hand, she is seductive, thus posing an obstacle that the men must surpass in order to successfully carry out their social enterprise. Surely,

> è afferrata da uno di loro, e, vinta, si offre in premio, gettando intorno i fiori fra l'agitazione sfrenata dei giovani che improvvisano una danza in tondo. Intanto i fiori ingigantiranno favolosamente prendendo proporzioni d'alberi e formando una vera foresta, all'ombra della quale si siederanno per riposarsi i quattro giovani. (*Vel* 16)

> [she is caught by one of them, and, defeated, offers herself as a reward, strewing flowers about amid the unrestrained agitation of the youths who improvise a round dance. Meanwhile, the flowers will miraculously grow gigantic assuming the proportions of trees and forming a veritable forest, in whose shade the four young men will sit down to rest.] (*Sp* 143)

By playing the role of the seductress, however, the Cousin also instigates the men's inner self-exploration. The abstract imagery that follows is a direct result of her actions, since it is the flowers that she throws about that turn into a gigantic forest. The oneiric images of nature that she introduces represent the men's attainment of a state of absolute purity and vitality, their discovery of a utopian register. This utopia is an indispensable source of inspiration for what follows, that is, the Futurist reconstitution of the world as a place replete with vitality. Furthermore, the discovery of this utopia may be seen as a *re*-discovery. In a psychoanalytic sense, the encounter with female sexuality, with which the utopia is here associated, suggests a return to a primordial union, a rediscovery of maternal plenitude.

One wonders whether Marinetti indeed suggests that there is a link between the Futurist revolution and the search for a lost utopian past. According to Lista, for a proper analysis of *Velocità*, one must also take into consideration the script's biographical dimension: 'The themes of sun and light as fertilizing forces and generators of future can be better understood when referred to Marinetti's Egyptian childhood.'[10] In *Il fascino dell'Egitto* (The Charm of Egypt, 1933), Marinetti recounts his impressions of his primeval land upon a later visit as an adult. The book's diary-like entries are infused with vivid childhood memories. Such memories are stirred by the traveller's encounter with specific images, such as the palms, the bananas, the huts, and the prevalence of the colours yellow and gold that suggest an intense sunlight, which correspond almost systematically to the images in the opening sequence of *Velocità* (*TIF* 1051–67). To Lista's general observation we may add a specific point: Marinetti selects those childhood images not at random, not merely because they happen to be readily retrievable from his mental database of images, but in a conscious attempt to seek therein the origins of a Futurist sensibility, one that continues to display the childlike traits of spontaneity, vitality, and action. This is evident in those moments in the Egyptian memoirs in which he seems to project the topoi of his Futurist ideology onto images the trademark of which is a childhood immersed in nature.

One such topos is the 'uomo moltiplicato,' or multiplied man. Crucial in this respect is the motif of the cave. When one of the brothers in *Velocità* enters a cave, 'si vede la discesa di lui, fra la meraviglia di stalagmiti fosforescenti, verso il centro della terra' [we watch his descent, amid the marvel of phosphorescent stalagmites, toward the center of the earth] (*Vel* 17; *Sp* 144). His immersion into such an essential yet obscure and bewildering space may be read as an inquiry into the unconscious, or as the discovery of a primordial truth. In the memoirs, it is in such a space that Marinetti seeks the spiritual force that mobilizes technological modernity. The traveller enters a cavern, where he witnesses a dervish ritual. In their ecstatic trance, the bodies indulge in swift rotational motions. In this 1933 work, however, the author projects onto this mystical ritual his by now amply articulated exaltation of modern technology:

Un rumore di officina mi richiama nella caverna sacra. Come trottole i Dervisci girano, le braccia aperte. La casacca e la gonna bianche si svasano nel movimento rotatorio. Una mistica ingenuità implorante immalinconisce il viso emaciato che guarda la volta.

Lassù vibra e ronza il santo motore. Funzionano ora 15 torni della grande acciaieria stellare. Limare la terra. Levigarne la superficie scabra . . .

La cenciosa orchestra ammucchiata stride:

'Imitiamo i ritmi dell'universo!

'*Meccanizziamo l'uomo-ingranaggio* del sistema planetario!' (*TIF* 1072; emphasis added)

[*The noise of a workshop* calls me back into the sacred cavern. The Dervish turn like spinning tops, their arms open. The white coat and skirt flare in the rotary movement. An imploring mystical naivety renders melancholy the emaciated face that looks at the vault.

Up there, the holy motor vibrates and hums. Now 15 lathes of the great stellar steel mill are at work. To polish the earth. To smooth its rough surface . . .

The ragged thronged orchestra squeaks:

'Let's imitate the rhythms of the universe!

'*Let's mechanize the man-gear* of the planetary system!']

The sounds of the dervish, originating in profound mysticism, are like 'the noise of a workshop,' while the 'man-gear' alludes to the 'multiplied man' as defined by Marinetti in 'L'uomo moltiplicato e il Regno della macchina' (Multiplied Man and the Kingdom of the Machine).[11] This ideal Futurist represents 'l'imminente e inevitabile identificazione dell'uomo col motore' [the imminent and inevitable identification of man with motor]. He is a 'tipo non umano e meccanico, costruito per una velocità onnipresente' [non-human and mechanical type, built for an omnipresent speed] (*TIF* 299). He is gifted with 'la grande divinazione meccanica o il fiuto metallico' [the great mechanical divination or the metallic instinct] (300). His identification with the machine rids him of a force detrimental to his vitality. He is immune to what Marinetti sees as the sickness of love for woman. This immunity is already evident in the attitude of some: 'Non avete mai osservato un macchinista quando lava amorevolmente il gran corpo possente della sua locomotiva? Sono le tenerezze minuziose e sapienti di un amante che accarezzi la sua donna adorata' [Haven't you ever observed a machinist when he lovingly washes the great powerful body of his engine? They are the meticulous and skilful acts of tenderness of a lover who caresses his adored woman] (298). Furthermore: 'S'incontrano oggi degli uomini i quali attraversano la vita quasi senza amore, in una bella atmosfera color d'acciaio' [Today we come across men who go through life almost without love, in a beautiful steel-coloured atmosphere] (300). The infiltration of the dervish ritual with metaphors evoking the 'multiplied man' displays Marinetti's wish to seek in the Egyptian experience the origin of his Futurist sensibility, to thus posit this sensibility as a product not strictly of his adult discovery of the Western industrial world, but also of that world's nourishment by a vital past defined as a mystical immersion in nature.

Another topos of Futurist discourse that Marinetti projects onto a childhood memory is the necessity for poetry to reject traditional linguistic forms, which he developed in his 1912 manifesto on Futurist literature. During his adult journey to Alexandria, Marinetti pays a visit to Costantino Cavafy, the 'celebre poeta greco che preferisce la sua Alessandria natale alla sua Atene lontana e distratta' [famous Greek poet who prefers his native Alexandria to his distant and detached Athens] (*TIF* 1078). He admires Cavafy not only as a poet but also for his dedication to his native Egyptian city that played a fundamental role in his poetry.[12] On his way to this visit, he walks by the Old Harbour, which stirs the memory of his mother. One's thoughts on poetry, the attachment to one's native land, and the memory of one's mother here become interwoven:

> valutavo le ragioni di nostalgia storica che possono legare l'animo di un poeta all'azzurro semicerchio del Porto Antico ora deserto ma certo ingombro di sontuose galere invisibili.
>
> Era questa la passeggiata serale preferita da mia madre che, sedicenne, accompagnavo cercando di armonizzare i miei passi sognanti coi suoi decisi e frettolosi. (*TIF* 1078)

> [I was assessing the reasons of historical nostalgia that are able to bind the soul of a poet to the blue semicircle of the Old Harbour, now deserted but surely cluttered up with invisible sumptuous prisons.
>
> This was the evening walk preferred by my mother, whom I used to accompany at the age of sixteen, trying to harmonize my dreamy footsteps with hers, which were firm and hurried.]

The nostalgia for a childhood attachment to one's mother and its ability to inspire poetry is not a concept pioneered by Marinetti. He reminds us, however, that he is not speaking of just any kind of poetry. His remarks on Cavafy that directly follow the stroll by the Old Harbour again project Futurist ideology onto this memory. Specifically, he admires Cavafy's philosophy of the Greek language, his preference for the *demotike*, the spoken language of the people. He perceives in Cavafy's thought a strong affinity with his own Futurist project, since the *demotike*, he states, 'ha una vitalità potente fuori e contro la grammatica classica che, rigidamente passatista, è ormai destinata a morire nelle biblioteche' [has a powerful vitality outside and against classical grammar that, strictly passéist, is by now destined to die in the libraries] (*TIF* 1081).[13]

It is important to note that insofar as scene 1 dramatizes the four brothers' need to overcome family pressures, Marinetti designates the grandparents, rather than the parents, as representatives of passéism, while the existence of the parents is mentioned nowhere in the script. This choice has a twofold effect. First, it represents more vividly the chasm between the two modes of thought, contrasting the new not merely with the old but with the much older. Second, it avoids constructing a scenario that would be readily interpreted in terms of psychological realism. Rather than assuming the roles involved in typical family dynamics, the characters serve as symbols, as the representatives of an era or a mode of thought. Yet this choice does not do away with psychology. As I have indicated, the mother enters the story symbolically in the figure of the Cousin. The tropical forest, with its sunshine, date palms, caves, magical animals, huts, and fruit, retrieves the childhood that in his later writings Marinetti designates as the bearer of the seeds of Futurism. From a narrative point of view, it represents a primordial state the rediscovery of which will fertilize the brothers' Futurist revolution. Furthermore, we have seen that the memory of the mother is not absent from the early formative experience. In 'Alessandria d'Egitto' Marinetti also recognizes the decisive influence of his mother's native city: 'Mia madre, che fu tutta una poesia delicatissima e musicale di tenerezze e lacrime affettuose, era milanese. Pur essendo nato ad Alessandria d'Egitto, io mi sento legato alla foresta di camini di Milano e al suo vecchio Duomo' [My mother, who was all a delicate and musical poetry of tenderness and affectionate tears, was Milanese. Though I was born in Alexandria of Egypt, I feel bound to Milan's forest of chimneys and to its old Duomo] (*TIF* 578). The Cousin's seductiveness, conveyed in her spreading flowers, themselves allusions to female sexuality, opens the gate to the vision of a primordial maternal kingdom. The man's descent into the cave, 'amid the marvel of phosphorescent stalagmites toward the center of the earth' (*Sp* 144), itself stages an inquiry into the unconscious, a pre-Oedipal reunion, something like the revisiting of the womb.[14]

The episode proceeds with what we may characterize as a metacinematic moment:

I fiori della foresta si metallizzano per formare il parapetto di *un palco* al quale è affacciata la ragazza (N. 5) che ha dietro di sé i quattro giovani in frak. Illuminazione di *gran teatro*, di cui si vedono 2 o 3 palchi e tutto il palcoscenico, contenente la scena precedente, cioè la foresta tropicale, coi 4 giovani e la ragazza (N. 5) seduti sotto gli alberi, ma *vista in lontananza e annebbiata di leggenda*. (*Vel* 17; emphasis added)

[The flowers of the forest metalize to form the parapet of *a theatre box* where the girl (N.5) leans out, behind her the four young men in tails. Illumination of *a grand theatre*, of which we see 2 or 3 boxes and the entire stage, containing the preceding scene, i.e., the tropical forest, with the 4 youths and the girl (N.5) seated under the trees, but *seen in the distance and shrouded in legend*.] (*Sp* 144; emphasis added)

The vision is 'seen in the distance and shrouded in legend' because it partakes of the archaic, unchangeable, and deterministic dimensions of the unconscious. Its attainment, as the primal inspiration for the revolution, takes the form of a show in a theatre, still witnessed under the leadership of the woman whose sexuality evokes the archaic mother. On a technical level, there is no doubt that the 'stage' performance within the diegesis is itself a film. Through techniques such as superimposition, dissolves, and time-lapse sequences, cinema would be the only medium capable of generating the scenes of transformation as described here. Being metacinematic means that the scene concerns more than the experience of the spectators *in* the film. To attain an unconscious utopia as a source of inspiration is also the task of the spectator *of* the film. It regards the didactic dimension of the script, the purpose of which is to engage its spectator in its ideology, urging him/her to participate in society's Futurist renewal. Thus, the spectator *of* the film, having watched the utopian forest for some time, is invited to witness 'her/himself' watching, insofar as s/he is to identify with the figures of the four brothers. In identifying with this alter ego of sorts, s/he is invited to follow a line of action similar to theirs.

Although *Velocità* follows a more literary style than typically characterizes the technical writing of a professional screenplay, certain details do imply the use of specific film techniques. For example, the depiction of flowers growing to monstrous proportions suggests an influence of scientific cinema, which depicted things such as flowers blooming in condensed time through the use of time-lapse sequences.[15] Furthermore, in the scene discussed above, the spectator of the film will evidently look at the on-stage vision by sharing the subjective view of the characters, who as spectators in the portrayed theatre act as agents of the look. While the description does not mention montage, camera distance, or camera angle, it suggests the deployment of the two-part point-of-view structure, which was to become essential in later narrative cinema.[16] First, we are told that the woman and the four men are sitting in a theatre box looking at a stage. Then, following what is understood as a cut, we are given the description of the theatrical stage containing the tropical forest that is 'seen in the distance.' It is certainly 'seen' by us, the spectators of the film, as well as the film's protagonists, spectators at the theatre that the film depicts, whose subjective view we therefore share. It is important to note that at the time of *Velocità* – provided that the script was indeed written in the 1910s – the point-of-view shot in narrative cinema had not yet acquired the consistent applicability and indispensable narrative function that it was to acquire in the classical Hollywood feature. It had nevertheless appeared in varied forms in both Italian and other national film narratives.

In discussing D.W. Griffith's contribution to 'the narrator system,' Gunning makes a distinction between 'earlier' and 'later' point-of-view shots. The former were common in the cinema of attractions, where the point-of-view, rather than being strictly narrativized, aimed at providing spectacle and scopic pleasure in its own right, revealing the characters' private views through things such as telescopes and keyholes. The later point-of-view shots, by contrast, have a specific psychological-narrative function because they present the subjective gaze of an individual character as decisive in the film's plot progression. In *The Redman and the Child* (1908), the shot of the Indian looking through a telescope is followed by a shot of the villains abusing the child, who are framed in a black circular matte to simulate the Indian's view through the telescope. This resembles earlier uses of point-of-view, such as the instances of 'trick work' in the cinema of attractions aiming at scopic pleasure. Gunning explains, however, that *The Redman* also pioneered in the narrative integration of point-of-view, because the Indian's view through the telescope is a source of awareness that determines narrative progression, namely, the need to pursue the villains and save the child. In *A Drunkard's Reformation* (1909), the point-of-view shot is essential to narrative progression, but still differs from its classical counterpart. The protagonist is not alone, but shares with numerous other characters, as spectators in a theatre, the view of the didactic stage play that urges him to abandon his drinking habit. In addition, the character's view of the stage does not convey an exact matching of position and angle.[17]

The use of the point-of-view shot in early 1910s Italian cinema was scarce. Its scarcity is evident in Pastrone's otherwise technically innovative and highly complex 1914 epic, *Cabiria*. Set in the third century BC, the film tells the adventures of little Cabiria, daughter of a Roman patrician living in Sicily, whose palace is destroyed by an eruption of Mount Etna. After the governess rescues the child from the volcanic eruption, they fall prey to Phoenician pirates and are taken to Carthage as slaves. The story unfolds during the Second Punic War. Rome's final victory over Carthage coincides with Cabiria's rescue, now a young adult, thanks to the heroic acts of Roman patrician Fulvio Axilla and his slave Maciste (see also chapter 2).[18] This originally three-hour film includes no more than one point-of-view shot in a style that approaches the concept of its classical counterpart. The eruption of Etna is depicted in an extreme-long-shot, juxtaposed with the reaction medium-shots of a group of alarmed characters looking through the window of the palace (figures 3.1 and 3.2). This structure partakes of the varied functions of point-of-view as discussed above, and thus differs from as well as resembles its classical counterpart. First, it is not a subjective shot aiding the viewer's identification with the protagonist. We share the view of the volcano not with a single character but with a group, most of them extras whose appearance in this scene may be their single appearance in the film. Second, the spatial relation between the two shots is not patterned upon a coherent eye-line match. Third, in an attractionist fashion, the view of the volcanic eruption provides a unique form of spectacle. The shot is nevertheless narrativized in that it marks the urgency to escape from the palace, thus determining Cabiria's fate and adventure, which informs the film's narrative development all the way to its finale.

As in *Cabiria*, the scene in *Velocità* suggests a point-of-view shot from the perspective of a group – the four Futurists and the Cousin – rather than one protagonist. It is also an occasion of great spectacle since it depicts the fantastic and legendary imagery of the tropical forest. It is also crucial, however, to the development of the film as narrative, since the characters' vision of the forest suggests the possibility for a psychological introspection that motivates the film's action. Indeed, the episode's further development involves the liberation of the four

Figure 3.1 The people of the palace look at the eruption of Etna in *Cabiria*. (Image provided by Kino Lorber Incorporated)

Figure 3.2 The eruption of Etna as seen by the people of the palace in *Cabiria*. (Image provided by Kino Lorber Incorporated)

Futurists from the prohibitions imposed by passéism as that is represented by family tradition: 'I due vecchi ricadono nelle loro poltrone che s'ingrandiscono come due tombe e vi si sprofondano lentamente, mentre intorno a loro i mobili si deformano, si decompongono e si disgregano per vecchiezza, cadendo a pezzi nella crescente oscurità' [The two old people fall back into their armchairs that grow large like two tombs and they sink into them slowly, while around them the furniture becomes deformed, decomposes, and comes apart due to age, falling to pieces in the growing darkness]. The grandparents' decrepit bodies themselves gradually decompose. This experience of initiation permits the now liberated Futurists to repay the Cousin, whose sexuality, in spite of – or because of – her seductiveness, led the way to the men's recovery of a primal vitality. A passéist family arranges the marriage of their 'effeminate' son to the Cousin. Trapped in the sinister villa of her future married life, the woman sees the huge laughing mouths of the four Futurists enter her bedroom through the four cracks on the wall. They help her escape by lowering her down from the window (*Vel* 17–18; *Sp* 144).

Following the dramatization of conflict in the realm of the family, the rest of the script is built upon a series of conflicts between the heroes and traditionalism, enacted successively in the spheres of work, city, and nation. Scenes 2–5 concentrate on representing conflict in various aspects of the sphere of work. 'Quadro 2°: Uno studio di giovani novatori' (Scene 2: A Studio of Young Innovators) is set in the art studio of the four Futurists. In what the artists experience as a nightmare, a group of rich men invade the studio and express their disdain for the Futurist canvases (*Vel* 18–19; *Sp* 144–5). As in scene 1, the abstract imagery that characterizes this episode is not there for its own sake or devoid of narrative linearity. Rather, in representing the passéist 'nightmare' that haunts the progressive artists, it affirms the urgency of society's Futurist renewal that is to follow. This sense of urgency is contrasted with the cultural stagnancy represented in 'Quadro 3°: I ricconi dai rigattieri' (Scene 3: The Rich Men at the Second-hand Store). A metaphor of the passéist artist who lacks in creativity and copies the exhausted forms of the past, the second-hand dealer receives a visit from a group of millionaires arriving in fancy automobiles. They eagerly purchase the inauthentic piece of antique furniture that the sly dealer presents to them, which they then handle with meticulous care. Evidently, these are the same rich men of scene 2, whose reappearance in scene 3 enhances the script's narrative continuity (*Vel* 19; *Sp* 145). 'Quadro 4°: Avanti i giovani!' (Scene 4: Young People, Step Forward!) depicts the interior of a sluggish workshop, which is paralysed thanks to a director who is described as gout-ridden and 'rammollito,' that is, a softy or a weakling. His sudden death results in his replacement by one of the four brothers, the Futurist engineer, who rapidly restores order and increases the shop's productivity (*Vel* 19–20; *Sp* 145). 'Quadro 5°: I diritti del genio' (Scene 5: The Rights of Genius) is set in a school of fine arts, where some professors, described as pedantic, achieve little more than caricatural gestures before illustrious marble statues, until the four Futurists rouse their companions towards a rebellion that results in turmoil and in statues being knocked over (*Vel* 20; *Sp* 145). Undeniably, the fact that the four Futurists appear in a fine arts school sustains narrative continuity, as it alludes to scene 2, where the brothers, in addition to being experts in different professional fields, are identified as artists.

Scene 5 thus concludes that part of the film that represents conflict in the sphere of work, specifically in the spheres of artistic and industrial production. This episode, however, is also unique. Compared to the previous episodes, it involves action at a larger scale. In representing the uprising of an entire school, it implies a form of revolutionary comradeship. Hence, it serves as a point of transition between lower-scale conflict and what is to follow, that is, the Futurist reorganization of entire cities. 'Quadro 6°: Una città galvanizzata' (Scene 6: A Galvanized City) is set in an unidentified city that is stained by an abundance of passéist symbols: cathedrals, flea-bitten beggars, cholera, and caricatures of tourists like those who typically frequent Pisa and Siena, as the writer specifies. The arrival of the four Futurists leading a crowd of young devotees immerses the old city in lively public activities and implements an overall spirit of cleansing and rejuvenation. The episode concludes with what Marinetti describes as the heroic vision of a *serata futurista*. As often happened with the *serate* in real life, the evening results in a battle inside the auditorium, which involves a shower of oranges, potatoes, and *maccheroni*, and ends with a 'Corteo eroico dei futuristi seguiti dagli studenti' [Heroic procession of the futurists followed by the students] (*Vel* 20–1; *Sp* 145). In 'Quadro 7°: Venezia futurista' (Scene 7: Futurist Venice), the four protagonists subject the city of Venice to a radical reconstruction, including the destruction of the old palaces, the paving of the canals, and the introduction of electricity, train tracks, and trams (*Vel* 21; *Sp* 146). It is not surprising that Marinetti devoted an entire segment to Venice. Attacking Venice as the passéist city par excellence was a topos in Futurist discourse. It had to do with the peculiarity of the city's physical configuration, free of automobile traffic and proud of its preserved centuries-old character.[19]

Velocità and the War Epic

'Quadro 8°: Voluttà e patria' (Scene 8: Pleasure and Fatherland) introduces the portrayal of Futurist struggle on a national scale, for the purposes of which war imagery serves as a most suitable signifier. Albeit its possible allusions are to Italy's participation in the First World War, 'war' in this segment is best understood as a metaphor for a Futurist artistic revolt against traditionalism. Only two of the four brothers appear in this segment: the Infantry Lieutenant and the Painter and Volunteer Soldier. The segment opens with a farewell scene between the lieutenant and his beloved. Still captivated by the woman's tenderness, the lieutenant finds it difficult to depart. The temptation that binds him is expressed in the image of the moonlight, a recurrent metaphor in Marinetti, which in contrast to the awakening and invigorating properties of the sun is associated with romance, languor, and paralysis, thus threatening to harness the Futurist's revolutionary spirit.[20] Scene 1, however, has shown that the protagonists have grown mature. In spite of love's temptations, the lieutenant resists the woman's entreaties. Hence, he is well on his way to attain the status of the 'multiplied man,' whose affinity to machines, according to Marinetti, makes him immune to the sickness of love.[21] Once in the trenches, he is found in the company of his brother, the Painter and Volunteer Soldier. Amidst fire and piles of corpses, the lieutenant engages in the recitation of verses, while the painter waves in the air a drawing that is immediately riddled with bullets. With art as a military weapon, the war as a metaphor for an artistic revolution concludes with the two Futurists' heroic victory (*Vel* 21–2; *Sp* 146).

To develop the theme of love and the necessity for the lieutenant to overcome it, the script relies on particular uses of montage that both support and defy Marinetti's condemnation of traditional narrative techniques. In describing the love affair, scene 8 relies on a montage sequence, a segment that condenses a period of time into a series of symbolic, brief, and diegetically interrelated images:

Evocazione cinematografica di 3 anni d'amore in paesaggi diversi, su piroscafi, in terre lontane. (*Vel* 21)

[Cinematic evocation of 3 years of love in different landscapes, on steamships, in far-off lands.] (*Sp* 146; …)

In spite of its abstract chronology, the montage sequence typically fulfils a well-defined narrative function. Here, it highlights the long duration and thus the solidity of the love affair, only to portray the lieutenant's liberation from it, and therefore his devotion to his Futurist vocation, as both more challenging and more pressing. Directly following, the woman's allure is depicted in a scene that aims to apply the ideas of the 1916 film manifesto to the letter:

Cinematografia analogica. Dare ogni immagine: '*Tu sei bella come una gazzella.*' Dare una gazzella. '*Il tuo sorriso è fresco e luminoso, lo contemplo come un viaggiatore, dopo lunghe fatiche, contempla il mare dall'alto della collina . . .*' Dare il mare. (*Vel* 22; ellipsis in original)[22]

[Analogical cinematography. Give each image: '*You're as lovely as a gazzelle.*' Give a gazzelle [sic]. '*Your smile is fresh and luminous, I gaze upon it like a traveler, after long labours, gazes upon the sea from the top of a hill . . .*' Give the sea.] (*Sp* 146; ellipsis in original)

As it declares Marinetti's intention to put his avant-garde notion of filmmaking into practice, the passage makes a mockery of conventional representations of romantic love, by transforming metaphors into images and thus rendering them literal. Furthermore, the fact that the lover's remarks appear in italics and quotation marks suggests that they are intended as lines spoken by the male character, most likely to appear as intertitles. The juxtaposition of the verbal utterance with its literal transposition into an image would surely tend to make a mockery of the former.

Such an effect, however, would only occur at the expense of 'analogical cinematography' itself, which the above description claims to achieve. To be precise, it would occur at the expense not of analogical cinematography in general but of the highly desired analogy *in absentia*, to borrow again Strauven's precise terminology (see chapter 1). Let us recall that this is the kind of analogy that suppresses the first term, leading to the invention of the 'imagination without strings,' hence to an expansion of the capabilities of the mind. The more readily communicative – hence, more conventional – form of analogy, by contrast, is the analogy *in praesentia*, that is, the kind that exposes both terms of the analogy side by side. As I explained in chapter 1, the definition of analogy in the 1916 manifesto on film is not as sharp as the 1912 definition of the literary analogy, as it oscillates between analogies *in preasentia* and analogies *in absentia* without acknowledging the distinction between the two kinds. I also noted that communicability vis-à-vis the audience is a greater concern in the film manifesto than in its literary counterpart. This explains to some extent why the definition of analogy in the film manifesto, even when it claims to suppress the first term, tends to presuppose a relatively well-defined narrative that would ascribe a comprehensible meaning to the images. *Velocità* in fact presents a case in which the necessity to communicate leads to a further downgrading of analogy. Not only does the technique described above restrict itself to the analogy *in praesentia*, the speech or intertitles spell out the thematic relationship between the two terms (as in the woman-gazelle example), a relationship that holds only in the diegetic context of a relatively realist narrative. Such process of spelling out abolishes the revolutionary, unsettling relationship of the 'deep love that connects distant, seemingly different and hostile things,' free of a traditional syntax that would smooth the transition and aid comprehension – which is how Marinetti first defines analogy in the 1912 literature manifesto (*TIF* 47–8). The spelling out negates distance, difference, and hostility, while remoulding the two terms into an ideal harmony with each other.[23]

If Scene 8 presents a metaphorical battle between two armies of unspecified nationality, 'Quadro 9°: Senilismo e gioventù futurista' (Scene 9: Senility and Futurist Youth) extends the theme of war into a scenario the historical specificity of which is more explicit. It takes place during a ball, aboard a battleship in an African port, carrying among its officers the young Futurist Navy Captain. Female sexuality is again a threat: an admiral described as old and 'rammollito' (soft, effeminate) is seduced by an extraordinarily beautiful spy who arrives on board with a group of guests comprising 'capi arabi e negri,' that is, Arab and Negro chiefs. It is only upon the swift intervention of the Futurist captain that the woman's operations of espionage are exposed. Her subsequent attempts at seducing the Futurist captain himself quickly fail, while he, in sharp contrast to the emasculated admiral, throws the woman into the sea. The dramatic character of the scene is intensified by several plot elements that lend a war-epic quality to the representation: a huge fire breaks out on the pier; Arab rebels climb up the rope-ladders to take possession of the ship; the Navy Captain leads the sailors and fights off the Arabs, who then fall into the sea; the heroes begin bombarding the African coast (*Vel* 23; *Sp* 146).

In contrast to the abstract imagery of scene 8, where Futurist art becomes a military weapon, the events of scene 9 are marked by both narrative linearity and strict verisimilitude. The segment displays an editing style that places shots in logical cause-effect relationships:

La donna fruga nei cassetti [dell'ammiraglio], ma s'arresta, atterrita, vedendo apparire al boccaporto la faccia del futurista capitano di marina. (Mostrare prima come questi discende per una scala di corda lungo il fianco della nave, per giungere al boccaporto e sorvegliare gli atti dell'avventuriera spia). (*Vel* 23)

[The woman rummages through (the admiral's) dresser drawers, but she stops, terrified, seeing the futurist navy captain's face appear at the porthole. (First, show how the captain descends down a rope-ladder along the side of the ship to arrive at the porthole and watch the actions of the adventuress-spy)]. (*Sp* 146)

In this scene, Marinetti not only breaks with his overall ideological rejection of verisimilitude, but also seems to cling to verisimilitude quite desperately. After he already stated that the woman sees the captain, he realizes that the viewer must also be informed as to how the captain arrived there, thus revealing a need to render the progression of events as clear and logical as possible. He thus adds a parenthetical statement that works retrospectively, explaining what the viewer will have seen 'First,' what diegetically should precede the woman's state of being 'terrified.' This necessity to be understood not only leads to a momentary adoption of verisimilitude, but also to a cause-effect style of editing that resembles what was later to be known as classical continuity. The woman's 'seeing the futurist navy captain's face' after the man watches 'the actions of the adventuress-spy' indicates an exchange of point-of-view shots the narrative function of which is clearly linked to an immediate and lucid line of action: terrified, she tries to seduce the captain as well. Hence, as compared to the inspirational function of the on-stage tropical forest in scene 1, this scene is closer to classical continuity, or what Gunning describes as the 'later' point-of-view shot (see above).

While this logical cause-effect mode of narration indicates a leap away from the 1916 film manifesto, the scene's particular subject matter recalls the popular genre of the *storico*, and specifically Pastrone's *Cabiria*. This seemingly literal war scenario, however, does not preclude the function of 'war' also as a metaphor referring to artistic revolution. That Marinetti is at least as concerned with questions of art and film history as with contemporary politics is indicated by the fact that neither in scene 8 nor in scene 9 does 'war' directly refer to Italy's contemporary anti-Austrian struggle. Set in an African port, scene 9 looks several years back, as it brings to mind the Italian 1911–12 victorious campaign in Libya. This event had also been the concern of *Cabiria*. As argued by Giovanna Finocchiaro Chimirri, although *Cabiria* is set during the Second Punic War, it is the recent war in Tripolitania that constitutes the implicit referent of the film's nationalism. This war restored a new viability to the victories of Scipione l'Africano, the Roman consul under whose leadership, as *Cabiria* shows, the Romans conquered Cirta, a victory that leads to the film's glorious denouement and the rescue of the female protagonist. Turning to the history of Ancient Rome offered an opportunity to justify colonial occupation, while the Punic Wars offered a chapter of history that had not yet been exploited by the new media.[24] If by spectacularly enacting ancient warfare *Cabiria* was able to kill two birds with one stone, that is, to celebrate both Italian nationalism and cinema's technical capabilities, *Velocità*'s allusion to *Cabiria* has a twofold function as well: it maintains a clear national conscience since it does not fail to exalt Italian heroism; it asserts Futurism's aesthetic vitality over what it sees as a persistently passéist mass culture. The script fails, however, to harmonize its two functions without running into an ideological impasse. Its rebuttal of traditional forms turns it against a film like *Cabiria*, the nationalism of which it shares.

Marinetti's allusion to *Cabiria* is found not only in the representation of an anti-African war but also in the specific scenes of the fire that breaks out on the pier and of the Arabs who are falling into the sea, which recall some of *Cabiria*'s visually most thrilling moments. While laying siege to the city of Syracuse, an ally of Carthage, the Roman fleet is set aflame and is burned in its entirety.[25] A striking difference between scene 9 and the scene in *Cabiria* is that the former concludes with the Futurist hero's victory, while the latter depicts a defeat of the Romans. Yet the film's specific diegetic element that is responsible for the defeat is exactly where Marinetti's implicit discourse on art comes into play. The destruction of the Roman fleet is owed to a scientific experiment performed by Archimedes, a native of Syracuse. As the intertitles announce, Archimedes 'crea per la difesa delle mura le macchine irre- sistibili' [invents irresistible machines for the defence of the walls].[26] The invention consists of an array of mirrors able to gather the rays of the sun and direct their concentrated energy against an object that then goes on fire. Archimedes is first shown in his workshop handling five square mirror plates, arranged in the shape of a cross onto a stand, each attached to the stand by a hinge. Each plate gathers light from the sun, which it then projects onto a white board, such that the shape of the cross is reproduced on the board (figure 3.3). By slightly tilting each plate, Archimedes directs the light emanating from all five plates onto a single spot in the centre of the board, thus setting it on fire (fig- ure 3.4). Archimedes is then shown at the top of the city walls, where he has installed a hexagonal mirror of immense proportions, several times the height of the men standing by it, each of its six triangles con- sisting of seventeen smaller mirror plates (figure 3.5). Once it is tilted in the appropriate direction, this impressive and perfect geometrical structure gathers the rays of the sun and projects them onto the Roman fleet that is parked outside the walls. Placed in the background of the set and occupying the upper half of the frame, the mirror, seen from the perspective of one of the ships in the foreground, blinds the spectator with its radiance (figure 3.6). The ship in the foreground is immersed in flames, throwing into panic the few soldiers in view. As the intertitles state, 'A sera il naviglio formidabile di Roma non è se non un rogo che si spegne sulle acque placate' [By evening the formidable Roman fleet is nothing but a dying bonfire on the calm waters]. The sequence pro- ceeds with a spectacular shot of ships buried in flames and gradually sinking to their extinction (figure 3.7).

What is particularly distinctive about Archimedes's mirror is that its physical configuration highly deviates from the film's overall

Figure 3.3 Archimedes gathers the rays of the sun in five mirror plates in *Cabiria*. (Image provided by Kino Lorber Incorporated)

Figure 3.4 Archimedes manages to create fire through his mirrors in *Cabiria*. (Image provided by Kino Lorber Incorporated)

Figure 3.5 Archimedes instals a huge set of mirrors on the walls of Syracuse in *Cabiria*. (Image provided by Kino Lorber Incorporated)

Figure 3.6 Archimedes's mirrors set the Roman fleet aflame in *Cabiria*. (Image provided by Kino Lorber Incorporated)

Figure 3.7 The Roman fleet is completely destroyed in *Cabiria*. (Image provided by Kino Lorber Incorporated)

mise-en-scène. The depiction of the mirror on the city walls is preceded by intertitles stating that 'l'ordigno non mai veduto si mostra all'improvviso, divinamente, simile a un fascio di folgori silenziose' [a device never before seen is suddenly, divinely revealed, like a sheaf of silent lightning bolts]. If such an impressive yet simple geometrical structure, made of pure straight lines arranged in perfect symmetry, was 'never before seen' by any of the characters in the diegesis, it is certainly not seen at any other point in the film by the film's spectator, whose eyesight is completely adjusted to the excessively ornate, flowery, and baroque mise-en-scène that alone establishes the royal and military decor of Roman and North African antiquity. Because of its geometrical simplicity, hence its 'synthetic' beauty (to use Marinetti's term), and its miraculous, as it were, technological function, the burning mirror is what strikes us as the film's most modern – or, if I may, most Futuristic – prop. That is to say, it allows us to think of *Cabiria*'s Archimedes as a Futurist of sorts.

As incorporated in the film, however, the image of the burning mirror is ideologically ambiguous. Perhaps Archimedes's scientific craftiness, in achieving 'miracles' by manipulating natural light, represents the craftiness of Pastrone himself, whose own handling of light rays creates the wondrous images that we enjoy. Yet the image of the mirror is impregnated with a threatening and destructive quality, since, on the diegetic level, it correlates with the Roman defeat. If Marinetti indeed evokes this scene, he does so in order to respond with an alternative and critical scenario. While *Cabiria* exalts ancient Rome, *Velocità* transports us to modern times. More important, if Pastrone stigmatizes *Cabiria*'s most 'Futuristic' personage and prop by associating them with defeat, Marinetti's Futurist protagonist stands for the supreme cause of victory. Thus, *Velocità*'s artistic struggle against traditionalism (represented metaphorically in its African 'war') ends victoriously only because its creator, Marinetti (represented metaphorically in the Navy Captain), adopts a swift Futuristic vision. In this manner, *Velocità* constitutes an implicit critique of *Cabiria* – as a film suffering from a fear of the new, a defeatist art form, a stage play 'without words,' a work that reaffirms an older tradition and bypasses the option of taking a victorious look to the future specifically through the lens of the new. Therefore, as in the case of *Vita futurista*, Marinetti seems to be ambivalent with respect to the popular culture that he sets out to refute. On the one hand, he shares the historical epic's nationalism, its celebration of victorious warfare. On the other hand, by infusing his own portrayal of warfare with metaphorical elements about an aesthetic revolution against passéism, he turns his back on the very cinema the national politics of which he shares and the aesthetic structures of which he simulates. Once again, the clash between 'war' as an aesthetic debate and war as a literal state of affairs exposes a dilemma that is inherent in Futurism.

Cinema and the 'New Divine'

The two final segments of *Velocità* proceed with a succession of images that celebrate modern technology at a pace worthy of the script's title, what Lista aptly describes as an inherently filmic 'exultation of a *spectaculum* conceived of as pure visibility of the world's polyphony.'[27] Concentrating on projecting the ideal city of the future, 'Quadro 10°: La città futurista fra cento anni' (Scene 10: The Futurist City in One Hundred Years) opens with what Marinetti describes as a highly accelerated depiction of the various operations taking place in large workshops, as well as the demolition of houses and their replacement with what we may describe as the 'polyphonic' vision of a city: illuminated streets, elevators, automobiles, airplanes, dirigibles, and subterranean rail lines. The city's exuberant spirit results also from misfortunes, such as automobile collisions, train derailments, and the collapse of a bridge, the debris of which is instantaneously recovered under the leadership of the Futurist *engineer*, which demonstrates the Futurist ideal of the fervent destruction of the old and its replacement with the new (*Vel* 23–4; *Sp* 147). 'Quadro 11°: L'uomo futurista fra 100 anni' (Scene 11: Futurist Man in One Hundred Years) concentrates instead on the individual, a *minister* – clearly another status of the previous scene's engineer, hence, the brother initially identified as Engineer and Minister. His life is portrayed as imagined in an established Futurist universe. Its prominent characteristics are its ubiquity and centupled duration, thanks to new technologies such as the telegraph, the telephone, and the phonograph, as well as revolutionary bedroom devices, such as those providing a massage or the so-called concentrated sleep – an electrical apparatus that makes it possible that five minutes of sleep are sufficient for the body's recovery – modelled upon the famous *Maison électrique* displayed in Paris at that time (*Vel* 24–5; *Sp* 147).[28]

In the ways discussed above, *Velocità* notably distances itself from the aims of the 1916 film manifesto, which rejected narrative, photographic realism, and theatricality. Despite its subdivision into eleven seemingly autonomous segments, some of which deploy abstract imagery and 'analogical cinematography,' the script may be viewed as a rather coherent story starting with the elaborate exposition of a psychological premise and tracing, from beginning to end, and in an epic manner, the adventures of the same four protagonists. Apart from narrative continuity, however, the thing that from a more practical standpoint situates *Velocità* in the realm of industrial film production is that its realization would have required a high production budget. Aside from the script's fantastic depiction of exotic forests, we must consider its linear narration of those episodes that take place in well-defined yet complex verisimilar settings: the events in the protagonists' art studio; the students' revolt at a fine arts school; the depiction of battles in the trenches and aboard a ship; and of course the profuse image of the future city, including things such as train collisions and crowds engaged in its reconstruction. Such scenes would have required complex sets, some perhaps shot on location but many necessitating large-scale studio shooting, as well as large crowds of extras; hence, a production budget comparable to that of any feature-length epic or upper-class melodrama that informed the genre cinema of the era. This does not surprise us, given that Marinetti, in envisioning the script's sumptuous style, may have relied on a contract with Cines of Rome, one that was never realized.

This is not to say that the script espouses exclusively the forms of representation of narrative cinema. Rather, the style of the script is marked by an oscillation between the avant-garde and narrativity. Marinetti's wish to participate in the institution of cinema is not exactly a betrayal of Futurism's avant-garde aspirations. It points, rather, to a peculiar aim to advance from the particular to the universal, that is, to grasp something of the world at large in the manner in which the Futurists themselves envisioned it. Thus, the degree of narrative continuity that marks the script indicates perhaps Marinetti's ambition to bring before the eyes something of an ultimate narrative, to tell the story of the recreation of the world in its totality, as realized in a series of diverse achievements carried out by four legendary Futurists.[29] From the practical point of view, the costly technical means that could be furnished by large-scale film production would serve towards a *verisimilar* portrayal of the world, one that at the same time would render the representation *abstract*. Of course, the representation of the world as abstract would have been linked to a new perception of it that arose side by side with the birth of the new century's scientific 'miracles.' One might expect that, in Futurist terms, this idea would be conveyed artistically through analogical representation, what in cinema may be explained as the juxtaposition of diverse images through montage. However, *Velocità*'s verisimilar-yet-abstract rendering of the world is a product of something other than the analogy. It involves not the montage of hostile and distant images but the succession of brief narratives aiming to portray the world as an oceanic collection of stories. At the same time, these are stories of enough diversity that in the end the world acquires an abstract dimension.

Yet there is something even more remarkable as regards the institution of cinema and its relation to Futurism. Apart from the concrete technical means with which large-scale film production would have been able to achieve this verisimilar-yet-abstract representation, the narrativity that defined the style of genre cinema, despite the adverse reaction that it provoked in Marinetti, is exactly what conditioned the perception of the world as what I called an oceanic collection of stories, since each product of the cinematic institution more-or-less tells a story. Hence, if Futurism rejected the linear narrative form of any *individual* film, seeing it as an extension of the traditional stage play 'without words,' it nevertheless aimed to emulate, as the script of *Velocità* achieves to some degree, the universal *ensemble* of cinematic works, that totality that is itself extremely verisimilar-yet-abstract, since it is defined by inner multiplicity and contradiction: historical epics, Dannunzian romances, working-class melodramas, Neapolitan cinema, comedy shorts, male comedians, female comedians, actualities, newsreels, war documentaries, scientific films, black and white films, colour films, divas, strongmen – an infinite clash of form that, *as a totality*, hence, not based on the viewing of any individual film but as a cumulative construct of memory and imagination comprising all films previously viewed, brings the world forward in an exuberant 'polyphonic' vision of speed, a vision that also reshapes, radically and decisively, human sensibility into something considerably new.[30]

Marinetti's *Velocità*, in spite of its status as a film work proper, is neither the single nor the predominant example of Futurism's adherence to this filmic rendering of the world during the second decade of the twentieth century. The parade of verisimilar and diverse narrative instances informs also the writing style of some of the manifestos. Noteworthy is the manner in which Marinetti lists the places where the 'divine' may be experienced in this exemplary excerpt from 'La nuova religione-morale della velocità' (The New Religion-Morality of Speed, 1916):

> **Luoghi abitati dal divino**: i treni; i vagoni-ristoranti (mangiare in velocità). Le stazioni ferroviarie; specialmente quelle dell'Ovest America, dove i treni lanciati a 140 km. all'ora passano bevendo (senza fermarsi) l'acqua necessaria e i sacchi della posta. I ponti e i tunnels. La piazza dell'Opéra di Parigi. Lo Strand di Londra. I circuiti d'automobili. Le films cinematografiche. Le stazioni radiotelegrafiche. I grandi tubi che precipitano delle colonne d'acqua alpestri per strappare all'atmosfera l'elettricità motrice. I grandi sarti parigini che mediante l'invenzione veloce delle mode, creano la passione del nuovo e l'odio per il già visto. Le città modernissime e attive come Milano, che secondo gli americani ha il *punch* (colpo netto e preciso, col quale il boxeur mette il suo avversario *knock-out*). I campi di battaglia. Le mitragliatrici, i fucili, i cannoni, i proiettili sono divini. Le mine e le contromine veloci: far saltare il nemico PRIMA che il nemico ci faccia saltare. I motori a scoppio e i pneumatici d'un'automobile sono divini. Le biciclette e le motociclette sono divine. La benzina è divina. Estasi religiosa che ispirano le centocavalli. Gioia di passare dalla 3ª alla 4ª velocità. Gioia di premere l'acceleratore, pedale russante della musicale velocità. Schifo che ispirano le persone invischiate nel sonno. Ripugnanza che io provo a coricarmi la sera. Io prego ogni sera, la mia lampadina elettrica; poiché una velocità vi si agita furiosamente. (*TIF* 133–4)

[**Places inhabited by the divine**: trains, dining cars (to eat at high speed). Railway stations; especially those of West America, where trains launched at 140 km per hour pass taking in (without stopping) the water they need and the mailbags. Bridges and tunnels. The Place d'Opéra in Paris. The Strand in London. Automobile racetracks. Cinematographic films. Radio-telegraphic stations. The large tubes that cast down the Alpine water columns in order to snatch electrical power from the atmosphere. The great Parisian fashion designers, who, through the swift invention of fashions, create passion for the new and hatred for the already seen. Very modern and active cities like Milan, which according to the Americans has *punch* (a sharp and precise blow, with which the boxer knocks out his opponent). Battlefields. Machineguns, rifles, cannons, missiles are divine. Swift mines and countermines: to blow up the enemy BEFORE the enemy blows us up. Internal combustion engines and the tires of an automobile are divine. Bicycles and motorcycles are divine. Gasoline is divine. Religious ecstasy inspired by hundred-horsepower automobiles. Joy of passing from the 3rd to the 4th gear. Joy of pressing the accelerator, a growling pedal of musical speed. Disgust inspired by people entangled in sleep. Repugnance I feel when I go to bed at night. I pray every night to my electric bulb; since in it some speed tosses about furiously.]

According to the central idea of this manifesto, the discovery of rapid movement by means of modern technology renders any previous religious-moral values obsolete. A new notion of 'good' is in place, which refers to any experience of an unprecedented intensity of speed, while its moral opposite, the new 'evil,' refers to any experience defined by slowness. If Christian morality, Marinetti claims, served to develop the internal life of man, defended his physiological structure from the excesses of sensuality, and moderated and balanced his instincts, the new Futurist morality will defend man from the decay caused by slowness, memory, analysis, rest, and habit. As the traditional opposition between good and evil surrenders to the Futurist principle of speed against slowness, Christian morality no longer has a raison d'être, as it has been emptied of its divine dimension and replaced by the new religion of speed (*TIF* 130).

More than a reflection on something already perceived as a new divine – or, in the terminology of semiotics, an order of signs pointing to their referents – the passage quoted above is itself an actualization of this divine, because of the rapidity with which it displaces the reader's mind from one image to the next, thus accomplishing a mental global journey, exuberantly swift, to multiple and diverse spaces. One wonders what this rendering of the divine has to do with cinema, and narrative cinema in particular. First, the passage is extremely 'visual.' In listing the 'places inhabited by the divine,' Marinetti composed a repertoire of distinct elements that pass through the mind as a series of verisimilar images. Second, as this repertoire transports us from West America, to Paris, to London, to the Alps, to Milan, and back to America, the global journey that it forms is so swift that it is impossible to realize in a concrete sense, because its rapidity exceeds the capacity not only of any obsolete means of transportation but of any revolutionary ones celebrated by Marinetti himself. Surely, modern and familiar means of transportation lend their capacities to the mind so that the journey may be realized in one's thoughts. Yet if the mind, be it the reader's or the writer's, is at all capable of picturing – that is, not merely forming arbitrary imaginary constructs but literally *picturing* – a series of such rapid translocations, that is a result of something much more concrete than what the mere familiarity with trains and airplanes can accomplish. It is a result of the human acquaintance with the very concrete images of the world that cinema brought forward in daily life.

Third, more than a series of verisimilar images, the 'places inhabited by the divine' are a series of brief *narratives*, every one of which is allowed to remain incomplete only to give way to the one that follows. That is to say, the images are narrativized. One does not simply eat at high speed, but one eats at high speed in a West American train, which after settling at a speed of 140 km per hour passes by train stations, gets quickly recharged, quickly picks up mail and resumes its swift journey, only to allow its passengers to keep enjoying the views of bridges and tunnels through the dining-car window – itself like a cinematic screen showing one of those early travelogues that were sometimes filmed by merely placing the camera at the train window. The Parisian fashion designers do not simply detest anything already seen, but their detestation is the logical result of the never-ending appearance of new styles. The image of the blown-up enemy is not static but part of a rational psychological scenario according to which one must destroy the enemy before the enemy destroys one. The euphoria of driving an automobile does not refer to an experience of speed actualized in a vacuum but to a logical progression that entails the act of switching from the third to the fourth gear, followed naturally by the pressing of the accelerator.

With respect to the above manifesto, *Velocità* aims to attain similar effects, but also to reach further. Owing to its multiple and interlaced brief narratives, the script is to some extent the manifesto's filmic equivalent. Each of its eleven episodes displays a given degree of autonomy. The epic adventure of the four brothers thematically links the scenes to one another, yet the sequence of the scenes does not convey a strong sense of continuity with respect to diegetic spatio-temporality. Like the reader of the above passage who imagines a swift global journey, the script's virtual spectator moves rapidly between different spaces and events, which vary considerably in their degrees of verisimilitude, historicity, exoticism, and intensity. This aspect of the script, its verisimilar-yet-abstract dimension, is testimony to its avant-garde temperament. Furthermore, insofar as it is the manifesto's filmic equivalent, *Velocità* pays cinema its dues. If the manifesto reflects a mindset informed by cinema's pervasive role in contemporary mass culture, with its tangible images *Velocità* reaffirms the relationship between cinema and this new mindset. Moreover, like the passage quoted above, the script goes beyond merely articulating the 'new religion-morality of speed.' The exuberance with which the virtual spectator receives its spatio-temporal displacements and diverse actions constitutes an actualization of the new divine. Hence, like other Futurist works, the script both articulates and to some extent proliferates modernity's sensibility.

To say that it articulates and somewhat proliferates this psychosocial condition, however, does not mean that it shapes it at its root. As I suggested at the opening of this chapter, in the medium of cinema, which was also an industry, Marinetti sought a means to control the shape of that sensibility with the same force with which other highly industrialized processes of modernity were able to control it. This is where the script's narrativity comes into play: in order for the script to transcend the local context of the *serata* and reach a universal audience, narrativity aims to unify the script's autonomous episodes, to contain its abstract dimension, thus establishing a tension between narrativity itself and avant-gardism. *Velocità* does not want to be merely an abstract manifesto-like succession of narrative fragments. In its wish to engage the contemporary mass audience, it must also be a story marked by unity and coherence, one the psychological realism of which is enhanced by the various structural elements that tend towards what was to become classical continuity, as we have seen. Furthermore, the script appeals to the contemporary audience also with its extravagant sets, numerous extras, and complex actions, the otherwise abstract meaning of which is fixed by the prevailing narrative context – an approach not unlike that of the industry's historical spectacles or its so-called Dannunzian melodramas, with their remote chateaux, paradisiacal gardens, and glittering heroines. This is not to say that Marinetti subscribed wholeheartedly to the demands of the 1910s film industry. I repeat that the script oscillates between an avant-garde style and narrativity. Not only does Marinetti not betray the fundamental ideals of Futurism, his choice to submerge the script's abstractness in an overarching narrative was also a way of communicating most effectively to the mass audience what is obviously the script's moral message: the need for all to be reborn as Futurists and take radical action for society's reorganization. Hence, the script does not want to merely articulate or somewhat proliferate the audience's new mindset; nor does it hope to incite the audience's intellectual contemplation of its own 'renewed sensibility.' Rather, *Velocità* wants to make Futurists, men (and perhaps women) willing to abandon thought for action. This is precisely where the dilemma lies: to attain its goal, *Velocità* deploys ways of communicating with the public that have been manufactured by the very culture that it wishes to abolish.

4

Forse che sì forse che no: Technological Inflections of a Decadent Text

A study of Gabriele D'Annunzio's *Forse che sì forse che no* (1910) provides an appropriate conceptual framework for the study of the Dannunzian cinematic projects that followed. Although it does not mention cinema, *Forse che sì* is the first major work in which D'Annunzio articulates his passion for modern technology – which, importantly, unlike the Futurists, he sees as an extension of the cultural tradition. Cinema itself is an area in which he will use modern technology to reaffirm tradition. What distinguishes *Forse che sì* from his earlier novels is that it represents the amalgamation of two sensibilities. The author adapts his nineteenth-century decadent temperament to the 'renewed sensibility' of the new century. We are struck, above all, by the exuberant celebration of new scientific discoveries, the experience of speed and the diverse perspectives on reality that technology implements, exemplified in the portrayal of motoring and aviation. This certainly does not make D'Annunzio an avant-gardist. If Marinetti claims to abolish tradition and invent culture anew, D'Annunzio reclaims the old from the angle of the new, that is, he reaffirms his adoration of tradition with the tools that modern technology affords culture. The glory of modern aviation is attributed time and again to its Daedalian origins and to the other legendary instances of man's aspiration to fly, such as Leonardo da Vinci's and Otto Lilienthal's, while the archetypal Dannunzian figure of the sadistic female lover is again pervasive. *Forse che sì* is therefore a most suitable framework for a study of D'Annunzio's work on cinema, since several years before his cinematic projects it institutes quite forcefully the union between old and new, which is the trademark of the cinematic projects themselves. As my next chapter will show, his reflections on film, his cinematic vision of the myth of Daphne, and his screenplay on Leonardo's *Gioconda* reassert the Dannunzian topoi of antiquity, myth, artistic tradition, and desire, now through techniques specific to the new medium. Moreover, as we will see in the present chapter, the novel's portrayal of aviation reaches its peak in the scene of a flying contest, the structure of which suggests that aviation, in all its mythical and historical associations, was also, for D'Annunzio, part of a culture of distraction that reflected the specific mood of early twenti-eth-century modernity, of which cinema itself was a significant factor.

Inspired by the novel's preoccupation with modern technology, crit-ics discuss *Forse che sì* as distinct from D'Annunzio's nineteenth-century work, which dominates, along with the work of Pascoli, the blossoming of the Italian decadent movement. To adopt a new attitude towards literary production was a conscious decision on D'Annunzio's part. In a 1908 letter to his publisher, he stated: 'Quando ti porterò il mio libro, voglio avere in me la sensazione reale di condurti un bel "puro sangue" tutto muscoli e nervi, palpitante in una rete di vene rilevate, fremente di rapidità. Il miglior libro è certo quello che somiglia a un animale vivente, che percota la terra con le sue quattro zampe svelte' [When I bring you my book, I want to have the feeling of bringing you a real 'thoroughbred,' all muscle and nerves, palpitating in a net of pro-truding veins, throbbing of rapidity. The best book is surely that which resembles a living animal, which strikes the earth with its four swift legs].[1] Niva Lorenzini explains the long break in the author's novelistic writing, from *Il fuoco* (1898) to *Forse che sì*, in terms of an inquiry into energy and action that arose in the first decade of the century. A new conception of life as a rush, of consciousness as action, and of expe-rience as movement and change informed a substantial production of narratives published in French dailies and periodicals with which D'Annunzio was well acquainted.[2] According to Federico Roncoroni, the main novelty of *Forse che sì* lies in its emphasis on action. A symp-tom of the ten years of recess during which D'Annunzio wrote primar-ily for the theatre, the novel is marked by a synthetic quality catering to the development of dramatic action, thus replacing the prosaic style of earlier novels the plots of which were 'poor in action and substan-tially static.' Furthermore, while the premise is again that of a love affair, D'Annunzio incorporated many new elements characteristic of other genres, such as the psychological novel, the adventure novel, the chronicle, and even the mystery novel. With respect to character, he abandoned the old bipolar model about a single man found in a dialec-tical relation of inferiority/superiority with one or two women, giving instead equal weight to a number of characters in addition to the central male and female protagonists.[3]

Forse che sì is divided into three books that tell the flying adventures of Paolo Tarsis and his agitating love affair with the young and seductive Isabella Inghirami, widow of a wealthy aristocrat. Book I opens with the lovers' automobile journey to Mantua, where Tarsis is to participate in a flying contest. In Mantua, they meet Giulio Cambiaso, Tarsis's fraternal companion with whom he shared years of adventures, such as travelling across the African desert and exploring the Orient. During the contest, Tarsis achieves a glorious victory while Cambiaso meets a tragic death caused by the mechanical failure of his aircraft. Book II takes place in Volterra, where Vana, Aldo, and little Lunella – Inghirami's younger siblings and financial dependents – find themselves imprisoned in the seventeenth-century palace that Inghirami inherited from her late husband. While Inghirami is away on a romantic holiday with Tarsis, the siblings engage in various artistic activities to alleviate their feelings of abandonment, which they perceive as a result of their sister's selfishness. Book III takes a turn towards a more dramatic and rapidly unfolding action. Haunted by jealousy, as she is herself in love with Tarsis, Vana secretly speaks to him of Inghirami's incestuous relationship with Aldo. Facing Tarsis's harsh confrontation, followed by the traumatic event of Vana's suicide and little Lunella's fears of complete abandonment, Inghirami experiences an overpowering crisis that leads her to madness. The closing chapter, alluding no further to the fate of Inghirami or her siblings, concentrates on Tarsis. Inspired by Cambiaso's immortal spirit and ready to meet his companion upon death, Tarsis defies danger and flies his plane from the coast of Lazio to 'the coast of Aeneas' in Sardinia, a heroic act that he completes victoriously.

This study will focus on book I, where the emphasis on automobiles and airplanes forms the basis of what we may describe as the novel's distinctly modern sensibility. Critics have aptly argued that *Forse che sì* constitutes not a radical shift but a negotiation of both rupture and continuity with respect to the author's nineteenth-century prose. To this widely shared view, I will contribute two points in particular, both of which draw on the details of the novel's style. First, revisiting the theme of the antagonistic male-female relation, I emphasize the fundamental role that technology plays in the characterization of the protagonists. While this theme recalls D'Annunzio's first novel, *Il piacere*, the figurative language through which it is developed reflects a historical actuality conditioned by the presence of modern machinery in everyday life.

The machine does not simply function as a crucial aspect of diegetic action, or as one element in the diegetic ambience, but penetrates the very core of the characters' psychology and thus the interaction among them.[4] Second, the flying contest, which epitomizes the novel's celebration of technology, exhibits a consciousness of modernity that is evident not only in its telling a story about airplanes but also in the specific configuration of the discourse. The flying contest is portrayed as a unique form of spectacle of which the audience displays a sensibility characteristic of this historical period. In a manner analogous to the case of the love affair, the aerial spectacle rehearses the author's decadent temperament now inspired by modern technology, while it also prompts the reader to engage in a social critique of the modern condition.

The Fatal Woman and the Superman

Renato Barilli draws a sharp distinction between those narrative segments concerned with 'feminine dramas' and those concerned with the 'sporting-agonistic trials of Tarsis and Cambiaso.' This structural split, he claims, gives the 'reader the possibility to make a choice, if he prefers the masculine and positive line, the novel of the motors . . . , or instead the feminine one, of turbid, mortuary, yet imposing, perturbing, love affairs.'[5] Rather, I argue, the two lines are inseparable. The omnipresence of the motor in the discourse is instrumental in what is agitating about the love affair because it adds its own dimension to both what is evasive and what is potentially controllable about the woman as perceived by the man. The novel opens in the middle of a conversation between the two lovers while driving to Mantua. The excerpt below demonstrates two things: first, the very opening summarizes the main preoccupations, both thematic and formal, that to varying degrees inform the unfolding of the narration all the way to the novel's finale; second, the verbal exchange alternates with descriptions of which the figures of speech reveal the author's intention to pay tribute to the era of modern technology:

- Forse – rispondeva la donna, quasi protendendo il sorriso contro il vento eroico della rapidità, nel battito del suo gran velo ora grigio ora argentino come i salici della pianura fuggente.
- Non forse. Bisogna che sia, bisogna che sia! È orribile quel che fate, Isabella: non ha alcuna scusa, alcuna discolpa . . . Che volete voi fare di me? Volete rendermi ancor più disperato e più folle?

– Forse – rispondeva la donna . . .
– Ah, se l'amore fosse una creatura viva e avesse gli occhi, potreste voi guardarlo senza vergognarvi?
– Non lo guardo.
– Mi amate?
– Non so.
– Vi prendete gioco di me?
– Tutto è gioco.
Il furore gonfiò il petto dell'uomo chino sul volante della sua rossa macchina precipitosa, che correva l'antica strada romana con un rombo guerresco simile al rullo d'un vasto tamburo metallico.
– Siete capace di metter la vita per ultima posta?
– Capace di tutto.
. . .
– Ora ho la vostra vita nelle mie mani come questo cerchio.
– Sì.
– Posso distruggerla.
– Sì.
– Posso in un attimo scagliarla nella polvere, schiacciarla contro le pietre, fare di voi e di me un solo mucchio sanguinoso.
– Sì.
Protesa, ella ripeteva la sillaba sibilante, con un misto d'irrisione e di voluttà selvaggia. E veramente l'uno e l'altro sangue si rinforzavano, balzavano; l'uno contro l'altro parevano ardere ed esplodere come l'essenza accesa dal magnete nel motore celato dal lungo cofano.
– La morte, la morte! (*PRII* 521–2)

[– Perhaps – the woman answered, almost holding out her smile against the heroic wind of speed, in the palpitation of her large veil, at times grey at times silvery, like the willows of the fleeting plain.
– Not perhaps. It must be, it must be! What you do is horrible, Isabella: it has no excuse, no defence . . . What do you want to make of me? Do you want to make me even more desperate and mad?
– Perhaps – the woman answered . . .
– Ah, if love were a live creature and had eyes, could you look at it without being ashamed?
– I don't look at it.
– Do you love me?
– I don't know.
– Are you playing with me?
– Everything is play.

The rage swelled the man's chest, bent on the steering wheel of his red on-rushing car that ran along the old Roman street with a warlike roar similar to the roll of a vast metallic drum.
 – Are you capable of putting life in the last place?
 – Capable of everything.
. . .
 – Now I have your life in my hands, like this steering wheel.
 – Yes.
 – I can destroy it.
 – Yes.
 – In one instant, I can hurl it in the dust, smash it against the stones, make out of you and me nothing but a bloody pile.
 – Yes.
Held out, she repeated the sibilant syllable with a mixture of derision and savage pleasure. And indeed the two bloods strengthened, jumped; the one against the other seemed to burn and explode like the essence kindled by the magnet in the motor hidden under the long hood.
 – Death, death!]

The passage re-establishes the familiar Dannunzian figure of the enigmatic woman who deprives the man of satisfaction.[6] The man's fear of going mad as a result of his unfulfilled desire is counteracted – ironically, because self-destructively – by his power of turning both her and himself into a bloody pile, evoking death as a solution. If these themes echo the early D'Annunzio, the figurative language takes its tropes from historical actuality. Her fleetingness is bound with the fleeting aspect specific to the movement of the automobile. Not only is it expressed in the conventional metaphor of the veil that she is wearing but also finds an objective correlative in the alternating colours of the willows, 'at times grey at times silvery,' described as such only because the fast movement of the machine creates frequent variations in the intensity of sunlight reflected by the surrounding landscape. The man, who here does not represent the conventional figure of the decadent aesthete, desperately attempts to negate the woman's control, not by transforming her into an aesthetic object through poetry or other artistic means but by grasping onto the power with which his dexterity in things technological endows him, that is, his ability to end this game of seduction by a random turn of the steering wheel.[7]

While the speed of the automobile inspires a historically updated configuration of the woman's fleetingness, her characterization in terms of the physical objects that surround her is not new in the writer's prose.

At the opening of *Il piacere*, anxiously awaiting the visit of Elena Muti, whom he has not seen in almost two years, the poet Andrea Sperelli is lost in the memory of past sensual encounters with the woman he still desires. Sperelli exemplifies the Dannunzian decadent aesthete. Typically an artist or intellectual, and constantly in the search of beauty, exquisite sensations, and refined pleasures, he surrounds himself with an abundance of precious objects and rare luxuries.[8] His material environs also serve the sensual characterization of his lover. Besides the descriptions of her face and body, Muti is associated with elements that excite the senses of touch and smell, such as wood, fire, fabrics, flowers, and perfumes. As compared to a motor, such elements maintain a high physical proximity to their derivation in nature:

> Proprio innanzi a quel caminetto Elena un tempo amava indugiare, prima di rivestirsi, dopo un'ora d'intimità. Ella aveva molt'arte nell'accumular gran pezzi di legno su gli alari ... Il suo corpo sul tappeto ... pareva sorridere da tutte le giunture, da tutte le pieghe, da tutti i cavi, soffuso d'un pallor d'ambra che richiamava al pensiero la Danae del Correggio ...
>
> ... Elena pareva presa da una specie di follia infantile, alla vista della vampa. Aveva l'abitudine, un po' crudele, di sfogliar sul tappeto tutti i fiori ch'eran ne' vasi, alla fine d'ogni convegno d'amore.[9]

> [Exactly in front of this fire, Elena loved to linger before redressing after an hour of intimacy. She had a way of piling big pieces of wood on the andirons ... Her body on the carpet ... seemed to laugh at all the junctions, all the folds, suffused by an amber colour which recalled the thought of the Correggio 'Danae' ...
>
> ... Elena seemed to have been seized by an infantile craze by the light of the fire. She had the habit, a bit cruel, to defoliate, on the carpet, all the flowers that were in the vases, after every session of love.][10]

If Inghirami's evasiveness is configured through her affinity to the speed of the automobile, Muti finds her objective correlative in the duplicity of a primary nature. Like the fire, she is radiant yet dangerous. Like the flowers, she is beautiful yet fragile, or, transient, ephemeral, evanescent.

Sperelli remembers his very last meeting with Muti of two years earlier. During a carriage ride, to his great dismay, she announces her departure. The scene anticipates the opening of *Forse che sì*. The two lovers are in a moving vehicle, the man admits his love while the woman is enigmatic, and the landscape that passes by, which his memory links to her departure, comes to signify her inaccessibility. Differently from

Forse che sì, neither the moving landscape nor the woman's allure is associated with high speed. Not yet replaced by the automobile, 'la carrozza chiusa scorreva con un romore eguale, al trotto' [the closed carriage ran on noisily, trotting horses], and the walls of the old patrician villas passed by, 'con un movimento continuo e dolce' [with a sweet and continuous movement]. As in the later novel, however, the moving landscape functions as her objective correlative. As though by natural necessity, its description leads directly to her: 'Elena taceva, avvolta nell'ampio mantello di lontra, con un velo su la faccia, con le mani chiuse nel camoscio. Egli aspirava con delizia il sottile odore di eliotropio esalante dalla pelliccia preziosa' [Elena was silent, wrapped in a cape of mink, with a veil covering her face, her hands in a muff. He breathed with delight the subtle odor of heliotrope emanating from the precious fur] (*PRI* 7–8; *Pleasure* 5). The landscape's idyllic beauty and the woman's sensuousness seem to reside in the same sublime universe, where they pose side by side, such that the landscape's 'sweet' mobility becomes indistinguishable from her evasiveness.

Hence, in each work, the journey confronts the man with his failure to secure the woman's love. It also serves as a frame for the representation of a flashback. The man seeks relief in recalling a past moment in which her companionship seemed more secure. When Muti announces her departure, Sperelli reminds her of sensual moments further in the past:

> – E quella sera de' fiori, in principio; quando io venni con tanti fiori . . . Tu eri sola, accanto alla finestra: leggevi. Ti ricordi?
> – Sì, sì.
> – Io entrai. Tu ti volgesti appena; tu mi accogliesti duramente. Che avevi? Io non so . . . Io pensai, scorato: 'Già ella non mi ama più!' . . .
> . . .
> – Poi, sul divano: ti ricordi? Io ti ricoprivo il petto, le braccia, la faccia, con i fiori, opprimendoti . . . Avevi la testa affondata nei cuscini, il petto nascosto dalle rose, le braccia nude sino al gomito; e nulla era più amoroso e più dolce che il piccolo tremito delle tue mani pallide su le mie tempie . . . Ti ricordi? (*PRI* 9–10; first and last ellipses in original)

> [– 'And that night of the flowers – in the beginning when I came with so many flowers . . . You were alone, near the window: you were reading – remember?'
> – 'Yes, yes.'

- 'I entered – you barely turned – you hardly received me. What was wrong? I don't know . . . I was disheartened: 'She does not love me' . . .
. . .
- 'Then, on the divan – remember? I covered your breast, your arms, your face with the flowers, suffocating you . . . Then – with your head buried in the pillows, your breast covered with roses, your arms bare to the elbows; nothing was so lovely and sweeter than the slight tremor of your hands on my temples. Remember?'] (*Pleasure* 6; first ellipsis in original)

Similarly, while driving, Tarsis thinks of Inghirami's first visit to his aviator's workshop:

Egli rivide in un lampo Isabella Inghirami sotto la tettoia che crepitava alla pioggia primaverile, là, fra i rotoli dei fili d'acciaio, fra le lunghe verghe di legno, fra i mucchi dei trucioli, negli stridori della sega, nei gemiti della lima, nei colpi del martello. (*PR II* 526)

[He saw again in a flash Isabella Inghirami under the roof that was rattling at the rain of the spring, there, amidst the rolls of the steel wires, amidst the long wooden bars, amidst the heaps of the shavings, in the screeching of the saw, in the groans of the file, in the blows of the hammer.]

Again, whereas the flashbacks of the early novel associate Muti with a lightly processed nature (soft-textured fabrics, such as the fur, the divan, the cushions) or nature that is still organic (the heliotrope, the roses), Tarsis's memory places Inghirami amidst a constellation of technological objects, or, amidst nature that has already been, or is now being, extensively processed.

Furthermore, in both cases the flashback contains a tension between two clashing forces. On the one hand, it promises to fulfil the man's wish to fix the woman in a static image, to thus enslave her in a fantasy drawn on a less threatening past. On the other hand, even in his recollection her enigma is persistent. Received with indifference on the night of the flowers, Sperelli suspects that Muti does not love him. Tarsis's memory does not evoke thoughts of such finality. Yet it triggers the awareness that despite his capability of building and controlling a structure as complex as an airplane, he is nonetheless mystified by the impenetrable mystery of that body, next to which the airplane becomes nothing but a 'dubious carcass':

Ah, perché d'improvviso quell'opera delicata e misteriosa come il lavoro dei liutai, fatta di pazienza di passione di coraggio, e di eterno sogno e di antica favola, perché era divenuta una incerta carcassa al paragone della somma di vita accorsa da tutti i punti dell'Universo e adunata maravigliosamente su quel volto quasi esangue i cui sùbiti rossori commovevano come gli accenti sublimi dell'eloquenza e come le grida dei fanciulli? Quanto ingegno teso e ostinato quanta accortezza e destrezza quante prove e riprove nel trovare i modi delle legature, delle giunture, degli innesti! E per qual segreto, a un tratto, ecco, le fragili falangi di quelle dita ripiegate all'angolo di quella bocca socchiusa potevano assumere un valore che aboliva tutto l'acume della ricerca e tutta la gioia dell'invenzione? (*PRII* 526–7)

[Ah, why suddenly that work as delicate and mysterious as the work of the lute-makers, made of patience, passion, courage, and eternal dream and ancient fable, why had it become a dubious carcass in comparison with the sum of life rushing from all points of the Universe and marvellously gathered on that almost bloodless face whose sudden blushes moved one like the sublime accents of eloquence and like the cries of children? How much tense and obstinate intelligence, how much wisdom and skill, how many trials and confirmations to find the ways of the bindings, of the joints, of the clutches! And by what secret, all of a sudden, there, could the fragile phalanxes of those fingers, folded at the angle of that half-closed mouth, assume a value that abolished all the acumen of the research and all the joy of the invention?]

The woman's static posture as found in the man's memory, either resting on the divan buried in a bouquet of flowers or standing next to an aircraft surrounded by the numerous objects pertaining to its construction, ascribes a painterly dimension to the representation: an immobility, serving his wish to counteract that opposing force that inevitably invades the recollection itself, namely, the fluidity, the inner mobility, that permeates her.[11]

One wonders how plausible it is to compare Tarsis's thoughts to a painting. In his poet's imagination, Sperelli compares Muti's posture to Correggio's Danae. Tarsis, however, differs greatly from Sperelli. First, he is not an aristocrat – a socio-economic status that goes hand-in-hand with the sensibility of the decadent aesthete – but a bourgeois.[12] Second, he is an aviator, a twentieth-century man of action, and not an artist who would like to capture his evasive lover by recreating her as an aesthetic object fixed in time and space. Yet his confidence in his ability to control sophisticated machinery, which he can render inanimate at will, is threatened by the utmost fluidity of that whimsical face and body. He wishes, perhaps, like the nineteenth-century aesthete who aspires to arrest her in an artwork, that the woman were as manageable as a machine. He senses that Inghirami shares something essential with the machine: 'Sopra la pulsazione del motore e sopra il riso della donna, che parevan salire *dalla stessa meccanica inconsapevolezza*, egli percepiva il silenzio senza confine' [Beyond the pulsation of the motor and beyond the woman's laughter, which seemed to rise *from the same mechanical unconsciousness*, he perceived an infinite silence] (*PRII* 526; emphasis added). He sublimates the wish to conquer her into his scientific ventures, as he senses the correlation between the two. In this sense, he undertakes an enterprise similar to that of the aesthete, whereby the 'art' of science displaces art proper – indicating again the relationship of both rupture and continuity between the two novels, separated by two decades marked by radical scientific discoveries.

It is appropriate to speak of Tarsis less as an aesthete than as a Superman, the figure that took shape in D'Annunzio's literature after *Il piacere* and before *Forse che sì*.[13] Among the Superman's essential attributes is 'the cult of a dominating energy that manifests itself as force.'[14] Although as a bourgeois he is relatively modest, what qualifies Tarsis as a Dannunzian Superman is the cultivation of force, vitality, and action, exemplified in his passion for flying, as seen especially in his heroic flight over the Tyrrhenian Sea at the novel's finale.[15] His intimate familiarity with the idiosyncrasies of modern machinery also distinguishes him from his predecessors. The latest among them, the poet Stelio Effrena, lived several years too soon to feel the exuberance that came along with the revolutionary inventions of the new century. Yet Dannunzio's Superman displays an unsettling combination of attributes. Inasmuch as he embodies the cult of force, he is marked by self-destructiveness, a fascination with death, an irresistible attraction towards nothingness.[16] The correlation between the woman and the machine indeed sustains this contradiction. Like the woman, the machine is evasive. In spite of its 'mechanical unconsciousness,' it presents a challenge. It incites the hero towards play with danger, a celestial exploration at the threat of annihilation. The conquest of the sky, or the secular yet sublime 'Assumption' that it promises (*PRII* 567), is no less perilous than the psychical annihilation entailed in surrendering to the 'fatal' woman's seductions.[17] Tarsis, who witnesses Cambiaso, his fraternal companion, fall to his death, may not deny this truth. Rather, he is lured by the fatal threat that celestial exploration poses. Insofar as he seeks self-destruction, he recalls one of his predecessors, Giorgio Aurispa, who puts an end to the torture that he receives from Ippolita Sanzio – *la Nemica*, or the Enemy, as he labels her – by pushing both her and himself over a cliff. Tarsis's analogous tendency is evident from the very beginning, when he threatens to put an end to his lover's game by turning both her and himself into a 'bloody pile' through a swift turn of the steering wheel.[18]

Tarsis's great faith in the machine brings to mind Marinetti's 'multiplied man' (see chapter 3). Let us recall that this 'non-human and mechanical type,' ready for 'the imminent and inevitable identification of man with motor,' is liberated from that menace that debilitates man's vital energy, namely, his desire for woman. He is immune to the sickness of love, as already witnessed in the machinist who washes the body of his locomotive with the same tenderness with which a lover caresses the woman he adores, or in those men who live well 'without love, in a beautiful steel-coloured atmosphere' (*TIF* 297–301). While flying his airplane during the contest in Mantua, Tarsis engages in these thoughts, which he would like to share with Cambiaso, his fraternal companion:

'Fratello, fratello, siamo solitarii, siamo liberi, siamo lontani dalla terra tormentosa!' . . . 'Non voglio più esser triste, non voglio più divorarmi il cuore, non voglio più nasconderti il mio supplizio . . . '

Egli lasciava dietro di sé la turbolenza della sua passione, il riso agitante d'Isabella, lo sguardo febrile e ostile dell'adolescente, la vanità delle amiche, la stupidità degli accompagnatori, tutto quello stuolo intruso che l'aveva assalito e oppresso. (*PRII* 587)

['Brother, brother, we are alone, we are free, we are away from the tormenting earth!' . . . 'I no longer want to be sad, I no longer want to devour my heart, I no longer want to hide my torment from you . . . '

He was leaving behind him the turbulence of his passion, Isabella's agitating laughter, the adolescent girl's febrile and hostile gaze, the vanity of the female friends, the stupidity of the companions, that whole crowd of intruders that had assailed and oppressed him.]

The analogy between Tarsis and Marinetti's type indicates that the former's motive to fly is ambivalent as regards woman. If the machine offers a means to capture her in his fantasy, it also represents the opposite. As in the case of Marinetti, it serves as a liberating force, a means of leaving woman behind. Furthermore, Marinetti's type enters also the character of Cambiaso, whose identification with his airplane corresponds neatly to Marinetti's exaltation of those men who are gifted with 'the great mechanical divination or the metallic instinct' (*TIF* 300):

> Giulio Cambiaso non aveva mai sentita così piena la concordanza fra la sua macchina e il suo scheletro, fra la sua volontà addestrata e quella forza congegnata, tra il suo moto istintivo e quel moto meccanico. Dalla pala dell'elica al taglio del governale, tutta la membratura volante gli era come un prolungamento e un ampliamento della sua stessa vita ... [E]gli credeva esser congiunto ai suoi due bianchi trapezii con nessi vivi come i muscoli pettorali degli avvoltoi, che aveva veduto piombarsi dalle rocce del Mokattam o aggirarsi su l'acquitrino di Sakha. (*PRII* 587)

> [Giulio Cambiaso had never felt so solid the concordance between his machine and his skeleton, between his trained will and that invented force, between his instinctive motion and that mechanical motion. From the propeller's blade to the rudder's edge, the entire flying structure was like an extension and enlargement of his very life ... He thought he was connected to its two white trapeziums with living joints like the pectoral muscles of the vultures that he had seen descent from the rocks of Mokattam or wander about on the marsh of Sakha.]

If D'Annunzio's novel shares this aspect of Marinetti's avant-garde, it also differs from it significantly.[19] The Dannunzian hero lacks that absolute confidence, stemming from a childlike enthusiasm, that marks his Marinettian counterpart. Whether the machine is a means to control woman or free oneself from her, it is the struggle with woman that gives meaning to the act of flying. Though Tarsis's aerial emancipation at Mantua occurs early in the novel, his efforts to resolve the agony of Inghirami's allure continue almost to the finale. Marinetti's type, by contrast, revels in vitality because he anticipates an ideal state of already being liberated. Furthermore, the thing from which the 'multiplied man' is to be liberated is not the essence of woman but an image of woman as created in romantic literature, the sentimentalism of which, for Marinetti, had subjected man to suffocating erotic passions. This literary phenomenon is at the core of the manifesto, which opens by declaring that the Futurists' main efforts 'consistono nell'abolire in lettura la fusione apparentemente indiscutibile delle due concezioni di *Donna* e di *Bellezza'* [consist in abolishing in reading the seemingly indisputable fusion of the two notions of *Woman* and *Beauty*] (*TIF* 297). Moreover:

> Noi siamo convinti d'altronde che l'arte e la letteratura esercitano un'influenza determinante su tutte le classi sociali, anche sulle più ignoranti, che ne sono abbeverate per via d'infiltrazioni misteriose.
>
> Noi possiamo dunque attivare o ritardare il movimento dell'umanità verso questa forma di vita liberata dal sentimentalismo e dalla lussuria ... [N]oi crediamo all'utilità di una propaganda artistica contro la concezione apologetica del dongiovanni e quella divertente del cornuto. (*TIF* 300–1)

> [We are also convinced that art and literature exercise a determining influence on all social classes, even the most ignorant, who absorb them through mysterious infiltrations.
>
> We can therefore activate or retard humanity's movement towards this form of life freed from sentimentalism and lust ... We believe in the usefulness of an artistic propaganda against the apologetic conception of the Don Giovanni and the amusing one of the cuckold.]

D'Annunzio's own veneration of the modern moves in the opposite direction. The fact that his man-machine identification is propelled by a vain attempt to overcome woman's allure sustains the fusion Woman-Beauty. Thus, his novel constitutes an example of the kind of literature that Marinetti attacks.[20] In the end Tarsis appears to overcome Inghirami, yet the role of the machine is not, strictly speaking, that of a liberator. Once he confronts Inghirami on account of her incest, she begins to fall into madness. Taken into custody by her parents, she becomes all the more inaccessible, and an anxious Tarsis makes numerous efforts to reach her. With no further reference to this unresolved affair, the novel closes with Tarsis's heroic flight over the Tyrrhenian Sea. The mysterious glossing-over of a romantic scenario that dominated the novel thus far suggests a denial, a suppression of an unfulfilled wish. The machine, one speculates, becomes an emotional outlet aiming to sooth Tarsis's pain of having lost Inghirami forever.[21]

An Aerial Spectacle

If the novel's celebration of movement and speed echoes Marinetti's exaltation of modernity, D'Annunzio's outlook differs from Marinetti's in ways beyond what I have suggested above. First, worship is not limited to the technological product. A recurrent motif in the first chapter is that of the swallows, which constitute an essential element of the fleeting landscape during the lovers' automobile ride through the country. Appearing as nature's counterpart to the man-made achievements of fast movement, the swallow is linked to one of the novel's philosophical preoccupations, that is, man's ability to surpass the prohibitions of nature, if by imitating its wonders. Second, the significance of technologically constructed speed has less to do with its implications for the future than with its origins in the far past. The opening of the second chapter traces the critical stages of humanity's aspiration to fly: the myth of Daedalus and Icarus; the writings of Leonardo da Vinci; the 1890s experiments of Otto Lilienthal; and the 1903 achievement of the Wright brothers. Third, in line with the author's earlier prose, this opening relies on a lyrical style that carefully excludes the names of the above figures.[22] Da Vinci is described as 'il nuovo Dedalo creatore d'imagini e di macchine' [the new Daedalus, creator of images and machines]. Lilienthal is presented as 'Un barbaro della Magna ... [che] aveva studiato il vento e ascoltato la parola del Precursore intorno al congegno: "Non gli manca se non l'anima dell'uccello, la quale anima bisogna che sia contraffatta dall'anima dell'omo"' [A barbarian of Germany ... who had studied the wind and listened to the words of his Forerunner about the device: 'It only lacks the soul of the bird, which must be forged by the soul of man'] (*PRII* 565).[23] The evocation of America as the peak of modern advancements is similarly lyrical: 'Alla vasta brezza costante dell'Atlantico, non al chiaro ponente meridiano del Mediterraneo, s'era rialzata e aggrandita la speranza della vittoria sul cielo cavo! ... Due fratelli silenziosi, figli del placido Ohio, infaticabili nel provare e nel riprovare, per spingere la macchina alata avevano aggiunto la forza di due eliche all'ostinazione dei due cuori' [At the vast constant breeze of the Atlantic, not at the clear meridian west wind of the Mediterranean, the hope of victory over the hollow sky had risen again and become greater! ... Two taciturn brothers, sons of the calm Ohio, tireless in trying and retrying, in order to push the winged machine, had added the force of two propellers to the obstinacy of the two hearts] (*PRII* 566). Aviation is described as the Assumption of the human species (*PRII* 567), only to reaffirm the sublimity of the phenomenon. Hence, although he sharès Marinetti's passion for modern technology, in a distinctly un-Marinettian style D'Annunzio celebrates technology with images of nature, myth, and a secular transcendence, thus displaying the continuity between this novel and the decadent temperament of his earlier prose.[24]

In spite of an overall mythical and sublime approach to the invention, the specific formal choices that make up the representation of the flying contest affirm the writer's attention to a contemporary sensibility. While the narration of the contest often refers to the pilot's thoughts and emotions, it emphasizes the exhilarated state of the crowd, whose experience seems to originate in a yearning for visual stimulation and is articulated primarily in terms of vision, of what they see. A scenario including the protagonist's performance in front of a large crowd is not new in D'Annunzio. In *Il fuoco*, the poet Stelio Effrena, under the aegis of the Queen, gives an oration to the Venetian public, who are left enchanted by his eloquent and profound statements.[25] However, this exaltation of a superior persona by a mass displays significant differences when it reappears in 1910: the airplane's violent movement replaces the 1898 speaker's static posture; the poet's intellectual exploration of the limitless depths of art gives way to the pilots' physical exploration of the limitless openness of the sky; the performer, who in the earlier novel is the poet alone, is now a multitude of pilots; and the mass of enchanted listeners now becomes a mass of avid lookers, anxious to indulge in an epic rendering of glory, danger, and death.

The flying contest was inspired by a real-life event. D'Annunzio had been present, as both a spectator and a flight passenger, at the 1909 Brescia International Air Meet.[26] Yet in turning the real experience into an aesthetic product, the author highlighted a particular view of the event. The recurrent descriptions of the various flights exactly as seen by the crowd grant the flying contest the status of a unique form of spectacle. Not only is the entire segment on flights dominated by the crowd's visual perspective, this visual inflection is also heightened by the frequent specification of the colour or shape of various objects. For example:

> La folla iterava il clamore inebriandosi a quel gioco grazioso e terribile, a quella gara di eleganza e di ardire, a quella disfida allegra tra due volatori della medesima specie [Tarsis e Cambiaso]. In un golfo ceruleo, lunato tra cumuli d'ambra, *apparvero* entrambi inseguendosi come due cicogne prima della cova, librate su le lunghe ali rettilinee; poi *si persero* bianche nella vasta bianchezza. (*PRII* 588; emphasis added)

> [The crowd repeated the outcry, becoming inebriated by that graceful and terrible play, by that race of elegance and boldness, by that jovial challenge between two fliers of the same species, Tarsis and Cambiaso. In a sky-blue gulf, half-moon shaped among amber cumuli, they both *appeared*,

following each other like two storks before brooding time, gliding on their long rectilinear wings; then they *disappeared* white in the vast whiteness.]

Significantly, the two pilots 'appeared,' and not simply flew, into the sky. Thus we receive the visual perspective of the mass as our primary means of spatial orientation in the diegesis. For this reason, 'si persero,' which in another context could be translated as 'they got lost,' is not misunderstood, because nothing in the text indicates that the pilots lose their way. Rather, it denotes the pilots' exit from the crowd's range of vision, hence, their 'disappearance.'

What is clearly the most prevalent aspect of this spectacle is the danger that flying entails. In numerous cases, a plane collapses and the pilot either approaches or meets death. The crowd then revels in the visualization of things such as a crashed wing, smoke, the blood and black oil spilled over the machine and its fallen pilot, and other horrid sights. A particular segment consists of a series of paragraphs, each narrating the misfortune of a different pilot – a formal structure that, next to the overall approach to the contest as spectacle, achieves something of a revue of falling planes. Each paragraph opens with the phrase, 'allora fu visto' ('then they saw' or 'then there was seen'), reiterating the performance value of the event:

> *Allora fu visto* uno dei grandi uccelli dedàlei inchinarsi verso terra, . . . urtare contro il suolo, restare immobile su l'ala infranta con alzata l'ala intatta senza il battito dell'agonia, esanime avanzo di vergelle e di canape, lordo di olio nero. L'uomo balzò dai rottami, si scrollò, guardò la sua mano sanguinante, e sorrise.
>
> *Allora fu visto* un altro velivolo . . . precipitarsi contro lo steccato, . . . [e] capovolgersi . . . La folla sbigottita e avida fiutò il cadavere, non apparendo dell'uomo se non le gambe prese nei fili d'acciaio aggrovigliati. Ma quegli fu tratto dall'intrico, fu dissepolto, fu rimesso in piedi. Pallidissimo, vacillò, si ripiegò, mozzò tra i denti il ruggito dello spasimo . . .
>
> *Allora fu visto* di subito apprendersi ad altre ali il fuoco senza colore, che non appariva nel giorno se non pel rapido annerirsi e involarsi della tela . . . [L]'ordegno percosse la terra con tale impeto che vi s'addentrò. Esplose nell'urto il serbatoio inondando la carcassa schiantata e l'uomo vivo . . .
>
> *E allora fu visto* l'uomo vivo avviluppato dal fuoco senza colore rotolarsi su l'erbe arsicce con una furia così selvaggia, che il suo cranio dirompeva il suolo friabile. La folla urlò, presa alle viscere *non dalla pietà pel morituro ma dalla frenesia del gioco mortale*. (PRII 590–1; emphasis added)

[*Then they saw* one of the great Daedalean birds bend towards the earth, ... crash against the ground, stand still on the broken wing, with the intact wing raised without the beat of agony, lifeless remainders of rods and hemp, besmeared of black oil. The man jumped out of the scraps, shook himself, looked at his bleeding hand, and smiled.

Then they saw another airplane ... hurl itself against the fence ... and capsize ... The astonished and avid crowd smelled the cadaver, nothing appearing of the man but the legs caught in the entangled steel wires. But he was pulled out of the tangle, he was unburied, he was put back on his feet. Very pale, he staggered, bent down, cut off the roar of agony through his teeth ...

Then they saw other wings caught by the colourless fire, which was not visible in daylight but for the quick blackening and vanishing of the cloth ... The device hit the ground with such force that it buried itself in it. The tank exploded in the collision, inundating the split carcass and the living man ...

And then they saw the living man, wrapped in the colourless fire, rolling on the scorched grass with such a savage frenzy that his skull broke the friable soil. The crowd shrieked, caught at the viscera, *not by pity for the dying man but by the delirium of the deadly game.*]

Allowing the crowd to indulge in the sensational spectacle of each plane crash and the ensuing human suffering, this revue both arouses and fulfils the crowd's *curiosity*, specifically in the sense explained by St Augustine in his *Confessions*: a curiosity that includes the desire to witness unsightly, repulsive, things.[27] Augustine makes a comparison between pleasure and curiosity, as regards the different ways in which they activate the senses: 'Pleasure pursues beautiful objects – what is agreeable to look at, to hear, to smell, to taste, to touch. But curiosity pursues the contraries of these delights with the motive of seeing what the experiences are like, not with a wish to undergo discomfort, but out of a lust for experimenting and knowing.' *Curiositas* is allied with the sense of vision – which, according to Augustine, plays the leading role among the senses in the acquisition of knowledge. However, this greed for knowledge through seeing, the 'lust of the eyes,' which is but a 'vain inquisitiveness dignified with the title of knowledge and science,' is not entirely devoid of a (perverse) form of pleasure: 'What pleasure is to be found in looking at a mangled corpse, an experience which evokes revulsion? Yet wherever one is lying, people crowd around to be made sad and to turn pale ... To satisfy this diseased craving, outrageous sights are staged in public shows.'[28] In recreating his air-meet public, D'Annunzio draws on Augustine's concept of *curiositas*. Attracted by the repulsive, the mass gathers around the suffering body and, eager to witness its breakdown, experiences a moment of enlightenment integrated with anxiety and pleasure.

Furthermore, the description reflects a sensibility that is marked by a wish to be ever stimulated, by the constant pursuit of distraction. The crowd's attention is drawn rapidly from one pilot to the next, leaving it no time to empathize with any one of the sufferers. If distraction is evident in the crowd's swift turns to ever new sensations of repulsion as driven by this uninterrupted series of misfortunes, it is seen even more vividly in the oscillation – which occurs without hesitation – between momentary feelings of repulsion and sudden outbursts of joy. The passage quoted above proceeds as follows:

> Un altro uomo, che volava nella nube, con un colpo temerario del timone d'altura calò giù a piombo come l'avvoltoio sul pasto; a poche braccia da terra si librò seguendo lo strazio dell'affocato che ancora s'avvolgeva sopra sé stesso invincibilmente, si sporse alquanto per riconoscerlo; lo guardò spento arrestarsi; rapido s'impennò, risalì per l'aria, s'inazzurrò nell'ombra, si dorò nel sole, continuò la sua rotta. Lo raggiunse l'urlo della folla in delirio:
> – Tarsis! Tarsis!
> . . .
> Un delirio crudele venò di rosso i mille e mille e mille occhi levati verso il convesso circo celeste. (*PRII* 591)

> [Another man who was flying in the cloud, with a rash blow of the rudder, came down, plumb, like a vulture onto its meal; he hovered at a few feet from the ground, tracking the agony of the burning man who still writhed and curled invincibly; he leaned out for a while to identify him; he watched him rest lifeless; he quickly reared up, went up again in the air, became blue in the cloud, gold in the sun, continued his route. The cry of the delirious crowd reached him:
> – Tarsis! Tarsis!
> . . .
> A cruel delirium painted with red veins the thousands, and thousands, and thousands of eyes, raised towards the convex celestial circus.]

Despite the sensational spectacle that firmly unites repulsion with pleasure, the flaming body of the writhing man grabs the crowd's attention only for an instant, before Tarsis's intact air route pulls a delirious cry out of the thousands of mouths, redirecting the thousands of eyes to the sky. What remains is neither an essential difference between the crowd's perception of fall and its perception of glory, nor one between the respective sensations of repulsion and joy; rather, a flattening succession of stimuli that, beautiful or hideous, grab the crowd's emotions with a steady force, revealing its affinity to distraction as a vital element of its psychological constitution.

Both the curiosity and the need for distraction that define D'Annunzio's crowd are psychosocial traits that received special treatment in this era. 'While the impulse to *curiositas* may be as old as Augustine,' argues Gunning, 'there is no question that the nineteenth century sharpened this form of "lust of the eyes" and its commercial exploitation.'[29] A particularly modern form of thrills, offered by new-sprung types of leisure, such as the cinema of attractions and the amusement park, relied on new technological discoveries to provide the public with extremely sensational views and bodily experiences.[30] Next to these phenomena, aviation itself was a form of spectacle that defined the sensibility of the era.[31] As D'Annunzio's work suggests, aviation played its own part in the fulfilment of the modern public's craving for thrills. Gunning draws on Maxim Gorky, Siegfried Kracauer, and Walter Benjamin, to speak of the modern public's affinity to distraction as the result of suffering a lack, as the loss of 'the coherence and immediacy traditionally attributed to reality [that] creates a consumer hungry for thrills,' a 'fragmentation of modern experience' the emotional void of which creates a taste for thrills and spectacle.[32] Let us recall that D'Annunzio's crowd 'shrieked, caught at the viscera, *not by pity for the dying man but by the delirium of the deadly game.*' The sensation occurs at the expense of compassion for the sufferer. If there is a lack that manifests itself in a modern fragmentation of experience and finds momentary fulfilment in a culture of distraction, part of the lost coherence is a human connection rooted in traditional values the erasure of which led to alienation. The delirium that grabs the air-meet crowd is D'Annunzio's way of describing that pressing 'hunger' for thrills, which bears alienation at its root.

If D'Annunzio's perception of the relation between alienation and distraction accords with Kracauer's and Benjamin's articulations of modern experience, one wonders whether his portrayal of modern spectacle nurtures the subversive potential that, according to the Frankfurt School thinkers, the culture of distraction and shock carries within. In

'Cult of Distraction: On Berlin's Picture Palaces' (1926), commenting on contemporary forms of film exhibition, Kracauer states that distraction carries a 'moral significance':

> Here, in pure externality, the audience encounters itself; its own reality is revealed in the fragmented sequence of splendid sense impressions. Were this reality to remain hidden from the viewers, they could neither attack nor change it; its disclosure in distraction is therefore of *moral* significance.
>
> But this is the case only if distraction is not an end in itself. Indeed, the very fact that the shows aiming at distraction are composed of the same mixture of externalities as the world of the urban masses; the fact that these shows lack any authentic and materially motivated coherence, except possibly the glue of sentimentality, which covers up this lack but only in order to make it all the more visible; the fact that these shows convey precisely and openly to thousands of eyes and ears the *disorder* of society – this is precisely what would enable them to evoke and maintain the tension that must precede the inevitable and radical change.[33]

While Kracauer does not specify exactly what physical shape this 'radical change' is to take, he most likely refers to the recovery of a form of life free of the alienation that industrial capitalism brought about. Thus, the 'moral significance' of distraction hinges on its dialectical function: not to deny fragmentation by privileging an artistic unity that fails to represent it, but to expose it and bring it to public awareness by making it the fundamental structural principle of spectacle.

Inasmuch as D'Annunzio is conscious of the correlation between distraction and alienation, nowhere does the narrative segment on flights state that this spectacle aims to make its audience conscious or critical of its own reality. To be exact, it does not do so *explicitly*, in that it makes no overt remark about the public's possible questioning, crisis, or gaining of awareness regarding its own experience or sensationalist reaction to the horror that it witnesses. Much less does the narration state that there is a need for any form of change. Rather, the discourse seems to maintain a morally detached attitude towards the crowd's own moral detachment. In this view, D'Annunzio's 'distraction,' along with the erasure of a basic human connection that it displays, reveals itself as an instance of pleasure for its own sake, or, to quote Kracauer, as 'an end in itself.' This aestheticist attitude that the novel maintains towards distraction (and destruction), along with its dematerialization of pain (which it turns into mere spectacle), attests to the novel's recourse to a decadent temperament.[34]

Nonetheless, as in the case of Inghirami's affinity with the machine, the violent and unpredictable aerial spectacle functions as the objective correlative of this crowd's subjectivity. It thus bears the potential to incite reflection, whether or not the author overtly says so. Kracauer introduces the notion of the spectacle as 'an end in itself' somewhat differently in 'The Mass Ornament' (1927). According to this essay, the legs of the Tiller Girls, arranged and moving in perfect linearity, resemble hands in the factory and reflect the instrumental or 'murky reason' that is 'the *Ratio* of the capitalist economic system.' They represent body parts devoid of human meaning, parts of a mass rather than 'individuals who believe themselves to be formed from within.' Whereas cinema has *'moral* significance ... only if distraction is not an end in itself,' regarding the 'mass ornament' Kracauer simply states that the 'ornament is an *end in itself.'*[35] He thus allows us momentarily to view the ornament as ideologically unidirectional, before he proceeds to address its value as the objective correlative of the urban masses, as 'the aesthetic reflex of the rationality to which the prevailing economic system aspires':

> Educated people – who are never entirely absent – have taken offense at the emergence of the Tiller Girls and the stadium images. They judge anything that entertains the crowd to be a distraction of that crowd. But despite what they think, the *aesthetic* pleasure gained from ornamental mass movements is *legitimate*. Such movements are in fact among the rare creations of the age that bestow form upon a given material. The masses organized in these movements come from offices and factories; the formal principle according to which they are molded determines them in reality as well. When significant components of reality become invisible in our world, art must make do with what is left, for an aesthetic presentation is all the more real the less it dispenses with the reality outside the aesthetic sphere. No matter how low one gauges the value of the mass ornament, its degree of reality is still higher than that of artistic productions which cultivate outdated noble sentiments in obsolete forms – even if it means nothing more than that.[36]

The mass ornament is an 'end in itself' when viewed on its own terms, whereas the critic seeks its dialectical function. Similarly, if D'Annunzio's aerial spectacle appears to be a form of pleasure for its own sake, 'an end in itself,' this does not preclude its ability to incite reflection, at least in the mind of the reader, if not also in the minds of its avid spectators. In a study that delivers D'Annunzio from conventional critical labels, aiming at a 'd'Annunzio without "isms" – not decadentism, not dandyism, not fascism, and symbolism only in part, or rather, d'Annunzio through – *isms*,' Paolo Valesio notes the moral, non-decadent, dimension of *Il piacere*. Sperelli's 'moral scruples were too definite, too firm. *Il piacere*, misunderstood as the immoral exaltation of pleasure, is in reality a moral narration, at times it is even moralistic.'[37] A moral position is unmistakable in D'Annunzio's remark that the crowd, I repeat, shrieked 'not by pity for the dying man but by the delirium of the deadly game,' which no doubt tends to elicit a critical response from the reader. It may not be the case that D'Annunzio anticipates Kracauer's rigorous critique of capitalism; but the technological inlays of *Forse che sì* surely expand the ideological horizons of this otherwise decadent tale, if subtly so.

That the portrayal of the historical event is radically conditioned by the author's temperament becomes clearest when examined against the aesthetic effect that aviation had upon another writer and one of D'Annunzio's contemporaries, namely, Marinetti. According to Jeffrey Schnapp, Marinetti's experience aboard Giovanni Bielovucic's biplane during the 1910 Milan International Air Week not only informs the opening statements of his 1912 'Manifesto tecnico della letteratura futurista,' but also opened a new range of cognitive possibilities that led the writer to formulate his radical concept of words-in-freedom.[38] The manifesto opens as follows:

In aeroplano, seduto sul cilindro della benzina, scaldato il ventre dalla testa dell'aviatore, io sentii l'inanità ridicola della vecchia sintassi ereditata da Omero. Bisogno furioso di liberare le parole, traendole fuori dalla prigione del periodo latino! . . .

Ecco che cosa mi disse l'elica turbinante, mentre filavo a duecento metri sopra i possenti fumaioli di Milano. E l'elica soggiunse: . . .

[In an airplane, sitting on the fuel tank, my stomach warmed by the pilot's head, I sensed the ridiculous inanity of the old syntax inherited from Homer. A furious need to liberate words, dragging them out of the prison of the Latin sentence! . . .

This is what the whirling propeller told me, while I was flying two hundred meters above the mighty chimney stacks of Milan. And the propeller added: . . .]

To tell us what 'the propeller added,' Marinetti enumerates those elements that will shape the formal structure of Futurist poetry: the abandonment of syntax, the use of verbs strictly in the infinitive, the elimination of adjectives, adverbs, and punctuation, and more (*TIF* 46–7).

According to Schnapp, these perceptual discoveries, later translated into the conception of a literary form, have much to do with the biplane's physical design. The latter accounts for the manifesto's oscillation between a 'poetics of agitated matter associated with aviation's links to the more "intuitive" senses of touch, smell, and hearing, and a poetics of image streams associated instead with aviation's impact on the faculty of sight.' Regarding the 'poetics of agitated matter,' the plane's design is such that the place designated for the passenger, which prevents him from communicating with the pilot because of the deafening noise, forces him to participate in the mechanical rhythms and physical vibrations emanating from the engine, thus intensely experiencing the machine's noises, weights, and odours. Moreover, the passenger's body, because of its post, forms a single physical unit with the engine. This 'body/machine complex,' particularly in connection with the conflicting sensations of power, unpredictability, and danger that flying involves, provides the structural model of Marinetti's poetics. For Marinetti, 'motors were meant to function as adversaries, as enemy doubles of a human subject who, in the process of taming the always menacing machine, was called upon to metallize himself and transform his own distinctive vital *scatti* [outbursts or fits], his own "breathing, sensibility, and instincts," into those of "metals, minerals, and wood."' Thus motors, for Marinetti, were not meant to be reliable and peril-free, as was the dream of turn-of-the-century mechanical and social engineers, exemplified in the Taylorist scientific management founded on 'notions of body/machine harmony, energy conservation, and freedom from fatigue.'[39]

In privileging the principle of discontinuity, unpredictability, and shock, Marinetti's poetics is clearly opposed to D'Annunzio's traditional style of narration. This is not to say that it aims further at the subversive effects that according to Kracauer and Benjamin inhere in the aesthetics of distraction and shock. Even if, on a strictly formal level, his poetics runs counter to the harmonizing aspirations of industrial capitalism, his valuing of aviation as the source of a structural model for poetry is aligned with his aestheticization of war. As regards the second component of his poetics, namely, the 'poetics of image streams' associated with aviation's impact on the faculty of sight, the experience aboard the biplane, again because of the precise position of the passenger's seat, provided a sense of unrestricted vision that strengthened Marinetti's 'conviction that aerial vision constituted an unmediated, accelerated, and synthetic mode of apprehending the real.'[40] This type of vision is not only the reverse of the perspective on aerial spectacle that is offered by D'Annunzio's crowd, but is also what fed Marinetti's aesthetics of analogy: the juxtaposition of things that appear mutually unrelated or hostile. The capacity to perceive similarities among seemingly unrelated things was born, as it were, out of modernity's novel experiences of movement, such as flying and other modes of rapid spatio-temporal displacements. Analogy itself involves an aesthetic of discontinuity, as a poem's juxtaposition of unrelated things is none but the successive layout of signs from the same linguistic category, such as a series of nouns not mediated by any elements of traditional syntax.

Yet during war, Schnapp explains, aviation was also valued in terms of efforts 'to develop aircraft for scouting, gunning, and bombardment purposes.' The battlefield's aerial vision that aviation provided instituted an absolute split between the earthbound perspective afforded the ordinary foot soldier and the overhead ubiquitous one of the commander. The latter, in spite of Marinetti's proposal to destroy the traditional 'literary I,' might engender a literary subject even more sovereign than that of traditional literature.[41] In fact, speaking of the 1911 Italian-Turkish conflict at the battle of Tripoli, where he worked as a war correspondent for a French daily – a battle that involved aerial surveillance, aerial photography, and aerial gunning, and that was filmed from the air by the documentary filmmaker Luca Comerio – Marinetti described it as 'the most beautiful aesthetic spectacle of my existence.'[42] It is this war that informs the content of his 'Battaglia Peso + Odore' (Battle Weight and Smell, 1912), a piece of writing exemplary of the words-in-freedom:

> Mezzogiorno ¾ flauti gemiti solleone **tumbtumb** allarme Gargaresch schiantarsi crepitazione marcia Tintinnìo zaini fucili zoccoli chiodi cannoni criniere ruote cassoni ebrei frittelle paniall'olio cantilene bottegucce zaffate (*TIF* 59)[43]

> [Noon ¾ flutes groans summer-heat **tumbtumb** alarm Gargaresch toburst crackling march Tinkling backpacks rifles clogs nails cannons manes wheels cases Jews pancakes bread-with-oil sing-songs workshops whiffs]

Tailored to the need of exalting 'the most beautiful aesthetic spectacle of [Marinetti's] existence,' the potentially subversive formal structure of these words-in-freedom does not escape his aestheticization of war, of which the affinity to Fascist imperialism Benjamin criticized in his famous essay 'The Work of Art in the Age of Its Technological Reproducibility.'[44] In this view, although Marinetti's response to aviation as a phenomenon that leads to the conception of an aesthetic of shock is sharply distinct from D'Annunzio's, the outcome is in no way less aestheticist than the product of D'Annunzio's decadent sensibility.

If Marinetti's discovery of aviation inspired the conception of a radical literary aesthetic, in D'Annunzio's case aviation provided the material for a fascinating subject matter to be well integrated within a conventional narrative form. The segment focusing on airplanes revolves around the two protagonists, Tarsis and Cambiaso, and is roughly divided into three stages: the heroes' preparations for the contest; their actual flying during which they witness the misfortunes of others and are reminded of aviation's deadly challenges; and Tarsis's victory and Cambiaso's death. The segment follows the conventional narrative climax that one would also expect to find in a traditional stage play. Having broken the record of altitude, Cambiaso experiences a moment of intense ambivalence. He tries to negotiate in his mind the knowledge of already being the winner against the desire to fly even higher. Like Icarus, he dares to realize that highest of ambitions. He gradually loses control until the plane dives headlong into the ground. The three plane crashes discussed above as distinct units of spectacle also constitute successive elements of narrative development, gradually building up the intensity of the action by presenting a steady increase in the volume of destruction and pain.[45] Yet all three pilots stay alive, only to reserve the final tragedy of death for the climactic scene that concerns the protagonist. It is during Cambiaso's flight alone that the crowd's cheering momentarily stops:

E nessuno più gridò, nessuno più respirò. Tutta quell'umana angoscia ebbe una sola faccia convulsa, un solo sguardo seguace: vide . . . la lunga fusoliera impennarsi, . . . urtare la terra con uno schianto che nel silenzio cavo dell'anima parve un tuono. (*PRII* 597–8)

[And nobody screamed any longer, nobody breathed any longer. All that human agony had one single convulsive face, one single following gaze: it saw . . . the long fuselage pitch, . . . crash into the ground with a blow that in the hollow silence of the soul seemed a thunder.]

While the previous crashes demand no pause or empathy, in Cambiaso's case the crowd is left dumbfounded and speechless. In a conventional fashion, the narrative elicits a unique emotional response from the reader when the protagonist's fate alone is at stake.

Nonetheless, while it primarily concerns the fate of the protagonist and does not fail, just before the fall, to describe his thoughts and emotions, this climax is also inseparable from the culminating point of arousal of the crowd's *curiosity*. The narration thus maintains the status of the flying contest as an exhilarating spectacle of danger and downfall until the very end:

> Poi di sopra gli steccati la folla si rovesciò sul campo, avida di vedere il sangue, di guardare la carne lacerata . . .
>
> – È morto? Respira? È schiacciato? Ha il cranio aperto? stronche le gambe? rotta la schiena?
>
> . . . Per vedere, i più avidi si chinavano sotto le pance dei cavalli, s'insinuavano tra le groppe, restavano stretti fra sprone e sprone.
>
> Come i rottami furono rimossi, districate le sàrtie, sollevate le tele, apparve il corpo esanime dell'eroe. (*PRII* 598)

> [Then the crowd threw itself over the fences onto the field, avid to see the blood, to look at the lacerated flesh . . .
>
> – Is he dead? Is he breathing? Is he smashed? Is his skull open? Are his legs cut off? Is his back broken?
>
> . . . In order to see, the most avid ones bent under the horses' bellies, crept in-between the horses' backs, rested straight between the spurs.
>
> As the scraps were removed, the shrouds disentangled, the cloths lifted, the hero's lifeless body appeared.]

If something in *Forse che sì* attests to D'Annunzio's initiation into the realm of modernism, it is neither a radical departure from the thematic premises of his earlier prose nor a ground-breaking formal structure marked by an all-encompassing discontinuity, as in Marinetti's words-in-freedom. Rather, it is the inclusion of a few stylistic elements that, quite inconspicuously, challenge his dominant adherence to the early D'Annunzio: the utilization of the specific signs of his time towards a reconfiguration of his protagonists; his insight into the correlation between an excitable public and modernity's unprecedented ways of providing thrills and spectacle – which, if not a rigorous ideological critique as in the writings of the Frankfurt School, tends somewhat towards the dialectical examination of spectacle that defines Kracauer's modernist humanism.

5

Through a 'Futuristic' Lens: D'Annunzio's Cinematic Re-Visions

The union of the old with the new, which D'Annunzio launched vigorously in *Forse che sì*, defines the core of his work on film, the inspiring force of automobiles and airplanes now giving way to the new aesthetic horizons delineated by cinematic technology. D'Annunzio's direct involvement with cinema, however, was rather sparse. Much of the critical work on the subject emphasizes not the author's creative engagement with the medium but his literary influence on the popular Italian cinema of the 1910s. It is said that his active interest in cinema began in 1908, when he visited a film studio and experimented with the tricks made possible by the medium's specific technology.[1] Yet his engagement with cinema is primarily associated with his intertitles for Pastrone's *Cabiria*, in which the extravagant mise-en-scène and pioneering use of the dolly, next to D'Annunzio's prestigious signature, are some of the things that secured the film's inclusion in the international silent cinema canon. After *Cabiria*, D'Annunzio wrote intertitles for a few other, much less celebrated, films.[2] He also completed three *soggetti*, or film scenarios, only one of which was realized as a film. The film adaptations of his novels and plays were much higher in number than the works that he wrote specifically for the screen. At least nineteen films were produced in Italy between 1911 and 1920 based on his works.[3]

Undeniably, the factor that accounts for Italian cinema's 'Dannunzianism' is not the quantity of work that D'Annunzio produced specifically for the film industry but a cultural climate permeated by his aesthetic outlook. 'Dannunzianism was in the air,' says Luigi Bianconi, one of the first to study D'Annunzio's relation to cinema. It was 'breathed by actors and directors, scriptwriters and cameramen . . . and by the public itself.'[4] As a critical category, 'Dannunzianism' denotes a mode of representation defined by stylistic excess, especially in the areas of acting and mise-en-scène, and by themes deriving primarily from antiquity and Decadentist literature. It is typically applied to two of the most popular Italian film genres of the 1910s: the *film storico*, of which *Cabiria* is exemplary, and the *cinema in frak*. The *storico*, aspiring to revitalize the glory of ancient Rome in the face of Italy's political campaign in North Africa, shared the writer's exaltation of antiquity and the national past.[5] The *frak*, in its glamorous depiction of an aristocratic class living in an antiquated era barely touched by technology's radical explosion, focusing on idle characters and fatal romantic passions unfolding in lavish parlours, nearby forests, and upper-class artists' ateliers, in a sense transported D'Annunzio's – or a D'Annunzioesque – high prose into the space of mass consumption.[6]

Inasmuch as Dannunzianism affirms literature's ability to influence film style, it fails to address other crucial aspects of that style itself, especially with respect to the medium's technical particularities, or its historical development in relation to factors other than Italian literature, such as other national cinemas. Also, while it confirms the industry's aspirations for cultural prestige through the exploitation of nineteenth-century literature, it overlooks what is indispensable for any study of D'Annunzio's relation to cinema, that is, the impact that cinema itself, as a dominant cultural phenomenon, may have had on the writer's own notion of art. In this chapter, I address the question of D'Annunzio and cinema by following a route other than the one defined by Dannunzianism. D'Annunzio's work dealing specifically with cinema illuminates an aspect of the author that his conventional reception as the 'prince' of Decadentism tends to obscure. His single and brief theoretical commentary on cinema, written in 1914, displays a strong affinity with the aggressive formulations of the Futurists. In line with the Futurist project, he proposes a film style that privileges an exhibitionistic display of technique, especially in its ability to show things unreal, while he envisions a space of exhibition that combines film with live performance. It is even uncertain whether D'Annunzio esteemed the aesthetic conventions and mode of exhibition associated with *Cabiria*, the epic with which scholarship has identified his relationship with cinema. This is not to say that his interest in film led him to refute traditional art with the conviction that characterizes Marinetti's outright rejection of it. D'Annunzio's *L'uomo che rubò la 'Gioconda'* (1920), a scenario that was never realized as a film, inspired by the possibilities that film technology introduced in the realm of aesthetics, presents an ambivalent view on the definition and social function of art in modernity.

Towards a 'New Aesthetic of Movement'

The single piece of non-fiction that D'Annunzio devoted to cinema is the short essay 'Del cinematografo considerato come strumento di liberazione e come arte di trasfigurazione' (Of Cinema Considered as an Instrument of Liberation and Art of Transfiguration, 1914). It is structurally peculiar in that it consists of the compilation of two sets of text, each produced on a separate occasion. D'Annunzio combined a number of newly written passages with the excerpts of an interview published in the *Corriere della Sera* on 28 February 1914, in anticipation of the imminent appearance of *Cabiria* in Italian theatres.[7] While the essay overall addresses the reasons for which D'Annunzio was drawn to cinema, the author's reassembling of the older parts alongside the newer ones resulted in a commentary that approaches the question of cinema's cultural significance from two different angles. The parts taken from the *Corriere* emphasize the medium's technical merits, such as the visual rendering of the marvellous and the spectacular portrayal of historical themes. The newer parts focus on cinema as an instrument with which to 'vindicate' the lost art of the theatre.[8] It is not surprising that an interview for a newspaper as widespread as the *Corriere della Sera*, insofar as it aimed to publicize *Cabiria* as an epic of unprecedented magnitude under the signature of Italy's most celebrated writer, concentrated on the medium's technical achievements. In revising the original document, however, perhaps intending to republish it as a more general reflection on the current state of the arts, D'Annunzio broadened the horizons of the subject matter to firmly situate and valorize cinema's technical inquiries in the context of what he saw as the crisis of the theatre.

The essay is divided into three sections. The first, written exclusively upon revision, attacks contemporary theatre for its state of degradation and proposes cinema as a solution. The acute polemical tone and specific figures of speech with which the essay opens recall Marinetti's similar criticism. The document grabs the reader with the urgency, boldness, and conviction of a Futurist manifesto. This sentiment emanates from the very first sentence, which speaks of renewal, movement, courage, and the need to destroy in order to rebuild.

> La recente industria del cinematografo – che pretende rinnovellare l'arte antica della Pantomima e potrebbe forse promuovere una novissima estetica del movimento – deve essere considerata come un'ausiliaria

provvidenziale di quegli artisti coraggiosi e severi che, nella ignobile dec-
adenza del Teatro d'oggi, aspirano a distruggere per riedificare. Bisogna in
verità augurare che il gusto sempre più vivo della folla per le rappresentazioni cinematografiche determini la rovina del basso commercio teatrale
ond'è disonorata l'epoca nostra. ('Del cinema' 115)

[The recent industry of the cinema – which wants to renew the ancient
art of the Pantomime and could perhaps promote a completely new aesthetic of movement – must be considered as a providential aid to those
courageous and severe artists who, in the ignoble decadence of today's
Theatre, aspire to destroy in order to rebuild. To tell the truth, we must
wish that the ever-livelier taste of the mass for cinema performances
brought about the ruin of the low commerce of the theatre, on account of
which our era is dishonoured.]

D'Annunzio does not specify what he sees as degraded in contemporary
theatre. In a tone that recalls Marinetti's disdain for passéism, he seems
to attack not all theatre but the kind of which the secure position in the
institution of art breeds complacency and idles creativity. Because of its
rapidly spreading popularity among the masses, he sees in cinema the
potential to effect a radical change. Exactly what shape this change is to
take and what the instrumental role of the masses will be are things that
to a large extent the essay leaves open to speculation. He wishes nonetheless to make his personal contribution to cinema's ability 'to destroy
in order to rebuild,' as we are told by a grotesque allegory the origin of
which he attributes to Leonardo da Vinci. In order to amuse himself, the
painter gathered a large amount of sheep entrails in his home. When visited by his most naive friends, he blew air into the entrails with a small
pair of bellows. The entrails grew to such proportions as to occupy the
entire room and make the friends run away in terror. Applying Leonardo's
allegory to the present, D'Annunzio compares the naive friends to those
foolish men from whom the modern stage is now liberated, thanks to
the 'improvviso e smisurato sviluppo della "pellicola" girante' [sudden
and excessive growth of the spinning 'celluloid']. He concludes, polemi-
cally: 'Ecco perché io stesso, col mio manticetto, mi adopero a gonfiarla'
[This is why I myself, with my little bellows, strive to pump it up] ('Del
cinema' 115). What reinforces the Marinettian spirit of this opening is the
amusingly grotesque image of the pumped-up entrails as a metaphor for
cinema, which, in contrast to the theatre's firm position in official culture,
invaded and destabilized the sphere of spectacle with a bold arrogance.

At the same time, D'Annunzio makes a leap away from the initial Marinettian spirit. The 'bellows' with which he 'pumps up' the 'spinning celluloid' is none but the author's pen, with which he wrote the celebrated intertitles of *Cabiria* and this very essay. What is clearly anti-Marinettian is that either project injects cinema with high literariness. As regards *Cabiria*, D'Annunzio was not the first *letterato* to write for the film industry. Years earlier, the industry had begun to exploit the creativity of numerous Italian writers – a phenomenon that Brunetta calls 'the great migration.' Yet as far as the final product was concerned, it was common for the contributions of these men of letters to go unrecognized, despite the respect that they may have enjoyed in the literary world. What was special about D'Annunzio's case is that his literary identity was not effaced. His contract with Itala Film was based on unique terms that reflected the industry's interest in the author's name itself as testimony to the film's artistic value and as an effective marketing strategy.[9] Pastrone, the producer and director of *Cabiria*, had already worked extensively on the film when he asked D'Annunzio to write the intertitles, invent a title, and assume the film's paternity. The poet received the exorbitant amount of 50,000 lire at a time when European film producers typically paid no more than 3000–4000 lire for the writing of a scenario.[10] As a result of assuming the film's paternity, D'Annunzio was received as the main figure responsible for its aesthetic qualities.[11] This obscured the role of Pastrone, whose unique craftsmanship, responsible, among other things, for the pioneering use of the dolly, secured *Cabiria*'s inclusion in the canon of silent film.[12] Furthermore, next to the film's publicity under the poet's signature, the intertitles brought a strong Dannunzian element into the viewing experience. By comparing a segment from D'Annunzio's intertitles to Pastrone's screen instructions, Brunetta demonstrates the highly lyrical prose with which the poet interpreted Pastrone's work. This resulted in a 'double textuality,' Brunetta claims, a stylistic rupture between image and verbal text. The latter produced its own autonomous connotations with an unprecedented effect on the mass audience's reception of the film.[13]

Despite the essay's Marinettian opening, D'Annunzio does not cite Marinetti as the inspiration of his polemic. Rather, he mentions Edward Gordon Craig (1872–1966), a practitioner and theoretician of the theatre: 'Come ben dice il precursore Gordon Craig, il primo passo verso il nuovo Teatro non dev'essere se non un passo verso una condizione di libertà' [As the precursor Gordon Craig rightly says, the first step towards the new Theatre must be but a step towards a condition of freedom] ('Del cinema' 115–16). Indeed, what D'Annunzio will propose for cinema is more in line with the views of the English writer whom he invokes. This is not to say that Craig and Marinetti have nothing in common. In fact, they share a critique of the theatre founded on the rejection of verisimilitude. Craig scorns European theatre for being haunted by the urge to carry out a photographic reproduction of nature. The 'business men' of the theatre, he argues, are extremely efficient in making the stage swarm with natural-seeming scenery and action. Yet they are not artists, because 'naturalism,' or 'realism,' insofar as it relies on the mere imitation of nature, has nothing to do with art.[14] Craig is not on Marinetti's side, however, as regards the necessity to propose an alternative. To be sure, he does not define his alternative in a mathematical fashion. The 'Art of the Theatre,' he advises, has its own laws, most of which are still waiting to be discovered.[15] Nonetheless, the idea that runs through his writings and contributions to theatre practice is contrary to Marinetti's indiscriminate passion against all 'Art with a capital A' (*TIF* 86). If Marinetti wished to make a mockery of traditional art by reducing all of Shakespeare to a single act (89), Craig conceived many of his creative 'stage-scene' designs specifically for some highly esteemed Shakespeare plays.[16]

What is it that distinguishes Craig's vision of 'the new Theatre' and how does that relate to D'Annunzio's idea of cinema as an art form? In its essence, according to Craig, the theatre is defined by the primacy of the visual over the verbal. He appeals to the 'first dramatist,' evidently the Greek who, knowing something that the modern dramatist ignores, namely, that the audience would prefer to '*see* what he would do than to *hear* what he might *say*,' 'spoke either in poetry or prose, but always in action: in poetic action which is dance, or in prose action which is gesture.'[17] The three basic materials out of which the artist of the future will create his masterpieces emphasize the theatre's performance more than its literary aspect:

> And when I say *action*, I mean both gesture and dancing, the prose and poetry of action.
> When I say *scene*, I mean all which comes before the eye, such as the lighting, costume, as well as the scenery.
> When I say *voice*, I mean the spoken word or the word which is sung, in contradiction to the word which is read, for the word written to be spoken and the word written to be read are two entirely different things.[18]

Craig's idea of 'action' has no relation to 'natural' action, which implies mere imitation. He rejects not nature but its imitation. The privileged position of dance in his concept of theatre derives from his belief in movement as a supreme force that gives birth to everything else, including music. Through the 'divine power of Movement' the artist is able to reveal 'invisible things, those seen through the eye and not with the eye.'[19] His idea of dance refers not to the cultivation of highly controlled and mechanical motions but to movement as a direct expression of the soul. Nature has a rhythm, he seems to imply, which the soul understands and may express through the body. 'In Art there must be created no feeling of disharmony between the Body and the Soul, yet in creating Art the body must be obedient, true, faithful to the Soul.'[20]

The second section of D'Annunzio's essay, excerpted from the *Corriere* interview, begins with a commentary that concentrates on some formal aspects of the theatre ('Del cinema' 116–18). Yet it provides a theoretical framework that gives insight into the author's comments on film form. While Craig is not mentioned here, this part bears a strong affinity with his vision of the theatre of the future. D'Annunzio speaks of what he calls a crisis of the word and an ever-broader predominance of music in theatre: 'I migliori spettacoli recenti . . . non sono se non azioni mimiche accompagnate dalla sinfonia e talvolta dal coro. Assistiamo a una improvvisa esaltazione del senso ritmico' [The best recent shows . . . are but mimic actions accompanied by the symphony and sometimes by the chorus. We are witnessing an unexpected exaltation of the rhythmic sense]. As they are accompanied by music, the 'mimic actions' denote not the mere imitation of life but the practice of mime, which relies on bodily movement and gesture rather than words. Furthermore, if Craig praises the 'first dramatist' for having perceived his audience's craving for dance and gesture, D'Annunzio himself invokes a specific figure from Greek drama: 'Sembra che ritorni fra noi l'imagine di quel Frinico il quale si vantava di aver nello spirito tante figure di danza "quante onde solleva una notte procellosa, durante l'inverno, sul mare"' [What seems to return among us is the image of that Phrynichus, who used to boast of having as many figures of dance in his spirit 'as a stormy night stirs waves, during winter, on the sea'].[21] Hence, in defining what he considers noteworthy contemporary spectacle, D'Annunzio shares Craig's belief in a primordial union between nature, soul, and dance. Those waves of a stormy night represent the rhythm of nature, of which the innumerable vibrations imprint themselves upon the soul and take the form of a dance. In a broader view, we learn something of the contesting positions on art inspired by the challenges and new horizons of this phase of modernity. For the ideal spectacle of the future both writers seek a model in antiquity, thus assuming a position diametrically opposed to Marinetti's, whose art, in defiance of anything that preceded it, is in search of an unknown future while guided by the invigorating noise of the propeller.

With reference to Craig, we may clarify some of D'Annunzio's lyrical statements. 'I personaggi sono lontani, così che qualunque contatto con essi ci sembra impossibile come con i fantasmi; ma la sinfonia rischiara il fondo reale che li produce' [The characters are faraway, such that any contact with them seems to us impossible, as with ghosts; but the symphony illuminates the real ground that produces them]. Like Craig, he values the predominance of music over naturalistic diegetic action. The characters' resemblance to 'ghosts' does not mean that they are unreal, but that the concept of character as based on verisimilitude is diminished. Their realness, Craig might say, is their intimate connection to nature, conveyed through the musical rhythm that accompanies their presence. D'Annunzio describes the pages of his novel *Il fuoco* as 'accese di presentimento' [kindled with foreboding], not to claim ownership of the ideas that he presents here but to draw on a specific thought – one that differs, but not irreparably, from Craig's *movement* as the primal divine source. Namely, it is *music* that, 'per mezzo de' suoi motivi, ci dà il carattere di tutti i fenomeni dell'Universo nella loro intima essenza' [by means of its motifs, gives us the character of all the phenomena of the Universe in their intimate essence].

To reaffirm the necessity of looking into the past, D'Annunzio again invokes Greek drama: 'Si sa che la strofe nella sua origine primitiva era una cornice destinata ad essere riempiuta da una serie ben composta di movimenti corporei' [We know that the strophe in its primitive origin was a frame destined to be filled by a well-composed series of corporeal motions]. In view of this new emphasis on rhythm, music, and dance in theatre, he raises this question: How can the poet balance the word with mime and symphony? He answers: 'bisogna ricordarsi che il concetto musicale perde la sua purità primitiva quando divien dipendente da rappresentazioni *estranee*, in sé, al genio della musica' [One must remember that the musical concept loses its primitive purity when it becomes subordinate to performances that are themselves *foreign* to the genius of music]. He thus implies that the modern poet, as a reincarnation of the Greek dramatist, must find a way to reconcile his love for words with his rediscovery of the primacy of music. By no means will he abandon literature for music; but he must not be a naturalist. Rather, his words must strive to have a rhythm, a musical sense. He must privilege the sound, the shape, and the texture of the utterance, not its verisimilitude. Nature is not to be imitated but interpreted and reassembled into aesthetic forms: 'sentimenti, passioni, luoghi, persone, costumi e altre particolarità estranee non sono – per il poeta – se non segni da interpretare e ... non han senso se non nei loro rapporti e nelle loro gerarchie. L'arte s'allontana dalla natura, per creare tipi impreveduti di bellezza' [feelings, passions, places, people, costumes, and other external details are not – for the poet – but signs to interpret and ... have meaning only in their interrelations and hierarchies. Art distances itself from nature, in order to create unexpected standards of beauty].

The essay's transition from the remarks on theatre to a discussion of cinema strikes us as somewhat abrupt. D'Annunzio smoothes the transition with a rhetorical device, a radiant metaphor that draws a direct, if short-circuited, link between antiquity and modernity – what further upholds the idea of the reincarnation of the Greek dramatist, now through the filmmaker:

> Sul fianco dell'Acropoli ateniese, che domina il Teatro di Diòniso, v'è un muro nudo, d'una nudità sublime, che sembra fatto per le apparizioni di domani. ('Del cinema' 118)

> [On the side of the Athenian Acropolis, which overlooks the Theatre of Dionysus, there is a nude wall, of a sublime nudity, that seems to be made for the apparitions of tomorrow.]

The analogy between the cinematic screen and an immense piece of white marble 'made for the apparitions of tomorrow' is unmistakable in an essay on cinema. In introducing cinema through the filter of classical sublimity, perhaps D'Annunzio wishes to elevate the medium's cultural prestige – not only because this was the industry's aim in imprinting *Cabiria* with his signature, but also to dignify his own, if more practical, motives for participating in a culturally 'lesser' medium. Though it is questionable that he esteemed cinema as an industry, *Cabiria* provided a major source of income such as he always welcomed. It is also possible that he viewed cinema as yet another means towards fame, next to journalism and literature.

Such utilitarian considerations do not diminish the theoretical weight of his insight into the film medium as a modern aesthetic form. Valentina Valentini makes relevant remarks on the relationship between theatre and cinema. In praising the predominance of music in the 'best recent shows,' Valentini notes, D'Annunzio was influenced by the Ballets Russes, whose success in Europe under the direction of Sergei Diaghilev was owed to their unorthodox spectacle, integration of action with music, dance, and painting, and exclusion of the traditional use of the word.[22] The style of the Ballets Russes, she specifies, also entered cinema. It was evident in the emerging genre of '"the musical cinematic drama," similar to the musical choreographic drama, created by the most modern Russian composers,' under which she lists *Cabiria*. Hence, according to Valentini's reading, although D'Annunzio does not mention cinema in this segment, cinema constitutes his more exact, if implicit, referent. She further suggests that D'Annunzio invokes Greek drama because it offers an aesthetic form that he would like to see implemented in cinema: 'Though confronting an essentially visual expression, such as cinema, D'Annunzio does not abandon the idea that, compared to all the arts, music is the dominating apparatus.' For this reason, she concludes, 'he was re-proposing also for cinema the ancient model of Greek theatre as a frame – through the strophe – in which to unitarily contain dance, music, and song.'[23]

Following Valentini's hypothesis regarding the 'musical cinematic drama,' we may speculate that, in describing characters as 'ghosts,' when speaking of 'the best recent shows,' D'Annunzio refers to their two-dimensionality and artificial colour on film. However, as regards the re-proposing 'for cinema the ancient model of Greek theatre,' Valentini does not define the form that such a union would assume. Furthermore, her suggestion that D'Annunzio's vision of cinema relies on the use of music in a literal sense contradicts the crucial statement with which the author decisively introduces his commentary on film form: 'Consideriamo intanto il Cinematografo come uno strumento di liberazione. Ma non potrebbe esso tuttavia divenire un'arte silenziosa, profonda e musicale come il silenzio?' [Meanwhile we consider Cinema as an instrument of liberation. But couldn't this anyhow become a silent art, profound and musical like silence?] ('Del cinema' 118). Let us note that D'Annunzio inserted this statement upon revising the *Corriere* interview, evidently to link two parts – one on theatre, one on cinema – the thematic continuity of which was not obvious. The statement resumes the essay's opening discourse about cinema as a form of liberation from the decadent state of the theatre, thus suggesting that the segment on theatre directly preceding it is parenthetical.

Hence, his praise of 'the best recent shows' may not relate to cinema as directly as Valentini suggests, but may serve to identify a cultural ambience ready to accept new and innovative forms of spectacle. If performances based on mime and music are one such form, cinema can be another. More important, the statement indicates that the use of music in cinema in a literal sense is not indispensable. He praises those innovative performances not only because they include music but also because they lean towards the mystical and sublime origins of drama that lie in musical rhythm. Cinema as well, to be an art, must cultivate its own musical rhythm – yet within the parameters of its technical specificity, which is silence. I agree with Valentini's remark that music dominates in D'Annunzio. Let me add, however, that this idea speaks not of music as a distinct form but of the *musicality* of *any* form: the emphasis on the phonetic value of language in literature, on the physical texture of the sign in any art, on the form as distinguished from the content. Like literature, cinema will have music in its very silence, because silence itself is, as he states, 'profound and musical.'[24] Giorgio Bertellini describes the idea accurately when he states that cinema, for D'Annunzio, was 'the realm of fantastic transfigurations, surprising metamorphoses which could *visually articulate melodic waves* and fascinate even the simplest minds of the masses' (emphasis added).[25]

It is in this context that we must read D'Annunzio's brief comments on film form, presented in his religiously cited – yet not adequately analysed – passage on Ovid's myth of Daphne. Several years back, he claims, thinking that the new medium of film could promote 'una nuova estetica del movimento' [a new aesthetic of movement], and give birth to an art the essential element of which was the 'meraviglioso' [marvellous], he spent many hours in a film studio in order to find out how he could benefit from those things that people of the trade called tricks. He was struck by the realization that Ovid's *Metamorphoses* was a true cinematic subject. He experimented by filming the transformation of Daphne's arm into the branch of a tree:

> Non feci se non un braccio: *il braccio che dalla punta delle dita comincia a fogliare sinché si muta in ramo folto di alloro,* come nella tavoletta di Antonio del Pollaiuolo che con gioia rividi a Londra pochi giorni fa. Mi ricordo sempre della grande commozione ch'ebbi alla prova. L'effetto era mirabile. Il prodigio, immoto nel marmo dello scultore o nella tela del pittore,

si compieva misteriosamente dinanzi agli occhi stupefatti, vincendo d'efficacia il numero ovidiano. La vita soprannaturale era là rappresentata in *realtà palpitante*. ('Del cinema' 118; emphasis added)

[I made but one arm: the arm that *from the tips of the fingers begins to grow leaves until it changes into a thick branch of laurel*, as in the canvas of Antonio del Pollaiuolo that I saw again with joy in London a few days ago. I always remember the great emotion that I experienced about the result. The effect was marvellous. The wonder, motionless in the sculptor's marble or in the painter's canvas, mysteriously took place in front of my astonished eyes, surpassing in effectiveness the Ovidian verse. Supernatural life was there represented in a *palpitating reality*.]

In asking how 'a silent art' can be 'musical like silence,' one thinks of those aspects of the medium – such as montage, camera movement, variations in the mise-en-scène – that produce changes in what the spectator sees, hence the 'musical' rhythm resulting from the frequency or pace with which the changes occur. Though D'Annunzio's passage on Daphne makes no mention of the film techniques that it presupposes, one thing is certain: the transformation is not the effect of a single cut. The arm '*begins* to grow leaves *until* it changes into a thick branch.' He speaks not of an instant change but of a slow and gradual process. A glance at Pollaiuolo's painting to which he compares the scene confirms this. At each shoulder, instead of an arm, Daphne bears a wooden branch that sustains a round green bush as large as her entire body (figure 5.1). Even a slow dissolve would not suffice, since the transformation, as he specifies, begins at the tips of the fingers and proceeds gradually towards the shoulders. A complex animation technique would be needed to depict the process as he describes it. We also imagine that only a slow and gradual process would convey the lyricism of Ovid, the Renaissance painting, or D'Annunzio's own. More important, if indeed it achieved the gradual accumulation of the countless leaves as in the painting, as well as conveyed the sense of repetition that defines anything that is 'palpitating,' the scene would acquire a sense of musical rhythm, something like a motif's repetition and variation. Each step of the process, each new leaf or set of leaves would resemble the one that preceded it. At the same time, the cumulative function of each individual step would only intensify the spectator's anticipation of the marvel's full realization.

Figure 5.1 Daphne turns into a tree in Antonio del Pollaiuolo's *Apollo and Daphne* (probably 1470–80). (© National Gallery, London / Art Resource, New York)

D'Annunzio proceeds with another Marinettian-like remark. The Ovidian experiment was interrupted because the immense creative effort required would not pay off in practical terms:

> I fabbricanti ad ogni *tentativo insolito* oppongono l'esecrabile 'gusto del pubblico.' Il gusto del pubblico riduce oggi il cinematografo a una industria più o meno grossolana in concorrenza col teatro. ('Del cinema' 118; emphasis added)

> [The manufacturers, against every *unusual attempt,* oppose the abominable 'taste of the public.' The taste of the public today reduces cinema to a more or less coarse industry in competition with the theatre.]

His interest in cinematic tricks involves not the tricks that serve verisimilitude, but those that depict the impossible, the otherwise nonseeable. Whatever film techniques the scene of Daphne would require, it constitutes an 'unusual attempt,' pointing to D'Annunzio's interest in form and his preference for an abstract style over verisimilitude. In describing cinema as a 'coarse industry in competition with the theatre,' he attacks the feature-length narrative film, which in 1914 was widespread in Italy. It is the kind of cinema that two years later Marinetti was to attack with words similar to the above, as a 'theatre without words' of which the adherence to narrative and verisimilitude suppressed the medium's Futuristic potential. In addition, like analogy, which constitutes the predominant aesthetic category in the Futurist film manifesto, D'Annunzio's 'unusual attempt' relies on film technology to show what the eye cannot otherwise attain.[26] This is not to overlook the crucial differences between the two tropes. If D'Annunzio brings to life the well-known myth of Daphne, a marvel that human imagination nurtured for centuries, analogy surpasses the concretization of a pre-existing idea. Like the new perspective that the airplane affords the eye, it opens a range of possibilities for *conceiving,* not merely *representing,* an idea. Let us recall that analogy 'connects distant, seemingly different and hostile things' (*TIF* 48). Furthermore, whereas D'Annunzio seeks a slow and gradual process in order to prolong the thrill of finally witnessing what always fled the eye's territory, Marinetti's application of analogy to cinema profits from the ability of a single cut to catch the viewer unawares.[27]

Yet D'Annunzio's Daphne is not strictly antithetical to the avant-garde project. The mere fact that the eye could bear witness to what only the mind had previously imagined bore revolutionary significance.

If analogy presumably turns its back on the past to generate a pure future, Daphne recreates the past anew, through a 'Futuristic' lens. Of course, cinema had achieved the visualization of the impossible long before D'Annunzio's interview or alleged film experiment. The use of tricks to represent the marvellous had appeared in Méliès films more than a decade earlier. Yet D'Annunzio announces – in 1914 – cinema's technical potential in the present tense, as though it were a novelty: 'Tecnicamente, non v'è limite alla rappresentazione del prodigio e del sogno' [Technically, there is no limit to the representation of prodigy and dream] ('Del cinema' 118). This indicates not that he ignored the facts, but that he was being polemical. He advocates exactly that style of representation, that 'unusual attempt,' for the suppression of which he criticized the film industry. In this view, his attention to the very moment in which the arm *begins* to grow leaves is significant. It speaks to that sensibility that in the early Lumière exhibitions required that the film were first presented as a still image, before the projector began cranking and the image moved.[28] Thus, the eye revelled not only in movement but also in that initial moment of transformation, when it had the first inkling that it was about to witness a 'miracle.' Does not D'Annunzio's Daphne, like the avant-garde, borrow from early attractions their 'exhibitionist confrontation,' to propose an alternative to narrative cinema?[29]

In view of D'Annunzio's rescuing the representation of the marvellous from marginality, valorizing its abstract quality and display of technique, his long eulogy of *Cabiria* in the essay's third and last section seems to be as much a contradiction as a marketing imperative ('Del cinema' 118–22). One wonders if *Cabiria* belongs, in his view, to the kind of cinema that the 'abominable taste of the public' reduces to a 'coarse industry.' As in his attack on the theatre, he offers no specific example of this 'coarse industry.' Let us recall that the interview was a form of publicity for *Cabiria*'s upcoming release. D'Annunzio never overtly states that he finds *Cabiria* aesthetically inferior to his vision of Daphne, yet he introduces his praise of *Cabiria* with irony:

Io stesso – per quella famosa carne rossa che deve eccitare il coraggio dei miei cani corsieri – ho lasciato cincischiare in *films* alcuni dei miei drammi più noti. Ma questa volta (oh disonore! onta indelebile!) m'è piaciuto di fare un esperimento diretto. ('Del cinema' 118)

[I myself – for that notorious red meat that ought to excite the courage of my greyhounds – let butcher some of my best-known plays into *films*. But

this time (oh dishonour! indelible disgrace!) I was pleased to perform a
direct experiment.]

Even if the single gain from having a contract with the film industry is financial rather than aesthetic, to distinguish *Cabiria* as a
Dannunzian experiment suffices, for the marketing purposes of
this interview, to ascribe aesthetic value to the film, in spite of what
D'Annunzio's definition of art may be. As a conscientious employee,
he gives a lengthy and grandiloquent account of the film's subject
matter, with references to mythology and the glory of Ancient Rome.
He describes *Cabiria* as 'il più grande e ardito sforzo che sia mai stato
fatto in quest'arte' [the greatest and most daring effort ever made in
this art].[30] Yet he does not relinquish his critical integrity as a poet:
'Non cesso tuttavia di pensare al delicato braccio di Dafne converso
in ramo frondoso. La vera e singolare virtù del Cinematografo è la
trasfigurazione e . . . Ovidio è il suo poeta' [I do not cease however to
think of Daphne's delicate arm converged in a leafy branch. Cinema's
real and single virtue is transfiguration and . . . Ovid is its poet] ('Del
cinema' 122).[31]

A sharper contradiction marks his attitude towards the cinema
public. If the 'abominable taste of the public' reduces cinema to a
coarse industry ('Del cinema' 118), we wonder how it is that the 'taste
of the mass for cinema performances' is our chance to overthrow the
base commerce of the theatre (115). Let us note that the remark about
the public's 'abominable taste' comes from the *Corriere* interview, while
the faith in cinema's mass public belongs to the part added upon revision. Perhaps the immense success in the interim of *Cabiria* launched
as a Dannunzian work appeased D'Annunzio's disdain for the masses.
The final excerpt from the interview, however, allows us to reconcile
the two parts more substantially:

> O prima o poi, la poesia delle *Metamorfosi* incanterà la folla che oggi si
> diletta di così sconce buffonerie . . . [D]ico, senza ombra d'ironia, che un
> buon bagno di mitologia mediterranea per il pubblico del Cinematografo
> sarebbe d'incalcolabile efficacia. ('Del cinema' 122)

> [Sooner or later, the poetry of the *Metamorphoses* will enchant the mass that
> today enjoys such obscene drolleries . . . I say, without a shade of irony, that
> a good bath of Mediterranean mythology for the Cinema public would be
> of incalculable effectiveness.]

As the essay's title announces, cinema is both 'an instrument of liberation and an art of transfiguration.' Let us look further into this dual qualification. 'Transfiguration' clearly refers to the portrayal of the 'marvellous' through 'tricks.' If it selects Ovid as its exemplary primary source, as in the case of Daphne, cinema will become art: it will divert attention from the criteria of verisimilitude to the musicality of form; it will secure its place in a millennia-old tradition, since it will now depict in a radical way those primal things that inspired artistic creation throughout the ages. The 'transfiguration' on the screen, however, is also a prerequisite for its counterpart, that is, the 'transfiguration' that must take place off screen. As the passage implies, with Daphne's metamorphosis, a transformation will befall the audience, once the latter is subjected to the medium's enchanting qualities. To be sure, its mass popularity gives cinema its strength, but not if the masses are moving in the 'wrong' direction, practising their 'abominable taste' unto infinity. First, a 'bath of Mediterranean mythology' is needed to refine their now vulgar sensibility – to thus put cinema's strength into a productive use, to let it actualize its revolutionary potential, to turn cinema into an 'instrument of liberation.'[32]

Whom is cinema to liberate, from what, and how? D'Annunzio's wish is not to abolish theatre and replace it with cinema. Evoking Craig, he states that theatre itself must be vindicated, must be liberated from the things that inhibit its creativity. The essay's opening offers an anthropomorphic, if misogynistic, metaphor that he also attributes to Craig:

> La scena è come una femmina isterilita da cui noi aspettiamo la nascita di qualche cosa . . . Ma lasciamola un poco in pace perché ella possa ritrovare in sé stessa un moto di fecondità . . . E, se pure ella non sia per ritornare più mai, manderà verso noi la sua figliuola o il suo figliuolo. 'Un figlio delicato e forte' augura Gordon Craig. ('Del cinema' 116)

> [The stage is like a sterilized woman from whom we expect the birth of something . . . But let us leave her in peace for a bit so that she can find again a flow of fecundity in herself . . . And if she is not to return ever again, she will send us her daughter or son. 'A delicate and strong son' augurs Gordon Craig.]

To be reborn, the stage needs cinema's intervention. The metaphor returns to conclude the essay:

> E quando, a imagine dei budelli fantastici ingegnati da Leonardo, la 'pellicola' gonfiata da soffii potenti e cresciuta a dismisura avrà invaso tutte le scene

e ne avrà cacciato la miseria e l'ignominia d'oggi, allora soltanto potremo
sperare di veder giungere verso noi l'Invocato e l'Aspettato: il fanciullo 'delicato e forte' concepito all'ombra delle colline armoniose. ('Del cinema' 122)

[And when, in the image of the fantastic entrails engineered by
Leonardo, the 'celluloid' pumped up by strong blows and grown out of
proportion will have invaded all the stages and driven away from them
today's poverty and shame, only then will we be able to hope to see the
Invoked and Expected reach towards us: the 'delicate and strong' young
boy conceived in the shadows of harmonious hills.]

We are speaking of cinema not as a separate institution but as an aesthetic element to be included in live performances, to thus penetrate
the stage and restore its fecundity. The 'delicate and strong' boy is not
cinema alone but the offspring of the union between stage and screen.
D'Annunzio does not provide enough details for us to ponder the
affinities of this 'delicate and strong boy' with Marinetti's designation
of the variety theatre and the *serata futurista* as spaces of film exhibition, or with the inclusion of films in early attractions. It is true, nonetheless, that aiming for a union between film and stage challenges the
model of the film auditorium proper, which next to the growth of the
feature-length narrative and explosion of *divismo* was becoming a dominant institution at the time. One still wonders, however, what exactly
the instrumental role of the masses is in the formation of this 'liberated' spectacle. Evidently, it is also a question of economics. Only after
their cultural metamorphosis is completed, having been enchanted by
D'Annunzio's 'bellows,' will the masses overthrow the institution of
cinema, as well as that of the theatre, because they will demand to see
cinematic magic on the theatrical stage – a demand that the producers
must fulfil if they wish to stay in business. If this romantic formula
strikes us as overly optimistic, not to say unrealizable, it is because it
leaves a fundamental question unanswered: What was it that made cinema so popular in the first place? D'Annunzio's ambivalent attitude
towards the masses reflects the confrontation between Art (with a capital A) and a rapidly spreading form of mass entertainment that is able,
so it seems, to 'pump up' its own 'spinning celluloid.'

Mona Lisa's Gaze

The definition of art in modernity is a central question in D'Annunzio's
L'uomo che rubò la 'Gioconda.'[33] Though never actualized as a film, the

scenario exemplifies the author's will to experiment with the aesthetic techniques specific to cinema. With a few exceptions, including an extensive study by Irene Gambacorti, the scenario has received little scholarly attention, in spite of – or perhaps because of – its atypical qualities vis-à-vis the D'Annunzio canon.[34] In her enlightening work, Gambacorti shows that D'Annunzio had a strong interest in the aesthetic possibilities of cinema, and in line with the aspirations of the avant-garde, he used the medium as a means to challenge the traditional barrier between high art and mass culture.[35] While I share Gambacorti's views, I will expose a further, essential dimension within D'Annunzio's text. In writing the scenario, being inspired precisely by cinema's technological specificity and ability to disrupt the high-low dichotomy, D'Annunzio envisioned the creation not only of a film that would entertain the movie-going public but also of a *film essay* – one that would address intellectuals and, by means of an allegory, articulate a 'thesis' concerning the very definition of art in modernity. Masterful artworks, the scenario teaches, are distinguished by an element of 'spirituality' that has its roots in the reverential function of art in religious ritual. The survival of this spiritual element is highly at stake in the face of technology's radical effects in the sphere of aesthetics. D'Annunzio articulates the phenomenon that Benjamin was to describe as the decay of the artwork's 'aura' in the age of its technological reproducibility – that is, notwithstanding the fundamental differences between the two writers' conceptual, ideological, and stylistic premises.

L'uomo che rubò la 'Gioconda' was inspired by the 1911 theft of Leonardo's masterpiece from the Louvre.[36] Through trials and sacrifices, and with a determination akin to that of a scientific explorer, the 'mystical Flemish painter' Peter Van Blömen, alias Orizzonte, discovers the alchemical principle that enables him to bring to life the human figures depicted in great paintings. For the preparation of the *cordastrum,* as Van Blömen names the invented substance, it is necessary to use the warm blood of a man's heart immediately after his death.[37] With the assistance of his young Italian accomplice Castruccio Lunelli, Van Blömen steals the *Gioconda* and brings it to one of her greatest admirers worldwide, the poet Gabriele D'Annunzio, now living in exile in Arcachon of France.[38] The Poet is possessed by the prospect of a flesh-and-blood encounter with Mona Lisa, whom he always perceived as his ideal love. He murders Lunelli and offers his blood to the alchemist. The experiment is successful but short-lived. Soon after she is brought to life, Mona Lisa dissolves. Hoping to bring the enigmatic woman back to the now deserted landscape, Van Blömen returns to his home and applies his alchemical operations onto the canvas. During a visit by Gian Giuseppe Vermeer, a man who wilfully blinded himself in an attempt to affirm his Christian faith, Van Blömen is astonished to see Mona Lisa reappear against her familiar background. He departs for Paris to redeliver the painting 'ai sogni del mondo' [to the world's dreams] (*TSM* 1198).

The scenario is as much a list of laconically described events, seeking their actualization in a visually complex film narrative, as it is a self-sufficient piece of literature. As a screenplay, it exploits the properties of film technology and adheres to existing patterns of cinema narration. Film technology facilitates the representation of things unreal, as exemplified in the animation of Mona Lisa, who walks away from the canvas and then dissolves. In addition, the scenario includes elements that suggest the use of montage and camera movement, as well as an expressive use of mise-en-scène, especially in the area of lighting.[39] Nonetheless, the scenario insists equally upon its status as a work of literature. This is not surprising, given that several years before completing this work, and inspired by the theft of the *Gioconda*, D'Annunzio had begun to write *L'uomo* as a novel, which however he never completed.[40] At its very opening, the scenario displays its lyrical tone and the narrator's culturally and historically informed approach to the subject matter: 'Un pittore mistico fiammingo, discendente da quella generazione di pittori che diede alla corte dei Papi lo *Standardo* [*sic*] e l'*Orizzonte*' [A mystical Flemish painter, descendant of that generation of painters who gave to the court of the Popes *Standardo* and *Orizzonte*] (*TSM* 1173). If this statement serves as intertitles aiming to introduce the protagonist to the spectator, it surely addresses a well-informed spectator, or at least one whose delight in the myth of Dannunzianism would compensate for the lack of comprehension, since nowhere will the narration make an explicit connection between the protagonist's actions and his cultural ancestry as presented here.[41] Yet the literary approach is mainly evident in the scenario's autonomy as a text, both in terms of its narrative closure, which is independent of its filmic realization, and in terms of the lyricism with which it strikes the reader. 'In spite of the narrative crystallization in detached scenes,' states Sergio Raffaelli, 'there exists a logical continuity from episode to episode that establishes a complete and autonomous fantastic universe.' Raffaelli observes that in the entire work only two statements constitute proper *didascalie*. They stand out, as they disrupt the narrative style of the fictional text.[42] Furthermore,

Valentini describes the scenario as the 'outline of a non-written novel' in the fragmentary style of D'Annunzio's *Notturno*.[43]

We may view the scenario's formal tension between a literary and a cinematic mode of representation as a symptom of D'Annunzio's hesitation to relinquish literature for a strictly instrumental use of language servicing an aesthetic project that officially lies elsewhere. This hesitation, however, is also part of the larger dilemma that informs the scenario's essayistic dimension, namely, the question of the artwork's fate in modernity.[44] The affinity between D'Annunzio's notion of 'spirituality' and Benjamin's 'aura' lies, among other things, in the inherent relationship that each one has with the utilitarian function of art in religious ritual. Van Blömen's adventure with the *Gioconda* is inspired by a spiritual incident. In this Flemish city resides Vermeer, '*L'Uomo che perdette lo sguardo*' [*the Man who lost his gaze*] while contemplating and adoring a painting of the Virgin at the altar of the local cathedral. His eyes 'vedono ma non guardano' [see but do not look], specifies the narrator, obviously to distinguish the faculty of vision from intellectual and inquisitive observation, the renunciation of the latter being a distinct mark of the eminently pious. Since that day, the canvas 'ha in sé qualcosa di più ricco, di più luminoso e di più patetico' [has within itself something richer, brighter, more pathetic] (*TSM* 1173). The following passage, which strikes us more as a philosophical reflection for its own sake than as a scene in a film, links the event to a universal phenomenon:

> La spiritualità che s'accumula intorno alle grandi opere d'arte, intorno ai grandi capolavori umani.
>
> I pensieri, i sentimenti, le imaginazioni, i sogni suscitati dai quadri famosi, dalle statue famose.
>
> La massa enorme di emanazioni umane, che grava su le imagini gloriose e ne dilata all'infinito la potenza e la bellezza.
>
> Gian Giuseppe Vermeer non soltanto ha lasciato lo sguardo ma la miglior parte della sua anima e della sua vita su quella tavola d'altare.
>
> Non s'è egli *transustanziato* nella figura divina? (*TSM* 1173–4)

> [The spirituality that accumulates around great works of art, around great human masterpieces.
>
> The thoughts, feelings, imaginations, dreams provoked by famous paintings, famous statues.
>
> The great mass of human emanations that weighs upon glorious images and expands endlessly their might and beauty.

Gian Giuseppe Vermeer has left not only his gaze but also the best part of his soul and life on that altar painting.

Has he not *transubstantiated* himself in the divine figure?]

At first glance, rather than being an inherent quality of the artwork, the supernatural semblance involves the projection of a human experience onto the object. As regards the religious painting in particular, its utilitarian appropriation for ritual may very well be arbitrary. The faith projected onto it will overshadow the arbitrariness. This projection is expressed in the metaphor of 'transubstantiation.' The lost 'gaze' of the faithful does not simply disappear but is retraceable in the image of the Virgin. In man's possession, the will for knowledge becomes the primary cause of secular progress. In the case of the genuinely humble, it is willingly and totally surrendered. Such is the case of Vermeer, a man of 'blind' faith, in whose eyes the Virgin appears to be alive. Having fully absorbed his soul, his will for knowledge, his critical consciousness, She gives him the impression of gazing back as omniscient.

The passage tidily separates secular categories from religious ones – thoughts, feelings, imaginations, dreams, or soul, transubstantiation – at the same time that it unites them under the indistinct notion of the 'human emanations' that weigh upon the images. Immediately following the telling of Vermeer's experience, this flexibility allows for a smooth shift of emphasis towards secular art:

V'è nel mondo un'opera d'arte, quasi magica, che per secoli ha affascinato l'imaginazione dei poeti. Generazioni di contemplatori e di sognatori hanno creato intorno ad essa un'atmosfera spirituale d'una intensità incalcolabile.

È la *Gioconda* del Vinci. (*TSM* 1174)

[There is in the world a work of art, almost magical, that for centuries fascinated the imagination of the poets. Generations of contemplators and dreamers have created around it a spiritual atmosphere of an incalculable intensity.

It is the *Gioconda* by Vinci.]

Thus, the *Gioconda*, like the Virgin, is enshrouded by her own 'spiritual' halo. In this case, however, the halo is stored up by the contemplation not of the eminently humble but of 'dreamers,' whom Van Blömen will see at the Louvre in a circle of 'ecstatic' men, who are fully absorbed in what the narrator now distinguishes as the painting's 'enigma seco-lare' [secular enigma] (*TSM* 1179). By juxtaposing the religious with the secular, D'Annunzio implies that the 'spirituality' of secular art is a result of reverential treatment that is carried over from the function of art in religious ritual.

In 'The Work of Art in the Age of Its Technological Reproducibility' (third version, 1939), Benjamin will also recognize the 'basis' of the aura in ritual. Unlike D'Annunzio, in whose narrative the two phenomena occur synchronically, Benjamin emphasizes the historical shift from rit-ual proper to 'secularized ritual.' 'The secular worship of beauty, which developed during the Renaissance and prevailed for three centuries, clearly displayed that ritualistic basis in its subsequent decline and in the first severe crisis which befell it.'[45] He explains this change in terms of a 'displacement':

> In the viewer's imagination, the uniqueness of the phenomena holding sway in the cult image is more and more displaced by the empirical uni-queness of the artist or of his creative achievement. To be sure, never com-pletely so – the concept of authenticity always transcends that of proper attribution ... [T]he concept of authenticity still functions as a determi-ning factor in the evaluation of art; as art becomes secularized, authenti-city displaces the cult value of the work.[46]

He has already defined 'authenticity,' an essential part of the aura, as a secular condition. It is 'the quintessence of all that is transmissible in it from its origin on, ranging from its physical duration to the historical testimony relating to it.'[47] No doubt, 'authenticity' as a product of histori-cal testimony is part of D'Annunzio's description of the *Gioconda*, and not only because of its centuries-long veneration in a museum. In antic-ipating the alchemist's miracle, the Poet thinks enviously of Bonaparte, 'che ebbe a Fontainebleau il quadro di Leonardo *nella sua camera da letto*' [who had Leonardo's painting *in his bedroom* at Fontainebleau] (*TMS* 1189). Furthermore, the synchronicity of the two 'rituals' in D'Annunzio does not negate the effect of 'displacement,' insofar as that is a social or psychological phenomenon as well as a historical one. In other words, the aesthete's or the non-believer's adoration of art is like a religion, which does not, however, eradicate from history the cult function of art in ritual proper. The text implies that what occurs in the case of the *Gioconda* is itself a form of 'transubstantiation,' another projection of human experience onto the painting – if not of religious faith, of the 'thoughts, feelings, imaginations, dreams' invested by 'generations of contemplators and dreamers' – as a result of which, in the eyes of its 'dreamers,' Mona Lisa appears to be gazing back.

The concept of the reciprocal gaze, which Benjamin presents in his essay on Baudelaire, is fundamental in the definition of the aura as experienced in natural objects. An essential characteristic of common human interactions, it refers to the anticipation that 'the person we look at, or who feels he is being looked at, looks at us in return.' The projection of this human response onto our encounter with inanimate objects accounts for their aura. 'To experience the aura of a phenomenon means to invest it with the capability of returning the gaze. This experience corresponds to the data of the *mémoire involontaire*.' Upon actualization of the experience, the reciprocating gaze is accompanied by the object's 'unique appearance of a distance.' In this case, 'distance' does not refer to the object's spatial proximity to the subject. It may be understood, rather, in terms of Freud's 'uncanny.'[48] It refers to a *temporal* distance, an unconscious past invoked by the encountered object, which instantaneously grabs the subject by way of *mémoire involontaire*, as the latter is explained in Proust.[49] The experience of the aura 'is neither immediate nor "natural,"' explains Miriam Hansen, but 'involves a sudden moment of transference' while 'the gaze that nature appears to be returning . . . confronts us with another self, never before seen in a waking state.'[50]

Benjamin alludes to the psychoanalytic basis of the phenomenon also in his comments on art. Like objects in nature, art has the capability of provoking an uncanny experience. When that occurs, we perceive it as beautiful. Drawing on Valéry, he defines our perception of the beautiful as something that infinitely regenerates itself: 'The painting we look at reflects back at us that of which our eyes will never have their fill. What it contains that fulfills the original desire would be the very same stuff on which the desire continuously feeds.'[51] From a psychoanalytic viewpoint, the 'stuff' refers to the trace of a pre-Oedipal memory, the vague invocation of which exhilarates because of its suggestiveness, while its immateriality sustains the desire: 'What makes our delight in the beautiful unquenchable is the image of the primeval world.' Art reproduces beauty when, upon its sight, the subject detects a familiar yet indefinable trace: 'Insofar as art aims at the beautiful and, on however modest a scale, "reproduces"' it, it retrieves it (as Faust does Helen) out of the depths of time.'[52]

The capability of awakening a primordial past is also an attribute of the *Gioconda* – not because Freud interpreted the enigmatic smile as

Leonardo's unconscious search for the smile of his mother (from whom he had been separated at a very early age),[53] but because D'Annunzio's scenario itself points in that direction from the start. Van Blömen begins to experiment with alchemy and painting only to bring back the life of a lost 'perfetto amore' [perfect love] (*TSM* 1173). More important, the 'beautiful,' in the sense of self-regenerating, is very much a trait of the *Gioconda,* whose 'spirituality,' upon her admirers' contemplation, 'di continuo si rinnova' [continuously renews itself] (1179). Furthermore, in speaking of the ecstatic admirers' enchantment with the female figure, the narrator emphasizes their status as her 'amanti solitarii' [lonesome lovers] (1179). This lonesomeness is the result of relinquishing human relations in the search for an ideal. It forewarns of the fate of the Poet who, known to be 'uno dei più acuti amanti della *Gioconda*' [one of *Gioconda*'s keenest lovers] (1180), will forever lose Sonia, his lover in flesh and blood, as a consequence of preparing the ritual of Mona Lisa's animation.

After Van Blömen and Lunelli arrive in Arcachon, the Poet conceals from Sonia his possession of the painting. Noticing the secrecy surrounding the two strangers, Sonia is overcome by jealousy, as she intuitively perceives that the situation concerns 'un segreto "femminile"' [a 'female' secret] (*TSM* 1188). To satisfy her curiosity, in a femme-fatale style that evokes her Dannunzian predecessors, she seduces Lunelli, who then falls madly in love.[54] They meet in the nearby forest during a fire, pictured in a spectacular sequence that leads to their death. Lunelli becomes the victim of the Poet's dagger in a duel inspired by jealousy. Horrified upon witnessing the extraction of Lunelli's heart for the preparation of the *cordastrum,* Sonia mounts her horse and rushes into the rapidly advancing flames. Her death provokes no immediate reaction on the Poet's part. Only later, while speaking to Mona Lisa during her brief animation, does the Poet mention Sonia for the first time. However, that is less an expression of longing for Sonia than a part of his love confession to Mona Lisa. His words imply that Sonia's death was necessary for the attainment of another love that is perceived as ideal: 'Ho ucciso il mio amore per te: il mio ultimo amore, per te che sei il mio amore unico e vero ... Ho dato tutto al fuoco ... perché tu m'eri stata promessa' [I killed my love for you: my last love, for you who are my only and true love ... I gave everything to the fire ... because you had been promised to me]. Any consummated love affair is a compromise, a substitute for a lost primordial love: 'Ho cercata te in tutte le amanti. Ho cercato su tutte le labbra voluttuose il tuo sorriso' [I looked for you in all my lovers. I looked for your smile on all the voluptuous lips] (1195–6).[55]

The unsettling tone of this love confession expresses the Poet's disappointment in seeing that once Mona Lisa is animated she bears the gaze of a mere stranger: 'Nessuna comunione. I secoli stanno tra lui e lei ... Non ha più il sorriso misterioso che Leonardo trasse con la musica da quell'anima mediocre e ignara' [No communion. The centuries stand between him and her ... She no longer has the mysterious smile that Leonardo drew with music from that mediocre and unaware soul] (*TSM* 1195). What she loses is her 'spirituality,' or her 'aura.' The dialectic of distance and closeness, essential in the experience of the aura, also defines the Poet's perception of Leonardo's painting. This is confirmed at the moment in which the aura is lost, when the Poet becomes suddenly aware of the centuries that separate them, and experiences the distance emanating from her now alienated gaze not as auratic but as absolute and impenetrable:

> Sei viva e respiri. Sei viva e parli.
> O eri più viva quando non respiravi, quando non parlavi?
> O eri più vicina a me quando avevi dietro le spalle le rocce inaccessibili e le acque tortuose? (*TSM* 1196)

> [You are alive and breathe. You are alive and speak.
> Or were you more alive when you weren't breathing, when you weren't speaking?
> Or were you closer to me when you had behind your shoulders the inaccessible rocks and the tortuous waters?]

The distance that now marks her gaze, bearing no familiar trace, is comparable to the stare of the eyes described by Baudelaire, in those verses that Benjamin reads as an expression of the demolition of the aura. Those eyes do not return the gaze but instead 'look at us with mirrorlike blankness.' Thus, they 'know nothing of distance,' insofar as 'distance' signifies what is also its opposite, that is, something familiar, a deep-rooted closeness.[56] To be sure, the enigmatic smile, which the alchemist unwittingly eradicates, is not exclusive to the figure of Mona Lisa but D'Annunzio's equivalent of the 'aura' in art. Its meaning reaches beyond its literal association with a person's facial composure: 'Nella tavola senza figura rimane il divino paesaggio di rocce, dove l'acqua tortuosa sembra perpetuare divinamente il sorriso umano'

[In the figureless painting remains the divine rocky landscape, where the tortuous water seems to divinely perpetuate the human smile] (*TSM* 1194). That the artwork's ability to grab the subject is not tied to the depiction of female beauty is confirmed when Mona Lisa disappears. Van Blömen and the Poet turn to the painting to see whether she resumed her original post: 'No. Non è ritornata. Lo sfondo è deserto. Ma il paese di rocce e di acqua *sorride* come Monna Lisa' [No. She did not return. The background is deserted. But the town of rocks and water *smiles* like Mona Lisa] (1196–7).

Benjamin finds a definition of the aura in Proust. He quotes a statement that displays a striking affinity with D'Annunzio's comments on 'spirituality':

'People who are fond of secrets occasionally flatter themselves that *objects retain something of the gaze* that has rested on them.' (The objects, it seems, have the ability to return the gaze.) 'They believe that monuments and pictures appear only through a *delicate veil which centuries of love and reverence* on the part of so many admirers *have woven* about them.' (emphasis added)

The idea that the admirers' gaze accumulates around the artwork leads to a different concept of the aura than what is suggested by its definition as a projection or transference. While the latter concerns the momentary invocation of a past that resides permanently within the subject, the former implies that the aura resides upon the object itself, and that it is stored up over time. Like Proust's 'veil,' D'Annunzio's 'spirituality' is the residue of the gaze that 'accumulates around the great works of art,' an 'atmosphere' that 'generations of contemplators and dreamers have created around' the *Gioconda*. Proust's narrator, however, views those 'people who are fond of secrets' with critical distance: 'This chimera ... would become truth if they related it to the only reality that is valid for the individual – namely, the world of his emotions.'[57] Similarly, the passage on 'spirituality' seems to represent the reflections not of the author but of the character of Van Blömen. It follows his conversations with 'l'Uomo senza sguardo' [the Man without a gaze], which Van Blömen carries because he is attracted 'da questo mistero' [by this mystery] (*TSM* 1173). From the alchemist's metaphysical perspective, 'transubstantiation,' which I have thus far interpreted as a metaphor, is literal: 'Has he not *transubstantiated* himself in the divine figure?' This rhetorical question favours the empirical verifiability of transubstantiation and posits Vermeer's testimony as proof.

D'Annunzio's text, however, establishes an ambivalent position as regards the permanence of 'spirituality' in the artwork. For one, the narrator's separation from the characters is not always evident. The scenario oscillates between the objective remarks of an omniscient narrator and those ambiguous ones that may or may not represent the characters' thoughts. For instance, the interrogative sentence mentioned above is not explicitly attributed to the mystic. The author possibly uses this ambiguity in order to mimic, with irony, the characters' sensibility. At the same time, he does not definitively mock the idea that a mystical element resides in art. It is important that Mona Lisa reappears in the presence of Vermeer, who now is not only 'without a gaze' but literally blind. Fascinated by the mystery of Vermeer's lost 'gaze,' Van Blömen steals the painting of the Virgin from the altar. He wants to collect its spiritual substance and apply it to the recovery of the man's 'gaze.' Vermeer, however, is profoundly opposed to this prospect. He rejoices in having donated something so precious to the Virgin. 'No. Tu non commetterai questo sacrilegio' [No. You will not commit this sacrilege], he tells Van Blömen. The zealous alchemist carries out his plan nonetheless. Vermeer instantly notices a change in the image: 'È diminuito lo splendore' [The splendour diminished]. He also recognizes his own image in a mirror. He realizes that his 'gaze' has been restored and the votive offering he made to the Virgin has been annulled. To compensate for the sacrilege, he grabs a knife and repeats 'l'atto disperato di Edipo' [the desperate act of Oedipus] (*TSM* 1175–6). Whether Vermeer's 'gaze' stands for empirical observation or the probing into one's repressed past, the knowledge that it bestows is of a secular kind. Vermeer blinds himself because he is confronted with his own capability of seeing truth with a secular eye. His self-sacrifice transforms him into a vessel of pure 'spirituality.' It is his mere presence that brings Leonardo's Mona Lisa back to her mysterious landscape. Perhaps, D'Annunzio allows us to speculate, what makes a secular artwork a masterpiece is that it is *not completely* secular. The painting of the Virgin, *any* painting of the Virgin, absorbs the soul of the pious by virtue of its religious function. May any secular painting, however, be arbitrarily deemed a masterpiece? What is it that makes it 'almost magical' and worthy of adoration? Perhaps something divine dwells therein, the essence of which evades the intellect, and for which reason D'Annunzio selects 'spirituality' as its name.

Despite the autobiographical allusions, the Poet alone does not represent the author's viewpoint. The scenario's thesis on art encompasses the diverse attitudes of the Poet, Vermeer, and Van Blömen. In the Poet, D'Annunzio rehearses his own public image as an aesthete, which he contrasts with the figure of Vermeer. If in different ways, the reference to Oedipus describes both characters. Vermeer's voluntary blindness is a reaction against the trauma of knowledge. It makes him a model of Christian faith, but also of repression. The Poet, by contrast, wishes to possess the enigmatic woman in flesh and blood. What attracts him to Mona Lisa is her 'aura,' her uncanny quality, that element of hers that is familiar yet alienated through repression.[58] This familiar trace arouses in the Poet a pre-Oedipal wish, the wish to return to a state of complete un-repression. Differently from Vermeer, the Poet would like to be an Oedipus whose eyes remain intact. He would like to have his cake and eat it too.[59] Overall, while Vermeer's religiosity affirms that art is sacred, the Poet's aestheticism draws a 'secular enigma.' The juxtaposition of the two attitudes, whether contesting or complementing each other, proposes a complex characterization of traditional art. However, the anachronism of meeting an alchemist in 1911 presents a case about the redefinition of art in the era of modern technology.[60]

As an alchemist, Van Blömen needs to reconcile his metaphysical outlook with his experiential one. Not only does he believe in transubstantiation, he also advocates its practical use: 'Con quale arte si può riconoscere, sceverare, isolare, restituire tali elementi accumulati?' [With which art can one recognize, sever, isolate, restore such accumulated elements?] (*TSM* 1174). Once he succeeds in restoring Vermeer's 'gaze,' he develops a higher ambition: 'La sostanza spirituale può essere alchimiata, può essere convertita in apparizioni sensibili' [The spiritual substance may be alchemized, may be converted into perceptible apparitions] (1177). He invents the *cordastrum* and is ready to steal the *Gioconda*. His wish to make the intangible tangible, next to his refusal to please Vermeer, upon whom he imposes a secular view of the world, indicates that his drive for empirical experimentation surpasses his reverence for the mystical. As in the case of the Virgin, his experiment with the *Gioconda* produces a woman without a 'smile.' Let us recall, however, that Van Blömen is above all a painter. His alchemical ventures, anachronistically set in 1911, refer allegorically to his role as an artist. He represents a time of ambivalence as regards the very notion of art: between an object of reverence and a phenomenon of which the negotiation with modern technology threatens its aura. Evidently, without Vermeer's presence, Van Blömen's devices fail to recover Mona Lisa. By this day, his sense of 'spirituality' is diminished.

Despite the qualities that 'spirituality' and 'aura' share, the waning of the phenomenon as represented in the allegory of the 'fallen' alchemist differs from Benjamin's analogous idea in 'The Work of Art.'[61] In this essay, the 'decay of the aura' bears a vast social significance. It rests on *'the desire of the present-day masses to "get closer" to things spatially and humanly,'* to overcome *'each thing's uniqueness by assimilating it as a repro-duction.'*[62] Van Blömen's attempt to animate Mona Lisa for the Poet's pleasure has little to do with the masses' takeover of culture. The Poet, who bears traits of the Dannunzian aesthete and Superman, is neither troubled by the reverential quality of the masterpiece nor excluded from the institution of high art. On the contrary, he is enchanted by those things that account for the painting's 'aura' – its authenticity, uniqueness, permanence, and inapproachability – while he considers himself entitled to the rare privilege of having unlimited access to the masterpiece. Furthermore, with respect to technique, the loss of Mona Lisa's 'spirituality' is an effect not of technical reproduction but of the alchemist's ability to transform the intangible – that is, the sacred, the enigmatic – into the tangible.

However, if the transition from Leonardo's painting to Van Blömen's 'dull' Mona Lisa constitutes an allegory, the allegory points to a jux-taposition that exceeds the diegesis, between Leonardo's painting and D'Annunzio's screenplay. As in the case of reproduction that entails the technological nature of the medium, it is D'Annunzio's consideration of cinema's technical specificity that warrants the literal depiction of the alchemist's achievement. Like Daphne's transformation, Mona Lisa's animation consists of a display of cinematic tricks:

> Il prodigio.
> L'animazione dell'immagine.
> La figura viva si stacca dalla tavola.
> Esce Intera. (*TSM* 1194)
>
> [The prodigy.
> The animation of the image.
> The living figure detaches itself from the painting.
> She exits entirely.]

Hence, compared to the Poet, the painter/alchemist, whose reverence for the mystical is in crisis, is a more accurate representative of D'Annunzio – the lover of sublime art, yet the real-life inventor of a 'dull' Mona Lisa.

Moreover, should this invention aspire to upset the social function of the traditional artwork as an object of reverence, it is only through the process of mechanical reproduction, insofar as the scenario is written with a film in mind, that its ideological repercussions would be actualized in the sphere of reception.

Does the scenario indeed question the status of the artwork as an object of reverence?[63] The Daphne experiment, which constitutes the visual translation of a literary work, does not seem to either question the cultural status or interfere with the aesthetic integrity of Ovid's treasure. To be exact, it does not self-admittedly do so. The poem's dissemination through its various adaptations in other artistic forms both defies its authority and modifies its aesthetic qualities, insofar as adaptations interpret the poem for us. What distinguishes the scene of the 'dull' Mona Lisa is the conspicuous manner in which it advocates, through cinematic tricks, not merely the *adaptation* of an artwork originating in another medium, which was common in cinema, but the visual *modification*, in a literal sense, of an already visual work. It thus promotes an intervention that leads to a candid distortion of the original. Furthermore, we do not fail to perceive the humour with which D'Annunzio conceived this distortion. Once we try to imagine Mona Lisa's animation through film, we think of the technical factors involved. Such is the question of acting. Which one of the Italian divas will play Mona Lisa? Will she appear with no make-up, or eyebrows, so as to reproduce her ethereal beauty? Will she be instructed to suspend the diva's usual histrionic gestures, to convey the sobriety that marks the Florentine lady? Or will she retain make-up, gestures, and all the rest, in order to draw out the enigmatic lady's 'fatale' side (adhering, of course, to the period's cinematic conventions of the femme-fatale style)?[64]

With its irony, the scenario participates in what was to become a tradition of *Gioconda* send-ups, still at an early stage in 1920. Its earliest known example is Sapeck's drawing of *Mona Lisa with a Pipe* (1887), while its most famous one from this early period is probably Marcel Duchamp's provocative *L.H.O.O.Q.* (1919) (figures 5.2 and 5.3).[65] Furthermore, the animated Mona Lisa is in line with the radical experiments proposed by Marinetti and the Futurists in their 1916 manifesto on film: specifically, filmic transcriptions of passéist poetry that faithfully turn metaphors into images, thus rendering them literal. The 'irreverent' result, for the amusement of modernity's ardent public, is the complete ridicule of the poem. Such would be, for instance, the aforementioned transcription of Carducci's 'my heart fled to the Tyrrhenian Sea,' showing the poet's

Figure 5.2 *Mona Lisa with a Pipe* by Eugène Bataille (aka Arthur Sapeck, French, 1854–1891 / Photo-relief illustration in C. Cadet, *Le Rire* [Paris, 1887], p. 5 / Collection Zimmerli Art Museum at Rutgers University, acquired with the Herbert D. and Ruth Schimmel Library Fund / 1992.0734 / Photo by Jack Abraham)

heart that 'pops out of his jacket and flies like a huge red balloon over the Gulf of Rapallo' (*TIF* 142–3). Likewise, to animate Mona Lisa means to render literal the 'enigma,' the live gaze, the chimera sustained by generations of 'dreamers'; and in the footsteps of Marinetti, to distract the contemporary viewer, whose adoration of high art, or his exclusion from it, shall yield to freshly articulated aesthetic and cultural horizons.[66]

Surely, this 'irreverent' treatment sheds further light on the question of 'spirituality.' It indicates a tongue-in-cheek attitude, rather than a sincere conviction, on the author's part when he speaks of art as sacred or enigmatic. This, however, does not definitively negate the ample space and thematic gravity granted the stories of Vermeer and the Poet, and thus their personal encounters, sacred or secular, with the artwork. The mockery, which contests, rather than rejects, tradition, produces an overall irresolute position regarding the question of art's

Figure 5.3 Mona Lisa with a goatee in Marcel Duchamp's *L.H.O.O.Q.* (1919). (CNAC / MNAM / Dist. Réunion des Musées Nationaux / Art Resource, New York; © 2011 Artists Rights Society [ARS], New York / ADAGP, Paris / Succession Marcel Duchamp)

role in society. In closing with the recovery of the *Gioconda*, D'Annunzio restates his respect for the Renaissance masterpiece; yet he does so only after declaring his separation from the masterpiece, after asserting his own scenario's distinctiveness as a non-traditional work of art. After all, he reminds us that Leonardo's *Gioconda* is shut inside the Louvre, while his own '*Gioconda*,' potentially a film, shall meet us in numerous other spaces.

6

The Humoristic Image
in Pirandello's *Si gira ...*

As in the case of D'Annunzio and other Italian authors of that time, financial necessity urged Luigi Pirandello to offer his literary talent to the film industry. He began writing original scenarios as early as 1911, soon to promote the adaptation of his novellas and plays.[1] However, whereas the critical work on D'Annunzio emphasizes the author's literary impact on popular film aesthetics, Pirandello's work has generated much reflection on the effect that cinema itself may have had on the author's world view, especially in response to the extensive treatment that cinema receives in his controversial and widely studied *Si gira*, first published in 1915 as a serial in *Nuova Antologia*, then as a single volume in 1916, and again in 1925 as *Quaderni di Serafino Gubbio operatore*.[2] Cameraman Serafino Gubbio, the novel's protagonist and first-person narrator, formulates a pessimistic critique of the institution of cinema, which he portrays as the emblem of the mechanization of life and alienation in industrial modernity. He describes himself as a thing, a 'hand that turns the handle,' and the camera as a monstrous beast that devours life only to regurgitate it in 'idiotic fictions.' The novel tends to perplex the reader regarding the extent to which the narrator's negative views on cinema and modernity stand for Pirandello's. It was not until the late 1920s that Pirandello expressed unequivocally his faith in cinema's potential as an aesthetic medium, as evident in his 1928–9 collaboration with Adolf Lantz in adapting his play *Sei personaggi in cerca d'autore* into a screenplay (never actually filmed), as well as his brief 1929 commentary 'Se il film parlante abolirà il teatro' (Will Talkies Abolish the Theatre?).[3] Studies have exposed, however, Pirandello's long-lasting and multifaceted relationship with the institution of cinema, suggesting that its condemnation in *Si gira* need not be taken at face value.[4]

They have addressed some prejudices that resulted from literal read-ings of the novel and explored its theoretical implications concerning film as a paradigmatic medium of modernity. They recast the novel's critique in the context of Pirandello's essay on humour, thus presenting his attitude towards the medium as ambivalent, to say the least.[5]

My analysis of several key elements in the novel will focus on cru-cial aspects of the relationship between cinema and humour that have not been adequately explored. This chapter will reinterpret Gubbio's multilayered portrayal of Varia Nestoroff, the enigmatic diva at the Roman production house where Gubbio is a cameraman, as well as his speculations on possible alternative methods of filming that exceed the camera's standardized use by the film industry. In spite of his over-all discontent, Gubbio endorses the cinematic medium insofar as it may assault the viewer with unconventional images that are able to intimate human truths otherwise suppressed by an illusory daily exis-tence. These are images of the kind that an industry devoted to 'idi-otic fictions' rejects. Yet we must not take Gubbio's faith in them at face value. Reading *Si gira* demands a constant reassessment of the degree to which Gubbio's views correlate with Pirandello's. On the one hand, in spite of his status as a character in the novel, which deprives him of narrative omniscience, Gubbio's authority as a narrator is so pervasive that we hesitate to disengage his thoughts from Pirandello's. On the other hand, the identification between the two figures is far from abso-lute. An important point of distinction concerns Gubbio's belief that an extraordinary image may signify obscure and otherwise ignored aspects of human experience. Contrary to Gubbio's belief, such images are no less fictional than the narrative films that he denounces. A study of the novel in light of Pirandello's theory of humour suggests that cinema may indeed allude to truth via its ability to enact a process of *reflection*, which entails not an investigation of the allegedly authentic qualities inherent in any single isolated image, but a continuous inter-play between diverse and competing – albeit fictional – images.[6]

Gubbio's notebooks comprise the events that unfold at Kosmograph, the Roman production house where he is employed, as well as his recol-lections of the past, alongside his obsessive hypothesizing on the psy-chological motives of the numerous individuals whom he encounters.[7] Inasmuch as Gubbio cynically boasts his impassibility as a mechanical hand, thus alluding to his ability to remain an objective observer, he has a personal stake in the events that he recounts and is not a reliable narrator. This is evident in his encounters with the alluring Nestoroff, a Russian émigrée and Kosmograph's leading star. Gubbio briefly met Nestoroff years earlier, before she became an actress, at the Mirelli country villa in Sorrento, which he often visited because of his friendship and intellectual bond with the Mirelli son and idiosyncratic artist Giorgio. Nestoroff came to the villa as Giorgio's fiancée, soon to have an affair with Aldo Nuti, who was at the time engaged to Giorgio's sister, Duccella. Her infidelity had tragic consequences for the Mirelli family. It drove Giorgio to suicide, which left an emotional scar on Gubbio and still infiltrates his perception of Nestoroff both as a person and as an actress.

Nestoroff's perfidiousness is not the only problem that Gubbio encounters in what he sees as the corrupt, alienating, and dehumanizing world of commercial film production. Despite her high status at Kosmograph, Nestoroff is considered a bad actress. She is still employed, Gubbio explains, only because she enjoys the favour of a high executive.[8] Yet the very notion of acting becomes precarious in this industry, where all actors, according to Gubbio, regardless of their professional merits, fare badly. For a large salary that makes cinema an option more lucrative than theatre, they sacrifice what used to be their richest reward, the ability to witness from the stage the audience's intense array of emotions. Now they feel as though they were in exile, not only from the theatre but also from themselves, since their performances consist of their mechanically reproduced and mute images, from which they themselves are permanently disconnected (*TR* 584–6; *Shoot!* 67–9). Those who develop the films are similarly alienated from their own bodies. A visit to Kosmograph's laboratories takes Gubbio into enormous rooms underground, barely lit by dim red lamps, where 'una mostruosa gestazione meccanica' [a monstrous mechanical birth] is taking shape. He sees not people but hands, innumerable, each making a contribution to this colossal fabrication of life, while the head and the heart exist only to assist the hands' mechanical function (*TR* 571–2; *Shoot!* 54–5). Gubbio poignantly asks himself: 'Ma come prendere sul serio un lavoro, che altro scopo non ha, se non d'ingannare – non se stessi – ma gli altri? E ingannare, mettendo sù le più stupide finzioni, a cui la macchina è incaricata di dare la realtà meravigliosa?' [But how are we to take seriously a work that has no other object than to deceive, not ourselves, but other people? And to deceive them by putting together the most idiotic fictions, to which the machine is responsible for giving a wonderful reality?] (*TR* 573; *Shoot!* 56).

The backdrop against which all current action at Kosmograph unfolds is the shooting of *La donna e la tigre* (The Woman and the Tiger), a film exemplary of the kind that Gubbio abhors and ritualistically calls 'idiotic.' The sparse information that he discloses regarding the story of the film, himself claiming to be vaguely familiar with it, is that it revolves around the trip of an English Miss to India while escorted by a group of male admirers. Several hundred thousand lire will be spent for the realization of the spectacular screenplay, which nonetheless is, according to Gubbio, 'quanto di più stupido e di più volgare si possa immaginare' [the stupidest and most vulgar that could be imagined] (*TR* 576; *Shoot!* 59). The dreary consequences of the alienated relationship between nature and a modern world obsessed with the fashionable manufacturing of illusions are evident in the cruel treatment that a tiger in flesh and blood, purchased from Rome's Zoological Gardens where it had been deemed indomitable, suffers on the grounds of Kosmograph. The tiger is locked inside a cage while awaiting its death in cold blood, during the shooting of what is projected as the film's most sensational scene. Gubbio laments: 'L'India sarà finta, la *jungla* sarà finta, il viaggio sarà finto, finta la *miss* e finti i corteggiatori: solo la morte di questa povera bestia non sarà finta. Ci pensate? E non vi sentite torcer le viscere dall'indignazione? [India will be a sham, the jungle will be a sham, the travels will be a sham, with a sham Miss and sham admirers: only the death of this poor beast will not be a sham. Do you follow me? And does it not make you writhe in anger?] (*TR* 576; *Shoot!* 59).

Not an 'Optical Unconscious'

In the midst of this industrial gloom, Gubbio surprises us with a few observations that seem to redeem the film medium. He contemplates the unique capabilities of the camera to intimate human truths that are otherwise irretrievable. The studio executives, usually shocked by Nestoroff's awkward gestures, discard much of the film in which she appears. In Gubbio's view, when Nestoroff watches her own image on screen, she is terror-stricken:

> Vede lì una, che è lei, ma che ella non conosce. Vorrebbe non riconoscersi in quella; ma almeno conoscerla.
>
> *Forse* da anni e anni e anni, a traverso tutte le avventure misteriose della sua vita, *ella va inseguendo questa ossessa che è in lei* e che le sfugge, per trattenerla, per domandarle che cosa voglia, perché soffra, che cosa ella dovrebbe fare per ammansarla, per placarla, per darle pace. (*TR* 557; emphasis added)

[She sees there someone who is herself but whom she does not know. She would like not to recognize herself in this person, but at least to know her.

Possibly for years and years, through all the mysterious adventures of her life, *she has gone in quest of this demon which exists in her* and always escapes her, to arrest it, to ask it what it wants, why it is suffering, what she ought to do to sooth it, to placate it, to give it peace.] (*Shoot!* 40; emphasis added)

Let us recall that everything we know of Nestoroff is presented through the eyes of Gubbio, who not only is the narrator but as a character in the novel also maintains a biased view of Nestoroff, one that is clouded by his memory of the Mirelli affair. In this respect, the introspection in which Nestoroff engages, the notion that for years 'she has gone in quest of this demon which exists in her,' more than an objective account of her inner experience, may reflect something that Gubbio himself construes, his subjective perception of Nestoroff, as Pirandello's use of the term 'forse' strongly suggests.[9] Before I resume this important point, which lies at the core of my reading of *Si gira*, let us establish that Gubbio's observations, subjective or otherwise, propose that certain film images, those the formal qualities of which the institution rejects, such as the one purportedly alluding to Nestoroff's 'demon,' are able to provoke such introspection.

This idea is complemented by the one that appears later in the novel, when Gubbio reflects upon his own profession in an atypical manner. He imagines how different things would be if the camera, instead of inventing fictions, were secretly used, without our knowledge, to record our daily actions as they unfold naturally: 'Chi sa come ci sembrerebbero buffi! più di tutti, i nostri stessi. Non ci riconosceremmo, in prima; esclameremmo, stupiti, offesi: "Ma come? Io, così? io, questo? cammino così? rido così? io, quest'atto? io, questa faccia?"' [Who knows how ridiculous they would appear to us! Most of all, our own. We should not recognize ourselves, at first; we should exclaim, shocked, mortified, indignant: 'What? I, like that? I, that person? Do I walk like that? Do I laugh like that? Is that my action? My face?'] (*TR* 614; *Shoot!* 97).[10] Gubbio's insights, regarding either his thoughts on Nestoroff or the camera's alternative applicability – in a manner that recalls the Futurists' polemics, who condemn the institution of narrative cinema, its 'theatre without words,' and aspire to an unprejudiced exploration of the medium's technical possibilities – imply two distinct notions of cinema: on the one hand, an institution, the commercial imperatives of which require the deployment of film technology in harmony with a rigidly defined set of aesthetic conventions; on the other hand, an apparatus in its pure form, free of conventions and able to inspire new and alternative forms of discourse.

At first glance, it is in this second notion of cinema, the liberation of the apparatus from its current subservience, that Pirandello invests his aesthetic endorsement. In support of this idea, critics have interpreted Gubbio's unconventional cinematic images – for their ability, as it were, to expose human truths that are otherwise irretrievable – as a precursor to Benjamin's notion of the 'optical unconscious.'[11] Prior to closer examination, the affinity appears to be unmistakable. In 'The Work of Art' essay Benjamin speaks of an otherwise unattainable exploration of space via particular camera techniques. With the use of the close-up to expand space, or slow motion to extend movement, cinema is able 'to assure us of a vast and unsuspected field of action,' inherent to the hidden details of otherwise familiar objects: 'just as enlargement not merely clarifies what we see indistinctly "in any case," but brings to light entirely new structures of matter, slow motion not only reveals familiar aspects of movements, but discloses quite unknown aspects within them.' For Benjamin, this unique trait of the camera resonates with the psychoanalytic process: 'Clearly, it is another nature which speaks to the camera as compared to the eye. "Other" above all in the sense that a space informed by human consciousness gives way to a space informed by the unconscious . . . It is through the camera that we first discover the optical unconscious, just as we discover the instinctual unconscious through psychoanalysis.'[12]

The inclination to compare Pirandello's novel to Benjamin's seminal essay is neither unwarranted nor limited to the idea of the optical unconscious. Critics have drawn further analogies between the two works, suggesting that Gubbio's condemnation of the mechanization of life and debasement of art in a rapidly industrialized society, in this novel represented by cinema, anticipates Benjamin's discourse about the decay of the artwork's aura in the age of its technological reproducibility.[13] The claim finds support in the fact that Benjamin himself cites *Si gira* in his essay. However, in drawing analogies between the two works, one must not overstate the influence that Pirandello had, as it were, upon his successor, or overlook their crucial conceptual differences. First, the single part of *Si gira* that Benjamin cites involves Gubbio's remarks on the actor, his state of being 'exiled,' feeling 'stripped of his reality, his life, his voice,' now that the apparatus 'will play with his shadow before

the audience, and he himself must be content to play before the apparatus.'[14] Second, it is likely that Benjamin had not read the novel in its
entirety, but found Pirandello's remarks on the actor as quoted in a secondary source.[15] Failing to account for this bibliographical detail, one
runs the risk of construing further intertextual influences by overvalu-
ing Benjamin's single explicit reference to the novel.[16]

Third, the condition of the actor, which for Gubbio exemplifies art's
debasement by an alienating institution servicing an alienated society,
is presented as desirable in Benjamin's Marxist analysis. It strengthens
his argument about the loss of the aura and the revolutionary prospects
that such loss opens for the inclusion of the masses in aesthetic experience. Reflecting upon Pirandello's remarks, he adds that in the case
of the stage actor, 'the aura is bound to his presence in the here and
now ... What distinguishes the shot in the film studio, however, is that
the camera is substituted for the audience. As a result, the aura surrounding the actor is dispelled.' Contrary to Gubbio's grudge, he sees
in the loss of the actor's aura the possibility for a revolutionary social
effect. That the film actor 'lacks the opportunity of the stage actor to
adjust to the audience during his performance ... permits the audience
to take the position of a critic ... *The audience's empathy with the actor
is really an empathy with the camera. Consequently, the audience takes the
position of the camera; its approach is that of testing.*' Furthermore: '*While
he stands before the apparatus, the screen actor knows that in the end he is
confronting the public, the consumers who constitute the market.*'[17]

It is not mistaken to juxtapose the two authors' reflections on the
socio-cultural phenomena of an early twentieth-century milieu that they
both inhabit, despite the divergent existential or ideological streams in
which they channel the implications of such phenomena. Indeed, when
comparing the two works, whether addressing Benjamin's comments on
the actor or a further range of implicit affinities, critics often address the
concerns that differentiate each work's appraisal of the industrial era.[18]
It is also true that each author's specific propositions may not be as conclusive as they appear. In noting above Benjamin's optimistic reversal
of Gubbio's grudge against industrial society, I refer to what Benjamin
presents as his overt argument in this section of the essay. However,
studies of the essay with respect to Benjamin's other works have chal-
lenged the very notion of the decay of the aura and its desirable social
effects.[19] As regards Pirandello, I have strategically referred to the condemnation of industrial society as a grudge that is held not by the author
but by Gubbio, whose dilemma – his ambivalent attitude towards a new

sensibility formed by an industrial rhythm of life and a degree of insincerity in his aversion to commercial cinema – I shall discuss more closely in the next chapter. Pirandello, by contrast, as a thinker who distinguishes himself from his narrator, though subtly and by no means absolutely, holds no such a grudge. To be specific, he neither rejects nor exalts industrial modernity. That he does not reject it does not mean that his views on cinema approach, even remotely, Marinetti's or D'Annunzio's zealous claims about speed, movement, a revolutionary spatio-temporality, the attainment of the marvellous, or any other exhilarating virtues that the new medium exhibits. Rather, he maintains a neutral and contemplative stance, reflecting upon the medium's unique ability to display, as I noted in the introduction to this book, the never-ending human struggle in quest of stable notions of truth and identity and the multiple illusions formed in its course – an idea that will become clearer as I discuss *Si gira* in terms of the author's theory of humour.

Irrespective of the degree to which the two authors converge or diverge as regards other controversial matters, when it concerns the capability of the film image to hint at evasive truths, one must acknowledge the fundamental difference between the optical unconscious and those unconventional images that inspire Gubbio to reflect. Although, as we shall see, any recourse to the Benjaminian metaphor fails to accurately explain the function of the Pirandellian images, an exploration of the incompatibility between the two allows for a better understanding of the Pirandellian trope itself – that is, the function that the author ascribes to those images – specifically in terms of his theory of humour. At the core of the incompatibility between them lies the decisive role that Benjamin attributes to the past in his view of subjectivity. By claiming an affinity between spatial revelations and psychoanalysis, Benjamin imbues spatial categories with temporality. The optical unconscious sustains his definition of the aura as nature's ability to return the gaze. As my discussion of D'Annunzio's Mona Lisa has explained, the reciprocal gaze entails the human projection of an unconscious past onto nature, which we thus invest with the capability of returning our gaze. In contemplating a natural object, the 'unique apparition of a distance, however near it may be,' an essential aspect of Benjamin's definition of the aura,[20] does not refer to the spatial proximity between subject and object. Interpreted in terms of the Freudian uncanny, it refers, rather, to a *temporal* distance, an unconscious past that the encountered object invokes when it grabs the subject by means of *mémoire involontaire*, as defined by Proust.[21]

From a psychoanalytic perspective, there is no doubt that a quest into the subject's past, prompted by things like Nestoroff's astonishment at the sight of her own image or the incredulity of the man who, having being caught unawares, sees his own everyday actions on screen, might lead to viable hypotheses regarding the subject's psychological make-up. In fact, psychoanalysis seems quite pertinent in Pirandello's case, where the images under question depict not just any object in nature but the looker him/herself, that is, where the image poses as an objective form of the subject. The shock results from the clash between the self-image that the subject carries within and cherishes and the contrasting version of that image with which the film projector assaults the subject.[22] The classical psychoanalyst, who may or may not think that one of the two images represents the subject more faithfully than the other, is interested in the shock that is caused by the clash between the two, insofar as the shock may be appraised with respect to a given hypothesis about the subject's repressed memories. The psychoanalyst knows, of course, that the unconscious is inexhaustible and the subject may never be able to un-repress sufficiently. Nevertheless, the thing that serves as the catalyst for the process, its raison d'être, is the firm belief that a trauma was once repressed and still lurks in the unconscious. Whether its unveiling is successful, the process is not in vain. Somewhat like Odysseus's invaluable discoveries during his ten-year return to Ithaca, it profits from the multiple things that it unveils along the way.

It is the existence of this *end*, psychoanalysis's putting forward a tangible goal, independent of its attainability or lack thereof, that distinguishes the spatial revelations provided by Benjamin's optical unconscious from the kind of revelations that the camera provides in Pirandello. Through the camera, Benjamin states, 'we first discover the optical unconscious, just as we discover the instinctual unconscious through psychoanalysis.'[23] The camera, in other words, may perform a function similar to analysis. The peculiar image of nature that it may reveal through a close-up or slow motion – peculiar, in that it is inaccessible to the naked eye – strikes the subject as uncanny, strangely familiar. As it grabs the subject by means of *mémoire involontaire*, it causes a shock the origin of which is *unconscious* and into the study of which the subject, as a result, may or may not wish to venture. The shock that Pirandello links to Gubbio's unconventional images, by contrast, in spite of the past trauma that the psychoanalyst might be inclined to seek in it, does not concern itself with either the unconscious or the past. It may not negate its possible psychological origin in the past, but it does not venture into it either.

Like the psychoanalyst, Pirandello is interested in the clash between the vague self-image that one cherishes and the distinct tangible version of that image as shown on the screen. Pirandello, however, who is not a psychologist but a novelist and dramatist, is interested less in the deeper psychological implications of the shock as triggered by the clash than in the clash itself. While he may not exclude the possibility of a past traumatic origin to the shock, he concentrates on the *conscious* recognition of the clash between the two images as it unfolds *here and now*. As Giuseppe Paradiso states in his comparative study of Pirandello and Freud, 'for Pirandello, objectivity is inconsistent and man hides so many truths inside himself that none of those is the definitive one. Freud, though convinced like Pirandello that it is necessary to dismantle appearance, is certain that one may arrive at a "reading" of the human mind that is close to reality.'[24] Pirandello's portrayal of the psyche through the invention of a set of peculiar images is not an odyssey. The coexistence of diverse perspectives free of any recourse to the past, the very clash between two variations of an evasive notion – that is, the self – and the dramatic effects that this clash makes possible *here and now*, take precedence in Pirandello and demand an interpretation of the shock with respect to his theory of humour.

Quite instructive in this regard is yet a third image, which appears near the end of *Si gira* and poses, with even more conviction than any of the other two, as a precursor of the optical unconscious – that is, before Pirandello throws into doubt the ability of this image to evoke any repressed past. Aldo Nuti, previously engaged to Duccella Mirelli and then lover of Nestoroff, hence responsible in part for Giorgio Mirelli's suicide and the family's ill fortune, is now an actor at Kosmograph, where he sought employment, possibly driven by a wish to reunite with Nestoroff. In the evening preceding the shooting of the finale of *La donna e la tigre*, for which Nuti has been selected to play the hunter who will shoot the tiger, Gubbio stumbles upon Nuti on the way home. Referring to the review of the dailies, which Gubbio was unable to attend, Nuti expresses his reaction to a close-up of himself on the screen: 'Quello che mi presenta solo, per un tratto, *staccato dal quadro*, ingrandito, con un dito così su la bocca, in atto di pensare. Forse dura un po' troppo . . . viene troppo avanti la figura . . . con quegli occhi . . . Si possono contare i peli delle ciglia. Non mi pareva l'ora che sparisse dallo schermo' [The one that shows me by myself for a minute, *detached from the scene*, close up, with a finger on my lips, like this, engaged in thinking. It lasts a little too long, perhaps ... my face is a little too prominent ... with those eyes ... You can count the eyelashes. I thought I should never disappear from the screen] (*TR* 724; *Shoot!* 203; emphasis added; ellipses in original).[25]

Upon viewing his own image, Nuti experiences a shock analogous to the one purportedly experienced by Nestoroff when viewing her own. His description of his image as 'detached from the scene' may seem ambiguous to today's reader. Extreme close-ups of the kind that allow the viewer to 'count the eyelashes' were uncommon in 1910s narrative cinema, while the *quadro*, or 'scene,' refers to a unit of action, consisting in one or more shots, dominated by what was then a commonly applied camera distance, namely, the tableauesque composition, or a static long-shot, to depict space in a manner akin to the theatrical stage. Nuti describes what today would be considered a common cut-in from a long-shot to a close-up as something out of the ordinary, 'detached from the scene,' hence, astonishing.[26] Of course, the deeper psychological aspect of the shock lies in the personal assault to which Nuti is subjected by such an enlarged and unexpected image of himself. The exposure of the minuscule details of the face recalls that state in which, for Benjamin, 'a space informed by human consciousness gives way to a space informed by the unconscious.'[27] Something held to be greatly familiar enters, suddenly, in a dialectical play with one's now revealed, seemingly unfamiliar, yet irrefutably most intimate traits. The unsettling nature of this play, its echoing the unwelcome layers of the psyche, renders the image disturbing for Nuti, who tries to gain distance from it, finding its duration 'too long,' the face 'too prominent,' and longing for the vanishing of 'those eyes' from the screen.

Acknowledging the curious effect of one's own photographed image, Nuti asks Gubbio why he thinks that it is so. Given the strong resemblance in the circumstances between this scene and Nestoroff's presumed shock, the reader expects Gubbio to offer a similar interpretation, perhaps to say that Nuti, like Nestoroff, sees in the image a part of himself that he does not know, a 'demon' that exists in him and that he fails to arrest; to suggest, in other words, that the image hints at a deep truth that is otherwise unnoted; to thus prompt us once again to study the image in terms of the optical unconscious. However, if Pirandello lets Gubbio's remarks on Nestoroff pass as such, in this second instance he leads elsewhere. It seems that Pirandello sets up the analogy between the two cases only to put Gubbio's shifting views on display. For if the narrator previously speculated on the veiled *living* cell of the actress's inner being as traceable in the image, he now attributes the odd effect of Nuti's own image to the fact that 'ci sentiamo lì fissati in un momento, *che già non è più in noi'* [we feel that we are fixed there in a moment of time *which no longer exists in ourselves*] (*TR* 724; *Shoot!* 204; emphasis added).

What further distinguishes Gubbio's present remarks from his earlier ones is that he now elaborates on the subject of temporality. The latter is essential in the earlier instance, though not discussed at length: 'Possibly for years and years, through all the mysterious adventures of her life, she has gone in quest of this demon which exists in her and always escapes her.' From a psychoanalytic perspective, the actress's evasive 'demon' as traced in the image may stand as the product of a repressed trauma. This would make Gubbio a Freudian reader of sorts. Yet Gubbio's discourse on temporality with Nuti does little to reaffirm his faith in the optical unconscious, not to say that it tends to dismantle that model altogether. The picture, he claims, ages also, just as we gradually age. However, it does not age in the same manner in which we age, in that it moves with us into the future; rather, it moves in the opposite direction, since the time represented in it 'si sprofonda sempre più nel passato' [recedes farther and farther into the past] (*TR* 724–5; *Shoot!* 204). Thinking psychoanalytically, we are tempted to seek a part of ourselves therein, forgotten or repressed, yet still alive in that aging image. Gubbio, however, banishes this possibility categorically: 'l'immagine, lì, *è una cosa morta* che col tempo s'allontana man mano anch'essa sempre più nel passato: e più è giovane e più diviene vecchia e lontana' [the picture itself *is a dead thing* which as time goes on recedes gradually farther into the past: and the younger it is the older and more remote it becomes] (*TR* 725; *Shoot!* 204; emphasis added). It is difficult to follow Gubbio's logic if we reason within a psychoanalytic frame of mind. Why would the picture's receding into the past make it a 'dead thing'? Gubbio implies that the temporal distance between subject and object abolishes any essential relationship between the two. Contrary to his interpretation of Nestoroff, this would make him an anti-Freudian raisonneur par excellence.

Nuti's response to Gubbio offers an alternative view, which brings to mind Benjamin's comments on early photography.[28] Nuti recalls a photographic portrait of his father, whom Nuti never met because the father died young. It is a photograph of the father at a very young age, taken before Nuti was even born:

L'ho custodita con reverenza, quest'immagine, benché *non mi dica nulla*. S'è invecchiata anch'essa, sì, profondandosi, come lei dice, nel passato. Ma il tempo che ha invecchiato l'immagine, non ha invecchiato mio padre; mio padre non l'ha vissuto questo tempo. E si presenta a me, *a vuoto, dal vuoto di tutta questa vita* che per lui non è stata. (*TR* 725; emphasis added)

[I have kept it reverently, this picture of him, although *it means nothing to me*. It has grown old too, yes, receding, as you say, into the past. But time, in aging the picture, has not aged my father; my father has not lived through this period of time. And he presents himself before me *in vain, from the void of all this life* that for him has not existed.] (*Shoot!* 205; emphasis added)[29]

Although Nuti, like Gubbio, finds the photograph lifeless, he implies that it would not have been so had his father lived long enough for Nuti to know him. We may relate his words to the perseverance of the aura that Benjamin finds in the portraits of nineteenth-century photography, a time prior to the medium's industrialization, when its cult value still exceeded its exhibition value: 'It is no accident that the portrait is central to early photography. In the cult of remembrance of dead or absent loved ones, the cult value of the image finds its last refuge. In the fleeting expression of a human face, the aura beckons from early photographs for the last time.'[30] The father's photograph, taken before Nuti was born, is old enough to be placed among the portraits in which Benjamin finds the surviving aura. Nuti's subsequent comments evoke the optical unconscious. In his father's gaze, he yearns for a reflection of himself, perhaps the trace of a repressed memory, which, as his words suggest, he may have experienced in the portraits of other loved ones. The picture, he says, 'non può dirmi nulla, *perché non sa neppure che io ci sia. E difatti è un ritratto ch'egli si fece prima di sposare; ritratto, dunque, di quando non era mio padre. Io in lui, lì, non ci sono*, come tutta la mia vita è stata senza di lui' [cannot say anything to me, *because he does not even know that I exist*. It is, in fact, a portrait he had made of himself before he married – a portrait, therefore, of a time when he was not my father. *I do not exist in him, there*, just as all my life has been lived without him] (*TR* 725; *Shoot!* 205; emphasis added).

From a historical viewpoint, Gubbio's own remarks seem to be aligned with Benjamin's. The time in which Gubbio, prompted by Nuti's close-up, describes the image as 'dead' is not the mid-nineteenth century, in the photographic portraits of which Benjamin finds the surviving aura, but the 1910s, the time of the medium's industrialization, when its exhibition value prevails over its cult value. Yet his reading of the close-up, in and of itself, makes no allusion to history. It strikes us, rather, as a blanket judgment on the photographic medium as a whole. Furthermore, Nuti's nuanced – Benjaminian, as it were – elaboration of Gubbio's view, does not make Pirandello a precursor of Benjamin. Nuti does not stand for Pirandello's beliefs any more than Gubbio does. Nor does Pirandello propose Nuti's nuanced discourse as a refinement of or complement to Gubbio's. Pirandello, rather, aims to expose the coexistence of multiple views on any given matter. He does so not only via the contrasting views of different characters but also with respect to a single character. As noted above, he sets up the analogy between Nestoroff's and Nuti's reactions to their own film images in order to put Gubbio's shifting views on display. As regards history, in tracing a lifetime's formation of a 'demon' in Nestoroff's image, Gubbio exhibits a Freudian stance of sorts, though observing an image contemporary to Nuti's. His appeal to temporality further exposes his inconsistency. In Nuti's case, he introduces temporality to demonstrate the rupture in the relationship between viewer and image, whereas with Nestoroff he evokes temporality ('for years and years, through all the mysterious adventures of her life') only to affirm such a relationship. He speaks of a different kind of temporality in each case. In conversing with Nuti, he underlines not, as in Nestoroff's case, the accumulation of psychic matter over time, but the distance between the moment in which the image is viewed and the moment of its creation. Had he been an objective observer, Gubbio would have applied the same standard of temporality to both images. He would have thus acknowledged that the temporal distance under question does not differ from one case to the next.

We may rest assured that the novel's premise is not that Gubbio is an objective observer or reliable reader of images but quite the contrary, despite his frequent claims to impassibility. We may in fact speculate on a deep personal cause of his shifting attitude towards the two actors' film images. His conviction that an object's state of receding into the past makes it a 'dead thing' may have a subjective basis. It may be the symptom of a recent disillusionment that made him feel betrayed by the past, shaking his faith in its ideal values and prompting a wish to sever his emotional ties with it. Shortly before his encounter with Nuti, Gubbio takes a journey to Sorrento to find Duccella and Nonna Rosa, her grandmother, in the hopes of resolving Duccella and Nuti's past trauma. Before that point, Gubbio's flashback recounting his visits to the Mirelli family, a passage the tranquil style of which sharply contrasts with the rest of the novel, thrives in nostalgia for a utopian country life immersed in an idyllic nature (*TR* 541–51; *Shoot!* 24–34).[31] His journey, in fact, perhaps less altruistic than he claims, may be a personal revisit of the past, triggered by a wish to relive the ideal moments that he has cherished all along, to thus gain a moment's relief from Kosmograph's mechanical rhythm. Yet upon arrival he faces the unexpected. Not only did Duccella and Nonna Rosa move from the idyllic villa to a squalid residence, they have also grown abhorrently ugly – fat, toothless, with facial hair. Even their Neapolitan accent bothers him now. Gubbio is so shocked that he hardly speaks to them before he rushes back to the railway station (*TR* 698–704; *Shoot!* 177–84).

Yet Gubbio's cynical view of Nuti's image, as opposed to his psychologically more intricate reading of Nestoroff's, is not only an automatic, uncritical reaction rooted in a recent personal ordeal but also a polemical gesture that conveys his discontent with the institution of commercial cinema. As previously noted, the image in which Gubbio detects a psychological riddle belongs to a category that the institution discards, namely, the takes in which Nestoroff's clumsy bodily movements attest to her lack of talent as an actress. To the same category belongs Gubbio's mental image of the non-actor whose spontaneous and unrefined everyday actions are captured by a hidden camera. That is not the case with Nuti's close-up, which was one of several scenes that the review of the dailies deemed agreeable, as we learn from the way in which Nuti introduces his description of it: 'Hanno fatto buona impressione a tutti. Non avrei immaginato che potessero riuscire così bene. Uno specialmente' [Everyone was pleased with them. I should never have imagined that they would come out so well. One especially] (*TR* 724; *Shoot!* 203). It is in those unrefined gestures, lacking proper institutional training, disqualified for inclusion in the industry's 'idiotic fictions' and thus thrust into its margins, that Gubbio seeks the surviving remnants of an authentic human reality. Hence, his persistent aversion to the institution justifies to some extent his shifting attitude towards Nestoroff's and Nuti's images. To be exact, his process of reflection is inconsistent insofar as it is conditioned, depending on the circumstances, by diverse ideological, philosophical, psychological, or other factors.[32]

His faith in those marginalized images confronts us again with the unrelenting optical unconscious, the camera's ability to evoke the subject's inner and previously unnoted truths. Indeed, my discussion of this model did not aim to demonstrate that Gubbio is immune to it. He clearly applies something like it to the first two images, if not to

Nuti's, as we have seen. What I aimed to demonstrate, rather, is that Pirandello, who is not Gubbio, is engaged not in investigating the repressed past traceable in any given image, but in exposing the *clash* between diverse images competing to portray an evasive notion (identity, the self), specifically as that clash takes place *here and now*. I am describing a phenomenon that constitutes the aesthetic concretization of Pirandello's humour. In *Si gira*, nowhere does it become as tangible as in the portrayal of Nestoroff, the novel's central and alluring object of desire, whose motives, both past and present, continue to leave Gubbio perplexed. Despite my earlier claim that Nuti's close-up, given Benjamin's own reference to the close-up in defining the optical unconscious, poses as the most obvious precursor to that model, of the three images discussed above, Nestoroff's is the one that most keenly relates to it. That is because, unlike Nuti's, Nestoroff's image incites something of a psychoanalytic reading on Gubbio's part, which extends, as we will see, to further parts of the novel. Hence, by focusing on Nestoroff, and in view of the fundamental distinction between Gubbio (who is more of a 'psychoanalyst' than Pirandello) and Pirandello (who is more of a humorist than Gubbio), we may observe more vividly the parallel conception and denigration of a Benjaminian-like model in Pirandello's novel; or, to be more specific, the predominance of a humoristic layering over a Freudian-like inquiry.

Humoristic Layering

The introspection prompted by the shocking image, be it that of Nestoroff or the non-actor who is caught unawares, is an instance of that 'reflection' that in the essay on humour Pirandello posits as the key factor of the humoristic response. He exemplifies such a response through the celebrated figure of the *vecchia signora imbellettata*, the old, dolled-up lady, which he added in 1920 upon revising the essay, evidently to answer Benedetto Croce's criticism of the 1908 version as lacking a precise definition of what he had called *riflessione* and *sentimento del contrario*.[33] In a brief narrative-like insert, Pirandello assumes the role of a narrator who at the sight of the old lady begins to laugh as he experiences the *avvertimento del contario*, the 'perception of the opposite,' that is, as he is struck by the disharmony between the gaudy youthful style of her make-up and his own notion of how a respectable old lady should be. Yet his laughter weakens upon reflection, when he speculates that the woman's appearance betrays her desperate wish to maintain the love of her much younger husband. He passes from the *avvertimento* to the *sentimento del contrario*, the 'feeling of the opposite,' of which the effect upon the narrator is to mix laughter with melancholy.[34]

When viewing Nestoroff in light of Pirandellian humour, one may fail to see what is laughable about her. It is important to note, however, that the comic effect, though it informs the example of the old lady, is not an indispensable component of humour. Pirandello also draws on humoristic literature in which the *avvertimento del contrario* incites a reaction other than laughter. One of the first examples that he presents in the second, theoretical, part of the essay is Giuseppe Giusti's *Sant'Ambrogio* (1846). The poet enters the Milanese church, which he finds full of Austrian soldiers. As he is reminded of his homeland's subservient state, a feeling of hate ('odio') permeates him. Yet when he hears the sound of the organ and the soldiers' chanting of their prayer, his hate makes room for sympathy. The intervention of reflection makes him contemplate the soldiers' own pain, who must leave their homeland in order to live in a country where they are hated (*SPSV* 128–9; *Humor* 114–15). Hence, the *avvertimento del contrario* incites not laughter but hate. It refers to the clash between the Austrian soldiers' presence in a Milanese church and the state in which, according to the poet, under normal circumstances both church and city should be, that is, free of foreign military control.

The thing that Pirandello postulates as constant in humour is not amusement, hate, sympathy, or any other isolated feeling. For humour to take effect, the only feeling that the humorist, writer and reader alike, must experience is the *sentimento del contrario*, which entails the coexistence of two or more distinct and often contradictory feelings. Such a state of mind results from the intervention of reflection, the function of which is to generate associations between contraries: 'le immagini cioè, anziché associate per similazione o per contiguità, si presentano in contrasto: ogni immagine, ogni gruppo d'immagini desta e richiama le contrarie, che naturalmente dividono lo spirito, il quale, irrequieto, s'ostina a trovare o a stabilir tra loro le relazioni più impensate' [the images, instead of being linked through similarity or juxtaposition, are presented in conflict: each image, each group of images evokes and attracts contrary ones, and these naturally divide the spirit which, in its restlessness, is obstinately determined to find or establish the most astonishing relationships between these images] (*SPSV* 133; *Humor* 119). Gubbio's insights indeed imply that the film camera may be transformed into a humoristic instrument. It is capable of provoking reflection, leading to an unsettling intellectual and emotional state defined by the subject's adherence to two or more conflicting versions of a single notion the essence of which remains evasive. Let us assume that Nestoroff, when she sees her own image, is indeed shocked, as Gubbio claims. The shock would be none but the *avvertimento del contrario*, insofar as the image on the screen, comical or otherwise, clashes with her pre-existent notion of self. Depending on her intellectual predisposition, the clash may instigate reflection, generating further self-images, thus leading to the *sentimento del contrario*. That is, she may respond with humour.

One may wonder whether such images relate to one another synchronically or diachronically. In claiming that humour entails the coexistence of diverse images, I speak of a synchronic relationship. Yet when Pirandello says that 'each image, each group of images evokes and attracts contrary ones,' he seems to describe a diachronic process. To convey a mental state we devise one image that *then*, upon reflection, awakes another. Such a diachronic process informs the narratives that Pirandello uses in order to render his idea of humour comprehensible. In the case of Giusti, the poet feels hate, then reflects, and then sympathizes. In the case of the old lady, the narrator laughs, then reflects, and then sympathizes.[35] This diachronic layout may be deceptive as it may imply the operation of a binary true-or-false model, according to which the narrator first misreads the lady's behaviour and then, like a psychoanalyst, gains insight into her real motives. The initial perception is thus discarded in favour of a later one that is presumably closer to the truth. Humour is nothing of the kind. Pirandello aims not to unveil a primordial truth but to expose its multiple portrayals. What we may call 'humoristic layering' does not refer to pre-existent layers the least accessible of which, in being farthest from the surface, is closest to the truth, but to an infinite process of elucidating – which means constructing – the new layers of the object under investigation, hence its layer*ing*. Since no single layer is verified as the object's absolute essence, each new layer, though formed diachronically, may reassert itself in various forms.

Nonetheless, the diachronic model is far from idle. Aesthetically, it constitutes a technical device that allows authors to convey humour via narrative form. Conceptually, it helps Pirandello to demonstrate the distinction between the *avvertimento* and the *sentimento del contrario*. Yet conceptually, humour must also be understood as a disposition: the ability of an author or reader to perceive, describe, and believe in two or more images simultaneously, even if those conflict with one another. In this synchronic relationship, the *avvertimento del contrario*, the *perception* of something as strange, is but one of the images. It is one of the components of the *sentimento del contrario*, the latter being the feeling that encompasses both that 'initial' and other images. Therefore, the diachronic process of laying out variables via writing, while in Pirandello it aspires to convey a synchronic state of affairs, makes it necessary that humour, which is not only a disposition but also an aesthetic form, constitutes an interactive phenomenon between diachronic and synchronic relationships among images.

As noted above, the essence of any given object under investigation remains unverified, while its single verifiable state is the constellation of its diverse portrayals. This idea is fundamental in the essay on humour: 'La vita è un flusso continuo che noi cerchiamo d'arrestare, di fissare in formi stabili e determinate' [Life is a continual flux which we try to stop, to fix in stable and determined forms]. Such forms are fictions, illusory fixities, which we construct through reason in order to comprehend life's elusive nature. We define identity, for example, the core of which is unreachable, according to the ideals that society dictates as norms. Such forms are fixed in themselves but their power is transitory, since the flux of life incites the conception of further forms: 'dentro di noi stessi, in ciò che noi chiamiamo anima, e che è la vita in noi, il flusso continua, indistinto, sotto gli argini, oltre i limiti che noi imponiamo, componendoci una coscienza, costruendoci una personalità' [within ourselves, in what we call the soul and is the life in us, the flux continues, indistinct under the barriers and beyond the limits we impose as a means to fashion a consciousness and a personality for ourselves] (*SPSV* 151; *Humor* 137). Though fictive and transitory, such constructs are not formed in vain. Life is not the triumphant unveiling of reality in a set of definitive forms but a process of re-forming any given aspect of reality into multiple constructs. Pirandello does not deny the existence of an absolute reality, but he thinks that it is imperceptible: 'una realtà vivente *oltre la vista umana, fuori delle forme dell'umana ragione*' [a reality living *beyond the reach of human vision, outside the forms of human reason*]. It reveals itself fleetingly in those rare vertiginous moments that Pirandello describes enigmatically as 'momenti di silenzio interiore, in cui l'anima nostra si spoglia di tutte le finzioni abituali' [moments of inner silence, in which our soul strips itself of all its habitual fictions]. Thereafter, we can no longer trust the ideas that constitute our ordinary consciousness, 'perché sappiamo ormai che sono un nostro inganno per vivere e che *sotto c'è qualcos'altro, a cui l'uomo non può affacciarsi, se non a costo di morire o d'impazzire'* [because we now know that they are deceptions which we use in order to survive and that *underneath them there is something else which man can face only at the cost of either death or insanity*] (*SPSV* 152–3; *Humor* 138; emphasis added).

Humoristic reflection 'scompone a una a una quelle costruzioni' [disassembles those constructions one by one] (*SPSV* 146; *Humor* 132). The humorist 'coglie subito queste varie simulazioni per la lotta della vita; si diverte a smascherarle' [readily perceives the various simulations used in the struggle for life; he amuses himself by unmasking them] (*SPSV* 148; *Humor* 134). Again, a seemingly diachronic model is tied with a synchronic state of affairs, in that the process is infinite. Disassembling 'one by one,' or 'unmasking,' does not lead to an underlying truth to which the humorist has privileged access, but implies an infinite layering. Beneath each mask another mask is revealed. Well aware of his inability to reach the truth, the humorist 'amuses himself' by exposing the various coexisting images of the object under investigation. Such is the case of the old lady:

> Ma se ora interviene in me la riflessione, e mi *suggerisce* che quella vecchia signora non prova *forse* nessun piacere a pararsi così come un pappagallo, ma che *forse* ne soffre e lo fa soltanto perché pietosamente s'inganna che, parata così, nascondendo così le rughe e la canizie, riesca a trattenere a sé l'amore del marito molto più giovane di lei, ecco che io non posso più riderne come prima. (*SPSV* 127; emphasis added)

> [But if, at this point, reflection interferes in me to *suggest* that *perhaps* this old lady finds no pleasure in dressing up like an exotic parrot, and that *perhaps* she is distressed by it and does it only because she pitifully deceives herself into believing that, by making herself up like that and by concealing her wrinkles and gray hair, she may be able to hold the love of her much younger husband – if reflection comes to suggest all this, then I can no longer laugh at her as I did at first.] (*Humor* 113; emphasis added)

The narrator reveals little, if any, of the woman's essence. Instead, he stages a parade of conventional identity constructs that he draws upon that face: the young-beauty ideal to which she aspires; the contemporary social norm of how a woman of that age should look; and the stereotype of a lonely person desperate for love. This third notion, though it aims to explain the coexistence of the first two, is itself a construct. The terms 'suggerisce' and 'forse,' the latter of which Pirandello reiterates, declare the impermanence of the humorist's explanation as one of numerous possibilities.

Gubbio's account of the scene in which Nestoroff sees her own image resembles in some ways the above example.[36] What we learn of Nestoroff is the product of a negotiation between diverse identity constructs. The dolled-up face, though it may seem comical to others, betrays the old lady's attempt to construct a specific self-image. Similarly, Nestoroff's acting, which Gubbio and the studio crew find peculiar – 'così scomposta la sua azione, così stranamente alterata e contraffatta la sua figura' [her action is so disordered, her face so strangely altered and disguised], and those things being true only in the rare cases in which she does not mistakenly move out of the picture – may be symptomatic of an attempt to project a specific self-image the psychological origin of which is unknown to Gubbio, the studio crew, us readers, and even herself. 'Ha in sé qualche cosa, questa donna, che gli altri non riescono a comprendere, perché bene non lo comprende neppure lei stessa. Si indovina però dalle violente espressioni che assume, senza volerlo, senza saperlo, nelle parti che le sono assegnate' [She has something in her, this woman, which the others do not succeed in understanding because even she herself does not clearly understand it. One guesses it, however, from the violent expressions which she assumes, involuntarily, unconsciously, in the parts that are assigned to her] (*TR* 555–6; *Shoot!* 39). In each case, the constructed self-image deviates from the norm. Like the dolled-up face, which defies the expectations associated with that woman's age group, Nestoroff defies the acting conventions of 1910s Italian cinema, which is another construct, culturally and historically determined.[37] Gubbio's perception of the clash between her gestures and the norm represents the *avvertimento del contrario*. It may provoke disturbance, laughter, or any reaction that betrays the onlooker's recognition of the clash.

Reflection intervenes, however, to complicate Gubbio's view and incite the *sentimento del contrario*. Like the humorist's speculation on the old lady's wish to win her husband's love, in Nestoroff's acting, besides failure, a sympathetic Gubbio sees a tortured soul: 'Possibly for years and years, . . . she has gone in quest of this demon which exists in her.' He implies that it is Nestoroff, not he, who experiences a shock by seeing 'this demon.' I have remarked on the humoristic effect that Nestoroff's image may have upon her, provided that she is shocked and bears a humorist's disposition. Let us note, however, that Gubbio barely describes any visible signs of shock on her face, concentrating instead on her inner reactions. This casts doubt on the objectivity of his report, allowing us to speculate that her presumed shock is instead Gubbio's projection of his own shock onto her, his own response to the *avvertimento del contrario*. If so, the suffering woman that he perceives is, as with the old lady, a third image that aims to explain the coexistence of the first two: her peculiar gestures and the era's conventions of acting. Furthermore, this image is again a construct. The term 'forse,' used instructively by Pirandello in both examples (translated as 'perhaps' and 'possibly'), implies that the image of Nestoroff in crisis, who for years 'has gone in quest of this demon,' is Gubbio's construct, hence, one of many possible interpretations.[38]

Undoubtedly, Gubbio's contemplation of her state of mind as inspired by that peculiar image allows us to think of film as a heuristic medium.[39] Yet if Gubbio tends to psychoanalyse her, treating the image like an optical unconscious where he might detect a primordial truth of the object, it is not so for Pirandello. If we recall his definition of reality as imperceptible, as that 'something else which man can face only at the cost of either death or insanity,' we understand that the heuristic ability of film does not lie within any single image, in its inherent physical qualities, such as the actor's body language, the props, costumes, colour, lighting, or camera angle. If reality is imperceptible, we must be wary of assuming that Pirandello discovers in film a medium able, more so than any other aesthetic medium, to render it perceptible. This relates not only to Gubbio's reading of Nestoroff's image but also to his idea of a non-actor caught on camera unawares. He wishes that his profession 'fosse applicata solamente a cogliere, senz'alcuna stupida invenzione o costruzione immaginaria di scene e di fatti, la vita, così come vien viene' [were applied to the recording, without any stupid invention or imaginary construction of scenes and actions, of life, life as it comes]; that it had the 'solo intento di presentare agli uomini il buffo spettacolo dei loro atti impensati, la vista immediata delle loro passioni, della loro vita così com'è' [sole object of presenting to men the ridiculous spectacle of their heedless actions, an immediate view of their passions, of their life as it is] (*TR* 614; *Shoot!* 97). It takes little effort to see the problem inherent in Gubbio's idealism. The notion of 'life as it is,' which is not definable, is best understood as a spontaneous action. Its filmed image is artifice nonetheless: two-dimensional, miscoloured, and shot from a specific angle, thus excluding much more than it includes of the physical environment and social conditions within which the action unfolds and which shape its meaning. Inasmuch as it may capture a spontaneous action, the image is also a synthetic abstraction of it.[40]

To dispel the idea that Pirandello invests such faith in the film image, suffice it to glance at his 'Illustratori, attori e traduttori' (Illustrators, Actors, and Translators, 1908), where he reflects upon the phenomenon of visual illustrations as found in works of literature. He compares various arts, such as music, painting, photography, and poetry, with respect to the formal limitations that they face in trying to convey the artist's feeling. He sees any visual illustration of poetry, through either painting or photography, as rigid and synthetic. If music, he claims, 'offende perché pone il sentimento vago, che è proprio delle sue forme e de' suoi modi, tra le idee e le rappresentazioni precise d'un dramma realistico; la vignetta offende perché determina troppo e quasi irrigidisce in un'espressione troppo precisa le immagini del poeta, quando non le falsi' [offends because it puts the vague feeling, which is typical of its forms and ways, among the precise ideas and representations of a realistic drama; the illustration offends because it determines too much and almost stiffens the poet's images in too precise an expression, if it does not falsify them] (*SPSV* 210). Furthermore, 'risulta evidente che la pittura è più limitata della poesia; e che perciò un illustratore, per quanto interpreti bene il sentimento del poeta non riuscirà mai, per la natura stessa della sua arte, a rendere quel che vi è di fluttuante nell'espressione poetica. Il sentimento reso visibile, rappreso per così dire nei contorni del disegno, diventa piuttosto sensazione' [it is clear that painting is more limited than poetry; thus an illustrator, however well he interprets the poet's feeling, will never manage, because of the very nature of his art, to render that floating element as found in poetic expression. The feeling made visible, clotted so to speak within the drawing's contours, becomes rather a sensation] (213). Poetry's own horizons, however, are limited: 'il poeta è meno limitato del pittore e meno libero del musico' [the poet is less limited than the painter and less free than the musician] (212).[41]

If poetry, less synthetic than painting and photography, faces its own limitations, and if music, freer than poetry, renders the feeling vague, what might allow us to imagine that Pirandello now seeks the object's primordial, repressed, and by his own definition imperceptible reality within the contours of the film image? One wonders whether Nestoroff's 'demon' and the non-actor's 'life as it is' are any less fictional than the 'idiotic fictions' that Gubbio abhors. They surely constitute Gubbio's subjective impressions. They are Gubbio's own fictions. I repeat that Pirandello allows us to think of film as a heuristic medium. Yet the inherent qualities of the image are not where its heuristic ability lies. The latter is found, rather, in the contrast between this and another image. Whether or not the viewer is also the object represented, such as Nestoroff or the non-actor, the image may lead through a course of discovery when and only when it enters a play of contrasts with other images, those that it contradicts or from which it differs considerably. This is, again, what Pirandello means by 'reflection,' the continuous process by which every image wakes its opposite. It is only by enacting such a process that images may allude to reality as he defines it. Not the unveiling of reality in any single isolated image, but *reflection*, as an infinite process of staging the coexistence of contraries, is the premise of humour. Insofar as Gubbio's disconcerting images fuel such a process, they are humoristic par excellence – not because they crush a fragile mental image with their authenticity, but because of the contrast itself as process, which they set forth.

Nestoroff's reality is not found in the 'demon' that Gubbio sees on screen but in the fluid intersections of her multiple and contrasting portrayals. She is configured like Vitangelo Moscarda, the protagonist of Pirandello's *Uno, nessuno e centomila* (One, No One, and One Hundred Thousand, 1925), who realizes that the Moscarda he always knew does not even exist, while countless Moscardas, those whom other people see, exist outside that body of his.[42] Her form lies in the constellation of her many images, some of which consist of Gubbio's speculations on her life experience, others of fixed visual renderings the meaning of which is filtered by Gubbio.[43] Regarding the former, in recounting the Mirelli tragedy, Gubbio does not indubitably blame Nestoroff as the disloyal fiancée, but reflects upon her motives like a humorist (*TR* 551–65; *Shoot!* 34–48).[44] He states from the start that he cannot know her entirely: 'Conosco bene adesso questa donna, o almeno quanto è possibile conoscerla' [I know this woman well now, as well, that is to say, as it is possible to know her] (*TR* 551; *Shoot!* 34). Noting that some compare her to Kosmograph's recently purchased tiger, he contrasts the cruelty of wild animals, which innocently kill humans out of hunger, to that of humans, whose hunting exploits justify the killing of innocent beasts for pleasure. Like a wild beast, Nestoroff suffered men's cruelty, yet 'non ne ha ucciso nessuno' [never killed anyone]. Mirelli's death was a suicide, which he committed not only for her but also for himself. Furthermore,. if a beast has no regrets about harming humans, Nestoroff is 'infelicissima. Non gode della sua malvagità' [most unhappy. She does not enjoy her own wickedness]. Despite the cold-blooded calculation with which she harms men, she lacks 'quella "sistemazione" tranquilla di concetti, d'affetti, di diritti e di doveri, d'opinioni e d'abitudini, ch'io odio negli altri' [that quiet 'systematization' of concepts, affections, rights and duties, opinions, and habits, which I abominate in other people] (*TR* 554–5; *Shoot!* 37–8). In describing others' condemnation of her seductiveness, Gubbio also suggests that her seduced lovers bear their share of responsibility for her cruel behaviour (*TR* 558–9; *Shoot!* 41–2).

As previously mentioned, he tends to psychoanalyse her, in the sense that he portrays her wickedness as rooted in a painful past. She met Mirelli at Capri, where the Russian community treated her with diffidence because she was believed to be the widow of a certain Nicola Nestoroff, who died in Berlin, probably as a political exile. It is said that after rescuing her as a young girl from Petersburg's most disreputable streets, Nicola Nestoroff educated and married her. Then, reduced to poverty by his own vices, he had her sing at infamous nightclubs, before abandoning her. If this story paints her as a victim, another honours her. According to her own account, to satisfy both a passion and an economic need, and despite her husband's objection, she eagerly worked as an actress in provincial theatres. Seeing his frail health, however, she followed him to Berlin, where she looked after him until his death. Gubbio's study of the Mirelli affair also challenges Nestoroff's reputation as wicked. An artist whose 'stato d'animo abituale era il rapimento e la meraviglia' [habitual state of mind was one of rapture and amazement], Mirelli neglected her pain, seeing only the figure that he himself created, an impression 'illuminata dalla luce che le diede' [illuminated by the light in which he beheld her], and in which she was neither allowed nor able to participate. Thus, like all men, he loved her for her body. What is worse, unlike the others, he adored her body not for a vulgar desire but for an ideal joy reserved for himself: 'Un angelo per una donna è sempre più irritante d'una bestia' [An angel, to a woman, is always more irritating than a beast]. Perhaps feeling emotionally neglected and excluded from that joy, in order to take revenge, she seduced him sexually, only to then deny him any access to her body, thus leading him to suicide. Yet it may also be true, Gubbio thinks, that she valued that pure friendship and was repulsed when Mirelli began to desire her sexually. Mirelli then desperately sought marriage as a way of fulfilling his own desire. Another possibility, he continues, 'a volere esser maligni' [if we wish to be ill natured], is that her repulse, her struggle against marriage, and her threats to abandon Mirelli were things carefully crafted so as to reduce him to despair and obtain various advantages from him, including being brought as his bride to Sorrento, where she met Nuti (*TR* 561–3; *Shoot!* 44–6).

Mirelli's failure to see Nestoroff outside of the figure of his own creation is crucial for at least two reasons, both of which sustain Pirandello's humoristic conception of her persona. First, it speaks to the impossibility of reaching the essence of identity, which in spite of how much love is involved, remains a construct of the onlooker's subjective state of mind. Second, it invites us to see Nestoroff as an aesthetic construct overall, that is, to apply the Mirelli model to other aspects of the novel, including both the 'images' produced by Gubbio's accounts of her life experience as discussed above and his descriptions of her various fixed visual renderings that occur throughout. In other words, it inspires us to receive all of her portrayals as mere images, none of which is closer than any other to her essence. Thus, the Mirelli model works like a bridge between her two sets of renderings – narrative and visual – the latter of which also serves, roughly speaking, as a synthetic abstraction of the former, as a more tangible display of her humoristic conception, or her layering. For instance, the images of her allegedly bad acting are offset by another, which highlights her sensuality and evidently satisfies the industry. She performs the savage so-called Indian dagger dance, 'quasi tutta nuda, con una sola fascia sui fianchi a righe gialle verdi rosse turchine' [almost completely naked, with nothing but a striped loincloth, yellow, green, red, and blue], during the filming of which Gubbio thinks that she tries to allure him with her suggestive gaze at the camera: 'Tra i penosi contorcimenti di quella sua strana danza màcabra, tra il luccichìo sinistro dei due pugnali, ella non staccò un minuto gli occhi da' miei, che la seguivano affascinanti. Le vidi sul seno anelante il sudore rigar di solchi la manteca giallastra, di cui era tutto impiastricciato' [Through the painful contortions of that strange, morbid dance, behind the sinister gleam of the daggers, she did not take her eyes for a minute from mine, which followed her movements, fascinated. I saw the sweat on her heaving bosom make furrows in the ocherous paint with which she was daubed all over] (*TR* 598–9; *Shoot!* 81–2).

This primitive layer of hers contrasts her ethereal impressions in Mirelli's six canvases that Gubbio sees during a visit at her apartment. These are products, evidently, of the artist's subjective state of mind and chaste ideal joy:

> L'assunzione di quel suo corpo a una vita prodigiosa, in una luce da qui
> ella neppure in sogno avrebbe potuto immaginare di essere illuminata e

riscaldata, in un trasparente, trionfale accordo con una natura attorno, di cui certo gli occhi suoi non avevano mai veduto il tripudio dei colori, era sei volte ripetuta, per miracolo d'arte e d'amore, in quel salotto, in sei tele di Giorgio Mirelli.

Fissata lì per sempre, in quella realtà divina ch'egli le aveva data, in quella divina luce, in quella divina fusione di colori, la donna che mi stava davanti che cos'era più ormai? (*TR* 688)

[The assumption of that body of hers into a prodigious life, in a light by which she could never, even in her dreams, have imagined herself as being bathed and warmed, in a transparent, triumphant harmony with a nature round about her, of which her eyes had certainly never beheld the jubilance of colors, was repeated six times over, by a miracle of art and love, in that drawing room, upon six canvases by Giorgio Mirelli.

Fixed there for all time, in that divine reality which he had conferred on her, in that divine light, in that divine fusion of colors, the woman who stood before me was now what?] (*Shoot!* 168)

Let us note the lyricism of the description, which reveals more about Gubbio's sensibility than Mirelli's. It recalls an earlier description of Nestoroff in flesh and blood, while she and some studio professionals, in a sultry afternoon, sit under a pergola waiting for an actress to arrive. Gubbio thinks that Nestoroff tries to avoid his gaze by pretending to be bothered by the sun, which, 'di tra i pampini del pergolato, la feriva in viso. Era vero; e mirabile su quel viso era il gioco dell'ombra violacea, vaga e rigata da fili d'oro di sole, che or le accendevano una pinna del naso e un po' del labbro superiore, ora il lobo dell'orecchio e un tratto del collo' [through the vine leaves of the pergola, was beating upon her face. It was true; and a wonderful sight was the play, on that face, of the purple shadows, straying and shot with threads of golden sunlight, which lighted up now one of her nostrils, and part of her upper lip, now the lobe of her ear and a patch of her throat] (*TR* 600; *Shoot!* 83).[45] His lyricism betrays a given degree of identification with Mirelli, whose subjective creations attest, as it were, to the sensibility of a true artist, foreign to the mechanically produced shams of the film industry: 'Là, nelle sei tele, l'arte, il sogno luminoso d'un giovinetto che non poteva vivere in un tempo come questo. E qua, la donna, caduta da quel sogno, caduta dall'arte nel cinematografo' [There, on the six canvases, the art, the luminous dream of a young man who was unable to live at a time like this. And here, the woman, fallen from that dream, fallen from art to the cinematograph] (*TR* 690; *Shoot!* 170). To be sure,

Gubbio's ideal film images, purportedly able to unveil hidden truths, such as Nestoroff's 'demon' or the non-actor's 'life as it is,' represent his lyrical side as well as exemplify the 'luminous dream' that the cinematic apparatus would have also been able to attain had it not been absorbed by a dreadful industry.

Yet the sincerity of Gubbio's scorn for 'the cinematograph' is questionable. The ambiguity of his judgment is nowhere more striking than in his accounts of Mirelli's art. He sees that body on the canvas in 'triumphant harmony with a nature round about her,' as a 'divine reality.' Nonetheless, he projects this primeval truth, an ideal harmony between nature and the divine, onto the same impressions that, as he reports elsewhere, were 'illuminated by the light in which [Mirelli] beheld her' and thus failed to capture her emotional state. As a humorist, he may be eager to acknowledge that this 'divine reality' is but the artist's construct. In that case, however, one would wonder why he is at all bothered by Nestoroff's having 'fallen from that dream, fallen from art to the cinematograph.' How is the woman on the canvas more of an artist's dream than the woman on the screen? What is it that makes the dream on the canvas superior to the dream on the screen in the first place? In calling it a 'fall,' Gubbio exposes his inconsistency. He conflates Mirelli's – which is to say, his own – subjective impression of Nestoroff as she appears on the canvas with the Nestoroff in flesh and blood. He would have liked the latter to realize unto herself the ideal image that Mirelli invented. He oscillates between the mindset of a humorist and that of a moralist; whereas the humorist, who is Pirandello, knows that neither the 'luminous dream' on the canvas, nor the 'demon' on the screen, nor the 'fallen' woman standing in front of him in flesh and blood is any less or more fictional than any other portrayal of her. Gubbio's insincerity, his wavering between humour and moralism – or rather, humour and irony, as we will see – demands that we revisit not only the authenticity of his idealized images, but also the very falseness of the 'idiotic fictions' that he professes to detest.

7

Cinema as Humour:
The *Oltre* and the *Superfluo*

Gubbio's construction of Nestoroff is worlds away from the mechanisms through which the Dannunzian hero tries to fix his elusive object of desire into something of a Renaissance painting. If Paolo Tarsis or Andrea Sperelli wish to arrest Isabella Inghirami or Elena Muti through the same means that enable them to design, remould, and control their technological or poetic creations, the Pirandellian narrator clings to his role as an impassive observer to whom the mesmerizing diva is but a thought-provoking object of study. This is not to say that Gubbio is all that sincere in describing himself as a mere observer. The clues to an unspoken desire for Nestoroff, though rare and faint, are indisputable. No other character inspires Gubbio to draw so many an image – a tale of a turbulent past, an awkward gesture in a film, a sensuous gaze at a camera, a clumsily aloof face under a grape vine, an ethereal body on a canvas. It is in their fluid exchanges, however, despite the momentary fixity displayed by each image alone, and in their refusal to congeal into the unequivocal symbols of an overtly stated desire, that the images sweep the souls of this story away from their Dannunzian counterparts. Gubbio is not an aesthete, a painter, a philosopher, a scientist, or a poet; rather, he is none and all of those things at once, spiritually flowing in and out of diverse possible temperaments. He is, in other words, a humorist.[1]

This does not make Gubbio his creator's equal. Pirandello magnifies Gubbio's idealism, fixed morals, and tendency towards bitter irony, most evident in his contempt for the institution of cinema, only so that a sharp contrast between this side of his character and his relatively amoral, humoristic side allows the latter to stand out as a genuinely Pirandellian mode of seeing the world, a way to see specifically modernity and its highly contested aesthetic paradigm: cinema. Unlike Pirandello as the narrator of the old dolled-up lady's story, Gubbio never claims that he is a humorist. Instead, he constantly displays his discontent. The reader, however, is asked to gather the clues to an interpretative model other than the one with which a bitter Gubbio assaults us throughout. In spite of its many melodramatic moments, *Si gira* is in some ways the kind of text that Roland Barthes calls 'writerly.'[2] Indeed, it is the urge to harmonize its many dramatic fragments, those occurrences presented through the 'lens' of the cameraman, like parts of a jigsaw puzzle, that turns the reader into the text's producer. It is nonetheless the failure to construe a clear-cut storyline, or a single moral/ideological perspective, that attests to the novel's essayistic dimension, its status as a text about humour. Nestoroff's role in this model is essential. She may flee any allusions to a love scenario, yet her enigma, the tactile texture of which I previously called her humoristic layering, is part and parcel of the interpretative model that Pirandello would like us to draw. She collaborates, that is, with Gubbio the humorist in the articulation of a Pirandellian view of the world and of cinema, hence, in the undoing of that bitterness that haunts Gubbio's other persona, the one that I call Gubbio the ironist.

The Humorist and the Ironist

In the essay on humour, Pirandello distinguishes the humorist from three other types of writers – the comic writer, the ironist, and the satirist – whom the hasty reader may confuse with the humorist. The *sentimento del contrario* is the condition that sets the humorist apart:

> E quest'appunto distingue nettamente l'umorista dal comico, dall'ironico, dal satirico. Non nasce in questi altri il sentimento del contrario; se nascesse, sarebbe reso amaro, cioè non più comico, il riso provocato nel primo dall'avvertimento di una qualsiasi anormalità; la contradizione che nel secondo è soltanto verbale, tra quel che si dice e quel che si vuole sia inteso, diventerebbe effettiva, sostanziale, e dunque non più ironica; e cesserebbe lo sdegno o, comunque, l'avversione della realtà che è ragione d'ogni satira. (*SPSV* 145–6)

> [This is precisely what distinguishes the humorist sharply from the comic writer, the ironist, and the satirist. The feeling of the opposite does not arise in any of the latter; if it did, the laughter provoked in the comic writer

by the perception of any abnormality would turn bitter and therefore would no longer be comical; the contradiction which in irony is only verbal, between what the writer says and what he wants understood, would become real and substantial, and therefore would no longer be ironic; and the scorn, or at least the aversion, for reality, which is the reason of any satire, would cease to exist.] (*Humor* 131)

For all its brevity, the passage is invaluable to our understanding of humour. In addition to differentiating the humorist, it implies that since the *sentimento del contrario* is unique to humour, its intervention in any of the other three forms of writing would transform those into humour. It thus enumerates, if indirectly, some of the conditions of humour. First, humour is never strictly comic. When it includes the comic, laughter is disrupted by compassion for the bearer of the abnormality, an example of which is the narrator's reaction to the dolled-up lady, as discussed above. Second, the remark on the ironist implies that the humorist's own response to any given phenomenon displays a contradiction that is 'real and substantial.' Unlike the ironist, whose single real conviction lies in the opposite of what s/he says, the humorist displays, in a concrete manner, multiple and contrasting responses to any given phenomenon. Third, differently from the satirist, the humorist does not feel sincere aversion for reality. Reflection generates in him 'il sentimento del contrario, il non saper più da qual parte tenere, la perplessità, lo stato irresoluto della coscienza' [the feeling of the opposite, to be in a state of mind of no longer knowing where to turn, of perplexity and irresoluteness] (*SPSV* 145; *Humor* 131). He thus perceives reality in multiple views, the agreeable and disagreeable among which tend to offset each other.

Just as the ironist and the satirist share the practice of critiquing reality, Pirandello's remarks on those two types share the implication that the humorist, differently from those, does not resort to moral judgments, since the *sentimento del contrario* prevents him/her from adhering to a single critical view of reality. Of course, the ironist and the satirist also differ from each other. While they both aim to critique a given phenomenon, they apply different methods to this end. Irony misrepresents its object by ascribing to it moral values that contradict the ones that, in the ironist's view, truly define it. This misrepresentation is exaggerated so as to make the reader suspicious of the sincerity of the statement, thus hinting at the ironist's real opinion. The satirist also uses exaggeration, but that may or may not involve a reversal of the object's moral qualities. Rather, the satirist uses various means to ridicule the object, usually aiming to provóke laughter. Irony, by contrast, may or may not aspire to be funny. In view of Pirandello's remarks on these four modes of discourse, Gubbio's character seems to oscillate between the humorist and the ironist. We have seen that his humorist's disposition conditions his account of Nestoroff's dubious past and relationship with Mirelli (see chapter 6). As regards the other modes of discourse, he is neither a comic writer nor a satirist, as his portrayal of the institution of cinema is hardly amusing. Even in the rare cases in which a character strikes us as laughable, laughter coexists with feelings of pity or sympathy, thus rendering the portrayal humoristic.

The most vivid example of such a character is Fabrizio Cavalena. Gubbio heard about this man from his friend and stage manager, Cocò Polacco. After his wife's pathological jealousy led him to abandon several professional engagements, such as his service in the armed forces as a lieutenant physician, his work as a journalist, and a post at a senior high school as an instructor of physics and natural history, Cavalena now dwells on the grounds of Kosmograph hoping to sell, yet without any luck, his tragic screenplays, the typical suicide plots of which earned him the nickname of Suicida (TR 602–3; Shoot! 86). Gubbio thinks that in order to alleviate his wife's suspicions, Cavalena described Kosmograph to her as an 'austero romitorio, da cui tutte le donne fossero tenute lontane, come demonii' [austere hermitage, from which all women were resolutely banished, like demons]. When Signora Nene, wishing to verify her husband's claims, accompanies him to Kosmograph, along with their daughter Luisetta and her little dog Piccinì, Gubbio reveals the comical spectacle that is this family: 'Cavalena, con la solita faccia di limone ammuffito, tra i riccioli della parrucca sotto il cappellaccio a larghe tese; la moglie, come una bufera a stento contenuta, col cappellino andatole di traverso nello smontare dalla vettura' [Cavalena, looking as usual like a mouldy lemon, among the curls of his wig that protruded under his broad-brimmed hat; his wife, like a cyclone barely held in check, her hat knocked askew as she dismounted from the carriage] (TR 625–6; Shoot! 108–9). Yet shortly thereafter we are told that Cavalena endures endless public humiliations by Signora Nene, that she turned his life into prison, and that now dejected and penniless he has become a public laughing stock.

Thus, laughter is only a part of the response that Cavalena elicits, especially when Gubbio, through the use of free indirect discourse, addresses Cavalena's dilemma, thanks to his ability as an educated man to recognize his wife's pathology: 'Che colpa ha la moglie, quella sua povera Nene, se è così gelosa? Egli è medico e sa che questa gelosia feroce è una vera e propria malattia mentale, una forma di pazzia ragionante. Tipica, tipica forma di paranoja, anche coi delirii della persecuzione' [What fault is it of his wife, his poor Nene, if she is so jealous? He is a doctor and knows that this fierce jealousy is really and truly a mental disease, a form of reasoning madness. Typical, a typical form of paranoia, with persecution mania, too]. Nene thinks that her husband and daughter conspire to kill her in order to take possession of her estate. Gubbio continues: 'E se egli, da medico, capisce tutto questo, non ne segue che dovrebbe trattar la sua povera Nene come un'inferma, irresponsabile del male che gli ha fatto e séguita a fargli? Perché si ribella? contro chi si ribella? Egli deve compatirla e averne pietà, starle attorno amoroso, sopportarne paziente e rassegnato l'inevitabile sevizia' [And if he, as a doctor, understands all this, does it not follow that he ought to treat his poor Nene as a sick patient, not responsible for the harm she has done him and continues to do him? Why rebel? Against whom? He ought to feel for her and to show pity, to stand by her lovingly, to endure with patience and resignation her inevitable cruelty] (*TR* 631–2; *Shoot!* 114–15). Pirandello's use of free indirect discourse, most evident in the repeated phrase 'his poor Nene,' has a twofold function. On the one hand, in the absence of tangible proof, it suggests that these remarks indeed represent Cavalena's thoughts and not Gubbio's speculations, thus allowing Gubbio's account to pass as an objective observation. Yet this same technique suggests that the thoughts are Gubbio's own, and that the study of the situation from diverse evaluative perspectives reflects his humorist's approach, more so than Cavalena's real motives or own humoristic temperament. This application of diverse perspectives, diverting us from Cavalena's comic dimension to his moral, psychological, and intellectual dilemma, is an effect of the *sentimento del contrario*, which despite the comical inflections makes Gubbio a humorist more than a comic writer or satirist.

Yet in many of the instances in which Gubbio does not think like a humorist he thinks like an ironist. He presents his contempt for modern reality, stated time and again, as his single real conviction. These are moments in which he is driven by a moral judgment, such as the idea that industrialization is loathsome because it is alienating, along with its flipside implication that the pre-industrial era preserved basic human values. The adherence to a single view of reality does not merely contradict Gubbio the humorist. It specifically makes him an ironist, as he often expresses his contempt in a celebratory tone that flaunts its falseness. He establishes his ironic stance at the opening of his 'notebooks.' First, he clearly states his qualms about modern life: 'Mi domando se veramente tutto questo fragoroso e vertiginoso meccanismo della vita, che di giorno in giorno sempre più si còmplica e s'accèlèra, non abbia ridotto l'umanità in tale stato di follia, che presto proromperà frenetica a sconvolgere e a distruggere tutto' [I ask myself whether really all this clamorous and dizzy machinery of life, which from day to day seems to become more complicated and to move with greater speed, has not reduced the human race to such a condition of insanity that presently we must brave out in fury and overthrow and destroy everything] (*TR* 520; *Shoot!* 4–5). He then meets a curious gentleman, a Pirandello look-alike as the description suggests,[3] whose face was 'gracile, pallida, con radi capelli biondi; occhi cilestri, arguti; barbetta a punta, gialliccia, sotto la quale si nascondeva un sorrisetto, che voleva parer timido e cortese, ma era malizioso' [delicate, pale, with thin, fair hair; keen, blue eyes; a pointed, yellowish goatee, behind which there lurked a faint smile that tried to appear timid and polite, but was really sly].[4] This man questions the very necessity of Gubbio's profession: 'Scusi, non si è trovato ancor modo di far girare la macchinetta da sé?' [Excuse me, but haven't they yet discovered a way of making the camera go by itself?]. This triggers Gubbio's first thought of himself as a machine: 'Con quella domanda voleva dirmi: "Siete proprio necessario voi? Che cosa siete voi? *Una mano che gira la manovella.* Non si potrebbe fare a meno di questa mano? Non potreste esser soppresso, sostituito da un qualche meccanismo?"' [By his question he meant to say to me: 'Is there any real necessity for you? What are you? A hand that turns the handle. Couldn't they do without this hand? Couldn't you be eliminated, replaced by some piece of machinery?'] (*TR* 521–2; *Shoot!* 6).

Gubbio reveals his ironist's skill by feigning to welcome the prospect of total mechanization:

Sorrisi e risposi:
– Forse col tempo, signore. A dir vero, la qualità precipua che si richiede in uno che faccia la mia professione è l'*impassibilità* di fronte all'azione che si svolge davanti alla macchina. Un meccanismo, per questo riguardo, sarebbe senza dubbio più adatto e da preferire a un uomo. Ma la difficoltà più grave, per ora, è questa: trovare un meccanismo, che possa regolare il movimento secondo l'azione che si svolge davanti alla macchina. Giacché io, caro signore, non giro sempre allo stesso modo la manovella, ma ora

più presto ora più piano, secondo il bisogno. Non dubito però, che col tempo – sissignore – si arriverà a sopprimermi. La macchinetta – anche questa macchinetta, come tante altre macchinette – girerà da sé. (*TR* 522)

[I smiled as I answered:
'In time, Sir, perhaps. To tell you the truth, the chief quality that is required in a man of my profession is impassivity in face of the action that is going on in front of the camera. A piece of machinery, in that respect, would doubtless be better suited, and preferable to a man. But the most serious difficulty, at present, is this: where to find a machine that can regulate its movements according to the action that is going on in front of the camera. Because I, my dear Sir, do not always turn the handle at the same speed, but faster or slower as may be required. I have no doubt, however, that in time, Sir, they will succeed in eliminating me. The machine – this machine, too, like all the other machines – will go by itself.'] (*Shoot!* 6)

He expresses more feelings of discontent and unrecoverable loss, followed nonetheless by his most emblematic ironic statement:

L'uomo che prima, poeta, deificava i suoi sentimenti e li adorava, buttati via i sentimenti, ingombro non solo inutile ma anche dannoso, e divenuto saggio e industre, s'è messo a fabbricar di ferro, d'acciajo le sue nuove divinità ed è diventato servo e schiavo di esse.
Viva la Macchina che meccanizza la vita! (*TR* 523; emphasis added)

[Man who first of all, as a poet, deified his own feelings and worshipped them, now having flung aside every feeling, as an encumbrance not only useless but positively harmful, and having become clever and industrious, has set to work to fashion out of iron and steel his new deities and has become a servant and a slave to them.
Long live the Machine that mechanizes life!] (*Shoot!* 7; emphasis added)

In such instances that define his mindset early on, Gubbio displays a contradiction that is not (to reiterate Pirandello's definition of irony) 'real and substantial' but 'only verbal, between what the writer says' (his welcoming of mechanization) 'and what he wants understood' (his condemnation of modernity).[5]

It is important to note that Pirandello's definition of irony as presented here refers to the kind that in his 1920 essay 'Ironia' (Irony) he calls 'rhetorical.' He distinguishes this kind from 'philosophical' irony, the latter having been inferred 'dai romantici tedeschi direttamente dall'idealismo soggettivo del Fichte, ma che ha in fondo le sue origini in tutto il movimento idealistico germanico post-kantiano' [by the German Romantics directly from Fichte's subjective idealism, though it essentially has its origins in the whole German post-Kantian idealist movement] (*SPSV* 1028). Drawing on Hegel, Tieck, and Schlegel, he describes philosophical irony as a 'forza,' a force, which deriving from the disposition to view the universe as a vain semblance allows poets to construct reality as they wish:

> Hegel spiegava che l'io, sola realtà vera, può sorridere della vana parvenza dell'universo: come la pone, può anche annullarla; può non prender sul serio le proprie creazioni. Onde appunto l'ironia: cioè quella forza – secondo il Tieck – che permette al poeta di dominar la materia che tratta: materia che si riduce per essa – secondo Federico Schlegel – a una perpetua parodia, a una farsa trascendentale. (*SPSV* 1028)

> [Hegel explained that the I, the only true reality, may smile about the vain semblance of the universe: as it lays it down, it may also annul it; it may not take seriously its own creations. Whence derives precisely irony: namely, that force – according to Tieck – that allows the poet to dominate the material that he treats: material that is reduced, by that force – according to Friedrich Schlegel – to a perpetual parody, to a transcendental farce.]

Irony is a force that allows one to understand the idea of a 'transcendental farce,' not in the common sense of the farce as a silly composition of vulgar hilarity, but as the self-parody and self-caricature that is inherent, for example, in tragedy, or as that arbitrary, illusory construct that constitutes our every notion of reality. He also states: 'Tra quella che suol chiamarsi ironia retorica e questa filosofica una certa parentela si può scoprire' [Between that which is usually called rhetorical irony and this philosophical kind, one may discover a certain relationship]. He refrains, however, from specifying exactly where their relationship lies. Instead, he proceeds to rhetorically encapsulate their dividing factor: 'La differenza tra l'una e l'altra è, che in quella non bisogna prender sul serio ciò che si dice, e in questa ciò che si fa' [The difference between the one and the other is that in the former (the rhetorical) one need not take seriously that which is said, and in the latter (the philosophical) that which is done] (*SPSV* 1029). While he does not elaborate on their alleged relationship, there is no doubt that the difference between them is crucial, specifically if we evaluate them with respect to humour. Whereas philosophical irony, in that it approaches reality as an illusory construct, is aligned with humour, rhetorical irony, which consists in 'una contradizione verbale tra quel che si dice e quel che si vuole sia inteso' [a verbal contradiction between that which one says and that which one wants to be understood] (1028), is essentially anti-humoristic, as the ironist in this case sustains a single view of reality, one that represents a stable moral or ideological conviction.[6]

Gavriel Moses compellingly discusses Pirandello's view of cinema from a perspective that unites irony with humour. In accordance with Pirandello's designation of philosophical irony, Moses seems to draw from *Si gira* a theory of cinema as a medium that is essentially marked by unreality, and which at the same time constitutes a selective and refined version of reality – a type of portrayal that does not unveil reality's pre-existent meaning as much as it points to the process of the creation of meaning.[7] Moses's analysis also incorporates Pirandello's definition of rhetorical irony, thus hinting at the relationship between the two kinds, which Pirandello leaves undefined: 'Very much in the limited sense of Pirandello's view of rhetorical irony, then, film *says* something that is untrue but leaves no clue in the text as to this untruth.'[8] The phenomenon that Moses describes, however, strikes me as an effect of *philosophical* irony, because it seems to differ from the rhetorical in at least three ways. First, as we have seen, in both the essay on humour and the essay on irony, Pirandello defines rhetorical irony as a form of *writing* that involves a *verbal* contradiction between what one says and what one wants understood. In the case of the film image, however, the material closeness between sign and referent renders the unreality of the representation quite subtle, thus bringing it closer to philosophical irony, for which any allegedly real event, be it reality itself or its most faithful reproduction, does not bear meaning except when diluted into an arbitrary, illusory construct. Let us note that in making his claim Moses seems to refer to a specific kind of film, the trick film, which exploits the immediacy between sign and referent to allow for things unreal to pass as real: 'It is the very immediacy of photographic reproduction which guarantees the reality-status of the silliest simplifications; the most fanciful flights of the imagination are "made real" by the medium.'[9] To be sure, in such cases, the filmmaker's discourse – like that of the rhetorical ironist, whose statement contradicts what the ironist him/herself considers real – defies a reality that the filmmaker him/herself recognizes as such. Moses, however, if the trick film is indeed his model, does not specify how its plainly unreal portrayal, though it shares something with rhetorical irony, carries over to cinematic narrative realism – where the rupture between the object and its representation is of greater subtlety, thus akin to philosophical more than to rhetorical irony, and which is – importantly – the prevalent style of filmmaking in *Si gira*, at least as far as Gubbio's few and brief descriptions of it allow us to presume.

Second, let us recall that in discussing rhetorical irony Pirandello speaks of a *contradiction* between what the writer says and the idea that s/he intends to convey. Film is unreal, on the other hand, not necessarily because it *contradicts* the filmmaker's belief or perception of reality, but because it involves a *selection* from reality, or as Moses himself expresses it by drawing on Merleau-Ponty, because 'it provides a new "finer-grained" and "more exact" picture of the world.'[10] In fact, owing again to the closeness between sign and referent, a filmic portrayal that contradicts the filmmaker's belief may easily result in the filmmaker's being misunderstood, more so than succeed as rhetorical irony. Third, Pirandello does not indicate, as Moses seems to assume, that rhetorical irony 'leaves no clue in the text as to this untruth.' Admittedly, Pirandello does not state the opposite either, namely, that the ironic statement in some tangible way reveals its own untruth. Yet while he leaves this question unresolved, his definition of rhetorical irony being quite brief, I insist that what points to the ironist's genuine conviction is a degree of exaggeration in his/her false evaluation of the phenomenon represented, as well as the contrast between the other, non-ironic, aspects of his/her discourse and the ironic statement itself – which does not come in a vacuum, and exemplary of which is, as we have seen, Gubbio's 'Long live the Machine that mechanizes life!'

I repeat that Moses's analysis of Pirandello's theory of film in terms of humour and irony is compelling – specifically in defining film's 'unreality' as a refined selection from the world, a 'more exact picture' of it, or, in Pirandellian terms, an ideal fiction drawn upon it – and I will again draw on Moses's contribution when I formulate my conclusions about the relationship between humour and narrative cinema as a pervasive cultural phenomenon. Furthermore, I agree with Moses's analysis insofar as it promotes the link between cinema and philosophical irony. I dwelled, however, on the distinction between the latter and rhetorical irony, because in my view it is precisely Gubbio's intermittent persona as a rhetorical ironist that contradicts, on the one hand, his humorist's persona, and allows us, on the other hand, to draw a picture of the degrees of convergence and divergence between him and Pirandello. As I stated at the opening of my study of *Si gira*, the reader has no choice but to engage in a constant reassessment of the extent to which Gubbio's views stand for Pirandello's. Certainly, while Gubbio's supreme narrative authority prevents us from entirely disengaging his views from the author's, the identification between the two figures is not absolute. This is not to say that they do not share something essential, and we must not assume that the two may be separated without qualification. In fact, Gubbio may be described as Pirandello's alter ego, to the extent that in Gubbio Pirandello creates a version of himself, yet one who is less advanced as a humorist. At any given moment, being more of a humorist and less of an ironist vis-à-vis Gubbio, Pirandello is found a step ahead of his protagonist, that is, a step ahead of his self under construction.

The reader may wonder why Pirandello, if he indeed wished to represent himself, would create a character that lagged behind by one step. A few suggestions may be put forth to address this question, all of which relate to the act of writing. For one, with *Si gira* Pirandello intended to write not yet another theoretical essay, one that now would have specialized on humour's relation to cinema, but a work of narrative fiction, one that despite its pervasive essayistic dimension – which undeniably directs us to its most essential meaning, be it historical, philosophical, or psychological – would have successfully integrated this dimension with its no less significant one, the mimetic. The latter requires the conception of a protagonist who, like most human beings, has the tendency to subscribe to fixed beliefs, to see life through the lens of a particular ideological conviction. In wishing to ascribe to his alter ego a familiar form, an identity that any reader would recognize and to which any reader would relate in some way, the author tends to transform his alter ego into an ideal fiction, that is, into a man who adheres to a fixed belief.

Moreover, the author himself, inasmuch as he enjoys the privilege of a humoristic disposition, is not entirely exempt from the tendency towards fixed beliefs. We may in fact speak of a mirror effect, insofar as Pirandello conceives of his mirror image in Gubbio the ironist. I am referring neither to some form of reciprocal mirroring between Pirandello and Gubbio, nor to Gubbio as an exact Pirandello look-alike. Rather, I am applying this metaphor in a way that respects the mirror's physiological property of providing a visually finite and exclusive, hence selective and limited, version of the subject. We may think of Gubbio as

Pirandello's mirror image in that his rhetorical ironist's persona, as one who subscribes to a fixed belief, represents Pirandello's own tendency to free himself from his humorist's 'state of mind of no longer knowing where to turn, of perplexity and irresoluteness' (see above) and adhere to a fixed belief, or, if I may sustain the metaphor, to dilute his 'irresoluteness' into a finite and crystalline image.[11] Furthermore, the metaphor of the mirror helps us to articulate the crucial difference between the two figures. In being the subject rather than the subject's mirror image, Pirandello fails to conform adequately to such an image – one that is marked by visual precision and a closed contour, and to which he makes the fictional Gubbio conform with more ease and steadiness – because he is quite prone to be dispersed in multiple directions, each one representing yet another possibility for evaluating any given phenomenon. His prevailing inclination is to value the coexistence of these multiple options and ascribe considerable weight to each one. This is what distinguishes him as a humorist. Hence Gubbio, inasmuch as he constitutes Pirandello's alter ego, being more of an ironist and less of a humorist vis-à-vis the author, lags behind by one step. His ironist's persona is a scapegoat of sorts, an exemplary and magnified carrier of those instances of fictional stability that serve to demonstrate that particular side of the author's dialectical process of self-portrayal. It works like a foil against which Pirandello the humorist reaffirms himself.[12]

Another way of addressing the relationship between the two figures is to question Pirandello's motive in writing this novel in the particular tone in which he wrote it, namely, with a consistent emphasis on Gubbio's overt condemnation of the cinematic institution and modernity throughout. The question is twofold, leading us simultaneously in what initially appear to be two opposite routes. On the one hand, we may rhetorically ask: Why would Pirandello, if he indeed shared Gubbio's views, devote an entire novel to a phenomenon that he detests? A likely answer is that a deeper analysis of the novel, perhaps with respect to his theory of humour (as is the case with the present study), exposes Pirandello's implicit appreciation of the medium, or at least his more complex view of it, one that in any case casts doubt on Gubbio's one-dimensional grudge. On the other hand, aiming to contest this view, one may ask: Why would Pirandello devote an entire novel to a narrator's contempt for the institution of cinema unless he himself shared this contempt at least in part? Both sides of the question are valid, which suggests not only that the author himself experiences a conflict, in that he, like Gubbio, if to a lesser degree, tends to adhere to a fixed belief, but also that the author, in devising a humoristic work of literature, and aspiring to elicit a humoristic response from the reader, wishes to neither validate nor invalidate his narrator's grudge. The latter, in fact, in addition to enforcing the novel's mimetic aspect, is instrumental to the novel's humour. As I have stated, it is like a foil against which Pirandello the humorist reaffirms himself. Furthermore, the fact that it is magnified as compared to Pirandello the subject or Pirandello the humorist is a further strategy that, like mimesis, relates to the act of writing. Let me further explain the notion of the magnified irony as a foil and the way in which it involves writing and, more precisely, narrative.

We have in our hands a humoristic work, one that involves the interaction between diachronic and synchronic relationships among images, which my previous chapter addressed in more general terms. Gubbio's coexisting personas as ironist and humorist, in order to suit narrative form, are laid out diachronically. We may view their alternation as a form of humoristic reflection, where contrasting states of mind awaken each other. Below we will consider the peculiarities of the type of reflection that I am proposing here. For the time being, let us agree that, in this specific context, Gubbio's irony is a case of the *avvertimento del contrario*, a reaction to the perception of an abnormality, that is, man's mechanization in modernity, which the humorist's persona would be eager to re-examine. The process, however, is not realized as such in the diegesis, since Gubbio the narrator does not claim awareness of the alternation. It operates instead on the extra-diegetic level, in Pirandello's relationship with his reader, whom the author wishes to espouse to humour. That Gubbio is not conscious of the alternation does not mean that he fails as a humorist. One of his personas is after all that of a humorist, but his recurrent recourse to mere irony indicates his lesser humorist's status vis-à-vis the author. If he does not, however, draw our attention to the alternation, that is, to the reflexive process by which the two diverse states awaken each other, how does Pirandello realize this process for the reader? The diachronic layout of the alternation renders tangible the contrast between the two personas, the ironist and the humorist. Irony is magnified only to sharpen the contrast, to thus allow the reader to refine his/her recognition of the humorist – an intellectual endeavour that the contrast itself tends to refine – and to weigh the two positions against one another time and again. Gubbio's status as a humorist, though highlighted diachronically, also constitutes a synchronic condition. This is true if we grasp the novel as a whole, as an overall impression, rather than as a diachronic process, to thus perceive Gubbio as an ensemble of his contradictory personas, as a set of images that relate to each other synchronically. Hence, his humorist's persona, the one that is highlighted diachronically, relates metonymically to Gubbio the humorist as a synchronic condition. The latter, in its turn, bears a metaphorical function, in that it stands for Pirandello the humorist, who constitutes a synchronic condition since he represents none but the novel's intellectual premise, the disposition that moulds it. In this indirect way, Gubbio's magnified irony is like a foil against which Pirandello the humorist reaffirms himself.

The novel hints at the reflexive process of two states of mind, humorist and ironist, early on, in Gubbio's encounter with the curious gentleman who resembles Pirandello, as noted above. The latter strikes us as relatively neutral, in that he is not, or he feigns not to be, as disturbed by mechanization as Gubbio is: 'Excuse me, but haven't they yet discovered a way of making the camera go by itself?' This neutrality, real or contrived, makes him look indubitably sly in Gubbio's eyes. As we have seen, Gubbio paraphrases the question in an elaborate fashion so as to articulate his first poignant ironic statement. In itself, however, the man's question poses as neutral, and it is strictly Gubbio who spells out its 'sly' intention to us readers. This suspicious neutrality, in its ambiguity, reflects that irresoluteness that marks the humoristic disposition of this Pirandello figure, yet Gubbio the ironist reshapes the question so as to drive it in a single direction. Nonetheless, it is his own deeper consciousness that Gubbio encounters in this figure, marked by ambivalence more than by irony, and which Mario Patanè describes as Gubbio's 'alter ego.'[13] Much of what follows this early encounter belongs to one of Gubbio's two conflicting temperaments, forming either a multidirectional discourse, or a unidirectional, contemptuous one. The latter is the one that encompasses his ironic mode, which is a symptom of his idealism as discussed in the previous chapter. Irony and idealism share the conceptual premise that the present state of the world is flawed, while an essential truth is somewhere to be found, from which to rebuild the world authentically. His tendency to psychoanalyse, to speculate on the psychic cause of Nestoroff's reaction to her own image, or his belief that a non-institutionalized camera, in capturing its object unawares, may reveal 'life as it is,' reflects his faith in a single, essential, and recoverable truth. His rhetorical irony, which scorns this truth's degradation, is another effect of this faith.

As I indicated, the humoristic reflection between Gubbio's two contradictory positions as proposed above is a peculiar one. First, my reader may have noted that here reflection involves no more than two positions, whereas my previous chapter spoke of reflection as an infinite formation of constructs. Second, the two positions do not constitute responses to the same phenomenon as in the case, for instance, of the dolled-up lady. Whereas Gubbio's ironic persona addresses his views on industrial modernity, his humoristic persona addresses various subjects, such as Nestoroff's past or the drama of the Cavalena family. Third, one of the two positions represents not a fixed belief, an ideal construct entering in a contrasting relationship with other ideal constructs, but the humoristic disposition itself, the mutual negation, reaffirmation, or revision of coexisting constructs. Let us also recall that here reflection is not presented as such in the diegesis, since Gubbio does not consciously weigh his two positions against one another. Furthermore, differently from a writer like Manzoni, whose Don Abbondio, regardless of Manzoni's intentions, lends himself to Pirandello's theorization of humour, Pirandello writes fiction while thinking theoretically about humour. Yet he does not, I repeat, wish to substitute theory for mimesis. Instead, via fiction, he sets up a process of reflection between two positions, not as takes on a single phenomenon (as with the dolled-up lady, Don Abbondio, Nestoroff, or Cavalena) but as *modes of thought*. He thus engages the reader in a humoristic process that operates extradiegetically and supersedes the single case study with its various interpretations. While reading fiction, the reader is urged to think in a theoretical vein about the two positions as diverse modes of thought, which s/he must weigh against one another time and again. Owing to this superstructure, *Si gira* works like an essay on humour. The extradiegetic reflection in which it engages the reader is essential to its essayistic dimension. As we will see, there is indeed a single phenomenon to which the reader him/herself, given Gubbio's failure to consciously do so, is incited to apply this type of reflection. It is the question of cinema, and specifically, Gubbio's disapproval of the film industry.

Furthermore, in the context of this particular form of reflection, given that reflection is also what constitutes one of the two positions, the process as a whole becomes self-regenerating. Thus, Pirandello's novel-essay points to an essential characteristic of humour, namely, that humour supersedes the mere clashes that occur within a set number of fixed images. Rather, it involves the multiple ways in which images intersect, interpenetrate, thus modify one another and form new images. That is because humour itself becomes one of the contrasting positions. As such, it has a twofold character. It is at once a mode of thought *and* a dynamic image that comprises the fluid interactions among images. In its twofold character, it invades and reshapes what appear as external and fixed images. To put it differently, the humorist is aware of being a humorist. S/he is not at the mercy of a limited number of clashing fixed views of one phenomenon, between which s/he then oscillates hopelessly. Rather, s/he adopts the humoristic position *consciously*, as a mental image that s/he applies to the revision of those images that appear as fixed. As this results in the infinite formation of new images, the process as a whole becomes self-regenerating. Hence, we may not think of 'humour' as a conclusive term. The thinker may have great faith in humour as a method for the study of reality, but that does not make it a fixed belief like those that attach a stable meaning to any given phenomenon. It is the belief in the disproving of all beliefs. We may thus think of humour only as an open and self-regenerating process.

What catalyses this process is a paradoxical wish to attain that imperceptible register that the essay on humour describes as reality in its absolute form, a 'reality living beyond the reach of human vision, outside the forms of human reason,' 'something else which man can face only at the cost of either death or insanity' (see chapter 6). This register finds its way into *Si gira* in various forms. Its strongest allusion is that mysterious aspect of all things that Gubbio calls 'oltre,' best translated as 'the beyond,' given his use of the term as a noun. At opening, he states: 'C'è un *oltre* in tutto. Voi non volete o non sapete vederlo. Ma appena appena quest'oltre baleni negli occhi d'un ozioso come me, che si metta a osservarvi, ecco, vi smarrite, vi turbate o irritate' [There is something more in everything. You do not wish or do not know how to see it. But the moment this something more gleams in the eyes of an idle person like myself, who has set himself to observe you, why, you become puzzled, disturbed, or irritated] (*TR* 519; *Shoot!* 4). It assumes more concrete forms in the themes of the tiger and religion – concrete insofar as the tiger is a body the physiological functions of which may be studied by rational discourse, while religion is an institution that entails organized practices. Nonetheless, each theme evokes a notion that is difficult to grasp. The tiger is here a metonym for nature, while religion evokes the divine. Both 'nature' and 'divine' are signs the referents of which are elusive. They share this quality with the *oltre*, of which they are parts. The elusive referent is what catalyses reflection and renders it a self-regenerating process. Of course, in the context of humour everything is deemed elusive. There is a difference, however, between these notions and things like identity or a person's motives. Whereas the former resist tangible and rational definitions, the latter lend themselves to ideal constructs drawn on tangible and rationally conceived phenomena. To say that Nestoroff is a film star presupposes some facts regarding income, lifestyle, professional activities, or appearance. To say that she tried to seduce Mirelli presupposes the operation of some explainable mechanisms. In other words, we may relate tangible referents to 'identity' or 'motives' more successfully than to 'the *oltre*' (or 'nature,' or 'the divine'). Let us see how the two groups relate to one another in the context of a humoristic response. At first glance, the ideal constructs drawn on apprehensible phenomena are products of what Gubbio calls *superfluo*, whereas the *oltre* is the imperceptible state that in the course of reflection – the infinite formation of constructs, products of the *superfluo* – vaguely reveals its existence to the humorist, yet all the while maintaining its indefinableness and continuing to catalyse the process. I repeat that this is how the two categories appear to relate to one another at first glance. As we proceed, we will examine whether there is an objective difference between them, whether the *oltre* indeed exists.

The Diva, the Tiger, and the *Oltre*

Gubbio's ironic mode dominates when he speaks of the tiger, insofar as the projected killing of the innocent beast for the most sensational scene of *La donna e la tigre* exemplifies the industry's alienation from nature, the latter's exploitation for the creation of 'idiotic fictions' and financial gain. Kosmograph purchased the tiger from Rome's Zoological Gardens, where it had been recently donated, shortly before it was condemned to death because it was found to be, 'assolutamente irriducibile, non dico a farle soffiare il naso col fazzoletto, ma neanche a rispettare le regole più elementari della vita sociale. Tre, quattro volte minacciò di saltare il fosso, si provò anzi a saltarlo, per lanciarsi sui visitatori del Giardino, che stavano pacificamente ad ammirarla da lontano' [absolutely incapable of learning, I do not say to blow her nose with a handkerchief but even to respect the most elementary rules of social intercourse. Three or four times she threatened to jump the ditch or, rather, attempted to jump it, to hurl herself upon the visitors to the gardens who stood quietly gazing at her from a distance].

Gubbio feels strong compassion for the tiger, the beastly innocence of which, he notes, led it to believe that the ditch had been built for no other reason than for it to jump it, and that those visitors stood there for no other reason than to be devoured. Furthermore, now locked inside a cage at Kosmograph, the animal is oblivious to the tragic end that awaits it. Gubbio is critical of either institution for bringing the tiger by force into an urban environment and awakening its natural instincts only to severely punish it for them. To his imaginary interlocutors who contest his views, he answers condescendingly: 'Ma non vi sembra uno scherzo pensare, ch'essa possa supporre che la teniate lì esposta per dare al popolo una "nozione vivente" di storia naturale?' [But does it not seem a joke to you to think that she can suppose that you keep her there on show to give the public a 'living idea' of natural history?] (*TR* 574–5; *Shoot!* 57–8). He admits, with irony, that his words of sympathy for the tiger are mere 'rhetoric,' and only with irony does he elaborate:

> Possiamo aver compatimento per un uomo che non sappia stare allo scherzo; non dobbiamo averne per una bestia; tanto più se questo scherzo a cui l'abbiamo esposta, dico della 'nozione vivente,' può avere conseguenze funeste: cioè per i visitatori del Giardino Zoologico, una nozione troppo sperimentale della ferocia di essa.
>
> Questa tigre fu dunque saggiamente condannata a morte. La Società della *Kosmograph* riuscì a saperlo in tempo e la comperò. (*TR* 575)

> [We may feel compassion for a man who is unable to stand a joke; we ought not to feel any for a beast, especially if the joke for which we have placed it on show, I mean the 'living idea,' may have fatal consequences: that is to say, for the visitors to the Zoological Gardens, a too-practical illustration of its ferocity.
>
> This tiger was, therefore, wisely condemned to death. The Kosmograph Company managed to hear of it in time, and bought her.] (*Shoot!* 58)

It is again with irony, now speaking directly to the tiger, that Gubbio informs us of Nestoroff's frequent visits to Kosmograph's menagerie, in order to study the tiger's behaviour – how it moves, how it turns its head, how it stares – in preparation of her part in the film under production: 'La Nestoroff. Ti par poco? T'ha eletto a sua maestra. Fortune come questa, non càpitano a tutte le tigri' [The Nestoroff. Is that nothing to you? She has chosen you to be her teacher. Luck such as this does not come the way of every tiger] (*TR* 578; *Shoot!* 61). He thus indirectly scorns the observation of the animal's behaviour, which is carried out not in order to ensure the animal's well-being, but strictly for the aesthetic refinement of a commercial film.

It is understandable that critics interpret the theme of the tiger as Pirandello's attack on industrial modernity, his lament for the loss of a more authentic existence as a result of modernization. Gubbio elicits our most tender feelings for the tiger, while no other element in the novel claims so tangibly, solely by virtue of its nature, its separate ontological status vis-à-vis industrialization, mechanization, and the triumph of human rationality that such categories entail. In commenting on Nestoroff's visits to the menagerie, Gubbio affirms: 'Non si sta invano, capirete, per una mezz'ora a guardare e a considerare una tigre, a vedere in essa un'espressione della terra, ingenua, di là dal bene e dal male, incomparabilmente bella e innocente nella sua potenza feroce' [It is no mere waste of time, you will understand, to spend half an hour in watching and considering a tiger, seeing in it a manifestation of Earth, guileless, beyond good and evil, incomparably beautiful and innocent in its savage power] (*TR* 579; *Shoot!* 62). Hence, the claim made by Giorgio Barberi-Squarotti, who sees the tiger as the only authentic entity in a world of mechanical artifice, appears incontestable: 'The tiger is the only authentic figure also in the world, outside the wings and fictions of the production house, when it lives in the zoological garden and behaves as its instinct commands.'[14] In a study that pits Pirandello's critique of the machine against Futurism's machine cult, Roberto Tessari sees the tiger's killing as 'the absolute triumph of artificial nature over real nature,' 'artificial nature' bearing film technology as its emblem, which Gubbio describes in terms analogous to the tiger's, as machines that devour life 'con la voracità delle bestie afflitte da un verme solitario ... La vita ingoiata dalle macchine è lì, in quei vermi solitarii, dico nelle pellicole già avvolte nei telaj' [with the voracity of animals gnawed by a tapeworm ... The life swallowed by the machines is there, in those tapeworms, I mean the films, now coiled on their reels] (*TR* 571; *Shoot!* 54).[15]

It is my view, nonetheless, that the critics paint only a partial picture of the relationship that Pirandello sets up between nature and industry, a relationship that is not, as it may seem at first glance, one of strict opposition. This partial picture corresponds to the viewpoint of Gubbio the ironist. From a humoristic perspective, however, one may question the very notion of nature as pure, innocent, and more 'real' than the 'artificial nature' into which technology and cinema immerse daily life, as a register of which the entanglement with technology and rationality leads to its degradation. One may view this pure nature as an ideal construct, a fiction that the humorist may wish to challenge with another fiction, one that would define nature differently. In *Si gira*, after all, it is institutions such as the Zoological Gardens and Kosmograph that promote this notion of authenticity, owing precisely to their reliance on rationality and the technological constructions that it enables, such as the stage sets that presumably reproduce that distant and utopian register in which we imagine the tiger's authentic existence. In making this claim I am not arguing that, when born and living in a distant jungle still unexplored by and imperceptible to man, the tiger fares any worse than when captured and locked in the zoo or the film industry's cage to await its execution. I am arguing, rather, that Pirandello – unlike Gubbio the ironist – claims to have no knowledge of what constitutes the tiger's authentic life and well-being, while he allows us to infer that modern institutions construct and market a particular image of that life. That is to say, he draws attention to our limited perspective, to our inability to know any more of reality than what our historically specific means – based on technology, given methods of exploration – permit. 'Nature,' in other words, here exemplified in the abyss conveyed by the tiger's gaze, is a sign the referent of which evades us. The tiger's 'manifestation of Earth,' its being 'guileless, beyond good and evil,' relieve it from the rationalist categories that govern human actions, placing it next to the divine in the realm of the *oltre*, or the beyond, in a 'reality living beyond the reach of human vision, outside the forms of human reason.'

That hypothetical other fiction, that which would define nature differently, although it is fiction, is not valueless. If our capacity to define reality is limited to ideal constructs, fixed beliefs, or fictions, these are the things that constitute truth for us. They are what we have that is perceptible and rationally conceivable.[16] The *oltre*, by contrast, is the imperceptible realm the existence of which the humoristic disposition, insofar as it incites reflection, brings to our awareness. Being aware of its existence does not mean that we may define it. I repeat that the *oltre* makes itself felt to the humorist while remaining indefinable. We may grasp it in one of two ways: schematically (that is, without humour), as a hollow concept, by settling with the thought that it is a sign with an elusive referent and leaving it at that; or substantially, as a state of emotional and intellectual unrest, the irresoluteness that marks the humorist's state of mind. This unrest grows out of the clash between the multiple fictions that strive to define a given phenomenon. For this reason, no fiction is valueless. This model finds support in a brief, yet crucial passage in which Gubbio philosophizes about life and the role of reason:

> Come sono sciocchi tutti coloro che dichiarano la vita un mistero, infelici che vogliono con la ragione spiegarsi quello che con la ragione non si spiega!
>
> Porsi davanti la vita come un oggetto da studiare, è assurdo, perché la vita, posta davanti così, perde per forza ogni consistenza reale e diventa un'astrazione vuota di senso e di valore. E com'è più possibile spiegarsela? L'avete uccisa. Potete, tutt'al più farne l'anatomia.
>
> La vita non si spiega; si vive.
>
> La ragione è nella vita; non può esserne fuori. (*TR* 662)

> [What fools all the people are who declare that life is a mystery, wretches who seek to explain by the use of reason what reason is powerless to explain!
>
> To set life before one as an object of study is absurd, because life, when set before one like that, inevitably loses all its real consistency and becomes an abstraction, void of meaning and value. And how after that is it possible to explain it to oneself? You have killed it. The most you can do now is to dissect it.
>
> Life is not explained; it is lived.
>
> Reason exists in life; it cannot exist apart from it.] (*Shoot!* 143)

Reason being our best tool and a product of life itself, it must grapple with life's distinct phenomena, but it may not explain life as a whole, which is a vast inconclusive process. Treating life as a unity leads to its labelling as a 'mystery,' which is similar to what I called a schematic grasp of the *oltre*. It means to assign closure to an infinite process, to settle with 'life' as a sign with no referent and leave it at that. It respects the limits of reason yet renders life an abstraction. The alternative is to preserve life's meaning by *living* rather that *explaining* it. This does not mean that one must abandon all contemplation, but the object of study must be any of life's countless phenomena and not life as a unity. Through reason, one is to dive into a constant inquiry with no pause, to grapple with the multiple rational constructs that strive to explain life's phenomena, to welcome the unrest that grows out of the infinite clash between such constructs.

The passage proceeds with one of the novel's rare, yet crucial references to religion, which we may view as a rationally more manageable synonym of the *oltre*:

Fuori della vita non c'è nulla. Avvertire questo nulla, con la ragione che si astrae dalla vita, è ancora vivere, è ancora *un nulla* nella vita: un sentimento di mistero: la religione. Può essere disperato, se senza illusioni; può placarsi rituffandosi nella vita, non più di qua, ma di là, in quel *nulla*, che diventa subito *tutto*. (*TR* 662)

[Outside life there is nothingness. To observe this nothingness, with the reason which abstracts itself from life, is still to live, is still *a nothingness* in our life: a sense of mystery – religion. It may be desperate, if it has no illusions; it may appease itself by plunging back into life, no longer here, but there, into that *nothingness*, which at once becomes *all*.] (*Shoot!* 144)[17]

Whereas life consists of innumerable perceptible phenomena every one of which we may explain through rational constructs, outside it lies a realm imperceptible, or, perceptible to the extent that we imagine it as a state of 'nothingness.' With the latter, Pirandello (or Gubbio the humorist) seems to allude again to that 'reality living beyond the reach of human vision, outside the forms of human reason,' which *Si gira* baptizes as *oltre*. By first putting 'nulla,' or 'nothingness,' in regular type, Pirandello differentiates its meaning from that of its subsequent use in italics. While the former refers to the imperceptible state itself, the latter refers to the act of defining that state. This act may involve again the formation of a hollow concept, as it employs reason to attach a label to an abysmal state, to render it rationally manageable, to thus ascribe closure to it – like when one says that life is a mystery, or that '*oltre*,' 'nature,' and 'divine' are signs with elusive referents and leaves it at that. The other option is to acknowledge the label as a mere label and proceed to further inquiry, to thus grasp 'nothingness' substantially.

'Religion' offers a compromise. It is a synonym to '*oltre*' or '*nothingness*,' but also a more comforting notion because it is conventionalized and institutionalized, and hence evokes things tangible. It thus poses as more manageable by reason. This is clearly a misapprehension. For all its tangible associations as practice, 'religion' proclaims the limits of reason, as its only legitimate referent is the divine. Religious discourse may reify things such as 'mysticism,' 'God's omnipresence,' and 'blind faith,' thus ascribing a form of illusory closure to any such notion, that is, by focusing on the sign and diverting attention from the elusive referent. Yet any active effort to grasp the divine, the most legitimate referent of 'religion,' would immerse one in a constant inquiry that exposes the limits of reason, in a state of unrest. Hence, like the *oltre*, 'religion' is grasped in one of two ways: as a sign with no referent (schematically) or as the constant inquiry that it may ignite (substantially). Pirandello claims that devising 'nothingness' and calling it 'religion' is 'still to live.' This is true provided that the second option, the constant inquiry, prevails. He adds that 'it [the act of defining nothingness, calling it religion] may be desperate if it has no illusions.' To be desperate means to articulate the notion (nothingness, religion) and *leave it at that*, to fail to acknowledge it as an illusion, to thus settle with a dead end. The humorist's state of irresoluteness, however, is not a state of desperation. The humorist recognizes the illusion as such and enters a process of inquiry so as to engage, via reason, in the articulation of innumerable other illusory constructs. These constructs do not aim to explain life as a unity (or nothingness, the *oltre*, nature, or the divine), because doing so would drive one back to where one started. Rather, they aim to explain those phenomena of life that lend themselves to reason. This is I think what Pirandello means by saying that the act may 'appease itself by plunging back into life, no longer here,' that is, no longer in this state of desperation where one settles with the sign of no referent, 'but there, into that *nothingness*,' that is, into the state of acknowledging *nothingness* as an illusion, to thus engage in the articulation of numerous new illusions, which is the humorist's reflection. It is in this sense – in that the recognition of *nothingness* as a construct leads to the articulation of numerous new constructs – that *nothingness* 'at once becomes *all*.'

Let us return to the theme of the tiger, the frequency of which in *Si gira* exceeds by far that of religion, while its relation to the question of cinema is more explicit, given the problem that it poses regarding the institution's treatment of innocent animals, as well as its associations with Nestoroff, a film diva. Along with religion, the tiger falls under the *oltre*. If 'religion' has the divine as its referent, the tiger is a metonym for nature. Like religion, the tiger allows us to explain some of its concrete functions. Nature, on the other hand, is like the divine, in that its referent is elusive; and like life, it allows us to explain its isolated phenomena, yet as a unity it exceeds the limits of reason. Furthermore, the tiger acquires unique importance because of its role in that reflection into which Pirandello aims to draw the reader *extra-diegetically*. As I argued, *Si gira* teaches us that humour itself becomes one of the contrasting images that reflection entails – an image that is not fixed or fictional but dynamic and that renders the whole process self-regenerating. It represents not a well-defined take on a given phenomenon but a mode of thought, one that invades and reshapes the other, seemingly fixed, images. Thanks to Nestoroff, a similar image enters the discourse on the tiger. Following Gubbio's ironic treatise on the tiger, his conversation with the diva at the menagerie offers an alternative perspective. As we will see, her remarks display an enigmatic logic that challenges Gubbio's viewpoint, urging him to insist, out of defensiveness, on his fixed beliefs. Her position perplexes both Gubbio and us readers and functions as a mode of thought more so than a fixed belief. It prompts us to question Gubbio's perspective, negating the absolute split between truth and fiction, nature and industry, 'real nature and artificial nature,' while it refrains from articulating a reconciliation scheme for any of those dichotomies such that would satisfy our moral and rational prejudices.

As noted above, Gubbio begins his account of Nestoroff's visit to the menagerie by marvelling at the tiger's innocence, 'manifestation of Earth,' being 'beyond good and evil'; that is, by hinting at 'nature' as a sign with an elusive referent. This hollow concept, or schematic grasp of the *oltre* as I have called it, in a manner that befits the humorist, leads Gubbio to its counterpart, to an inquiry that leaves him suspended in irresoluteness, what I called substantial grasp of the *oltre*. I repeat that the first response, the schematic grasp, is not a humoristic state. It is, however, a possible point of transition, a discovery that offers the option to either enter a humoristic mode or linger in nonhumour; the latter means to confront the mystery under question – be it nature, the divine, or the *oltre* – by giving it a fantastic definition, treating it as though it were a conclusive notion, an ideal construct, a fiction, that is, by labelling it as a sign with no referent and leaving it at that. Gubbio succeeds in crossing the threshold of humour. Yet once there, he diverts his attention from the tiger to Nestoroff. We wonder what it is that brings about this displacement. The novel has already promoted the analogy between the diva and the tiger: 'la Nestoroff è stata paragonata da qualcuno alla bella tigre comperata, qualche giorno fa, dalla *Kosmograph*' [Nestoroff has been compared by someone to the beautiful tiger purchased, a few days ago, by Kosmograph] (*TR* 552; *Shoot!* 35). The title of the film under production, *La donna e la tigre*, also suggests the analogy, and that may be related to Nestoroff's study of the animal in preparation of her role. The displacement lies in the fact that these elusive notions – nature, the divine, or the *oltre* in which those two reside – are not *themselves* the object of the humorist's reflection. Rather, they are interior states that serve as a motivating force behind every tangible, rationally conceived, exterior phenomenon. Gubbio introduces the *oltre* as a thing inherent to all: 'There is something more in every-thing ['C'è un *oltre* in tutto']. You do not wish or do not know how to see it.' The object of the humorist's reflection is not the *oltre in itself* – the humorist is not necessarily a metaphysicist – but an exterior phenom-enon that lends itself to tangible and rational definitions. The humorist senses the existence of this abysmal state upon reflection, while dealing with constructs that are tangible and rationally devised. In the case of nature, the humorist grapples with that of which nature represents an interior state. Hence, when Gubbio crosses the threshold of humour, the tiger gives way to the diva, whose unreachable interiority is what the tiger represents, while the facts of her life as a socialized human being (income, lifestyle, professional activities, appearance, and so on) read-ily lend themselves to ideal constructs drawn on tangible and rationally conceived phenomena.

Once he begins to converse with Nestoroff, Gubbio senses a mysteri-ous tone in her voice, which makes him suspect that she is aware of his friendship with Mirelli and his familiarity with the villa by Sorrento into which she brought so much grief. He admits that having such awareness on her part is something that he would dislike intensely. This concern of his leads to one of the strongest manifestations of his humorist's persona, not to say a short treatise on Pirandello's theory of identity, in a passage that might well be drawn from *Uno, nessuno e centomila*:[18]

> Non ho amore, ripeto qua, né potrei averne, per questa donna; ma odio, neppure. Qua tutti la odiano; e già questa per me sarebbe ragione for-tissima di non odiarla io ... Ho conosciuto Giorgio Mirelli, ma come? ma quale? Qual egli era nelle relazioni che aveva con me. Tale, per me, ch'io l'amavo. Ma chi era egli e com'era nelle relazioni con questa donna? Tale, ch'ella potesse amarlo? Io non lo so! Certo, non era, non poteva essere uno – lo stesso – per me e per lei ... Si spiega così, come uno, che a ragione sia amato da me, possa con ragione essere odiato da un altro. Io che amo e quell'altro che odia, siamo due: non solo; ma l'uno, ch'io amo, e l'uno che quell'altro odia, non son punto gli stessi; sono uno e uno; sono anche due. E noi stessi non possiamo mai sapere, quale realtà ci sia data dagli altri; chi siamo per questo e per quello. (*TR* 581–2)

> [I feel no love, I repeat again, nor could I feel any, for this woman; but neither hatred.[19] Everyone hates her here; and that by itself would be an overwhelming reason for me not to hate her ... I knew Giorgio Mirelli; but

how, in what capacity? Such as he was in his relations with me. He was the sort of person that I liked. But who and what was he in his relations with this woman? The sort that she could like? I do not know. Certainly he was not, he could not be, one and the same person to her and to myself . . . This explains how someone who is reasonably loved by me can reasonably be hated by a third person. I who love and the other who hates are two: not only that, but the one whom I love and the one whom the third person hates are by no means identical; they are one and one: therefore they are two also. And we ourselves can never know what reality is accorded to us by other people, who we are to this person and to that.] (*Shoot!* 64)

He explains that if Nestoroff knew of his friendship with Mirelli she might think that he hated her. She would then present only one aspect of herself to him, hiding the rest. This would prevent him from studying her, 'com'ora la studio, intera' [as I am now studying her, as a whole] (*TR* 582; *Shoot!* 65). She would hinder, that is, his humoristic view of her.

It is therefore as a sudden relapse to his ironist's persona that we receive his ensuing dialogue with Nestoroff. Here, not only does he reassert his fixed ethical view of the tiger, but given the diva's dispute of his view he also grasps onto a single and fixed judgment on the diva herself, thus obliterating the humoristic effusion of the previous lines. He thinks that Nestoroff does not share his feelings for the tiger not because she may have a perspective worth contrasting to his own, but because the tiger's fate serves a personal motive of hers; perhaps that the risky part of the hunter who will shoot the tiger in *La donna e la tigre* is still assigned to Carlo Ferro, Nestoroff's present lover: 'le relazioni, che tra lei e la belva si sono stabilite, non le consentono né pietà per essa, né sdegno per l'azione che qui sarà compiuta' [the relations that have grown up between her and the animal do not allow her to feel either pity for it or anger at the deed that is to be done]. What is crucial, however, about Nestoroff's response is that the logic based on which she justifies the brutal deed shatters both his ethical perspective and the very split between truth and fiction: 'Finzione, sì; anche stupida se volete; ma quando sarà sollevato lo sportello della gabbia e questa bestia sarà fatta entrare nell'altra gabbia più grande che figurerà un pezzo di bosco, con le sbarre nascoste da fronde, il cacciatore, per quanto finto come il bosco, avrà pur diritto di difendersi da essa, appunto perché essa, come voi dite, non è una bestia finta, ma una bestia vera' [A sham, yes; stupid too, if you like; but when the door of the cage is opened and the animal is driven into the other, bigger cage representing a glade in a forest, with the bars hidden by branches, the hunter, even if he is a sham like the forest, will still be entitled to defend himself against it, simply because it, as you say, is not a sham animal but a real one]. Gubbio attempts to clarify that the problem lies precisely in the operations of the cinematic institution, the ethics of which we tend to leave unquestioned: 'Ma il male è appunto questo, . . . servirsi d'una bestia vera dove tutto sarà finto' [But that is just where the harm lies, . . . in using a real animal where everything else is a sham] (*TR* 582; *Shoot!* 65).

His appeals are to no avail, as she either stays unmoved or fails to follow his rationale:

> – Chi ve lo dice? – rimbeccò pronta. – Sarà finta la parte del cacciatore; ma di fronte a questa bestia *vera* sarà pure un uomo *vero*! E v'assicuro che se egli non la ucciderà al primo colpo, o non la ferirà in modo d'atterrarla, essa, senza tener conto che il cacciatore sarà finto e finta la caccia, gli salterà addosso e sbranerà *per davvero* un uomo *vero*. (*TR* 582)

> ['Where do you get that?' she promptly rejoined. 'The part of the hunter will be a sham; but when he is face-to-face with this real animal he will be a real man! And I can assure you that if he does not kill it with his first shot or does not wound it so as to bring it down, it will not stop to think that the hunter is a sham and the hunt a sham, but will spring upon him and *really* tear a *real* man to pieces.'] (*Shoot!* 65)

What essentially distinguishes Nestoroff from Gubbio is her absolute disinterest in questioning the ethics of the institution. For all her cynicism, Nestoroff strikes me as wiser than Gubbio, in that she hints at Pirandello's humoristic concept of cinema. Her cynicism with respect to the institution, though expressed in a rather spontaneous tone, recalls that neutrality – perhaps real, perhaps contrived – expressed by the Pirandello look-alike at the novel's opening. Beneath her coldness or failure to comprehend there hides the recognition of an irrefutable historical reality: like any era, this one has invented its own systems for the production of fictions, ideal constructs, or fixed beliefs, which are, I repeat, the things that constitute truth for us, all we have that is perceptible and rationally conceivable. In other words, she knows, consciously or instinctively, that our touch with reality is mediated by our historically specific means. Furthermore, from her words we infer that each of these fictions is *not wholly* fictional. Rather, like the sham hunter facing the real tiger, it involves an arrangement of elements artificial and real, a dynamic of elements subjective and objective. If Pirandello selects cinema as the prototypical metaphor of this arrangement, an aesthetic structure able to conceal its technical means and create the illusion of perfect diegetic homogeneity, we may speak of the numerous 'fictions' that govern human life as perfect amalgams, constructs in which truth and fiction congeal into and become indistinguishable from one another. To look at it differently, even if we view life through the lens of our illusory constructs, it is with these illusions that we must then live, and like the sham hunter facing the real tiger, it is their real consequences that we must face.

In this respect, Gubbio's rationale is the one that appears less coherent after all. In failing to accept, on amoral grounds, with the required cynicism or the humorist's suspicious neutrality, that cinema is today paradigmatic of humanity's perception of the world, Gubbio the ironist strives, in his idealism, to cherish an absolute separation between truth and fiction, such that would allow one to opt for truth as the basis of perception. In reading his words, we sense that he denounces the formal rupture between sham and truth, the tiger's killing as the *only real* act in a fake world, no less than the killing itself. We do not doubt his sympathy for animals, vigorously expressed before his discussion of the tiger, in the parable of the hunter, the engineer, and the snipe, which criticizes the practice of hunting for its pitiless killing of innocent animals solely as a sport.[20] His scorn for recreational hunting, however, next to the zoo and the film industry, speaks again to his idealism, his yearning for a pure nature free of human intervention, a utopian, ahistorical register that is barely knowable. A non-idealist Nestoroff, now irritated by his refusal to share her view, strikes him back with his own idealism, by mocking its ahistoricity, feigning a belief in the viability of pure fiction as a way of preventing nature's exploitation: 'Vi sta tanto a cuore? Ammaestratela! Fatene una tigre attrice, che sappia fingere di cader morta al finto sparo d'un cacciatore finto, e tutto allora sarà accomodato' [Do you feel it too deeply? Tame her! Make her a stage tiger, trained to sham death at a sham bullet from a sham hunter, and then all will be right] (*TR* 583; *Shoot!* 66). Though emotionally charged, her irony reaffirms her aloofness with respect to the ethics of the institution, her tranquil cynicism in defiance of Gubbio's morality. Overall, she assaults us with an enigmatic logic in refusing to provide a model for industry's relationship with nature such that would confirm our moral and rational prejudices. Her cynicism puzzles the reader, whose sensitivity, slight though it may be, prevents him/her from losing the sympathy that Gubbio elicits for the innocent beast. The dynamic interplay between her irrefutable common sense, based on the acceptance of the institution's historical reality, and the reader's no less irrefutable sympathy for the animal puts the reader in a state of moral-rational perplexity, as moral and rational concerns become entangled with one another. Thus, her view does not represent a fixed belief with which to agree or disagree. Rather, like Gubbio's humoristic persona, it is at once a dynamic image *and* a mode of thought. It casts doubt on Gubbio's fixed belief, drawing the reader into a reflexive process structurally akin to that peculiar reflection between the humorist and the ironist as discussed above.

This process is not intended to define nature, although the discussion of the tiger is what initiates it. Like the reflection between the humorist and the ironist, which the reader may apply to the question of cinema regardless of the specific object of the humorist's musings, it incites the reader to apply this mode of thought to other issues. There are two main issues at stake here, which are inextricably linked to each other. One is cinema, which I briefly addressed above and to which I will return. The other is Nestoroff herself, whose unreachable interiority is what the tiger, a metonym for nature, represents. Like the tiger's entrapment in a zoo or a studio for man's aesthetic gratification, Nestoroff is oppressed, as Gubbio the humorist suggests, by men's view of her as a body. Like the tiger's wish to devour those who oppress it, Nestoroff wishes to punish those who see her as just a body, including Mirelli, who may have seen but the figure created by his artist's imagination (*TR* 561; *Shoot!* 44). Hence, when Gubbio later supposes that only in vain does Nestoroff come to study the tiger, as the role of the Miss, 'più tigre della tigre' [more tigerish than the tiger], will not be assigned to her after all and perhaps she does not yet know this, he only reaffirms his ironist's persona (*TR* 578; *Shoot!* 61). He neglects what Gubbio the humorist suggested earlier: that Nestoroff's cruelty is a symptom of the oppressed state that she shares with the tiger – which means that her identification with the tiger may be the true reason that she continues to visit the menagerie, and not her ignorance of the reassignment of the role, as Gubbio the ironist now supposes. It is perhaps this identification, or the encounter between the exterior and interior aspects of one and the same entity, that Pirandello reaffirms in the dramatic finale that brings the death of both. After Nuti replaces Ferro in the part of the hunter, he devises a scheme to avenge himself against the diva, under whose spell he still lingers. During filming, instead of shooting the tiger, he turns around and shoots Nestoroff; and once the tiger starts tearing Nuti to pieces another man intervenes and shoots the tiger (*TR* 732–3; *Shoot!* 211–12).

Humour, Cinema, and the *Superfluo*

Nestoroff's enigmatic view of nature, as it provides a mode of thought rather than a fixed belief, added to her affinity with the tiger, summons the enigma of her own identity. It offers a Pirandellian approach for the study of Nestoroff herself, whose multiple, competing, yet tangible identity constructs are found in what I called her humoristic layering (see chapter 6). Some of these layers, such as her appearances in films, belong to her image as created by the institution of cinema, her star-image: a product of diverse media texts, including films, promotion, publicity, interviews, or criticism, which add up to the creation of an artificial personality for the fulfilment of the public's curiosity, an image launched by the institution as the revelation of the person behind the scenes.[21] This points to a further affinity between the diva and the tiger, the authentic life of which is purportedly re-enacted by the stage sets in the zoo and the film studio, not to mention the analogies between the Italian silent divas and the mystery, irrationality, and indomitableness of nature, as often suggested by the structural relations that the films set up between the diva's character, her appearance, and the rest of the mise-en-scène.[22] It must be with these analogies in mind that Pirandello, in asking Anton Giulio Bragaglia to turn *Si gira* into a film, proposed the mesmerizing Pina Menichelli for the role of Nestoroff.[23]

If Nestoroff's enigmatic view of nature summons, as I suggested, the enigma of her own identity, we need not be concerned by the contradiction involved in her cynicism towards the tiger's killing, which according to my reading would symbolize the killing of her own interiority. If need be, we may explain the contradiction by suggesting, for instance, that Nestoroff's concern for Ferro's safety (at the scene of the menagerie, the hunter's part has not yet been reassigned to Nuti) surpasses her own existential attachment to the animal. She may also be disturbed by the fact that the tiger's reality, like her own, is suppressed by the image that Kosmograph, a commercial institution, constructs around its body. Hence, she may wish to eliminate, if symbolically, that inner part of hers that elicits its own exploitation. Any such explanation, however, is partial. First, it constitutes what I have all along called an ideal construct, a fixed belief, or a fiction. Despite the notion that any fiction, as Nestoroff's words allowed us to infer, is an amalgam of elements objective and subjective, adopting it *tout court* would be following the steps of Gubbio the ironist, who assumes, for instance, that Nestoroff's cynicism has a personal motive, probably her concern for Ferro – not to exclude, as a wildly speculative Gubbio adds, her eagerness to receive the dead tiger's skin, promised to Ferro by the terms of the contract, 'per i piedini di lei; tappeto prezioso' [for her little feet; a costly rug] (*TR* 583; *Shoot!* 66). Second, any such explanation is exclusive to the diegesis, as it treats Nestoroff's motives like those of a real person. Here, instead, as with the contrast between Gubbio's humoristic and ironic personas, what takes precedence is the reflexive process in which Pirandello aims to draw the reader, a process that is not acknowledged by the character in the diegesis (we do not know whether Nestoroff considers herself a humorist) and that occurs extra-diegetically. The reader need not be as concerned by the psychological justification of Nestoroff's words as by their function as a mode of thought, a method that s/he may apply to things other than the explicit subject matter of her words. In his novel-essay, Pirandello aspires not only to create characters that reaffirm the conventions of literary realism but also to compose a theoretical interpretative model.

One wonders why Pirandello selects Nestoroff of all people for the fuelling of the reader's reflection. The author seems to play with the reader's expectations as formed by traditional representations of romantic love. The diva is not alone in this function. She is the counterpart of Gubbio the humorist. In Pirandello's theoretical model, the two voices complement each other. In the diegesis, their encounters constitute a love affair *manqué*. Several things allude to a possible love scenario, at least in the mind of Gubbio, whose narrative voice dominates. The suggestion of his identification with Mirelli in his lyrical descriptions of the six canvases, his lyrical account of Nestoroff while she sits under a pergola, his idea that she pretends to be bothered by the sun only to avoid his gaze, or that she gazes at him seductively while performing her sensual Indian dance to his camera, his talk about not loving her but not hating her either – are allusions to a love story that never quite departs. Pirandello stirs up the theme of love only to displace it with a relationship of complementarity concretized on the extra-diegetic, essayistic level. Both voices incite the reader to approach any issue with humour. They thus collaborate against Gubbio the ironist. The scene of the menagerie is crucial because here the diva promotes the humoristic mode when Gubbio reverts to irony. The ethical views that he presents to her, though they are not ironic in themselves, are an extension of his ironic treatise of the tiger that immediately precedes this scene. They thus sustain the magnified irony that, as we saw it in relation to Gubbio the humorist, works as a foil against which Pirandello the humorist reaffirms himself – now in Nestoroff's enigmatic logic.

This is not to say that Nestoroff and Gubbio the humorist are identical voices. Certainly, they both incite the reader to confront any issue with humour, cinema being the central issue in this work. The enigma of Nestoroff's identity is not an alternative to the question of cinema but a vital component of it. What distinguishes her from Gubbio is how she evokes cinema, which she achieves by means of two interrelated operations. The first concerns the structure of the image, the fact that she herself constitutes its physical texture. As I argued in the previous chapter, she is portrayed by means of a 'humoristic layering.' I suggested that although this layering also comprises the competing narratives that Gubbio construes around her past, her visual renderings are at the forefront because they serve as synthetic abstractions of those narratives, as tangible displays of her overall humoristic conception. In the present chapter, her words allowed us to expound on the filmic image, to see it as an amalgam of the artificial and the real, the subjective and the objective, the sham hunter and the tiger, the latter conveying her unreachable interiority. Hence, in many respects, the novel aligns her with the concrete, physical texture of the visual, a vital dimension of which is the photographic component of her star-image. Let us note that her star-image comprises not only her filmic images as found in the novel (which are rare), but also our projection onto her character of star-image fragments with which we are familiar before our reading of *Si gira*. Thus, her star-image, her status as a diva, in its multiple and interpenetrative visual connotations, pervades any attempt to seek her identity. Her enigma is inextricably linked to the cinema question, insofar as the latter is incarnated in the tangible layers of the former. The second of the two operations that distinguish her from Gubbio concerns the intellectual manner in which she promotes humour. Her role as one who fuels the reader's humoristic reflection is realized not through rational discourse but through an enigmatic logic that finds its tangible echoes in the ambiguity of her every visual rendering, which despite its dominating artificiality, like the image of the tiger's killing, bears a trace of truth. Gubbio the humorist, by contrast, is defined by his rational weighing out of narrative alternatives.[24] The two voices are thus complementary but not identical. The one highlighting the humoristic image in its physical texture, the other providing a rational tool for the re-elaboration of narrative – a structure of which the former constitutes the physical core, the two collaborate in the dismantling of Gubbio the ironist, of his conviction that cinema is a futile mass of 'idiotic fictions.'

The fictions that Gubbio abhors are products of the human quality that he calls *superfluo*, what distinguishes humans from animals and serves as another term for rational thought.[25] He introduces the *superfluo* in response to an odd remark made by his friend and philosophical interlocutor, Simone Pau: 'Il monte è monte, perché io dico: *Quello è un monte. Il che significa: io sono il monte.* Che siamo noi? Siamo quello di cui a volta a volta ci accorgiamo' [The mountain is a mountain because I say: 'That is a mountain.' In other words: '*I am the mountain.*' What are we? We are whatever, at any given moment, occupies our attention] (*TR* 526; *Shoot!* 10). Pau implies that experience has no meaning outside of the constructs that we attach to it, which are formed dialectically by elements subjective and objective. Gubbio does not disprove Pau's observation, yet he questions the act of philosophizing. He sees it as the outcome of a *malattia*, a 'malady,' the capacity to reason, from which he admits that he suffers also. He envies the condition of animals, which he sees as more fortunate:

> La terra non è fatta tanto per gli uomini, quanto per le bestie. Perché le bestie hanno in sé da natura solo quel tanto che loro basta ed è necessario per vivere nelle condizioni, a cui furono, ciascuna secondo la propria specie, ordinate; laddove gli uomini hanno in sé un superfluo, che di continuo inutilmente li tormenta, non facendoli mai paghi di nessuna condizione e sempre lasciandoli incerti del loro destino. Superfluo inesplicabile, chi per darsi uno sfogo crea nella natura un mondo fittizio, che ha senso e valore soltanto per essi, ma di cui pur essi medesimi non sanno e non possono mai contentarsi, cosicché senza posa smaniosamente lo mutano e rimutano. (*TR* 526)

> [The earth was made not so much for mankind as for the animals. Because animals have in themselves by nature only so much as suffices them and is necessary for them to live in the conditions to which they were, each after its own kind, ordained; whereas men have in them a superfluity which constantly and vainly torments them, never making them satisfied with any conditions and always leaving them uncertain of their destiny. An

inexplicable superfluity, which, to afford itself an outlet, creates in nature an artificial world, a world that has a meaning and value for them alone, and yet one with which they themselves cannot ever be content, so that without pause they keep on frantically arranging and rearranging it.] (*Shoot!* 10)

Pau thinks that humans are superior to animals because animals are content always to repeat the same actions. Gubbio disagrees:

Che giova all'uomo non contentarsi di ripeter sempre le stesse operazioni? Già, quelle che sono fondamentali e indispensabili alla vita, deve pur compierle e ripeterle anch'egli quotidianamente, come i bruti, se non vuol morire. Tutte le altre, mutate e rimutate di continuo smaniosamente, è assai difficile non gli si scoprano, presto o tardi, *illusioni o vanità, frutto come sono di quel tal superfluo*, di cui non si vede su la terra né il fine né la ragione. (*TR* 527; emphasis added)

[Of what benefit is it to a man not to be content with always repeating the same action? Why, those actions that are fundamental and indispensable to life, he too is obliged to perform and to repeat, day after day, like the animals, if he does not wish to die. All the rest, arranged and rearranged continually and frantically, can hardly fail to reveal themselves sooner or later as *illusions or vanities, being as they are the fruit of that superfluity*, of which we do not see on this earth either the end or the reason.] (*Shoot!* 11; emphasis added)

Hence, the *superfluo*, as the capacity to reason, is what triggers the infinite generation of constructs, 'illusions or vanities,' to define experience, which then lead to the 'arranging and rearranging' of society with no repose.

Gubbio may not question Pau's claim that we construct meaning subjectively ('The mountain is a mountain because I say: "That is a mountain."'), but he probably sees this practice as a misfortune, since the *superfluo*, whence comes the ability to diversify meaning, is what 'constantly and vainly torments' humans. As elsewhere, he longs for a pure nature uncontaminated by human reason, as seen in his envy of animals that lack the capacity to perform any act in excess of basic survival needs. The person speaking is Gubbio the ironist. He boosts his rejection of human reality by using the term *superfluo* (superfluous), which denotes what exceeds need, what is not useful. If reason is not even a necessity for life, its pervasive application is quite harmful, especially at a time when technological progress renders human endeavours, the incessant 'arranging and rearranging' of 'an artificial world,' more complex than ever, making humanity all the more alienated and anxious, a condition exemplified by cinema's production of countless fictions. However, if Gubbio the ironist likes the term *superfluo* for its common usage, it is for a different reason that Pirandello prefers this term to any rough synonym, such as *inutile* (useless). His use of it is relativistic. Composed of the adverb *super*, often used like *sopra*, meaning 'above,' and a derivative of the verb *fluire*, or 'to flow,' the term refers to what 'flows above,' what lies in excess of something. Whether this excess is undesirable depends on the value ascribed to the thing that lies below. If life's value lies strictly in physical survival, as Gubbio finds in animals, rational thought is useless; but if humans ascribe value to the capacity to reason, the latter is 'superfluous' not in the sense of useless, but as a privilege specific to humans or, to avoid value judgments, a structure lying above the physical. To equate without qualification Pirandello and Gubbio the ironist, and to thus imply that the author rejects the human capacity to reason, would be absurd.[26] The analogy holds only to the extent that Pirandello, in his own tendency to adhere to fixed beliefs as part of his self-construction, may fleetingly find in Gubbio the ironist his mirror image, that is, in the sense in which the metaphor of the mirror is explained above.

The relationship between the *superfluo* and the *oltre* is fluid and one wonders whether they represent two different concepts or one and the same. At first glance, they differ. As I suggested earlier, the *superfluo* is what permits the production of ideal constructs drawn on tangible and rationally conceived phenomena, whereas the *oltre* is the imperceptible register to which the multiple constructs allude in the course of a self-regenerating reflexive process. The *superfluo* is reason, the instrument with which one strives, paradoxically, to attain the *oltre*, which thus serves as catalyst for the process. Yet one wonders whether Pirandello speaks seriously or tongue-in-cheek when he describes reality as what 'man can face only at the cost of either death or insanity,' what *Si gira* evokes with the *oltre*. For the alive and sane, this 'reality,' in its utmost inaccessibility, is defined as that *nothingness*, which as we have seen, if we allow it to lead us to further inquiry, 'at once becomes *all*.' If the *superfluo* creates *all* that is perceptible and rationally conceivable, and if the *oltre* is that state of nothingness that once defined becomes *all*, then the two seem to represent the same state of affairs. They share, after all, the connotation of *more*, the existence of something in addition to something else, whether it refers to excess (the superfluous, which is relative in Pirandello) or simply to something more (found *oltre*, beyond). Inasmuch as the *oltre*, given the elusiveness of its imperceptible utopia, is the catalyst for reflection, it may also be but that surge of faith which arises as we negotiate the viability of each ideal construct, the faith in yet another possibility, a better view, another construct. That is to say, the *superfluo* and the *oltre* are one and the same insofar as they are mutually generative. Thomas Harrison encapsulates his remarks on the relationship between the two notions as follows: 'If life creates form, it is also life that undoes it, perpetually restructuring its own organization. If this life is anything in itself, it is aesthetic transcendence, a continuous "rewriting" in search of ever more adequate articulations.'[27]

Gubbio is the first to allude to the fluid relationship between the two, in what appears to be a transition from his ironist's persona to further insight. As the *superfluo* never finds rest,

cerca e chiede altrove, oltre la vita terrena, il perché e il compenso del suo tormento. Tanto peggio poi l'uomo vi sta, quanto più vuole impiegare su la terra stessa in smaniose costruzioni e complicazioni il suo superfluo.

Lo so io che giro una manovella.

Quanto al mio amico Simone Pau, il bello è questo: che crede d'essersi liberato d'ogni superfluo, riducendo al minimo tutti i suoi bisogni, privandosi di tutte le comodità e vivendo come un lumacone ignudo. E non s'accorge che, proprio all'opposto, egli, così riducendosi, s'è annegato tutto nel superfluo e più non vive d'altro. (*TR* 527–8)

[it seeks and demands elsewhere, beyond the life on earth, the reason and recompense for its torment. So much the worse, then, does man fare, the more he seeks to employ, upon the earth itself, in frantic constructions and complications, his own superfluity.

This I know, I who turn a handle.

As for my friend Simone Pau, the beauty of it is this: that he believes that he has set himself free from all superfluity, reducing all his wants to a minimum, depriving himself of every comfort and living the naked life of a snail. And he does not see that, on the contrary, he, by reducing himself thus, has immersed himself altogether in the superfluity and lives now by nothing else.] (*Shoot!* 12)

He implies that the frenzy reflects a wish to find recompense 'else-where.' He does not claim a firm belief in this *oltre* more than in the need of man to nurture a hope, one that may only be realized in *yet one more* construct, thus propagating the frenzy. His criticism of Pau speaks to the fusion of the two states. If this Gubbio believed in the *oltre*, he would praise Pau's frugal life, closer to nature and even God. Instead, he sees such riddance of superfluity as a mere denial, an illusion, or a schematic grasp of the *oltre*. In Pau's case, of course, the grasp occurs not in mere thought but in actions. Yet any action acquires meaning in its conceptualization. With his actions Pau erases the *superfluo* insincerely, implies Gubbio the humorist. He turns a blind eye to the numerous endeavours prompted by reason and leaves it at that. The alternative is to recognize the illusion as such and welcome the infinite struggle that the possession of reason makes inevitable.

Just as the *superfluo* and the *oltre* both merge and part, so do the voices of Gubbio and Pau, reflecting perhaps Pirandello's own ambivalence as a humorist. In a later passage, it is Pau who claims the inseparableness of the two states. He implies that Gubbio himself is insincere for believing in their separation, particularly with respect to his contempt for his own profession:

Tu non sei nella tua professione, ma ciò non vuol dire, caro mio, che la tua professione non sia in te! ... Noi possiamo benissimo non ritrovarci in quello che facciamo; ma quello che facciamo, caro mio, è, resta fatto: fatto che ti circoscrive, ti dà comunque una forma e t'imprigiona in essa. Vuoi ribellarti? Non puoi ... [N]eanche dopo morto. Stai fresco, caro mio. Andrai a girare la macchinetta anche di là! (*TR* 611)

[You do not enter into your profession, but that does not mean, my dear fellow, that your profession does not enter into you! ... We may easily fail to recognize ourselves in what we do, but what we do, my dear fellow, remains done: an action which circumscribes you, my dear fellow, gives you a form of sorts and imprisons you in it. Do you seek to rebel? You cannot ... Not even after death. Keep calm, my dear fellow. You will go on turning the handle of your machine even beyond the grave!] (*Shoot!* 94–5)

Di certo, non sappiamo niente. E non c'è niente da sapere fuori di quello che, comunque, si rappresenta fuori, in atti. Il dentro è tormento e sec-catura. Va', va' a girar la macchinetta, Serafino! Credi che la tua è una professione invidiabile! *E non stimare più stupidi degli altri gli atti che ti combinano davanti, da prendere con la tua macchinetta. Sono tutti stupidi allo stesso modo, sempre*: la vita è tutta una stupidaggine, sempre, perché non conclude mai e non può concludere. (*TR* 613; emphasis added)

[We know nothing for certain. And there is nothing to be known beyond that which, in one way or another, is represented outwardly, in actions. Within is torment and weariness. Go, go and turn your handle, Serafino! Be assured that yours is a profession to be envied! *And do not regard as more stupid than any others the actions that are arranged before your eyes, to be taken by your machine. They are all stupid in the same way, always*: life is all a mass of stupidity, always, because it never comes to an end and can never come to an end.] (*Shoot!* 96; emphasis added)

Indeed, for all his discontent with 'idiotic fictions,' apart from a meagre description of *La donna e la tigre*, or one or two scenes or images, Gubbio refrains from describing the content of the films that he shoots. It seems that their alleged stupidity lies in the mere fact that they are fictional. We wonder where the alternative is to be found, what would qualify as non-stupid reality. We look for it in the off-screen events, only to realize that, apart from Gubbio's musings or occasional philosophical exchanges with other characters (such as Nuti and Pau), all of which prompt us to contemplate the notion of humour, thus serving as theoretical inserts of sorts, his accounts of the purportedly real events, such as the Mirelli tragedy, Nestoroff's turbulent love affairs, or the drama of the Cavalena family, strike us as the fragments of a melodrama.[28]

Outside of these fragments, the novel refuses to affirm any tangible objective reality. The *oltre* is the only other reality that arduously finds its way in the pages of the 'notebooks.' The classical analyst may search for truths in the subject's past, aiming to unearth it, to render it tangible, to raise it to consciousness. For Pirandello, however, objective reality, in its aloofness, does not make concessions to our reconstructions of the past, which are but ideal constructs (or fictions) drawn upon it, however rigorous and inquisitive they may be. In *Si gira*, the past comes in utopian film-like episodes, such as Gubbio's flashbacks of the idyllic country life at the Mirelli villa in Sorrento, or romantic tragic ones, such as his reports on Mirelli's suicide. His present-day journey to Sorrento, allegedly to resolve Duccella and Nuti's past trauma, is a personal revisit of the past, one triggered by nostalgia (see chapter 6). With this journey, Pirandello stages the wish to unravel the past and the truths that we believe that lie therein. Only with shock and disgust, however, does Gubbio discover the physical and social deterioration that his beloved Duccella and Nonna Rosa have undergone in the meantime. His report on the visit, in its formal qualities – quick, dramatic, and grotesque, is no less film-like than his utopian memories. More so than evidencing an objective reality, it is the inflated product of his panic, his harsh condemnation of the scene that crushed his other illusion. He escapes hysterically, finding himself squeezed in the middle of two colliding illusions. The past is nowhere to be found.[29]

These film-like fragments are Gubbio's constructs, products of his *superfluo*. They reflect the mindset of a man whose profession creates the tendency to view the world as a stage. For Gubbio, this tendency is a symptom of mechanization. When he speaks of his job to his visitor and Pirandello look-alike, he emphasizes, as we have seen, its 'impassivity,' the need to stay emotionally and intellectually detached from the actions that he records: 'La qualità precipua che si richiede in uno che faccia la mia professione è l'*impassibilità* di fronte all'azione che si svolge davanti alla macchina' [The chief quality that is required in a man of my profession is impassivity in face of the action that is going on in front of the camera] (*TR* 522; *Shoot!* 6). His claim to impassivity, however, is no more sincere than his rejection of cinema. It would be wrong to just label him an impassive person. He sympathizes with the Mirelli family, feels compassion for the tiger, has a crush on Luisetta Cavalena, has feelings of dislike for Ferro and Nuti, and his attitude towards Nestoroff is hardly immune to the bewildering effects that her enigma rehearses upon his mind. Is he impassive only when he rolls his camera? He refrains, in fact, from isolating any such instance, just as he fails to recount the plots of the fictions that he abhors. The absence of these two sets of facts from his 'notebooks' is the flipside of his constant dwelling on 'real' events – which as a result become this novel's only version of cinematic fiction, and in which Gubbio is entangled in various ways, just like a spectator who is not impassive towards the melodrama on the screen. Not only are his daily reports film-like, they are neither more nor less fictional than the purported truths that he seeks in those images that the industry discards, such as Nestoroff's 'demon' or the 'life as it is' of the man captured by the camera unawares. However Gubbio reckons the act of filming – loathsome, impassive, or otherwise – his cameraman's craft becomes a way of life. He is an expert in gazing at life from within the parameters of the filmic lens. As he himself declares, 'Già i miei occhi, e anche le mie orecchie, per la lunga abitudine, cominciano a vedere e a sentir tutto sotto la specie di questa rapida tremula ticchettante riproduzione meccanica' [Already my eyes and my ears, too, from force of habit, are beginning to see and hear everything in the guise of this rapid, quivering, ticking mechanical reproduction] (*TR* 524; *Shoot!* 8).[30] His cinematic mindset shapes the novel's narrative point of view. In Moses's words, he is 'our constant camera eye.'[31] In the figure of the cameraman, Pirandello finds a supreme example of cinema's role as the paradigm of perception in modernity.

Each of Gubbio's film-like reports displays two attributes that are crucial to this study. First, they are neither entirely fictional nor entirely true. Second, though an ideal construct, each is not a conclusive narrative but a narrative fragment. We have addressed the fusion between truth and fiction in terms of Nestoroff and Gubbio's dispute about the ethical implications of the tiger's killing. As we recall, the diva's cynicism assumes that each so-called fiction inevitably entails an amalgam of things real and artificial, a dynamic interplay of the objective with the subjective. It is a construct where truth and fiction congeal into one another. This fusion is not limited to a single scene. It applies to any narrative in its entirety, as well as any single image – what would be, for example, a still shot of Nestoroff, one of the multiple components of her star-image. We may feel the urge to isolate the real components from the artificial ones and examine how the two interact to form the whole. To be sure, observing the collapse of the extra-diegetic fact into the diegetic is a way to begin, the tiger's 'snuff' shot being one of countless examples that we could name. Such a project, however, would soon assault us with the hopeless task of agreeing on what is 'real' or 'artificial,' 'objective' or 'subjective,' terms that we may find it difficult to define *objectively*. In a Pirandellian context, a fact's extra-diegetic status does not guarantee its 'realness,' since the latter is radically bound up with the meaning that the individual subjectively assigns to it. Pirandello does not urge us to dissect discourse into its real and artificial components. Again, he finds in cinema an ideal metaphor for the fusion between truth and fiction, precisely because of its ability to camouflage its technical means and create the illusion of perfect diegetic homogeneity. By displacing cinematic fiction with Gubbio's storytelling, or rather, by obscuring their differences, Pirandello implies that each image, scene, or story, *as a whole*, is at once real and fictional, objective and subjective, a construct where truth and fiction congeal into one another. *Si gira* exercises that 'philosophical irony' deriving from German philosophy as discussed by Pirandello in 'Ironia,' a disposition to view the universe as a vain semblance, to thus portray reality as a 'perpetual parody,' a 'transcendental farce' (see above).

The dynamic interplay between truth and fiction lies at the core of the second attribute of Gubbio's reports, namely, their status as fragments. In the course of reflection, the humorist senses that the construct under question is not all that viable, that it is a mere construct despite its objective dimension (deemed as such only subjectively). This doubt does not shatter the drive to seek truth. Rather, it collaborates with it. It is this doubt that urges the search for the next possibility, the formation of a new story, a new image, the awakening of a new construct, which will form an interpenetrative relationship with the other constructs. It is therefore this doubt that incites that faith that is the *oltre* – generated thus by the *superfluo*, itself generated all the while by the *oltre*, as previously suggested. Hence, the interplay between truth and fiction fragments the construct and proliferates reflection as a self-regenerating process. By obscuring the difference between cinematic fiction and Gubbio's film-like reports, which are not only amalgams of truth and fiction but also fragments, Pirandello proposes a notion of narrative films as themselves fragments, in spite of their formal closure. Indeed, a mutual exchange marks the relationship between cinema and humour. Each narrative film, what Gubbio names 'idiotic fiction,' is an ideal construct, a plainly presented moral or ideological view of reality, and of course a product of the *superfluo*. However, despite the film's clear storyline, verisimilitude, spatial and temporal coherence, and strong moral message – in a few words, its organic structure – a humoristic disposition prompts us to seek its inherent element that fragments it. Seen as a fragment through the lens of humour, each narrative film always evokes the next narrative film, thus working as a metonym for cinema as a whole. Conversely, narrative cinema, developing in the 1910s into a multitude of seemingly intact yet somewhere punctured stories, and used by Pirandello as a paradigm of perception, itself prompts one to view the world through the lens of humour. Each narrative film, as a product of the *superfluo*, suggests that there is something more, beyond itself, some (thing) *oltre*.[32]

The metonymic displacements that the mind incurs in the face of cinema as a pervasive cultural phenomenon in the 1910s brings to mind Marinetti's notion of speed as a new 'divine,' what I attributed to the medium's ability to make the world look like an 'oceanic collection of stories,' a constellation of narratives the multiple colours and inter-penetrations of which result in a 'verisimilar-yet-abstract' image of the world lingering in the back of one's mind (see chapter 3). Let us recall that this model refers not to the single film but to cinema as a totality, a universal ensemble defined by formal diversity and contrast, with its historical epics, bourgeois melodramas, comedies, newsreels, documentaries, divas, strongmen, and more. It is a cumulative construct of the mind that brings the world forward in a polyphonic vision of speed, what Marinetti apparently hoped to capture with his ambitious script *Velocità*. Indeed, the interpenetration of constructs in the humorist's reflection recalls the Futurist aesthetic principle of *compenetrazione* (interpenetration) of artistic forms or spatio-temporal registers. Each of the two outlooks, however, is quite distinct. First, the fragments that inform Marinetti's vision of the new 'divine' primarily consist, as we have seen, of events defined by speed as achieved by modern technology. As a humorist, however, and unlike Gubbio the ironist, Pirandello may not condemn technology, but he does not celebrate it either. Rather, with that cynicism or dubious neutrality of the humorist, he accepts it as the means by which this historical era, like any other, manufactures its own illusions. Second, it seems that *Velocità*, despite its abstract imagery and *compenetrazione* of diverse spatio-temporal registers (as seen, for instance, in the oneiric transformations of scene 1), aspired to contain this 'verisimilar-yet-abstract' notion of the world in a relatively conclusive narrative. *Si gira*, by contrast, not only makes an inconclusive tale, a 'romanzo da fare,' a 'novel in the making,' as described in Giacomo Debenedetti's seminal study,[33] but also promotes a view of the world via a self-regenerative reflexive process. Humour itself, I have argued, becomes one of the images, one that is also a mode of thought and invades other images, thus leading to the formation of new images. Third, in submerging the world's constellation of narrative fragments in a rather conclusive narrative, Marinetti also attaches a clear moral message to it, namely, the need for all to be reborn as Futurists, to abandon thought for action and begin the world's radical Futurist resurgence.

As regards this third point, Pirandello's difference from Marinetti is less sharp. If Marinetti's conclusive script promotes Futurism, Pirandello's inconclusive novel promotes humour. Yet the action sought by *Velocità*'s proselytizing scenario represents a fixed belief. It celebrates industrial modernity and the need to rebuild the world accordingly. It is ideologically the exact opposite of Gubbio the ironist's equally fixed belief, about the mechanization of man in an alienated world. In spite of the opposition, Pirandello himself seems to send a moral message: if not to be reborn as Futurists, or overthrow modernity, to study the world with humour. Let us recall, however, that unlike the first two, humour is not a fixed belief. The humorist has faith in humour as a method for the study of reality, but humour is always the belief in the disproving of all beliefs. It is in light of humour that we must read *Si gira*'s finale, which may otherwise pass as a conclusive *un*happy ending where Gubbio's bitterness proves triumphant. The finale follows the filming of the tiger's killing. When to everyone's devastation Nuti shoots down Nestoroff, and the overexcited tiger begins to tear Nuti to pieces, Gubbio falls into a state of shock. Being the only human inside the cage other than Nuti, he fears that it is his turn to fall into the tiger's jaws. His hand stays fixed to the camera, mechanically turning the handle and unable to stop, until the tiger is shot down. The result is quite lucrative, as the monstrous film of a real man being devoured by a real beast brings a fortune to the industry, making Gubbio rich and free of the need to work. His life of ease, however, has a price. Since the day of the shooting, thanks to the overpowering shock, he forever loses his speech. When he narrates the event, he begins with irony: 'Nessuno intanto potrà negare ch'io non abbia ora raggiunto la mia perfezione. Come operatore, io sono ora, veramente, perfetto' [No one henceforward can deny that I have now arrived at perfection. As an operator I am now, truly, perfect] (*TR* 729; *Shoot!* 208). The state of perfection is none but the absolute mechanization of man in modern times. Gubbio's permanent muteness is his *silenzio di cosa*, the 'silence of an object,' which he mentions elsewhere in relation to his role as a thing, a hand that turns the handle.[34] The literal silence in which he must now remain is a metaphor for his total conversion into a thing. In his bitter outlook, such conversion is imminent if one is to live by the times, the mechanical muteness of which finds in cinema its paradigm. Now that human life is sacrificed to mute fictions, the camera indeed becomes a devouring beast; and in thus assuming the role of the tiger, it affirms the 'triumph of artificial nature over real nature.'[35]

The meaning of silence, however, is not strictly negative. Gubbio usually evokes his *silenzio di cosa* when he addresses his tender feelings for Luisetta Cavalena, who apparently sees in him a mysterious combination of man and machine. He then evokes his *silenzio* not with irony or bitterness but with a sincere concern for his suppressed humanness.

When in an earlier moment he imagines speaking to Luisetta directly, he states:

> Sì, avete ragione. Misterioso. Se sapeste come sento, in certi momenti, *il mio silenzio di cosa*! E mi compiaccio del mistero che spira da questo silenzio a chi sia capace d'avvertirlo. Vorrei non parlar mai; accoglier tutto e tutti in questo mio silenzio … perché tutti dentro di me trovassero, non solo dei loro dolori, ma anche e più delle loro gioje, una tenera pietà che li affratellasse almeno per un momento. (*TR* 607)

> [Yes, you are quite right. Mysterious. If you knew how I feel, at certain moments, my inanimate silence! And I revel in the mystery that is exhaled by this silence for such as are capable of remarking it. I should like never to speak at all; to receive everyone and everything in this silence of mine … so that all might find in me, not only for their griefs but also and even more for their joys, a tender pity that would make us brothers if only for a moment.] (*Shoot!* 90)

As described here, silence represents a state that once accessed provides a deep knowledge of life in its pains and joys. It is, I think, the discovery of the *oltre*, which the essay on humour associates with silence, in this highly cited passage:

> In certi momenti di silenzio interiore, in cui l'anima nostra si spoglia di tutte le finzioni abituali, e gli occhi nostri diventano più acuti e più penetranti, noi vediamo noi stessi nella vita, e in se stessa la vita, quasi in una nudità arida, inquietante; ci sentiamo assaltare da una strana impressione, come se, in un baleno, ci si chiarisse una realtà diversa da quella che normalmente percepiamo, una realtà vivente oltre la vista umana, fuori delle forme dell'umana ragione. (*SPSV* 152)

> [In certain moments of inner silence, in which our soul strips itself of all its habitual fictions and our eyes become sharper and more piercing, we see ourselves in life, and life in itself, as if in a barren and disquieting nakedness; we are seized by a strange impression, as if, in a flash, we could clearly perceive a reality different from the one that we normally perceive, a reality living beyond the reach of human vision, outside the forms of human reason.] (*Humor* 138)

It is Gubbio the idealist, the one who believes in the *oltre*, but at a moment in which his suppressed humanness does not seek respite in bitter irony, that reveals the humoristic meaning of silence. The *silenzio di cosa* is thus revealed as an ambivalent state. It merges the idealist with the humorist, which again suggests that the *oltre* does not exist, that it is one with the *superfluo*, a *nothingness* that is at once *all*, both evoking reflection as an infinite process.[36]

At closing, Gubbio reaffirms his state of being 'perfect,' irony now giving way to powerful suggestiveness: 'Io mi salvo, io solo, nel mio silenzio, col mio silenzio, che m'ha reso così – come il tempo vuole – perfetto' [I have found salvation, I alone, in my silence, with my silence, which has made me thus – according to the standard of the times – perfect] (*TR* 734; *Shoot!* 213). In reframing silence as salvation, he evokes the humorist's 'inner silence,' salvation signifying the coming to terms with life's riddles, welcoming reflection as a never-ending state. Importantly, he relates this suggestive state of being 'perfect' to the 'standard of the times.' He thus also reframes cinema's muteness, allowing us to think of cinema, a multitude of stories, as an ongoing metonymic displacement that incites reflection, as discussed above. It is Gubbio's 'constant camera eye' that exposes these stories – at once real, fictive, and fragile – as able to set forth such a process. It is the same Gubbio who at the sight of Mirelli's six canvases crafts a Nestoroff with the lyricism of a romantic painter. If a 'camera eye' makes images of such lyricism, then cinema must not fare badly in competing with the traditional arts. As Pirandello says elsewhere, traditional art is not closer to truth: 'Anch'essa l'arte, come tutte le costruzioni ideali o illusorie, tende a fissar la vita: la fissa in un momento o in varii momenti determinanti; la statua in un gesto, il paesaggio in un aspetto temporaneo, immutabile. Ma, e la perpetua mobilità degli aspetti successivi? e la fusione continua in cui le anime si trovano?' [Art, like all ideal or illusory constructions, also tends to fix life; it fixes it in one moment or in various given moments – the statue in a gesture, the landscape in a temporary immutable perspective. But – what about the perpetual mobility of the successive perspectives? What about the constant flow in which souls are?] (*SPSV* 157; *Humor* 142). In its deceitfulness, cinema is neither inferior nor superior. If Pirandello is uninterested in unveiling underlying truths, he is as uninterested in the paradigmatic qualities of the image – its truthfulness, lyricism, subjectivity, falseness, impassibility, or objectivity. To be exact, he is uninterested in those qualities *for themselves*, but he likes to observe their participation in modernity's constellation of contrasting images, infinitely refuelling that reflection that is the essence of the humoristic temperament. The multiple and contrasting images of Nestoroff, comprising both paintings and films, are key in Pirandello's crafting of this constellation in *Si gira*, precisely because therein the old coexists with the new. Cinema is modernity's special tool for manufacturing its own illusions. In its intense polyphony, it provides a unique thrust for reflection, unravelling infinite possibilities for articulating one's fluid existence. It is not only its alternative prospects – the emancipation of the apparatus, Nestoroff's 'demon,' or the 'life as it is' of the man captured by the camera unawares – that guarantee its aesthetic validation, but any application of it, including those 'idiotic fictions,' the creator of which, the 'devouring beast,' is a deeply ambivalent metaphor. It does not merely epitomize technology's traumatizing of experience; it also offers its lens, its technological outlook, as the leading tool for constructing one's life in modernity.

Conclusion

As I mentioned at the opening of this study, each of the three authors under discussion grapples with two distinct notions of 'cinema.' One is the institution of narrative cinema as developed and established in Italy by the mid-1910s. It is a historically and culturally specific phenomenon, not only because it occurred at a given moment in history, but also because it involved the industry's particular use of a developing technological apparatus towards the systematization of a well-defined aesthetic as a way of anticipating and conditioning the expectations of an audience across class, intellectual, and national boundaries, attaining thus the status of a largely widespread form of mass entertainment. Marinetti, D'Annunzio, and Pirandello confronted the institution of narrative cinema in different ways, relating to it both positively and negatively to varying degrees. The extent to which each author relates to it negatively is what allows us to address a second notion of cinema, an *abstract* notion that involves the medium's essence, its status as a technological apparatus in its pure form that is available to a diverse range of practical applications, one of which is what pertains to the film industry of the 1910s. The reason that my study of Marinetti, though the youngest of the three authors, precedes the discussion of the other two in the layout of this book is not only that the Futurist manifestos, in their theoretical dimension, articulate the era's cultural features against which I also gauge the works of the others. More specifically, the notion of cinema as an apparatus in its pure form reaches its most explicit and exclusive level of conceptualization in Marinetti. The film aesthetic that the Futurists promote in the fervent language of their 1916 manifesto aims quite aggressively to emancipate the apparatus from its industrial exploitation and passéist, as it were, narrativization. Against the institution of narrative cinema, Marinetti's conceptualization of the medium strikes us as a form of rebellion. After defining his radical position, I examine the extent to which his comprehensive involvement with the medium, comprising also its more implicit theoretical layers and practical applications, sustained indeed that rebellious impetus, before examining whether D'Annunzio's and Pirandello's own works, clearly less aggressive in their approaches, were informed by the same idealistic premise of cinema as a pure apparatus to be emancipated and restored.

Despite their largely diverse approaches to aesthetics, Marinetti's and D'Annunzio's encounters with the medium of cinema tend to neutralize the differences between them. This occurs in at least three areas, the most evident of which is one that transcends the distinction between cinema as institution and cinema as pure apparatus. It involves each author's appraisal of the medium in terms of the new horizons that it opens in the sphere of nationalism. The attempt of the 1916 film manifesto to 'frame' its conception of avant-garde aesthetics within its politics, to valorize the Futurist emancipation of the apparatus for its ability to lead Italy to cultural hegemony, complements D'Annunzio's discourse on *romanità* in his commentary on *Cabiria*, a spectacular epic based on a traditional narrative form, which the author exalts for its ability to kindle the nationalistic spirit of the young Italian nation. To be sure, the fact that the Futurists appropriated avant-gardism for their politics suggests that the notion of cinema as a pure apparatus to be emancipated and restored is not a realizable one; that it is a designated ideal, a catalyst for cultural change, more so than a concrete and attainable state of affairs in and of itself. For this reason, I characterize it as an *abstract* notion. Before I resume this crucial point, which ties together my analyses of all three authors, let us consider the other two areas in which Marinetti's and D'Annunzio's encounters with cinema tend to neutralize their differences.

We may consider a second affinity between Marinetti and D'Annunzio, one that has to do with the extent to which the two authors share a *positive* response to cinema as an institution. By writing the celebrated intertitles of *Cabiria*, by exalting the film in *Corriere della Sera*, and by allowing the cinematic adaptation of his works, D'Annunzio proclaimed himself as a supporter of popular narrative cinema, that is, the very institution that the Futurists attacked as the passéist appropriation of an otherwise revolutionary and 'eminently Futurist' medium. Yet an affinity between them may be sought in that 'aberrant' aspect of

Futurism, in its inherent contradictions, which involves the extent to which Marinetti's own work with the medium, comprising not only the manifesto's radical proclamations but also its implicit conceptual layers and the medium's practical applications, shares the characteristics of popular narrative cinema. We have noted that the manifesto, despite its search for an unprecedented abstract aesthetic to extend the limits of imagination, displays an ambivalent attitude with respect to the question of communicability, the necessity to engage the film spectator in his/her present state. We have also seen that *Vita futurista*, despite its indisputable avant-gardism, and contrary to the aspirations of its makers, instigated a mode of reception that in some ways resembled that of narrative cinema. A juncture of factors, both historical and stylistic, contributed to this effect: a widely diffused patriotic sentiment related to Italy's fighting in the First World War; Marinetti's interventionism as portrayed in the scenes in which he fights a so-called passive neutralist, thus appealing to the audience's patriotism; the photographic naturalism of these 'duels' that countered the film's avant-garde aspirations; and the *arditismo* demonstrated in these segments, which echoed the *attractionist* dimension of the *forzuto*. We have also seen that Marinetti's *Velocità*, in spite of its essayistic enterprise of demonstrating Futurism's superiority over traditionalism, displays ideological and stylistic affinities with the war epic, and with *Cabiria* in particular.

Nonetheless – even if Futurism displayed a more ambivalent relationship with popular culture and a less radical aesthetic program than Marinetti was eager to proclaim – we may not speak of a direct aesthetic affinity between Marinetti and D'Annunzio specifically with respect to cinema. One might argue that the *forzuto* provides a link between Futurist film and D'Annunzio. The *forzuto* has been described as a popularized form of D'Annunzio's myth of the Superman and as an expression of the *arditismo* that marked the author's military excursions.[1] The figure of Maciste, whose popularity expedited the growth of the *forzuto* as a genre, was appropriated during war for the genre's cultivation of nationalism. Maciste's nationalism was present from the start, with his inception in *Cabiria*, the nationalism of which D'Annunzio exalted. Marinetti's 'duels' themselves, in their striking *arditismo*, recall Maciste's boldness and bravery, and perhaps even those same traits in D'Annunzio the fighter. Yet we may not speak of a direct affinity between the two authors, because Maciste is not in effect Dannunzian. Only with caution may we compare him to the Dannunzian Superman.[2] His immense physical strength, working-class status, lack of education, supreme morality, and abstention from romance, are not traits of the typical Dannunzian hero. Furthermore, as I suggested earlier, the notion of the Italian cinema's 'Dannunzianism' presents limitations. To call Maciste Dannunzian is to overvalue the phenomenon. When cheering Maciste's or Marinetti's acts of bravery, audiences were not necessarily having a Dannunzian experience. We must certainly not preclude narrative cinema as the basis of a comparison between the two authors, but we must recognize that the affinity is indirect. Cinema was an ideological vehicle. Discretely emulated by Marinetti and unabashedly exploited by D'Annunzio, the institution of cinema aided for both authors the transmission of a nationalist ideal to the public. This involves not the aesthetic exchange between the specifically Decadentist and the specifically Futurist, but the participation of either movement in the era's political climate. It is the subjection of aesthetics to politics.

The third area in which the two authors' encounters with cinema tend to neutralize their differences involves the extent to which they relate to the institution of cinema *negatively*, hence, their promotion of an alternative concept of cinema as essence, as a technological apparatus in its pure form to be emancipated and restored. In this case we may speak of a more direct affinity. To be exact, we may speak of D'Annunzio's sharing of the specifically Futurist. As noted above, Futurism's conceptualization of cinema via its radical proclamations is a form of rebellion against the traditionalist appropriation of the medium. An alternative to the cinematic institution is also what D'Annunzio advocates in describing his experiment with Daphne as an 'unusual attempt.' His praise of the *meraviglioso* refers to tricks aiming not at verisimilitude but at the astonishing actualization of strange, unfamiliar, or 'unusual' things. In his essay he reveres the non-realist capabilities of the apparatus while questioning its institutional application. We have also observed the avant-garde urge in the *Gioconda* piece, its conception of a 'dull' Mona Lisa, whose caricatural animation, inspired by film technology and its extended aesthetic horizons, like a surgeon's intervention, shatters the aura of the Renaissance masterpiece. This is not to say that D'Annunzio becomes a full-fledged avant-gardist, or that his project is driven by an impetus as rebellious as Marinetti's. In neither work does D'Annunzio reject the cultural tradition. With respect to the *Gioconda* in particular, I suggested that its structural oscillation between a script proper and a literary work betrays his hesitation to relinquish literature for an instrumental use of language in the service of a medium other than literature. I also interpreted the script as a both meta-discursive and allegorical

statement about the necessity to redefine art in view of the new aesthetic possibilities offered by film – a statement nonetheless that casts
no doubt on the author's deep-rooted adoration for Leonardo's painting. Rather than largely espousing avant-gardism, D'Annunzio inte-
grates avant-gardism with aestheticism. He flirts with the radical tools
that technology confers on the realm of aesthetics so as to explore new
mesmerizing ways of revering the old. Still an aesthete, he now gazes
at the past through a 'Futuristic' lens.

The concept of cinema's essence, a pure apparatus to be emancipated and restored vis-à-vis any institutions historically formed, is an
abstract one, a mere concept. Its single concrete value is the inspiration
that it may provide to the artist, to the Futurists and to D'Annunzio
alike. In its pure form, the medium promises art's ability to resist what
is already established and to create an alternative and unfamiliar view
of the world. In order to refute the institution, Marinetti appeals to
the medium's technological essence, where its subversive potential
presumably lies. Aesthetically speaking – not politically – the wish to
create art that is subversive is what grants Futurism its status as an
avant-garde movement. Yet once the medium is put into practice there
begins the process of its institutionalization. In asking why Futurism
did not engage further in filmmaking, I suggested that it had to do
with the failure to implement a revolutionary spectator response, one
defined by the spectators' belligerent spirit and participation in the
spectacle, what we may describe as the implementation of an aesthetics of war. This failed, I argued, because of Vita futurista's slippage into
a conventionalized mode of reception, given its inability to resist the
wish to incorporate a patriotic discourse during war. What Vita futurista's case study suggests is that, once applied to a specific practice, the
medium's adherence to an institution becomes inevitable. Whether
this refers to the medium's adherence to an already existing institution
or its tendency to form one of its own, its institutionalization of sorts
diminishes its subversive potential. It is thus contrary to the goals of the
Futurists, who posed as anarchic. A similar phenomenon characterizes
D'Annunzio's 'dull' Mona Lisa, his own invention of a Gioconda send-
up, several examples of which preceded his scenario. This is also true of
the meraviglioso in Daphne, which had been preceded, one might say, by
the cinema of Méliès. Yet in his essay D'Annunzio implies that now, in
1914, the meraviglioso is a novelty, most likely in order to be polemical.
Perhaps refreshing one's memory of the revolutionary potential of the
apparatus – or, to be exact, allowing oneself to be inspired by the notion

of a pure and emancipated apparatus without marring this inspiration with empirical investigations of the notion itself – refreshes and invigorates one's revolutionary artistic spirit.

If Marinetti espouses the utopia of the pure apparatus with the spirit of a rebel and D'Annunzio with the contentment of an aesthete, Pirandello gazes at it with the apprehension and emotional detachment of a sage. This is not to say that he is immune to the cultural dilemmas sprung forth by the era's technological novelties. However, what distinguishes him both from Marinetti's unidirectional euphoria and from D'Annunzio's erudite rehearsals is a vigorous investigation of the modern condition leading to the conscious articulation of a fragmented subject. Yet with the detached neutrality of the humorist, a position that no doubt is itself an intellectual construct, he dexterously assigns his own tendency towards any extreme and unidirectional views on modernity to his fictional creation, to his mirror image as I described it earlier, which is Gubbio the ironist. Unlike the Futurists, Gubbio the ironist scorns industrial modernity. Much like the Futurists, however, he also scorns the institution of narrative cinema, an alternative to which he seeks in those unconventional images that fail to fulfil the institution's prerequisites, where film technology renders the represented object strange, unfamiliar, and awkward, and where the suppressed human instincts and the remnants of authenticity are presumably found and unveiled. In other words, Gubbio the ironist seeks the institution's alternative in the subversive potential of the medium's essence, driven by his faith in a pure apparatus to be emancipated and restored. It is Pirandello, to whom Gubbio's other persona – that of the humorist – points metaphorically, that encourages us to think of this alternative image, this highly sought achievement of the emancipated apparatus, as yet another fiction – and what is more, a fiction the multilayered meaning of which does not evade the conventional processes that determine the ways in which the subject grasps any phenomenon. By thus inviting us to view modernity through the lens of humour, Pirandello paints cinematic practice in its entirety – industrial and alternative alike, narrative and abstract alike – as a process that adheres to pre-existent patterns of thought, hence, to thought that is informed by institutions historically formed. In blurring the boundaries between institutional and alternative practice, Pirandello prompts us not only to accept the cinematic institution as a historical fact, as modernity's own means to confront the dilemma that always hovered and will always hover over humans – that is, the struggle to define truth and identity and the multiple illusions formed in its course – but also to seek the unfamiliar, the awkward, and the irresolute in the ideal structure itself; hence, to perceive the organic narrative structure as itself a fragment, one that lies in wait of its own completion via the arrival of the next narrative fragment.

The infinite process by which every fragment that seeks completion awakens the next fragment acquires in Pirandello's novel a tangible form in the figure of the diva, whose identity consists of multiple, diverse, and contrasting visual renderings, as well as narrative hypotheses about her behaviour and experience, none of which suffices in itself to define her. The reader's initial perception of Nestoroff may be conditioned by his/her familiarity with a popular view of the Italian silent diva-image as a femme fatale, defined by seductiveness, secrecy, a menacing disposition, corporeality, and strong associations with nature. Insofar as these traits represent the explosion of a traditional literary conception of woman as an alluring object of desire, they are also the ones that Marinetti claims to dispel via his conception of the 'multiplied man,' the ideal Futurist who does away with desire and replaces his love for woman with his love for the machine. If we bracket momentarily the presumed misogyny that underlies Marinetti's 'multiplied man' and focus strictly on the fragmentary aesthetic that his machine cult inspires in him – to consider, for instance, the concepts of *analogy* and *imagination without strings* and the conceptualization of an anti-realist, anti-narrative, avant-garde cinema that those inspire – we may speak of an affinity between Futurism and Pirandello's diva. This is true to the extent that Nestoroff's portrayal through her multiple, diverse, and unconventional visual renderings and contrasting narrative fragments may be interpreted in light of Futurist aesthetics, while it undercuts the reader's tendency to view Nestoroff as little more than the incarnation of the familiar cinematic femme fatale.

This avant-garde portrayal of woman, as it were, does not make Pirandello more Marinettian than Dannunzian. As we have seen, the dilemma between woman and technology triumphs in *Forse che sì forse che no*. Against its affirmation of the female protagonist as the catalyst for man's desire and action, D'Annunzio's novel portrays technology as a liberating alternative to the oppressiveness of desire, what immediately brings to mind the 'multiplied man.' Both Paolo Tarsis and the 'multiplied man' are *arditi* – active, bold, brave – to the core. Yet they also differ in a significant way, in that Marinetti, who wishes to undo the old-fashioned ideals of woman, beauty, and love, claims to abolish desire altogether, whereas D'Annunzio exploits the power of desire all the way to the novel's finale. Inasmuch as the tortuousness of the love affair threatens male integrity, D'Annunzio applies modern technology to the invention of new tropes only to reaffirm his adoration of feminine allure, the traditional notion of the elusive object of desire, now through a 'Futuristic' lens. This is true not only of Isabella Inghirami, but also of his cinematic conceptions Daphne and Mona Lisa, the avant-garde component of which does very little to negate their status as seductive ethereal figures, relocating instead their centuries-old allure in a modern setting. Hence, as in the case of film technology and aesthetics in general, with regard to female representation in particular D'Annunzio does not share Marinetti's rebelliousness but flirts with a modern aesthetic tool as a way of venerating the old.

The traces of the traditional notion of woman as alluring, ethereal, sadistic, ambiguous, and so on, are unmistakable in Pirandello's representation of Nestoroff – whether in the canvases made by the hand of a tortured soul, a sensual dance in front of a camera, her suspicious involvement in tragic love affairs, or her blending with the rays of the sun while sitting under a pergola. Yet it is through the coexistence of these diverse images, and through the failure of any one of them to affirm itself as her real identity, that Pirandello mixes traditionalism and avant-gardism. To say that he mixes the two does not mean that he achieves an amalgam like the one achieved by D'Annunzio, who exploits modernity's aesthetic tools in order to retell an old story in new mesmerizing ways. Rather, he mixes the two via humour. Once again, he gazes at his object neither as a rebel nor as an aesthete, but with neutrality. The old beauty is constantly dismantled and reconstituted in varied forms. That we are dealing with a film diva reminds us that cinema – be it an institution or alternative practice, whether we view it as an industry established in the second decade of the twentieth century or as the utopian search for an apparatus in its pure form – in this historical moment not only revolutionizes the sphere of aesthetics, it also multiplies rapidly the possibilities of conceiving reality through that ever-existing and infinite process in which the fragmented images of the past, the present, and the future merge with and reconstitute one another.

Notes

Introduction

1 According to Luciano De Maria, although the 'heroic period' generally refers to 1909–15, that initial impulse persisted for several additional years, manifest especially in the writings on theatre and film. He thus dates the 'heroic period' alternatively as 1909–20. Filippo Tommaso Marinetti et al., *Teoria e invenzione futurista*, ed. Luciano De Maria, 3rd ed. (Milan: Mondadori, 1996) xxxi. Further references to this volume appear in the text (abbr. *TIF*). Unless otherwise noted, all translations of secondary text are mine.

2 The passage is from Marinetti's manifesto 'Distruzione della sintassi / Immaginazione senza fili / Parole in libertà' (1913). Unless otherwise noted, all translations of Futurist works are mine, and where available with consultation of F.T. Marinetti, *Let's Murder the Moonshine: Selected Writings*, ed. R.W. Flint, trans. R.W. Flint and Arthur A. Coppotelli (Los Angeles: Sun & Moon Press, 1991) and/or F.T. Marinetti, *Critical Writings*, ed. Günter Berghaus, trans. Doug Thompson (New York: Farrar, Straus and Giroux, 2006).

3 Starting with Marinetti's 'Fondazione e Manifesto del Futurismo,' appearing on 20 February 1909 in the Parisian newspaper *Le Figaro* under the title 'Le Futurisme,' the Futurists continued to publish manifestos up until Marinetti's death in 1944, the year that Mario Verdone designates as marking the end of the Futurist movement. Mario Verdone, *Il movimento futurista* (Rome: Lucarini, 1986) 112–13.

4 See Marinetti's 'La nuova religione-morale della velocità' (1916) in *TIF* 130–8.

5 See Marinetti's 'Manifesto tecnico della letteratura futurista' (1912) in *TIF* 46–54.

6 Renato Poggioli, *The Theory of the Avant-Garde* (Cambridge, MA: Harvard University Press, 1968) 27–40, 61–8.

7 'Surely antitraditionalism was more polemical and programmatic in Italian
   futurism than in any other avant-garde movement; surely in no other
   country did it express itself in such clamorous demonstrations against tradition, the academy, and the temples thereof, the library and the museum.'
   Ibid. 52–3.
8 Peter Bürger, *Theory of the Avant-Garde*, trans. Michael Shaw (Minneapolis:
   University of Minnesota Press, 1994) 35–54.
9 Claudia Salaris, 'Marketing Modernism: Marinetti as Publisher,' trans.
   Lawrence Rainey, in *Marinetti and the Italian Futurists*, ed. Lawrence
   Rainey and Robert von Hallberg, special issue of *Modernism/Modernity* 1.3
   (1994) 121–2.
10 'The concept of the historical avant-garde movements used here applies
   primarily to Dadaism and early Surrealism but also and equally to the
   Russian avant-garde after the October revolution ... With certain limitations that would have to be determined through concrete analysis, this is
   also true of Italian Futurism and German Expressionism.' Bürger 109n4.
11 Ibid. 49–50.
12 For more on the divergent ideological approaches to technology on the
   part of Italian Futurism and other avant-garde movements see Andreas
   Huyssen, *After the Great Divide: Modernism, Mass Culture, Postmodernism*
   (Bloomington: Indiana University Press, 1986) 9–13.
13 Bürger 78.
14 Poggioli 95.
15 Emilio Gentile, 'The Conquest of Modernity: From Modernist Nationalism
   to Fascism,' trans. Lawrence Rainey, in Rainey and von Hallberg, eds,
   Marinetti and the Italian Futurists 59–65.
16 In 1920, when the Fascist party, initially left wing, turned officially right
   wing, Marinetti and the Futurists accused the *fasci* of being reaction-
   ary and traditionalist and withdrew from the party. It took several years
   before Marinetti revised his position and the positive relationship was
   re-established. On the relationship between Fascism and Futurism see *TIF*
   l–lxiii; Verdone, *Il movimento futurista* 15–22; and Gentile 55–6.
17 Mario Verdone, *Cinema e letteratura del futurismo* (Rome: Centro
   Sperimentale di Cinematografia, Edizioni di Bianco e Nero, 1968) 39.
18 For a theorization of the style of representation and mode of exhibition
   during cinema's first decade, as well as cinema's social and structural
   affinity with the aims of the avant-garde, see Tom Gunning, 'The Cinema
   of Attractions: Early Film, Its Spectator and the Avant-Garde,' in *Early
   Cinema: Space, Frame, Narrative*, ed. Thomas Elsaesser (London: BFI, 1990)
   56–62. As regards the venues of exhibition, in the north of Italy, quite

common also was the *cinema ambulante* (travelling cinema), which took place at seasonal city and village fairs. These public events offered a meeting place for the coaches of travelling artists who rode all the way from Spain and France, through Austria-Hungary, to Italy. Aldo Bernardini, *Cinema muto italiano: Ambiente, spettacoli e spettatori 1896/1904* (Bari: Laterza, 1980) 65–70, 109–10.

19 Aldo Bernardini, *Cinema muto italiano: Industria e organizzazione dello spettacolo 1905/1909* (Bari: Laterza, 1981) 15–22.

20 Ibid. 194–5.

21 Such were the two successes produced by Ambrosio, *Gli ultimi giorni di Pompei* (1908) and *Nerone* (1909). Bernardini, *Cinema 1905/1909* 220–3.

22 Aldo Bernardini, *Cinema muto italiano: Arte, divismo e mercato 1910/14* (Bari: Laterza, 1982) 40–54.

23 Ibid. 62–77. For an extensive discussion of the development of the narrative film and the prevalent genres through the middle of the 1910s see also Gian Piero Brunetta, *Storia del cinema italiano I: Il cinema muto 1895–1929* (Rome: Riuniti, 1993) 130–230.

24 Bernardini, *Cinema 1910/14* 79–97.

25 Ibid. 111–15.

26 Ibid. 192–211. For an extensive discussion of Caserini's film, see Jacopo Comin, 'Ma l'amor mio non muore,' in *Antologia di Bianco e Nero 1937–1943*, ed. Leonardo Autera, vol. 3.2 (Rome: Edizioni di Bianco e Nero, 1964) 934–59. Comin's essay first appeared in *Bianco e Nero* 1.4 (1937) 99–116. For more on this genre, see Eugenio Ferdinando Palmieri, *Vecchio cinema italiano* (1940; Vicenza: Neri Pozza, 1994) 91–128. Palmieri's expressionistic yet informative study, written in 1940, is one of the first attempts to write a comprehensive history of the Italian cinema.

27 Giuliana Bruno, *Streetwalking on a Ruined Map: Cultural Theory and the City Films of Elvira Notari* (Princeton: Princeton University Press, 1993) 30–1. In this seminal work, Bruno provides an in-depth cultural study of the major contribution to Italian film history by the female Neapolitan filmmaker Elvira Notari. She exposes Notari's cinema as a form of realism that is superior to the film *verista*, in that it is marked, among other things, by its modest means of production, reliance on non-professional actors, and portrayal of the real Neapolitan underworld. She explains that traditional historiography had obscured Notari's cinema, displacing it with the film *verista*, thanks to the latter's professionally more legitimate conditions of production and strong associations with official culture.

28 Angela Dalle Vacche, *Diva: Defiance and Passion in Early Italian Cinema* (Austin: University of Texas Press, 2008) 2–3.

29 Brunetta, *Storia* 86–90. For extensive treatments of the *forzuto* see Monica
  Dall'Asta, *Un cinéma musclé: Le surhomme dans le cinéma muet italien
  (1913–1926)*, trans. Franco Arnò and Charles Tatum, Jr (Crisnée [Belgium]:
  Editions Yellow Now, 1992) and Alberto Farassino and Tatti Sanguineti,
  eds, *Gli uomini forti* (Milan: Mazzotta, 1983).

30 For the international commerce of the Italian cinema in 1912–18, with a sta-
  tistical table of exports and revenues in its ten largest markets (countries of
  Europe, South America, and the United States), see Brunetta, *Storia* 53–5.

31 Initially describing the 1880s Parisian movement of the *Poètes maudits*
  (damned poets), the term 'Decadentism' finds its way into Italy mainly
  through the works of D'Annunzio and Giovanni Pascoli (1855–1912). See
  Guido Baldi, Silvia Giusso, Mario Razetti, and Giuseppe Zaccaria, *Dal
  testo alla storia, dalla storia al testo: Letteratura italiana con pagine di scrittori
  stranieri, analisi dei testi, critica*, ed. Gigi Livio, vol. 3.2.a (Turin: Paravia,
  1994) 11.

32 A notion yet to be theorized by Freud, the 'unconscious' is an obscure
  psychical state where individuality disappears in a fusion with all, promising the discovery of an authentic and ineffable realm of experience.
  Ibid. 12–13.

33 For D'Annunzio and Decadentism I am especially indebted to Baldi et al.
  11–22; Walter Binni, *La poetica del decadentismo italiano* (Florence: G.C.
  Sansoni, 1936); Maria Teresa Marabini Moevs, *Gabriele D'Annunzio e le
  estetiche della fine del secolo* (L'Aquila: L.U. Japadre, 1976); Mario Praz, *The
  Romantic Agony*, trans. Angus Davidson (New York: Meridian Books,
  1967); Carlo Salinari, *Miti e coscienza del decadentismo italiano: D'Annunzio,
  Pascoli, Fogazzaro e Pirandello* (Milan: Feltrinelli, 1986); and Barbara
  Spackman, *Decadent Genealogies: The Rhetoric of Sickness from Baudelaire to
  D'Annunzio* (Ithaca: Cornell University Press, 1989).

34 '*Vampe vampe vampe*' is from Marinetti's 1914 epic poem in words-in-
  freedom, *Zang Tumb Tuuum*, reprinted in *TIF* 639–779 (this part, 775). The
  quoted segment is from D'Annunzio's *Notturno*, as quoted by Marinetti. It
  appears in smaller print in *TIF*. In translating it, I have consulted Gabriele
  D'Annunzio, *Nocturne and Five Tales of Love and Death*, trans. Raymond
  Rosenthal (Marlboro, VT: The Marlboro Press, 1988) 231.

35 Noted by Rosenthal in D'Annunzio, *Nocturne* 6.

36 See, for example, Rudyard Kipling's 'Boots,' also a poem about war: 'We're
  foot – slog – slog – slog – sloggin' over Africa! Foot – foot – foot – foot –
  sloggin' over Africa – (Boots – boots – boots – boots – movin' up an' down
  again!) There's no discharge in the war!' Rudyard Kipling, *Collected Verse of
  Rudyard Kipling* (New York: Doubleday, Page & Co., 1910) 370.

37 D'Annunzio, *Nocturne* 6.

38 'Prince of Italian Decadentism' is how Walter Binni, in his seminal study, characterizes D'Annunzio. Binni 58.

39 Gabriele D'Annunzio, *Prose di romanzi*, vol. 2, ed. Niva Lorenzini (Milan: Mondadori, 1989) 566–7. Further references to this volume appear in the text (abbr. *PRII*). All translations from the novel *Forse che sì forse che no* are mine.

40 For the definition of 'objective correlative' see T.S. Eliot, *The Sacred Wood: Essays on Poetry and Criticism* (London: Methuen, 1928) 100.

41 A *soggetto*, which may be translated as 'scenario' or 'screenplay,' is a story outline with occasional allusions to dialogue or style. It lacks the detailed specifications of dialogue and technique that characterize, for instance, the standard screenplay of a Hollywood studio.

42 Gabriele D'Annunzio, *Tragedie, sogni e misteri*, vol. 2, ed. Egidio Bianchetti (Verona: Mondadori, 1966) 1129. My translation. Further references to this volume appear in the text (abbr. *TSM*).

43 Gian Piero Brunetta, 'La conquista dell'impero dei sogni: D'Annunzio e Pirandello,' *Annali d'Italianistica* 6 (1988) 22–3.

44 Commenting on the heroine of *Ma l'amor mio non muore*, Comin describes Borelli's figure as 'ethereal and Dannunzian to the core.' Comin 952. Lisetta Renzi notes that the typical motifs surrounding the diva – animals, flowers, forest, sea – place her on the side of the irrational, making her both attractive and threatening to the male ego. The denouement eliminates the threat with repentance, illness, death, or other sacrifice or punishment. The diva character represents, according to Renzi, the transition of a Dannunzian theme from literature to film: 'In the case, however, of the irreducible ones, who persevere in their perversity, rests the Dannunzian judgment on Ippolita Sanzio: "the Enemy" who must be defeated.' Lisetta Renzi, 'Grandezza e morte della "femme fatale,"' in *Sperduto nel buio: Il cinema muto italiano e il suo tempo (1905–1930)*, ed. Renzo Renzi (Bologna: Cappelli, 1991) 128.

45 Pietro Bianchi, *Francesca Bertini e le dive del cinema muto* (Turin: UTET, 1969) 10–13.

46 Mario Verdone, 'I film di D'Annunzio e da D'Annunzio,' *Quaderni del Vittoriale* 4 (1977) 24.

47 On D'Annunzio's 'stardom' and popularity, see also Enrico Mazzuoli, 'Attori e attrici nei film dannunziani,' in *Quaderni del Vittoriale* 4 (1977) 37–44. For the ambiguous relations between D'Annunzio and Mussolini see John Woodhouse, *Gabriele D'Annunzio: Defiant Archangel* (Oxford: Clarendon Press, 1998) 353–80.

48 Bianchi promotes an unqualified identification between literary
   Decadentism and the film diva: 'We have insisted on the influence, though
   indirect (*Cabiria* is not an example), that Gabriele D'Annunzio had on
   our silent cinema, precisely because through the poet from the Abruzzi
   European Decadentism made a triumphant entry in Italy. In actresses like
   Lyda Borelli, Italia Almirante, Francesca Bertini, and Pina Menichelli, the
   femme damnée found cinematic models whose success among the spectators of the western world ['del mondo civile'] was undisputed for years.'
   Bianchi 227.
49 Verdone, 'I film di D'Annunzio e da D'Annunzio' 24.
50 Whereas D'Annunzio's literary heroine is a catalyst for the hero's desire,
   her cinematic counterpart is herself the protagonist and it is her own desire
   that the film underlines. Perhaps this reversal is owed to the transition of
   an idea from literature to film. A trope of the diva film is a static shot of the
   diva looking seductively at the camera. A decade after the cinema of attractions, this kind of image exhibits an *attractionist* quality. Highly charged
   with erotic appeal, it suspends narrative progression and indulges the
   spectator in the pleasure of seeing, while it alludes to the diva's revered
   image outside this specific narrative. Perhaps the mass audience found the
   diva's antics more appealing than the aesthete's spiritual quandary. For the
   perseverance of attractions in narrative cinema see Gunning, 'The Cinema
   of Attractions' 61.
51 The scholarship on Pirandello's humour is vast. I am especially indebted
   to Paola Casella, *L'umorismo di Pirandello: Ragioni intra- e intertestuali*
   (Fiesole [Florence]: Cadmo, 2002); Arcangelo Leone de Castris, *Storia
   di Pirandello* (Bari: Laterza, 1962); Thomas Harrison, *Essayism: Conrad,
   Musil and Pirandello* (Baltimore: Johns Hopkins University Press, 1992);
   Catherine O'Rawe, *Authorial Echoes: Textuality and Self-Plagiarism in
   the Narrative of Luigi Pirandello* (London: Legenda, 2005); and Adriano
   Tilgher, *Studi sul teatro contemporaneo*, 3rd ed. (Rome: Libreria di Scienze e
   Lettere, 1928).
52 Walter Benjamin, *Selected Writings*, vol. 4, trans. Edmund Jephcott et al.,
   ed. Howard Eiland and Michael W. Jennings (Cambridge, MA: Belknap
   Press of Harvard University Press, 2003) 266.
53 Gaspare Giudice, *Luigi Pirandello* (Turin: UTET, 1963) 265–9.
54 Ibid. 415, 441. In his chapter on Fascism (412–64) Giudice discusses
   Pirandello's public stance on many aspects of the regime, addressing both
   honours and controversies.
55 Quoted ibid. 422. My translation.
56 Ibid. 416.

57 Bernardini, *Cinema 1896/1904* 91–107. For Fregoli's own account of his
   Parisian experience and subsequent success in Italy, see Leopoldo Fregoli,
   Fregoli raccontato da Fregoli: Le memorie del mago del trasformismo (Milan:
   Rizzoli, 1936) 214–20.

58 *Maestri di musica* and other films by Fregoli are held at the Cineteca of the
   Centro Sperimentale di Cinematografia in Rome. On some uncertainties
   regarding the conditions of production of *Maestri di musica* see Bernardini,
   Cinema 1896/1904 94 and Luigi Colagreco, 'Il cinema negli spettacoli di
   Leopoldo Fregoli,' *Bianco e Nero* 63.3–4 (2002) 44–5.

59 Bernardini, *Cinema 1896/1904* 95–7.

60 For an extensive commentary on Fregoli in relation to Futurism see
   Colagreco.

61 *TIF* 89. Fregoli himself claims that Marinetti once met him in Naples and
   gave him an article that he had written, entitled 'Il dinamismo di Fregoli.'
   Fregoli 220.

62 See Luigi Pirandello, *Tutti i romanzi*, vol. 2, ed. Giovanni Macchia (Milan:
   Mondadori, 1973) 612. For the English translation see Luigi Pirandello,
   Shoot!: The Notebooks of Serafino Gubbio, Cinematograph Operator, trans. C.K.
   Scott Moncrieff (1926; Chicago: University of Chicago Press, 2005) 95. As
   'rientrante' means 'sunken,' a form marked by a concavity, the opposite of
   'protruding,' Moncrieff's description of the tripod as 'knock–kneed' is most
   appropriate. The image of the spider as a metaphor for the camera appears
   in slightly varied forms also on pages 586, 598, 607, and 679 of the Italian
   text, and on pages 68, 82, 91, and 159 of Moncrieff's translation.

1. Film Aesthetics of a 'Heroic' Futurism

1 'La cinematografia,' signed by Marinetti and Ginna, appeared in 1938 in
  Bianco e Nero and was noted as having originated in *La Gazzetta del Popolo*,
  but without a specific date. *TIF* cxxxiv. The Futurists made more written
  interventions on issues related to cinema, the most noted of which, both
  signed by Marinetti, are 'La cinematografia astratta è un'invenzione italiana,' published on 1 December 1926 in *L'Impero*, and 'La morale fascista del
  cinematografo,' published in April 1934 in *Sant'Elia*. For an extensive discussion and reprints of Futurist writings on cinema see Wanda Strauven,
  Marinetti e il cinema: Tra attrazione e sperimentazione (Pasian di Prato:
  Campanotto, 2006) 82–121, 228–38.

2 It is likely that Marinetti wrote *Velocità* in the late 1910s, although that
  remains uncertain. See Giovanni Lista, 'An Unpublished Work by
  Marinetti: "Speed," Futurist Film,' in *Oltre l'autore I*, ed. Alberto Boschi and

Giacomo Manzoli, special issue of *Fotogenia* 2 (1996) 139 and Strauven 190–1. Several film projects realized on the initiative of artists working outside of the movement may also be discussed in terms of the Futurist endeavour. For comprehensive accounts see Giovanni Lista, *Cinema e fotografia futurista* (Milan: Skira, 2001) and *Il cinema futurista* (Recco, Genoa: Le mani, 1910); Strauven; and Verdone, *Cinema*. Most relevant in this respect are the experiments in abstract cinematography realized by the brothers Arnaldo and Bruno Ginanni Corradini (renamed by Balla as Arnaldo Ginna and Bruno Corra upon their initiation in the movement), whose examples of *cinepittura*, or cine-painting, preceded the movement's official cinematic exordium by several years. See Lista, *Cinema e fotografia* 20–6; Strauven 83–5; and Verdone, *Cinema* 2–38. In addition, Aldo Molinari's narrative film *Mondo Baldoria* (1914), of which the self-proclaimed association with Futurism infuriated Marinetti, was inspired by Aldo Palazzeschi's 1913 manifesto, 'Il controdolore.' See Lista, *Cinema e fotografia* 31–7. Moreover, Anton Giulio Bragaglia, in collaboration with Enrico Prampolini as art director, made four narrative films of variable length, of which only *Thaïs* (1916) is extant. For more on Bragaglia and his problematic relationship with the movement, as well as detailed analyses of *Thaïs*, see Lista, *Cinema e fotografia* 61–7 and Millicent Marcus, 'Anton Giulio Bragaglia's *Thaïs*, or, The Death of the *Diva* + the Rise of the *Scenoplastica* = The Birth of Futurist Cinema,' *South Central Review* 13.2–3 (1996) 63–81.

3 Verdone, *Cinema* 118–19.

4 Lista, *Cinema e fotografia* 11–18, esp. 12. See also Lista, *Il cinema futurista* 15–19.

5 Strauven 20–4, 86. More scholars addressed this question. Brunetta posits that the concept of cinema as proposed by the 1916 film manifesto represents potentially one of the most productive theoretical hypotheses of Futurist discourse. If it did not find a direct application in Italian film practice, it did so in other national avant-garde cinemas, such as Russian, German, and French. Brunetta, *Storia* 215. Franca Angelini argues that the late arrival of the 1916 film manifesto as compared to Futurist writings on the other arts suggests not a real interest in the expressive value of the new medium but a mere necessity for the Futurists to write on cinema in order to render their expressive code complete. She explains the lack of Futurist film production as the Futurists' inability to perceive the symbolic significance of the medium for a modern industrial mass culture. Franca Angelini, *Serafino e la tigre: Pirandello tra scrittura teatro e cinema* (Venice: Marsilio, 1990) 56–8.

6 Strauven 54–9.

7 For a historical account of Italian theatre in the late nineteenth and
  early twentieth centuries, see Günter Berghaus, *Italian Futurist Theatre,
  1909–1944* (Oxford: Clarendon Press, 1998) 11–25. The genres of the Italian
  stage in the period preceding the Futurist debut consisted primarily of
  well-crafted comedies, usually set in a contemporary upper-class milieu
  and catering to a low-brow taste, and serious drama in the form of tragedy,
  the 'problem play,' taking place in a contemporary or historical setting and
  catering to a somewhat sophisticated audience while providing material
  for discussion in literary journals of the time. Berghaus 19–20.

8 In general terms, besides the comparison with cinema, theatre offered
  an ideal means for the instigation of action, which was one of Futurism's
  foundational principles. According to Berghaus, 'Futurism assumed the
  role of a violent jolt that set ablaze the somnolent and stultified cultural
  scene in Italy. The means to achieve this aim could not be conventional
  literature alone. The publication of a manifesto, however controversial
  and polemical its language, remained an act of literary discourse. The
  true transformation of art into life began only when Futurism entered into
  the public arena by means of live performances and theatrical actions.'
  Berghaus 5–6. See also Lia Lapini, *Il teatro futurista italiano* (Milan: Mursia,
  1977) 31–43.

9 An early treatment of the topic discussed in chapters 1 and 2 appears in
  Michael Syrimis, 'Film, Spectators, and War in Italian Futurism,' in *Italian
  Cultural Studies 2001: Selected Essays*, ed. Anthony Julian Tamburri et al.
  (Boca Raton, FL: Bordighera Press, 2004) 168–85.

10 For a detailed, step-by-step reading of the 1916 film manifesto see Strauven
  85–111.

11 The manifesto reads: 'Col nostro Manifesto *Il teatro sintetico futurista,* con
  le vittoriose *tournées* delle compagnie drammatiche Gualtiero Tumiati,
  Ettore Berti, Annibale Ninchi, Luigi Zoncada, coi 2 volumi del *Teatro
  Sintetico Futurista* contenenti 80 sintesi teatrali, noi abbiamo iniziato
  in Italia la rivoluzione del teatro di prosa. Antecedentemente un altro
  Manifesto futurista aveva riabilitato, glorificato e perfezionato il *Teatro di
  Varietà.* È logico dunque che oggi noi trasportiamo il nostro sforzo vivifi-
  catore in un'altra zona del teatro: il *cinematografo'* [With our Manifesto *The
  Futurist Synthetic Theatre,* with the victorious tours of the theatre compa-
  nies of Gualtiero Tumiati, Ettore Berti, Annibale Ninchi, Luigi Zoncada,
  together with the 2 volumes of the *Futurist Synthetic Theatre* containing
  80 theatrical syntheses, we have launched the revolution of the theatre of
  prose in Italy. Prior to that, another Futurist Manifesto had rehabilitated,
  glorified, and perfected the *Variety Theatre.* It is therefore logical for us

today to carry our vivifying effort into another zone of the theatre: the *cinema*] (*TIF* 139).

12 Emphasis in original. The use of boldfaced type for emphasis was common in Futurist manifestos.

13 As the manifesto proceeds to explain, the concept of *poliespressività* had been expressed in 'Pesi, misure e prezzi del genio artistico,' a 1914 manifesto by Corra and Settimelli, reprinted in Mario Verdone, ed., *Manifesti futuristi e scritti teorici di Arnaldo Ginna e Bruno Corra* (Ravenna: Longo Editore, 1984) 167–73.

14 Strauven 90.

15 Ibid. 34; Brunetta, *Storia* 23.

16 Isabella Innamorati, 'Marinetti nella cinematografia futurista,' in *Marinetti il futurista*, ed. Carlo V. Menichi (Pistoia: Tellini, 1988) 118n13.

17 For extensive commentaries on analogy see Luca Somigli, *Legitimizing the Artist: Manifesto Writing and European Modernism, 1885–1915* (Toronto: University of Toronto Press, 2003) 141–4 and Strauven 59–73.

18 Strauven 67.

19 On the expansion of the viewer's imagination see also Lista, *Il cinema futurista* 60–5.

20 In the case that this is the idiomatic use of the future tense that conveys probability, then the image of the gazelle will suggest that those are the words that the man 'probably says.'

21 See Somigli's remarks on the equivalents in literature and theatre. In analysing the 1912 literature manifesto's definition of analogy, Somigli addresses Marinetti's renunciation of 'being understood' and explains that meaning is produced by the active participation of the reader, a model that also extends to Futurist theatre and the role of the audience. Somigli 143–4.

22 Marinetti praised the variety theatre not because it constituted a paradigm of Futurist theatre proper, but because it exhibited the ideal spirit necessary for its actualization. For extensive commentaries on Futurism's relationship to the variety theatre and to the *meraviglioso* see Michael Kirby, *Futurist Performance* (New York: Dutton, 1971) 19–27 and Strauven 73–82.

23 Kirby 41–2.

24 Gunning, 'The Cinema of Attractions' 59.

25 Strauven notes that the comment on variety's inclusion of films does not appear in Marinetti's original version of 'Il Teatro di Varietà,' as published in the journal *Lacerba* on 1 October 1913. Instead, it was added in his revised version that was included in *I Manifesti del Futurismo*, a volume published by *Lacerba* in 1914. Yet the later and longer version is mistakenly

presented in all anthologies (including the one edited by De Maria that I cite here) as the original 1913 version. Strauven 46.

26 A brief account of the program of this event is found in newspaper reviews of the time. For reprints see Giovanni Antonucci, *Cronache del teatro futurista* (Rome: Abete, 1975) 115–16. For more information regarding the organization of the event see Isabella Innamorati, 'Nuovi documenti d'archivio su "Vita Futurista": Peripezie di una pellicola d'avanguardia,' *Quaderni di Teatro* 9.36 (1987) 47.

27 Salaris, 'Marketing Modernism' 112.

28 Kirby 18.

29 For this reason, the 1914 performance at the Teatro del Verme in Milan may be considered as the last major instance of this paradigm. See Berghaus 133.

30 Ibid. 133–4.

31 For more on this change in direction see R.S. Gordon, 'The Italian Futurist Theatre: A Reappraisal,' *Modern Language Review* 85.2 (1990) 352–3.

32 I am using the term 'spectator' as defined by Miriam Hansen in her analysis of the emergence of spectatorship in American cinema during the same period. 'Spectator,' as Hansen explains, does not refer to the empirical moviegoer, whose response is diverse and unpredictable, but is a structural term that developed along with cinema's move towards the classical narrative codes during the 1910s. It refers to the deployment of specific narrative strategies that made it possible for the industry to conceive of a standardized model of audience response as a way of anticipating the empirical one. Miriam Hansen, *Babel and Babylon: Spectatorship in American Silent Film* (Cambridge, MA: Harvard University Press, 1991) 76–86. Although the Italian cinema's level of industrialization was not as advanced as that of its American counterpart, and while Italian 'spectatorship' in its specificity still needs to be elucidated, the nonetheless standardized narrativization of the prevalent genres, along with the increasing popularity of American narrative film in Italy, allows us to speak of Italian spectatorship in similar terms. For an account of the ups and downs of the Italian film industry during this period and the aesthetic development of the narrative system and genre see Brunetta, *Storia* 26–56, 130–230.

33 Lista, *Cinema e fotografia* 48.

34 Gunning, 'The Cinema of Attractions' 59.

35 Lista warns against a hasty identification between Futurism and Eisenstein's 'montage of attractions.' Whereas Eisenstein's sensorial shock was meant to educate the spectator by leading to 'a final thematic effect' or 'the work's ideological conclusion,' the Futurists wanted only to instigate a

vital intensity capable of 'liberating the spectator from his servile immobility and setting him in motion.' Lista, *Cinema e fotografia* 50–1. In discussing the structural relations between montage and analogical discourse, Strauven also addresses this distinction. If Eisenstein's attraction is calculated 'mathematically' in order to produce a number of shocks in a given order, Marinetti aims at an intuitive sequence of images that relies on the maximum degree of disorder. In addition, Eisenstein seeks the production of meaning in the dialectical fusion between the juxtaposed concepts, whereas Marinetti privileges an 'illogical sequence' in which every component maintains its own distinct meaning. Strauven 66. For Eisenstein's comments on attractions as addressed by these critics see Sergei Eisenstein, *The Film Sense*, trans. and ed. Jay Leyda (New York: Harcourt Brace Jovanovich, 1975) 230–3.

36 Gunning, 'The Cinema of Attractions' 59.
37 For further information on existing resources, efforts to reconstruct the film, extensive commentaries on it, and reprints of archival documents, see among others Maurizio Fagiolo Dell'Arco, ed., *Balla: Ricostruzione futurista dell'universo: Scultura, teatro, cinema, arredamento, abbigliamento, poesia visiva* (Rome: Bulzoni, 1968); Isabella Innamorati, 'Un "manifesto" fatto d'immagini,' in *Il 'Fronte interno' de L'Italia Futurista (Firenze 1916–18)*, ed. Luciano Caruso (Florence: S.P.E.S., 1992) 31–6; Innamorati, 'Marinetti' and 'Nuovi documenti'; Kirby 120–42; Lista, *Cinema e fotografia* 42–55 and *Il cinema futurista* 45–69, 199–208; Strauven 161–88; *TIF* cxxviii–cxxx; and Verdone, *Cinema* 103–9.
38 Lista, *Il cinema futurista* 51–60.
39 An analytical table that juxtaposes vividly the four versions is offered in Strauven 177.
40 The Niccolini poster is also one of Innamorati's discoveries from that time. See Innamorati, 'Nuovi documenti.'
41 For more on the film's length see ibid. 53–61; Kirby 123; Strauven 165–6; and Verdone, *Cinema* 103–4.
42 Lista, *Il cinema futurista* 51–2.
43 Kirby 138.
44 Strauven 182–5.
45 For reprints of the Nulla Osta document see Innamorati, 'Marinetti' 133–5 and 'Nuovi documenti' 54–8; and Lista, *Il cinema futurista* 180–6.
46 Arnaldo Ginna, 'Note sul film d'avanguardia "*Vita futurista*,"' *Bianco e Nero* 26.5–6 (1965) 157.
47 Innamorati, 'Un "manifesto"' 34–5. For a reprint of Venna's account see Innamorati, 'Marinetti' 141.

48 See, for instance, Kirby 130 and Lista, *Il cinema futurista*.

49 Kirby 129; see especially the extensive commentary on a recently discovered fragment from this episode in Lista, *Il cinema futurista* 57–60.

50 'Ricerche d'ispirazione – Dramma d'oggetti' enjoys a rather detailed description in the advertisement titled 'Alcune parti del film *Vita futurista*,' appearing in issues 8 (15 Oct. 1916), 9 (1 Nov. 1916), 10 (15 Nov. 1916), and 11 (1 Dec. 1916) of *L'Italia Futurista* (reprinted in *TIF* cxxviii–cxxx). Parts of this segment also appear in the Teatro Niccolini poster.

51 See Tom Gunning, 'An Unseen Energy That Swallows Space: The Space in Early Film and Its Relation to American Avant-Garde Film,' in *Film before Griffith*, ed. John L. Fell (Berkeley: University of California Press, 1983) 357. Strauven demonstrates the existence in the cinema of Méliès of most of the techniques of abstract cinematography as proposed by the film manifesto. Strauven 77–9, 94–110. According to Lista, the origins of the film's abstract aesthetics may also be linked to *cerebrismo*, a movement in which Ginna and Corra had participated, or traced back to French symbolist poetry. Lista, *Cinema e fotografia* 20–6, 47–8.

52 Ginna, 'Note' 158.

53 Lista also notes a 1928 testimony by Settimelli, who claims that the scene took place outdoors and included one single dancer whom the Futurists bombarded with mirror reflections of collected sunrays. Lista, *Cinema e fotografia* 44, 47.

54 On Loïe Fuller see ibid. 11–13.

55 See Verdone, *Cinema* 107; Innamorati, 'Marinetti' 126; and Strauven 178.

56 According to Lista's recent account of this episode, based on the discovery of multiple frames from it, the white-bearded Futurists were two in number. Lista, *Il cinema futurista* 55.

57 Bernardini, *Cinema 1896/1904* 229–30. A sample of Remondini actualities shot and shown in Florence in 1902 attests to this phenomenon: *Cinematografie di Firenze, La piazza Santa Trinità di Firenze, Garden-Party in Boboli, Feste del Grillo alle Cascine, Il giuoco del calcio a S. Maria Novella, Feste di Firenze*. Ibid. 255–6. For more on Alberini and Remondini see ibid. 155–71.

58 Dai Vaughan, 'Let There Be Lumière,' in *Early Cinema: Space, Frame, Narrative*, ed. Elsaesser, 64–5.

59 Quoted in Lista, *Cinema e fotografia* 42. Marinetti himself quotes Pavolini's commentary in 'La cinematografia astratta è un'invenzione italiana' (reprinted in Strauven 232–3).

60 The four episodes are listed so, with minor variations in the titles, in both *L'Italia Futurista* and the Niccolini poster. This differs from the Nulla Osta

document, which includes only 'Scherma e boxe.' We may observe analogies between the remaining three and other items found in the Nulla Osta, but in the absence of definitive evidence the analogies remain tentative.

61 Innamorati, 'Marinetti' 127.

62 Lista, *Cinema e fotografia* 52. For more on Fregoli and Futurism see Fregoli 220 and Colagreco (see also Introduction). On the relations of Futurist film to early popular cinema see also Lista, *Il cinema futurista* 20–8.

63 Aldo Bernardini, 'Appunti sul cinema comico muto italiano,' in *I comici del muto italiano,* ed. Paolo Cherchi Usai and Livio Iacob, special issue of *Griffithiana* 24/25 (1985) 28–30.

64 This is evident in the following titles, some of which are extant: *Cretinetti cerca un duello* (1909), *Cretinetti lottatore* (1909), *Jolicoeur ama la boxe* (1910), *Ravioli ama la boxe* (1910), *Il duello di Robinet* (1910), *Tontolini boxeur* (1910), *Tontolini si batte in duello* (1910), *Amore e boxe* (1912), *Il sestuplo duello di Cretinetti* (1912), *Il duello di Fricot* (1913), *Il duello di Kri Kri* (1913), *Kri Kri boxeur per forza* (1913), *Kri Kri campione di lotta* (1913), *Kri Kri gladiatore* (1913), *Il primo duello di Polidor* (1913), *Robinet boxeur* (1913), *Robinet e Butalin duellanti* (1913), *Kri Kri boxeur* (1915), *Kri Kri ha un duello* (1915), *Il tredicesimo duello di Polidor* (1915). For an extensive list of titles of the *comica* as assembled by Aldo Bernardini see 'I comici del cinema muto,' in *I comici del muto italiano,* ed. Cherchi Usai and Iacob, 63–134. For more on the *comica* see Brunetta, *Storia* 192–99. For additional articles on the genre see *I comici del muto italiano.*

65 Gian Piero Brunetta, 'Il clown cinematografico tra salotto liberty e frontiera del West,' in *I comici del muto italiano,* ed. Cherchi Usai and Iacob, 15–18.

66 See also Bernardini, 'Appunti' 34.

67 Brunetta, *Storia* 192–9.

68 Ibid. 192.

69 Bernardini, 'Appunti' 34.

70 Kirby 132.

71 On the film's implications for spectatorship see Hansen, *Babel and Babylon* 25–30.

72 It is possible that the film manifesto mentioned in this announcement does not refer to the well-known version of the 1916 Futurist film manifesto. As Innamorati explains, although in later reprints the Futurists specified the date of 11 September 1916 as the official date of the manifesto's conception, the manifesto was first published in *L'Italia Futurista* on 15 November 1916, that is, a month after the above announcement, which first appeared on 15 October. In addition, the name of Remo Chiti, which is listed among the writers of the manifesto on 15 November, is not listed among the writers'

names in the opening of this announcement. It is likely, Innamorati concludes, that the manifesto mentioned here refers to a document that is still
in progress. Innamorati, 'Nuovi documenti' 61.

73 A scornful reviewer signing as E.C.O., whom Lista identifies as the 'traditionalist painter Cipriano Efisio Oppo' (Lista, *Il cinema futurista* 51),
referring to the film's exhibition in Rome, indicates that such introduc-
tory text was part of the film: 'Come tutte le *film* di questo mondo anche
questa comincia con la presentazione dei personaggi: *Marinetti, Balla,
Settimelli, Corra* ecc. tutta gente che ha voglia di scherzare (si vede subito).
Le iscrizioni che precedono i quadri ve le risparmio per le parole grosse
e le assurde pretese che annunciano e poi basta che vi dia un sunto delle
azioni perché vi facciate un'idea della inutilità di tante chiacchiere dinanzi
all'evidenza di così poveri fatti' [Like all films of this world, this one too
begins with the presentation of the characters: *Marinetti, Balla, Settimelli,
Corra* etc., all people who want to joke (it's immediately obvious). I spare
you the inscriptions that precede the pictures, for the big words and
absurd claims that they announce, and it's enough to give you a summary
of the action for you to get an idea of the uselessness of so much chatter
in face of the obviousness of such poor facts]. E.C.O., 'La prima della film
futurista "Uccidiamo il chiaro di luna,"' *Il Cinema Illustrato* [Rome], 23 June
1917: n.p.; repr. in Innamorati, 'Marinetti' 139.

74 Lista, *Cinema e fotografia* 54.

75 Innamorati, 'Un "manifesto"' 36.

2. An Aesthetics of War

1 'Gli spettacoli futuristi al Niccolini pro famiglie dei richiamati,' *La Nazione*
[Florence], 29 Jan. 1917: 3; 'Le rappresentazioni futuriste al Niccolini,' *Il
Nuovo Giornale* [Florence], 29 Jan. 1917: 3. Further citations of the reviews
refer to the reprints in Antonucci, *Cronache* 115–16. Settimelli included
both reviews in 'La prima del mondo della cinematografia futurista,' an
article addressing many aspects of the film's production and exhibition,
published in *L'Italia Futurista* on 10 February 1917; repr. in Innamorati,
'Marinetti' 136–8. On 28 January the Niccolini offered both an afternoon and an evening show of the Futurist program. Innamorati, 'Nuovi
documenti' 47.

2 Antonucci, *Cronache* 115.

3 Ibid. 116.

4 Giovanni Antonucci, *Storia del teatro futurista* (Rome: Studium, 2005) 15.

5 Antonucci, *Cronache* 37–41.

6 The founding manifesto of Futurism appeared in Paris's *Le Figaro* more than a month later, on 20 February. Turin's newspapers announcing the upcoming show did not fail to express their wishes to the budding playwright. Gigi Livio, *Il teatro in rivolta: Futurismo, grottesco, Pirandello e pirandellismo* (Milan: Mursia, 1976) 10–11. The performance also preceded by a whole year the first *serata*, which took place in Trieste on 12 January 1910. For a chronology of the *serate* see Simona Bertini, *Marinetti e le 'eroiche serate'* (Novara: Interlinea, 2002) 47–9.

7 Antonucci, *Cronache* 37–8, 40.

8 Livio 10–13.

9 The manifesto appeared in different versions between 1910 and 1915. It was signed by a large group of Futurists, including Marinetti. See the notes by Berghaus in Marinetti, *Critical Writings* 183–4 and De Maria in *TIF* cxxxviii.

10 For vivid descriptions of the notorious *serate* see Antonucci, *Storia* 14–45; Berghaus 85–155; and Bertini 15–49. Vivacious and witty reports are also found in Francesco Cangiullo's autobiographical novel, written in 1923 and first published in 1930, *Le serate futuriste: Romanzo storico vissuto* (Milan: Ceschina, 1961). Berghaus warns that Cangiullo's reports may be unreliable as historiographic documents. As Cangiullo did not officially join the movement until 1912, his accounts of any *serate* previous to that year are based on the reports of others, including those of Marinetti, who often intentionally falsified the events. Berghaus 85–6.

11 Antonucci, *Storia* 43.

12 Berghaus 85–6.

13 Ibid. 85–155; Bertini 47–9.

14 'Vita futurista,' *La Nazione* [Florence], 15 May 1916: 6.

15 'Cinematografia futurista al Niccolini pro famiglie richiamati,' *La Nazione* [Florence], 27 Jan. 1917: 3.

16 'Il più bizzarro spettacolo pro "famiglie dei richiamati" Domenica 28 Gennaio,' *Il Nuovo Giornale* [Florence], 22 Jan. 1917: 3.

17 'Il primo esperimento di "cinematografia futurista" al Teatro Niccolini,' *Il Nuovo Giornale* [Florence], 25 Jan. 1917: 3.

18 'La [*sic*] grandi rappresentazioni futuriste di domani al Teatro Niccolini pro famiglie richiamati,' *Il Nuovo Giornale* [Florence], 27 Jan. 1917: 3.

19 Antonucci, *Cronache* 115. The Compagnia Ines Masi and associates, under the direction of Giulio Ricci, comprised amateur actors active in the vicinity of Florence. See Antonucci, *Cronache* 113.

20 Ibid. 115–16.

21 See Innamorati, 'Nuovi documenti' 50–1; Strauven 185–8; Verdone, *Cinema* 103–9; and Mario Verdone and Günter Berghaus, '"Vita futurista" and

Early Futurist Cinema,' in *International Futurism in Arts and Literature*, ed. Günter Berghaus (New York: Walter de Gruyter, 2000) 398–421.

22 Ginna, 'Note' 157.

23 Verdone, *Cinema* 108.

24 Verdone and Berghaus 419. I warn my reader that note 54 of their essay includes some typographical errors as regards the specific dates of the cited issues of *Il Nuovo Giornale*.

25 Ibid. 420.

26 Ginna, 'Note' 158.

27 Maria Ginanni, 'La prima a Roma della Cinematografia futurista,' *L'Italia Futurista* [Florence], 17 June 1917: 1.

28 'Cronaca di Roma,' *Il Cinema Illustrato* [Rome], 16 June 1917: n.p.

29 Ginanni announces the 14 June premiere in the present tense ('lo spetta-colo è dato'), which suggests that she wrote the article before or perhaps on that day. The article did not appear in *L'Italia Futurista* until Sunday, 17 June, only because the paper, as the first page of the issue cited here indicates, was printed only every Sunday.

30 Cited in chapter 1. An editorial comment following the review associates the reviewer with the art of painting, yet without naming him. In identify-ing the reviewer, Lista states that 'the film is blasted ['stroncato'] by the traditionalist painter Cipriano Efisio Oppo.' Lista, *Il cinema futurista* 51. By evoking the painter's traditionalism, Lista certainly casts doubt on the objectivity of the review.

31 Verdone and Berghaus 420.

32 Teatro dell'Opera, ed., *Dal Costanzi al Teatro dell'Opera, 1880–1968* (Rome: ATENA, 1969) 1.

33 Bertini 48.

34 See Berghaus 111–18.

35 Vittorio Frajese, *Dal Costanzi all'Opera: Cronologia Degli Spettacoli (1880–1960)*, vol. 4 (Rome: Edizioni Capitolium, 1978) 127.

36 Ibid. 128.

37 See 'Teatri di questa sera,' *Il Giornale d'Italia* [Rome], 14 June 1917: 3; 'Cronaca di Roma,' *La Tribuna* [Rome], 15 June 1917: 2; and 'Teatri di Roma,' *Il Travaso delle Idee* [Rome], 17 June 1917: n.p.

38 'Teatri di questa sera.'

39 Innamorati, 'Marinetti' 126.

40 Frajese 5.

41 'Cronaca di Roma,' *Il Cinema Illustrato* [Rome], 30 June 1917: n.p. *La batta-glia da Plava al Mare* was a new film with footage from the current war. The same issue of *Il Cinema Illustrato* includes a full-fledged article on this film.

Sangue bleu is a 1914 film directed by Nino Oxilia, starring the popular diva Francesca Bertini.

42 'Cronaca di Roma,' *Il Cinema Illustrato* [Rome], 23 June 1917: n.p. *Come le foglie* is a 1916 film directed by Gennaro Righelli, starring the popular diva Maria Jacobini.

43 Strauven 186–7.

44 Ginna, 'Note' 157–8. Although Innamorati, unlike Strauven, does not claim that Ginna addresses the Costanzi, her commentary on the Roman events may also convey such a message, if implicitly. See Innamorati, 'Nuovi documenti' 51.

45 Strauven 187.

46 Gio:livo, 'Argomenti minimi di gio:livo: Cinematografia futurista,' *Cine-gazzetta* [Rome], 11 Aug. 1917: 7.

47 Verdone, *Cinema* 104.

48 All citations of Venna's letter refer to its reprint in Innamorati, 'Marinetti' 141. The original is held at the Fondazione Primo Conti, Fiesole. See ibid. 126–7n47.

49 The private and promotional nature of the Marconi screening, exclusive to critics and lessees, is also indicated in Lista, *Il cinema futurista* 49.

50 Arnaldo Ginna, 'Le vicende di un film,' *Il Secolo d'Italia* [Rome], 21 Feb. 1969: 3. Also cited in Lista, *Cinema e fotografia* 43.

51 Ginna, 'Note' 157.

52 Innamorati, 'Nuovi documenti' 48–9.

53 See Claudia Salaris, *Marinetti: Arte e vita futurista* (Rome: Riuniti, 1997) 166 and Walter Vaccari, *Vita e tumulti di F. T. Marinetti* (Milan: Omnia, 1959) 328–31.

54 See also Salaris, *Marinetti* 160–211.

55 The first *serata*, held at Trieste's Politeama Rosetti on 12 January 1910, if not explicitly political, was nevertheless coloured by Marinetti's local reputation as an irredentist. This reputation had been established by his previous political acts in Trieste, one of which led to his arrest. His irredentism and blatant criticism of Austrian control in north-east Italy and of the Triple Alliance shaped the tone of the *serate* that followed. Exemplary is the one at Milan's Teatro Lirico on 15 February 1910. For detailed accounts of these events see Berghaus 85–97.

56 Noted in Salaris, *Marinetti* 160.

57 Also discussed in Innamorati, 'Nuovi documenti' 49.

58 'Il grande spettacolo di beneficenza alla Pergola,' *Il Nuovo Giornale* [Florence], 6 Jan. 1917: 3.

59 Many sources refer to this Mascagni work by the alternative title 'Inno del sole.' See, for instance, Alan Mallach, *Pietro Mascagni and His Operas* (Boston: Northeastern University Press, 2002) 126–7.

60 Antonucci, *Storia* 48–9.

61 Antonucci, *Cronache* 115.

62 'Dichìarazione di guerra,' *L'Italia Futurista* [Florence], 8 April 1917: 4.

63 'Attacco di aeroplani austriaci,' *L'Italia Futurista* [Florence], 10 Feb. 1917: 3.

64 Innamorati, 'Nuovi documenti' 54. The episode was a re-elaboration of the synthesis *Gorizia uccide Cecco Beppe*, written by the same authors and previously published in *L'Italia Futurista* [Florence], 10 Aug. 1916: 3.

65 The episode had already been filmed before it was censored and Giulio Spina had received praise for his performance in the role of the emperor. See 'Attività futurista,' *L'Italia Futurista* [Florence], 15 Oct. 1916: 2.

66 Innamorati, 'Nuovi documenti' 57–9.

67 Ibid. 59. More recently, Innamorati makes an even stronger connection between politics and the film's structure: 'The important sequence that was censored used to conclude the entire filmic operation under the banner of that bellicose and nationalistic engagement that had mobilized a large part of Futurism in war operations and of which the film was meant to be a further instrument of propaganda.' Innamorati, 'Un "manifesto"' 35.

68 For further details on the event see Berghaus 91–7.

69 Vaccari 329–30.

70 For a history of the *forzuto* and its ideological connections to Futurism see Dall'Asta; and Alberto Farassino, 'Anatomia del cinema muscolare,' in *Gli uomini forti*, ed. Farassino and Sanguineti 29–49.

71 Farassino 35.

72 *Maciste* may be viewed at the Cineteca del Museo Nazionale del Cinema in Turin.

73 As regards Maciste's overpowering of the national other, the case of *Cabiria* is more complex than the other two films. As noted by Monica Dall'Asta, *Cabiria*'s celebration of Roman victory in Carthage reflects the imperialist ideology of Italy's colonial expedition in Libya in 1911–12. In this context, Maciste's construction as a dark-skinned slave whose goodness and loyalty function in favour of the Romans and against the Carthaginians constitutes an ideologically subversive image that is eroded by his properly Italian bourgeois identity in the later films, especially his wearing a military uniform in *Maciste alpino*. Dall'Asta 25–40, 59–61.

74 Bernardini, 'Appunti' 35.

75 For the *comica*'s subversive qualities in relation to the feature-length genres
    see ibid. 34 and Brunetta, *Storia* 192.
76 Cf. Farassino 42.
77 Gunning claims that 'the cinema of attractions does not disappear with the
    dominance of narrative, but rather goes underground.' He finds a vivid
    example in the 1924 version of *Ben Hur*, which was shown in a Boston
    theatre with a timetable announcing the moments of its prime attractions.
    This Hollywood advertising policy shows the 'primal power of the attrac-
    tion running beneath the armature of narrative regulation.' Gunning, 'The
    Cinema of Attractions' 57, 61.
78 *Cabiria* played at the Pergola on 17–29 January. See *Il Nuovo Giornale*
    [Florence], 9 Jan. 1917: 3 and 29 Jan. 1917: 3.
79 'Il grande successo di Cabiria al R. Teatro de la Pergola,' *Il Nuovo Giornale*
    [Florence], 18 Jan. 1917: 3. Similar reviews of *Cabiria* appeared in this news-
    paper on 22, 24, 25, 27, 28, and 29 January.
80 'Cronaca di Firenze,' *La Nazione* [Florence], 14 Feb. 1917: 3; 'Cronaca
    Fiorentina,' *Il Nuovo Giornale* [Florence], 22 Feb. 1917: 3.
81 'Cronaca di Roma,' *Il Cinema Illustrato* [Rome], 16 June 1917: n.p.
82 Luca Cottini characterizes *Maciste alpino* as an 'original form of *comic epic*'
    (*epica comica*). Luca Cottini, 'La novità di *Maciste alpino*,' *Italian Culture* 27.1
    (2009) 56.
83 The film's depiction of violence raised controversy and issues of censor-
    ship upon its release. See Folchetto, 'Tutela e controllo della cinemato-
    grafia: Mutiamo indirizzo,' *Il Cinema Illustrato* [Rome], 16 June 1917: n.p.
    Maciste alpino may be viewed at the Cineteca del Museo Nazionale del
    Cinema in Turin.
84 In April 1915, for instance, the main program at the Excelsior consisted
    of a series of reports on 'The Great Fleets,' showing the English fleet in
    the North Sea, the Russian in the Black Sea, the German in the Baltic, and
    the Italian in the Adriatic. The program ended with two love comedies,
    Amor pacifico and *Quando Robinetti ama*. 'Cinematografi,' *Il Nuovo Giornale*
    [Florence], 12 Apr. 1915: 2. More programs depicting the war and followed
    by a *comica finale* are announced in this newspaper on 3 May, 2 June,
    6 October, and 13 October 1915.
85 For instance, in January 1915, that is, only four months before Italy's dec-
    laration of war, after the 'beautiful drama' *La finestra illuminata*, the Libia
    closed its show with *Polidor dichiara la Guerra*. In February at the Excelsior,
    the 'strong drama of passion' *La campana fatale* was followed by *Polidor
    guerriero*. See 'Cinematografi,' *Il Nuovo Giornale* [Florence], 2 Jan. 1915: 5
    and 27 Feb. 1915: 2.

86 Bernardini, 'I comici' 80.

87 *Cretinetti e la paura degli aereomobili nemici* may be viewed at the Cineteca del Museo Nazionale del Cinema in Turin.

88 Innamorati, 'Marinetti' 133 and 'Nuovi documenti' 55; Lista, *Il cinema futurista* 182.

89 Innamorati, 'Marinetti' 135 and 'Nuovi documenti' 53.

90 Berghaus 99–102.

91 Lista, *Il cinema futurista* 55–6; Strauven 180–1.

92 For more on the crowd see Venna's letter to Ginna in Innamorati, 'Marinetti' 141. Also noted in Innamorati, 'Un "manifesto"' 33, 36.

93 Lista, *Cinema e fotografia* 45; Strauven 185.

3. *Velocità*

1 The manifestos were not merely reflections on other cultural phenomena, but constituted in themselves a literary aesthetic form with its own structural and stylistic patterns. For a detailed discussion of this phenomenon see Marjorie Perloff, *The Futurist Moment: Avant-Garde, Avant Guerre, and the Language of Rupture* (Chicago: University of Chicago Press, 1986) 80–115.

2 By 'local' presentations, I do not mean that the Futurists did not perform outside Italy. In England, for instance, Marinetti's *serate* met with much success, their provocations drawing the attention of the public and the press to a large degree. See Lawrence Rainey, 'The Creation of the Avant-Garde: F. T. Marinetti and Ezra Pound,' in *Marinetti and the Italian Futurists,* ed. Rainey and von Hallberg, 195–219. As I will explain, I call this activity 'local' in contrast with the superior volume of universal appeal enjoyed by narrative cinema, evident in the high popularity that Italian features gained internationally or that foreign features gained in Italy. For a detailed account of this international film activity see Brunetta, *Storia* 43–56.

3 The script was published for the first time both in Italian and in its English translation in *Oltre l'autore I,* a special issue of *Fotogenia,* edited by Boschi and Manzoli. In this issue see Marinetti, 'Velocità' 15–25 and 'Speed' 143–47. Further citations of the script refer to this issue and appear in the text (abbr. *Vel* and *Sp*). Each version of the script is preceded by Lista's introduction in the corresponding language. See Lista, 'Un inedito marinettiano: "Velocità," film futurista' 6–14 and 'An Unpublished Work' 139–42. In his later work, Lista also acknowledges Verdone's claim to having received his own copy of *Velocità* from Marinetti's family before Lista's discovery. Lista, *Cinema e fotografia* 128n58. Reprints of the script are also found in Lista, *Il cinema futurista* 209–18 and Strauven 255–61.

4 Strauven mentions additional film scripts in which Marinetti was involved and proposes possible later dates for the writing of *Velocità*. See Strauven 189–91.

5 Lista, 'An Unpublished Work' 139–40. See also Lista's further remarks on *Velocità* in *Cinema e fotografia* 55–7 and *Il cinema futurista* 65–9.

6 Lista, 'An Unpublished Work' 139.

7 Strauven notes specific technical similarities with *Vita futurista:* the brothers' arrival creates a sharp contrast between light (Futurism) and dark (passéism), the frame being described by Marinetti as ¼ bright and ¾ dark, thus achieving a split-screen effect much in the style of 'Come dorme un futurista'; the grandfather's long white beard recalls Venna's appearance as a traditional old man in 'Colazione futurista'; and the grandmother's skeleton-like figure recalls Madame Death in 'Perché Francesco Giuseppe non moriva.' Strauven 193.

8 Strauven relates the fantastic imagery to the work of various figures, such as Lewis Carroll, Méliès, Balla and Depero, Loïe Fuller, Pathé, Lumière, and D'Annunzio. She relates the scenes of transformation to Ovid's *Metamorphoses,* which, as we will see in chapter 5, D'Annunzio characterized as the best source of inspiration for the art of film. Ibid. 194–5.

9 My reading thus differs from Strauven's, who seems to agree with Lista on the question of narrativity: 'Except for the girl's engagement and subsequent escape [clear-cut narrative events that conclude the episode] nothing narratively significant happens.' Ibid. 193.

10 Lista, 'An Unpublished Work' 140.

11 The manifesto was first written in 1910, although it was not published until several years later. See De Maria's note in *TIF* cxxxvii.

12 See Phillip Sherrard, 'Cavafy's Sensual City: A Question,' in *The Mind and Art of C. P. Cavafy: Essays on His Life and Work* (Athens: Denise Harvey and Co., 1983) 94–9.

13 In another essay, 'Alessandria d'Egitto,' Marinetti openly attributes his distaste for passéism and 'monotony,' as well as the formation of his 'futura sensibilità rumoristica' [noise-based future sensibility], to specific experiences from early childhood and adolescence. In addition, he praises both the Alexandrian experience, where he lived till the age of sixteen, and that of Milan, his mother's native city. See *TIF* 577–82. De Maria notes that the first version of this essay was published in 1927. See ibid. cli.

14 The script's allusions to a utopian childhood may seem to contradict one of the values of Futurist aesthetics, namely, the abolition of psychology from art. According to Marinetti's 1912 literature manifesto, one must destroy the 'I' in literature and replace human psychology with the exploration

of matter, including the breath, sensibility, and instincts of metals, stones, or wood (*TIF* 50). Also, as regards spectacle, we know that he praised the variety theatre for replacing psychology with 'body madness.' Yet his use of the term *psicologia* is specific. It refers to man's subordination 'a una logica e ad una saggezza spaventose' [to a frightening logic and wisdom], deriving from libraries and museums (50), as well as traditional theatre's exaltation of 'la meditazione professorale, la biblioteca, il museo, le lotte monotone della coscienza, le analisi stupide dei sentimenti' [professorial meditation, the library, the museum, monotonous struggles of conscience, stupid analyses of feelings]. 'Body madness,' by contrast, exalts 'la vita all'aria aperta, la destrezza, l'autorità dell'istinto e dell'intuizione' [life in the open air, dexterity, the authority of instinct and intuition] (87), things that by no means contradict *Velocità*'s fantastic retrieval of an innocent childhood immersed in nature.

15 Strauven's extensive remarks on the episode's implied film techniques are enlightening, concluding nonetheless that the episode works in the service not of narration but of what she calls 'truccalità,' or cinematic tricks. Strauven 195–7.

16 The point-of-view structure, which prevails in classical Hollywood cinema, usually consists of a shot A that depicts a character looking off frame, succeeded by a shot B, which through eye-line match is understood to contain the object of the look of the character in shot A. For a detailed layout and discussion of the point-of-view structure see Edward Branigan, *Point of View in the Cinema: A Theory of Narration and Subjectivity in Classical Film* (New York: Mouton, 1984) 103–21.

17 Tom Gunning, *D. W. Griffith and the Origins of American Narrative Film: The Early Years at Biograph* (Chicago: University of Illinois Press, 1991) 70–4, 169.

18 *Cabiria* revealed Pastrone as a great craftsman. The film is known, among other things, for its invention of the dolly between foreground and background while keeping the image in sharp focus, for its opulent mise-en-scène, and for its employment of an extravagant amount of extras. On Pastrone and the importance of *Cabiria* in film history see, among others, Silvio Alovisio and Alberto Barbera, eds, *Cabiria & Cabiria* (Milan: Il castoro, 2006); Paolo Bertetto and Gianni Rondolino, eds, *Cabiria e il suo tempo* (Milan: Il castoro, 1998); Brunetta, *Storia* 173–7; and Paolo Cherchi Usai, ed., *Giovanni Pastrone: Gli anni d'oro del cinema a Torino* (Turin: UTET, 1986).

19 See Marinetti, Boccioni, Carrà, and Russolo's 'Contro Venezia passatista' (1910) in *TIF* 33–8.

20 See Marinetti's 'Uccidiamo il Chiaro di Luna!' (1909) in *TIF* 14–26.

21 It is important to note that when Marinetti speaks against 'love' he specifically refers to a debilitating form of desire for woman that had been cultivated by romantic literature. See 'L'uomo moltiplicato e il Regno della macchina,' in *TIF* 297–301. See also chapter 4.

22 For the almost identical passage in the 1916 film manifesto see *TIF* 141–2.

23 While Strauven's distinction between analogy *in praesentia* and analogy *in absentia* is extremely useful in discussing this scene's dilemma between abstract imagery and narrativity, in her own analysis of scene 8 Strauven highlights other significant aspects of style, without however addressing the discourse of analogy. See Strauven 67, 199–200.

24 Giovanna Finocchiaro Chimirri, *D'Annunzio e il cinema: Cabiria* (Catania: C.U.E.C.M., 1986) 33.

25 The image of the Arabs falling into the sea recalls another attraction in *Cabiria:* while besieging Cirta before their victory, the Romans fall in numbers from the top of the city walls.

26 The intertitles as quoted are from *Cabiria,* videocassette, Mondadori Video S. p. A., 1992 and *Cabiria,* Restoration Eighteen Frames Inc., Charles Affron, 1990, DVD, KINO, 2000. The intertitles of the Mondadori edition are the ones written by D'Annunzio and also appear in *TSM* 1136 (see also Introduction and chapter 5).

27 Lista, 'An Unpublished Work' 140.

28 As Lista explains, the *Maison électrique* was opened in Paris in 1911 to exhibit the technological marvels associated with electricity. Ibid. 140.

29 Quite relevant in this respect is Lista's observation that, despite their criticism of the traditional notion of the artwork as organic, 'the Futurists never put emphasis on the work's processing method, namely, on the fact of connecting and assembling materials with each other; they instead put emphasis on the final result. They thus excluded words like *assemblage, collage, montage,* which suggest a materialist reading of the artwork as a technical process, as the artist's "process of doing." Although they preconized the "anti-graceful," the Futurists were nevertheless Italian, that is, they belonged by training to a culture nourished by Catholicism and naturally imbued with the concept of art as "beautiful synthesis" ['bel composto'], a device arranged in concert into a whole, following Gian Lorenzo Bernini.' Lista, *Cinema e fotografia* 48–9.

30 Verdone speaks of 'cinema' as indispensable to the conceptualization of Futurist aesthetics, evidently referring to cinema in its totality as I describe it here, although he does not specify this. More than any other medium, he notes, cinema brought to the world 'movement' and 'montage,' things that bear a distinct affinity to the Futurist principles of 'speed,' 'analogy,' and

'synthesis.' Verdone, *Cinema* 39–46, 119. Whereas Verdone emphasizes how certain properties of film are appropriated by Futurist works of specific aesthetic forms (how montage, for instance, inspires the literary analogy or the theatrical synthesis), my intention is to emphasize the affinity of cinema as a totality, as an oceanic collection of stories, if I may call it so, to Futurist thought – not only to Futurist works of specific forms but also to the movement's articulation of the state of the world at large as found in what we may consider its theoretical writings, namely, the manifestos.

4. *Forse che sì forse che no*

1 Quoted in Federico Roncoroni, 'L'ultimo romanzo,' in *D'Annunzio moderno? 'Forse che sì forse che no,'* ed. Laura Granatella (Rome: Bulzoni, 1990) 204. My translation.

2 See Lorenzini's commentary on *Forse che sì* in *PRII* 1315. See also Niva Lorenzini, 'Itinerario attraverso le fonti del *Forse che sì forse che no*,' in *D'Annunzio moderno?* ed. Granatella, 165.

3 Roncoroni 197–212, esp. 204, 210–12. On the redistribution of the characters' narrative significance see also Renato Barilli, 'Motivi di contemporaneità,' in *D'Annunzio moderno?* ed. Granatella, 276.

4 The above argument is developed below in the section titled 'The Fatal Woman and the Superman.' The latter is an expanded version of Michael Syrimis, 'Decadent Repetitions, Technological Variations, in Gabriele D'Annunzio's *Forse che sì forse che no*,' *Romance Notes* 45.2 (2005) 141–50.

5 Barilli 282–3.

6 In tracing the literary origins of the Dannunzian 'fatal woman,' out of all D'Annunzio's characters Mario Praz finds Inghirami to be 'the most obviously sadistic – and that in a novel which is completely transfused with sadism.' Praz 265.

7 Cf. Roberto Tessari, *Il mito della macchina: Letteratura e industria nel primo Novecento italiano* (Milan: Mursia, 1973) 183–4. In the dialogue Tessari also notes a trace of humour 'that makes a subject matter aspiring to epic and tragedy sink in a comical tone.'

8 On Sperelli's 'aesthetic hedonism' and the novel's influence by the English Aesthetic movement see Marabini Moevs 124–32.

9 Gabriele D'Annunzio, *Prose di romanzi*, vol. 1, ed. Annamaria Andreoli (Milan: Mondadori, 1988) 6–7. Further references to this volume appear in the text (abbr. *PRI*).

10 Gabriele D'Annunzio, *Il piacere (The Pleasure)*, trans. Virginia S. Caporale (Bloomington: 1st Books Library, 2000) 4. Further references to the translation

appear in the text (abbr. *Pleasure*). For an alternative translation of *Il piacere* see Gabriele D'Annunzio, *The Child of Pleasure,* trans. Georgina Harding (New York: Boni & Liveright, 1925). Harding's translation omits the novel's first chapter, including the sensual descriptions of Muti, which I quote above. Writing in 1898, Harding faced censorship regulations effective in 1890s Victorian society. See Woodhouse 85.

11 For the role of the art of painting in D'Annunzio's literature see G. Donati-Pettèni, *D'Annunzio e Wagner* (Florence: Felice Le Monnier, 1923) 89–135. 'While poets generally receive the cue and origin of their inspirations from other poets, D'Annunzio appeals to painters and musicians . . . And among the Renaissance men of letters, one may compare him to da Vinci, Vasari, Cellini, Leon Battista Alberti, from whom he learns the vigour of images, the accuracy and variety of words, the decorative splendour of phrases.' Donati-Pettèni 103–4.

12 Roncoroni states: 'In fact, things had changed since the times of Andrea Sperelli, Tullio Hermil, Giorgio Aurispa and Stelio Effrena and, in the new world, there was no longer a place for the refined aesthetes, the incurable dreamers and intellectuals spoiled by snobbism, incapable of putting on their boots without the help of a servant . . . Now the new "heroes" know how to drive the automobile, smoke cigarettes, ride the airplane, use the telephone . . . Paolo Tarsis . . . is not of noble origins and is not even an intellectual: he is a bourgeois and is not involved in literature: he does not have a "decadent" soul and is perfectly comfortable in the modern world, among women and motors.' Roncoroni 212–13.

13 Making his first developed appearance in the character of Claudio Cantelmo of *Le vergini delle rocce* (1895), the Superman also characterizes Giorgio Aurispa of *Trionfo della morte* and Stelio Effrena of *Il fuoco*. For an extensive analysis of the Dannunzian Superman with emphasis on his rela-tion to contemporary Italian politics, sensuality, and partial derivation in his Nietzschean counterpart see Salinari 29–105. For remarks on *Il fuoco* as a critique of Nietzsche see Paolo Valesio, *Gabriele D'Annunzio: The Dark Flame,* trans. Marilyn Migiel (New Haven: Yale University Press, 1992) 31–6.

14 Salinari 38.

15 As regards the ideology of the Superman in the case of Tarsis, Roncoroni states: 'D'Annunzio could not eliminate or replace it completely . . . but could and had to modify it. . . . The Superman, though without refusing to define himself as such, made himself into a bourgeois, descending from his pedestal and avoiding playing the trumpet of his incommensurable supe-riority with the usual frequency.' Roncoroni 213. For an extensive discus-sion of Tarsis as Superman see also Tessari 185–201.

16 Baldi et al. 19.

17 Cf. Tessari 192–6. Rather than a correlation, Tessari sees a neat opposition between Inghirami and the aerial invention. He reads the woman as a terrestrial entity that obstructs the realization of the Superman's celestial ambitions: 'woman of the earth and symbol of tellurian love irreducibly armed against every prospect of transcendence of matter' (ibid. 193). This is part of Tessari's general reading of the novel in terms of a philosophical duality expressed in the opposition between the automobile, as an earthbound and thus constricting structure that fails to realize the freedom that its speed promises, and the airplane, as a truly liberating structure that permits the Superman's self-actualization. In this reading, Inghirami corresponds to the earthbound aspect of the automobile, the 'mechanical unconsciousness' of which she indeed shares, as I noted. Yet such 'unconsciousness' undeniably marks every man-made apparatus, including the airplane, which allows me to address the affinity between Inghirami and moving machines *in general.* I redirect my reader to my earlier remarks on Tarsis's remembrance of her body as an organic entity against which the aircraft seemed a 'dubious carcass,' which supports my reading of his scientism as a paradoxical attempt to imitate and contain her organicity.

18 In accordance with his distinction between the 'sublime hero' of the earlier prose and Tarsis as 'an "applied" hero' who 'loses on the level of ideas [and] intellectual and aesthetic endowment,' Barilli also draws a distinction between the nature of Tarsis's death drive and the '"beautiful death" that is so theoretical, so worthy of a "transcendental I," like the one with which Giorgio Aurispa afflicts himself ... The death of Giulio Cambiaso, Paolo Tarsis's *alter ego,* is of a dry, sober, aseptic, nature that adapts to this new key of "applied" masculinism: a death that may or may not come, and that should therefore be counted among the accidents of the job; so much so that Paolo Tarsis himself looks for it, in the novel's finale, himself pushed by an inevitable spirit of remorse and self-punishment.' Barilli 276, 278.

19 It is unclear whether either writer directly influenced the work of the other. Marinetti wrote 'L'uomo moltiplicato' in 1910, the year of publication of *Forse che sì.* See De Maria's note in *TIF* cxxxvii. According to Lorenzini, although *Forse che sì* recalls the 1909 founding manifesto of Futurism, it is likely that both writers were influenced by Mario Morasso's *La nuova arma: La macchina* (1905) and *Il nuovo aspetto meccanico del mondo* (1907), works in which the veneration of modernity sees the machine as a modern monument and locus of beauty, admires the new cult of speed, and is both contemplative and imperialistic. See Lorenzini's commentary

in *PRII* 1316. On Morasso and the authors under discussion see also Tessari.

20 Barilli overemphasizes D'Annunzio's 'march' towards Futurism and thus obscures the distinction that I am highlighting: 'All this means that "this" D'Annunzio marches resolutely towards Futurism; . . . it no longer seems permissible, therefore, to argue only in opposing terms, between the Symbolism-Decadentism of the one and just the Futurism of the other; . . . It should be noted that D'Annunzio goes as far as to anticipate [Marinetti] in the contempt for woman, if she is meant as a lazy and idle instrument of seduction.' Barilli 281–2.

21 Moreover, before reading this denouement as a real victory over the woman's seductions, which would enforce the D'Annunzio–Marinetti affinity, let us note that it is thematically consistent with D'Annunzio's earlier work, where the hero's ability to conquer the female lover often coincides with her fall into a state of physical or mental incapacity. As Praz notes: 'Both Tullio Hermil [of *L'innocente* (1892)] and Giorgio Aurispa have intercourse with women who are scarcely convalescent from diseases of the womb. Elena gives herself to Sperelli when she is ill. In Ippolita Giorgio possesses an epileptic, and Paolo Tarsis, in Isabella Inghirami, a lunatic.' Praz 257. The erotic implications of each of these illnesses, though at the exclusion of the case of Inghirami, are discussed extensively in Spackman 152–91.

22 For more on D'Annunzio's idiosyncratic historical overview see Peter Demetz, *The Air Show at Brescia, 1909* (New York: Farrar, Straus and Giroux, 2002) 30–8. Demetz notes that D'Annunzio's brief history over-looks the significant contribution to aviation made by Louis Blériot, who appears only later in the novel, though without explicit reference to his name and often used as a source for the development of the character of Tarsis. Demetz 30, 36, 167–8.

23 The 'Precursore' possibly refers to Nietzsche's Zarathustra. See Demetz 33–4.

24 For more on D'Annunzio's exaltation of aviation in the context of myth and divine archetypes, as well as remarks comparing D'Annunzio to Marinetti with respect to aviation, see Dalle Vacche 106–8; Demetz 30–1, 166–7; and Tessari 185–9.

25 *PRII* 233–59. For an English translation see Gabriele D'Annunzio, *The Flame of Life,* trans. Kassandra Vivaria (New York: Howard Fertig, 1990) 45–77.

26 See Demetz; Jeffrey T. Schnapp, 'Propeller Talk,' in *Marinetti and the Italian Futurists,* ed. Rainey and von Hallberg, 156; and Robert Wohl, *A Passion for*

Wings: Aviation and the Western Imagination 1908–1918 (New Haven: Yale University Press, 1994) 114–22.

27 For the relation of modern spectacles to Augustine's *curiositas*, I am indebted to Tom Gunning, 'An Aesthetic of Astonishment: Early Film and the (In)Credulous Spectator,' in *Viewing Positions: Ways of Seeing Film*, ed. Linda Williams (New Brunswick, NJ: Rutgers University Press, 1995) 124–5.

28 St Augustine, *Confessions*, trans. Henry Chadwick (New York: Oxford University Press, 1998) 211.

29 'Expanding urbanisation with its kaleidoscopic succession of city sights, the growth of consumer society with its new emphasis on stimulating spending through visual display, and the escalating horizons of colonial exploration with new peoples and territories to be categorised and exploited all provoked the desire for images and attractions.' Gunning, 'An Aesthetic of Astonishment' 125–6.

30 Ibid. 122. In this essay Gunning sheds light on the mood of the modern public. He challenges the accounts of early cinema that take literally the Parisian audience's terrified reaction to Lumière's *Arrival of a Train at the Station* (1895) and portray early audiences as naive and mistaking the image for reality. He argues that one must view the experience historically, to account also for the attraction that astonishment involved. Rather than real fear resulting from credulity, the on-rushing train produced 'the particularly modern entertainment form of the thrill, embodied elsewhere in the recently appearing attraction of the amusement parks (such as the roller coaster), which combined sensations of acceleration and falling with a security guaranteed by modern industrial technology.'

31 Schnapp 157.

32 Gunning, 'An Aesthetic of Astonishment' 126–8.

33 Siegfried Kracauer, *The Mass Ornament: Weimar Essays,* trans. and ed. Thomas Y. Levin (Cambridge, MA: Harvard University Press, 1995) 326–7.

34 Aestheticism, one of the dominant attributes of Decadentism, is amoral. Rejecting customary distinctions of good and evil, art designates beauty as the principle by which to judge reality. Baldi et al. 13–14. Giulio Marzot theorizes aestheticism in its relation to the barbarism of the instincts. The suffering that barbarism entails is itself a function of pleasure, the primary motive of decadent art. See Giulio Marzot, *Il decadentismo italiano* (Bologna: Cappelli, 1970) 156–66. 'In D'Annunzio, civilization and barbarism are identical; one is order, which comes from the constant work of the centuries, present in works of taste and thought; the other is the force that operates outside time, thoughtless, because purely instinctive, revealing what

intellect and consciousness themselves ignore, imperious in imposing its own law, demolishing the structures manufactured by small reason for everyday practice.' Marzot 157.

35 Kracauer 76–81, 326.
36 Ibid. 79.
37 Valesio 3–4.
38 Schnapp 153–4.
39 Ibid. 160–1.
40 Ibid. 166.
41 Ibid. 167.
42 Quoted ibid. 168.
43 The work appeared as an appendix to the 1912 literature manifesto. See *TIF* cxxiv.
44 Benjamin, *Selected Writings* 269–70.
45 As noted, the first pilot is not seriously hurt since he 'looked at his bleeding hand, and smiled'; the second is worse off: 'Very pale, he staggered, bent down, cut off the roar of agony through his teeth'; but the third is 'wrapped in the colourless fire, rolling on the scorched grass with such a savage frenzy that his skull broke the friable soil' (*PRII* 590–1).

5. Through a 'Futuristic' Lens

1 Gianni Rondolino, 'Gli impacchi taumaturgici dei miti di celluloide,' in *Gabriele D'Annunzio: Grandezza e delirio nell'industria dello spettacolo: Atti del Convegno Internazionale, Torino, 21–23 marzo 1988,* Centro Regionale Universitario per il Teatro del Piemonte (Genoa: Costa & Nolan, 1989) 215–16.

2 Sergio Raffaelli, 'Il D'Annunzio prosatore nelle didascalie dei suoi film,' *Quaderni del Vittoriale* 4 (1977) 46–7.

3 Only one of these is extant: *La Nave* (1920), from his 1905 play under this title, directed by his son, Gabriellino D'Annunzio. For an extensive list of films from the silent era based on D'Annunzio's literature, as well as his completed and incomplete projects written specifically for cinema, see Mario Verdone, 'Gabriele D'Annunzio nel cinema italiano,' *Bianco e Nero* 24.7–8 (1963) 20–1. Verdone notes that the list must be considered incomplete and further research may enrich our knowledge of the writer's activity in the field of cinema. Ibid. 2. More recent work by Ivanos Ciani documents D'Annunzio's negotiations with the film industry over a period of two and a half decades, discussing in particular the numerous potential contracts that failed to come to fruition. See Ivanos Ciani, *Fotogrammi dannunziani:*

Materiali per la storia del rapporto D'Annunzio – Cinema (Pescara: Ediars, 1999).

4 Luigi Bianconi, '"Arte muta" e letteratura: Il verismo e il dannunzian-esimo,' *Bianco e Nero* 6.2 (1942) 16. See also Luigi Bianconi, 'D'Annunzio e il cinema,' *Bianco e Nero* 3.11 (1939) 3–57.

5 On *Cabiria*'s relation to the war in Libya (1911–12), see Finocchiaro Chimirri 33 (see also chapter 3). On *Cabiria*'s relation to D'Annunzio's historical play *La nave*, see Brunetta, 'La conquista' 21–3 (see also Introduction).

6 For more on Dannunzianism see Verdone, 'Gabriele D'Annunzio' 18–19 and Brunetta, *Storia* 97–103.

7 For a reprint see Cherchi Usai, *Giovanni Pastrone* 115–22. All citations of the essay refer to this source and appear in the text (abbr. 'Del cinema'). The reprint alternates between bracketed and non-bracketed segments. The former are from the *Corriere* interview and the latter are D'Annunzio's additions upon composing the essay, during or shortly after *Cabiria*'s opening. The film opened in Turin, its birthplace, on 18 April 1914. Cherchi Usai, *Giovanni Pastrone* 26, 45. To my knowledge, the essay has not been translated in English. The translations are mine.

8 Ibid. 25–6.

9 Brunetta, *Storia* 92–101.

10 Tommaso Antongini, *D'Annunzio* (Boston: Little, Brown and Co., 1938) 130–4.

11 Brunetta, *Storia* 97–8.

12 For instance, publicity posters of the film's 1914 release include no other written text than, 'CABIRIA/ DI GABRIELE D'ANNUNZIO.' For reprints of such posters see, among others, Paolo Cherchi Usai, '*CABIRIA*, an Incomplete Masterpiece: The Quest for the Original 1914 Version,' *Film History* 2 (1988) 160, 163 and Cherchi Usai, *Giovanni Pastrone* 64.

13 'The audience is promoted to a kind of privileged experience, completely new with respect to its linguistic standards and no longer founded on a series of data of an informative character.' Brunetta, *Storia* 99–101, esp. 100.

14 Edward Gordon Craig, *On the Art of the Theatre* (Toronto: Heinemann, 1957) 106. This selection of works written between 1905 and 1911 includes some of Craig's main essays, as well as two 'dialogues,' named as such by the author perhaps to highlight their Platonic structure: through conversation, a 'Stage-Director' shares his wisdom with an eager 'Playgoer.' See in particular 'The Actor and the Über-Marionette' (54–94); 'Some Evil Tendencies of the Modern Theatre' (95–111); and 'The Art of the Theatre: The First Dialogue' (137–81).

15 Craig, *On the Art of the Theatre* 111.

16 See the illustrated volume Edward Gordon Craig, *Towards a New Theatre: Forty Designs for Stage Scenes with Critical Notes by the Inventor* (Toronto: J.M. Dent & Sons Ltd, 1913).

17 Craig, *On the Art of the Theatre* 141.

18 Ibid. 180–1.

19 Ibid. 46–7.

20 Arnold Rood, ed., *Gordon Craig on Movement and Dance*, by Edward Gordon Craig (London: Doance Books, 1977) 94–101.

21 One may wonder to which Phrynichus D'Annunzio refers. The phrase that he puts in quotation marks is from his novel *Il fuoco* (*PRII* 297). As Lorenzini explains, he refers to Phrynichus the tragedian (*PRII* 1256n2). An older contemporary of Aeschylus, Phrynichus was one of the first dramatists to leave evidence of his work. Though only fragments are extant, he is known for his contribution to the music and dance of drama. There was also the Phrynichus who wrote comedies, a competitor of Aristophanes. In his case as well, only fragments are extant. Moreover, there was Phrynichus the tragic actor, of whose existence we know from the works of Aristophanes, who in fact ridicules the manner in which this Phrynichus used to dance. See William Smith, ed., *A Dictionary of Greek and Roman Biography and Mythology*, vol. 3 (London: John Murray, 1880) 359–61.

22 Valentina Valentini, *Un fanciullo delicato e forte: Il cinema di Gabriele D'Annunzio* (Rome: Biblioteca del Vascello, 1995) 24. Of course, this would place D'Annunzio in opposition to Craig, who saw the Ballets Russes as a case of degradation of contemporary performance. Craig disliked, among other things: an excessively decorative and commercially founded scenery and costume as conceived by Léon Bakst; a dancing style undeservedly praised as original (which for Craig copied the style of Isadora Duncan, whom he esteemed); and a charming yet artificial style that overemphasized the mechanical capabilities of the body and failed to capture the Rhythm of Nature. Rood 75–108. Despite Valentini's argument, D'Annunzio's essay does not cease to display a firm affinity with Craig's ideas as discussed above.

23 Valentini 24–5.

24 Valentini instead interprets D'Annunzio's comment on a 'silent art' as an inconsistency in his writing, which she attributes to the influence of Eleonora Duse: 'A part of him, the one that did not give up the taste for speculation and intellectual risk, was able to imagine new situations for spectacle: cinema, exterminator of theatre's ugly things, would have been able to suddenly sweep away from the stage both the spoken word and

music and leave only images, evoking a curious agreement with Duse's ideas on cinema.' Ibid. 26.

25 Bertellini asks: 'How could D'Annunzio talk about the musicality of film's images when, apparently, they were mute . . . ?' To provide an answer, he explains, it is necessary to 'unearth what is now a lost perception of early film shows: the mere rhythmical succession of images and the pantomimic performance of actors and actresses. By equating cinema with the "art of silence," the Italian poet meant to stress the speechless uniqueness of an optical flow which still displayed phonic features in the musical stream of its shifting tableaux.' Giorgio Bertellini, 'Dubbing *L'Arte Muta*: Poetic Layerings around Italian Cinema's Transition to Sound,' in *Re-viewing Fascism: Italian Cinema, 1922–1943*, ed. Jacqueline Reich and Piero Garofalo (Bloomington: Indiana University Press, 2002) 44–5.

26 I redirect my reader to Marinetti's remarks on the cinematic analogy in *TIF* 139–42.

27 See chapter 1 on analogy as either a literary or a film technique.

28 Gunning, 'An Aesthetic of Astonishment' 119.

29 Gunning, 'The Cinema of Attractions' 59.

30 While he speaks of narrative themes, D'Annunzio does not mention the film techniques that made *Cabiria* famous. This is not surprising, given that the interview took place in Paris on 27 February 1914, that is, two months before the film's release. Rondolino 228. Evidently, D'Annunzio had not seen the film before the interview. Antongini, who claims that D'Annunzio never saw the film, mentions that Pastrone, when he visited the author in Paris in order to draw the contract, brought hundreds of still photographs from the film so as to provide the author with a 'complete idea of the mise-en-scène.' Antongini 130–2.

31 D'Annunzio was to remain faithful to the 'marvellous' as the core of film aesthetics. In a 1933 letter to his son Gabriellino he states: 'Il *cinema* deve dare agli spettatori . . . il "meraviglioso," il "meravigliosissimo" dei tempi moderni e degli spiriti di domani . . . "Trucco, trucchi, truccherie . . ." Non chiamate così le stupende frodi che tessono lo schermo col ritmo dei rapsodi? So che oggi i "trucchi" sono innumerevoli e penso che nei "trucchi" appunto sia la potenza vera e invincibile del Cine' [*Cinema* must give spectators . . . the 'marvellous,' the 'very marvellous' of modern times and of the spirits of tomorrow . . . 'Trick, tricks, trickeries . . . ' Isn't this how you call the wonderful deceits that weave the screen with the rhythm of the rhapsodists? I know that today 'tricks' are innumerable and I think that precisely in 'tricks' lies the true and invincible power of Cinema]

(3rd ellipsis in original). Gabriele D'Annunzio, 'Le stupende frodi,' in *Letteratura e cinema*, ed. Gian Piero Brunetta (Bologna: Zanichelli, 1976) 16.

32 Valentini addresses D'Annunzio's self-image as a 'savior of the "Seventh art" from vulgarity and tastelessness' and notes his similar attitude in previous years regarding his 'dream to regenerate the theatre.' Valentini 26.

33 The following discussion comes from Michael Syrimis, 'Mona Lisa's Gaze: D'Annunzio, Cinema, and the "Aura,"' *Quaderni d'Italianistica* 27.1 (2006) 69–88.

34 Irene Gambacorti, *Storie di cinema e letteratura: Verga, Gozzano, D'Annunzio* (Florence: Società Editrice Fiorentina, 2003). See also Valentini 15–17.

35 Gambacorti 293–315.

36 For a reprint of the scenario see *TSM* 1171–99. All citations of the scenario refer to this source and appear in the text. The translations are mine. An anonymous English translation, dating back to 1920, was discovered in D.W. Griffith's papers and is now part of the D.W. Griffith Collection at New York's Museum of Modern Art. For a reprint as well as the editor's introduction, both bilingual, see Russell Merrit, 'L'uomo che rubò la "Gioconda": Introduzione' and 'The Man Who Stole the Gioconda: Introduction,' *Griffithiana* 21.64 (1998) 50–9; and Gabriele D'Annunzio, 'L'uomo che rubò la "Gioconda"' and 'The Man Who Stole the Gioconda,' *Griffithiana* 21.64 (1998) 60–79.

37 The term *cordastrum*, which does not appear in standard references of classical Latin (such as *Harpers' Latin Dictionary* or the *Oxford Latin Dictionary*), may have attracted D'Annunzio because it comprises the Latin *cor* (heart) and *astrum* (star, heavenly body, constellation). I am indebted to Susann Lusnia for providing me with enlightening information regarding this term.

38 The Arcachon setting is autobiographical. In August 1911, when the *Gioconda* was stolen, D'Annunzio was in France, where he lived in self-exile from 1910 to 1915 in fleeing his Italian creditors. After spending several months in Paris, he settled in his secluded rented residence in Arcachon. See Woodhouse 249–82. For further details on D'Annunzio's obsession with the *Gioconda* episode during his sojourn in France see Gambacorti 271–4. Henceforth, I will refer to the D'Annunzio in the diegesis as 'the Poet,' who, as I will explain, differs significantly from D'Annunzio, the author of the scenario.

39 See, for example, the scene of the robbery. While Van Blömen and Lunelli are hiding behind a curtain, they see: 'Il passaggio periodico delle ronde con le lanterne . . . La luce della lanterna su l'imagine [della *Gioconda*], che sola vive di luce nella tenebra enorme' [The periodic passing of the

patrols with flashlights . . . The light of the flashlight onto the image of the *Gioconda,* which alone glows in the great darkness] (*TSM* 1181). For a detailed analysis of the work's cinematographic qualities see Gambacorti 293–303.

40 Gambacorti 273–7.

41 The opening refers to two Flemish brothers, both painters, who worked in Italy. Pieter Van Bloemen (1657–1729), the less renowned of the two, was nicknamed *Stendardo* (Banner) because of the military content in his paintings. Jan Frans Van Bloemen (1662–1749) was nicknamed *Orizzonte* (Horizon) because he was known for his landscapes of a wide perspective. Andrea Busiri Vici, *Jan Frans Van Bloemen Orizzonte e l'origine del paesaggio romano settecentesco* (Rome: Ugo Bozzi, 1974) 18. D'Annunzio's protagonist combines both figures. He is named Peter Van Blömen, but also calls himself Orizzonte, 'in memoria del suo Antico e per nostalgìa dell'Italia bella e di Roma città dell'Anima' [in memory of his predecessor and because of nostalgia for Italy the beautiful and for Rome, city of the Soul] (*TSM* 1173).

42 Raffaelli, 'Il D'Annunzio prosatore' 46. As applied to silent cinema, *didascalie* is the equivalent of the English *intertitles*, though it also denotes *screen directions*. The *didascalie* that Raffaelli mentions serve as instructions for the filmmaker or anyone who would rewrite the scenario tailoring it specifically to the process of filming. For example, when the *Gioconda* is returned to the Louvre, D'Annunzio gives the following instructions, in parentheses: '(Seguire le *tracce reali*, seguire l'episodio così come fu narrato dai giornali dell'epoca)' [(To follow the *real traces*, to follow the episode as it was told by the newspapers of the period)] (*TSM* 1198).

43 Valentini insists, nonetheless, that the style bears an inherent affinity with screenwriting proper. The scenario's literary dissolution of traditional syntax is legitimized, she notes, by its transitional status as preliminary to the shooting of a film. She also notes that the scene of the robbery resembles a detective story ('un racconto poliziesco'), where the 'febrile rhythm of the fast action is congenial to the "screenplay form."' Valentini 15–16.

44 Valentini also notes that the text often presents 'interrogative sentences, cues submitted to the reader towards a reflection . . . , which contribute to ascribe to the text the state and tone of the page of a diary, a conversation of the author with himself.' Ibid. 15.

45 Benjamin, *Selected Writings* 256. The quoted statement is directly preceded by these remarks: 'As we know, the earliest artworks originated in the service of rituals – first magical, then religious. And it is highly significant that the artwork's auratic mode of existence is never entirely severed from

its ritual function. In other words: *the unique value of the "authentic" work of art has its basis in ritual, the source of its original use value.* This ritualistic basis, however mediated it may be, is still recognizable as secularized ritual in even the most profane forms of the cult of beauty.'

46 Ibid. 272n12.

47 Ibid. 254.

48 Freud defines the uncanny by observing human encounters with things perceived as frightening: 'among instances of frightening things there must be one class in which the frightening element can be shown to be something repressed which *recurs.* This class of frightening things would then constitute the uncanny; and it must be a matter of indifference whether what is uncanny was itself originally frightening or whether it carried some *other* affect . . . [T]his uncanny is in reality nothing new or alien, but something which is familiar and old-established in the mind and which has become alienated from it only through the process of repression.' Sigmund Freud, 'The "Uncanny,"' in *The Standard Edition of the Complete Psychological Works of Sigmund Freud,* trans. and ed. James Strachey, vol. 17 (London: Hogarth Press, 1955) 241.

49 For the above remarks on the aura I rely on Miriam Hansen, 'Benjamin, Cinema and Experience: "The Blue Flower in the Land of Technology,"' *New German Critique* 40 (1987) 186–8. The quoted parts are from Benjamin's 'On Some Motifs in Baudelaire' and are presented here as translated by Hansen. Cf. Benjamin, *Selected Writings* 338.

50 Hansen, 'Benjamin' 188.

51 Benjamin also distinguishes the painting from the photograph, the technological reproducibility of which he considers exemplary of modernity's demolition of the aura: 'to the gaze that will never get its fill of a painting, photography is rather like food for the hungry or drink for the thirsty.' Benjamin, *Selected Writings* 337–8. As I will argue, in an analogous manner, Mona Lisa's aura is abolished at the moment Van Blömen succeeds in 'animating' her figure through alchemy – a practice that I will interpret as a metaphor for film technology.

52 Ibid. 338. The reference to Faust is significant. The underworld is a register of both past and present. Like the unconscious, where past memories still survive as repressed, it is the place where Helen, who once lived, still lives as dead. Her return is a vision of 'beauty': it stirs up the longing for a past world that is otherwise known as beyond one's grasp.

53 Sigmund Freud, 'Leonardo da Vinci and a Memory of His Childhood,' in *The Standard Edition of the Complete Psychological Works of Sigmund*

Freud, trans. and ed. James Strachey, vol. 11 (London: Hogarth Press, 1957) 107–18.

54 'Sonia, ebra d'imaginazioni, folle di curiosità perversa, vendicativa e crudele, ha dato convegno al giovine Italiano nella foresta ardente. Ella lo ha spinto, con provocazioni sapienti, alla più disperata demenza dell'amore e del desiderio' [Sonia, inebriated with imagination, mad with perverse curiosity, vindictive and cruel, gave a rendezvous to the young Italian in the blazing forest. She pushed him, with wise provocations, to the most desperate madness of love and desire] (*TSM* 1190). Sonia is also described as 'la "nemica"' [the 'enemy'] and a 'bellissima belva' [very beautiful beast] (1187). By putting the former in quotation marks, D'Annunzio evokes his *Trionfo della morte*, where 'nemica' describes the heroine, Ippolita Sanzio. Seductive and irresistible, yet made of a 'carne inferma, debole e lussuriosa' [ill, weak and lecherous flesh], only when she dies will Giorgio Aurispa be freed from her 'impero' [empire] (*PRI* 850).

55 The search for an ideal in art at the cost of sacrificing one's lover is also the central theme in Edgar Allan Poe's 'The Oval Portrait' (1842). Struck by the lifelikeness of a female portrait, the protagonist traces the painting's history. A painter's total devotion to the making of his lover's portrait made him overlook the physical suffering of his lover in flesh and blood. When she died, the life that had left her body was retraceable in the painting. Edgar Allan Poe, *Selected Tales: With an Introduction by Kenneth Graham*, ed. Douglas Grant (London: Oxford University Press, 1967) 235–8.

56 Benjamin, *Selected Writings* 340.

57 Ibid. 338–9. For the French original see Marcel Proust, *Le temps retrouvé* [1927], *À la recherche du temps perdu III*, ed. Pierre Clarac and André Ferré (Bruges: Librairie Gallimard, 1954) 884. Benjamin, who agrees with Proust's conclusion, though he calls it 'evasive,' further elaborates on it, drawing on Valéry and Baudelaire.

58 See Freud, 'The Uncanny' 241. The Poet's desire for Mona Lisa also recalls those encounters that, according to Freud, evoke the mother's body and thus involve a play of the unfamiliar and the familiar: 'It often happens that neurotic men declare that they feel there is something uncanny about the female genital organs. This *unheimlich* place, however, is the entrance to the former *Heim* [home] of all human beings, to the place where each one of us lived once upon a time and in the beginning. There is a joking saying that "Love is home-sickness."' Moreover: 'the *unheimlich* is what was once *heimisch*, familiar; the prefix "un" ["un-"] is the token of repression' (square brackets in original). Freud, 'The Uncanny' 245.

59 Needless to say, any fulfilment of the wish can only be imaginary, a fantasy the transience of which is confirmed by the brevity of Mona Lisa's rebirth. The 'distance' is not really overcome, Mona Lisa is elsewhere, the landscape, which still 'smiles,' retains its physiognomic quality, and the desire is sustained.

60 Generally speaking, alchemy was outmoded by chemistry in the eighteenth century. See John Read, *The Alchemist in Life, Literature and Art* (New York: Thomas Nelson and Sons, 1947) v. For a more extensive discussion of this historical transition, see F. Sherwood Taylor, *The Alchemists: Founders of Modern Chemistry* (New York: Henry Schuman, 1949) 190–212.

61 If we associate Van Blömen's loss of spirituality with alchemy's transformation into chemistry, we may speak of his 'fall': 'From the alchemist's point of view, chemistry represented a "Fall" because it meant the secularization of a sacred science.' Mircea Eliade, *The Forge and the Crucible*, trans. Stephen Corrin (New York: Harper & Brothers, 1962) 11.

62 Benjamin, *Selected Writings* 255. This essay seems to present a resolute apology for the *decay* of the aura, while Benjamin's view of the aura is neutral in the essay on Baudelaire. Both essays speak of a 'unique apparition of a distance,' historically based on the cult function of art: 'The *essentially* distant is the unapproachable. Unapproachability is, indeed, a primary quality of the cult image.' Ibid. 255, 272n11, 338. The Baudelaire essay, however, underlines the notion of the aura as the return of the gaze, evoking the psychoanalytic dimension of 'distance.' For an extensive commentary on the redemption of the aura, indicating that its indispensability to aesthetic experience is already implied in Benjamin's notion of the 'optical unconscious' as presented in 'The Work of Art' essay, see Hansen, 'Benjamin' 202–24.

63 For D'Annunzio's desecration of the *Gioconda* see also Gambacorti 311–15.

64 Relying in part on Mario Praz's seminal study of the femme fatale in literature, Donald Sassoon argues that it was not until the nineteenth century, when the femme fatale became a standard type comprising the traits of beautiful, seductive, and castrating, that the image of Mona Lisa underwent a 'transmutation ... from a cheerful housewife into a mysterious, ironic woman.' Donald Sassoon, *Becoming Mona Lisa: The Making of a Global Icon* (New York: Harcourt, 2001) 92, 93–117.

65 Gambacorti 312. This is one of Duchamp's 'readymades,' his radical challenge of the institution of high art: ordinary objects of no aesthetic worth by traditional standards, sometimes slightly modified by the artist, displayed in a context that endows them with artistic status. On a postcard of the *Gioconda*, Duchamp drew a moustache and a beard, adding underneath

the image the infamous *L.H.O.O.Q.* When it is read uninterruptedly in French, this series of letters produces the phrase *elle a chaud au cul* (she is hot in the butt). For more on this work in the context of Duchamp's avant-gardism, see Jerold Seigel, *The Private Worlds of Marcel Duchamp* (Berkeley: University of California Press, 1995) 115–47. Another famous *Gioconda* send-up preceding D'Annunzio's work is Kasimir Malevich's *Composition with Mona Lisa* (1914), a collage in which the Mona Lisa image is almost hidden by the other elements, while her face and neck are each marked with a red cross. For more on the *Gioconda* send-ups, including other famous and more recent examples, see Sassoon 207–14. For the transformation of the Mona Lisa image into an icon of mass and consumer culture, especially following her theft in 1911, see also Molly Nesbit, 'The Rat's Ass,' *October* 56 (Spring 1991) 7–20.

66 The 'irreverence' for tradition is also found in the casual use of personal names that bear cultural significance. Orizzonte (see above) was a younger contemporary of the Dutch painter Vermeer (1632–75). A secondary character, the young Antonio Van Diemen, who willingly dies in order to donate his heart to Van Blömen for the invention of the *cordastrum*, is named after a Dutch colonialist in the East Indies (1593–1645). It is unlikely that we may draw any consistent allegories based on these names. Some observations may be made, however, regarding the choice of a 'Flemish city' as the place where the *Gioconda* theft is planned. In creating a Flemish protagonist who is both a painter and an alchemist, D'Annunzio may have been inspired by the many Flemish and Dutch painters known for their depictions of alchemy. See Read 63–84. Furthermore, following the *Gioconda*'s theft in 1911, the main suspect was the starving artist Géry Piéret, friend of Apollinaire and Picasso, and apparently of Belgian origin, who had previously stolen two statuettes from the Louvre. Nesbit 10. Obsessed with the *Gioconda* and the tales about her theft, D'Annunzio invented his own tale, telling his French translator, André Doderet, that he had received the stolen *Gioconda*. Sassoon 196.

6. The Humoristic Image in Pirandello's *Si gira* . . .

1 See Francesco Càllari, *Pirandello e il cinema: Con una raccolta completa degli scritti teorici e creativi* (Venice: Marsilio, 1991) 25–34; Nino Genovese and Sebastiano Gesù, eds, *La musa inquietante di Pirandello: Il cinema*, vol. 2 (Palermo: Bonanno, 1990); and Liborio Termine, *Pirandello e la drammaturgia del film* (Turin: Fiornovelli, 1997) 39–40, 60–73.

2 Càllari 21.
3 For an original English translation of both texts, as well as a reprint of the original German text of Pirandello and Lantz's screenplay, see Nina daVinci Nichols and Jana O'Keefe Bazzoni, *Pirandello and Film* (Lincoln: University of Nebraska Press, 1995).
4 I am especially indebted to Càllari; daVinci Nichols and O'Keefe Bazzoni; Manuela Gieri, *Contemporary Italian Filmmaking: Strategies of Subversion* (Toronto: University of Toronto Press, 1995); Gavriel Moses, 'Film Theory as Literary Genre in Pirandello and the Film-Novel,' *Annali d'Italianistica* 6 (1988) 38–68; Gavriel Moses, *The Nickel Was for the Movies: Film in the Novel from Pirandello to Puig* (Berkeley: University of California Press, 1995); and Termine, *Pirandello e la drammaturgia del film*. See also Jennifer Stone, 'Cineastes' Texts,' *Yearbook of the British Pirandello Society* 3 (1983) 45–66 and Alessandro Vettori, 'Serafino Gubbio's Candid Camera,' *MLN* 113.1 (1998) 79–107. For collections of diverse views on Pirandello and film see, among others, Genovese and Gesù, eds, *La musa inquietante di Pirandello: Il cinema*, vol. 1; Maria Antonietta Grignani, ed., *Il cinema e Pirandello (atti del convegno di Pavia 8–10 novembre 1990)* (Florence: La Nuova Italia Editrice, 1992); Enzo Lauretta, ed., *Il cinema e Pirandello* (Agrigento: Centro Nazionale Studi Pirandelliani, 2003); and Enzo Lauretta, ed., *Pirandello e il cinema: Atti del convegno internazionale* (Agrigento: Centro Nazionale di Studi Pirandelliani, 1978).
5 See especially daVinci Nichols and O'Keefe Bazzoni 12–18; Gieri 1–81; and Moses, *Nickel* 3–36.
6 The following discussion is an expanded version of Michael Syrimis, 'The Humoristic Lens in Pirandello's *Si gira*,' *Journal of the Pirandello Society of America* 21 (2008) 45–63.
7 For an extensive contextualization of the story in relation to the 1910s Italian film industry and cinematic culture in general, see daVinci Nichols and O'Keefe Bazzoni 3–12.
8 See Pirandello, *Tutti i romanzi* 555–6 and *Shoot!* 39. Further citations of both the novel and Moncrieff's translation appear in the text (abbr. *TR* and *Shoot!*).
9 Maria Antonietta Grignani underscores the aesthetic and literary-historical importance of the subjective dimension in Gubbio's narration. In 1915, she claims, the loss of faith in the ontological impassivity typical of naturalism was a given for Pirandello. She advises the reader not to be deceived by Gubbio's repeated claims of being impassive. Pirandello rejects the pseudo-objectivity of the omniscient narrative and adopts the principle of subjectivity as expressed by a single voice and a clearly individualized point of

view. Maria Antonietta Grignani, 'Quaderni di Serafino Gubbio operatore: Sintassi di un'impassibilità novecentesca,' *Rivista di Studi Pirandelliani* 5.3 (1985) 7. Pirandello presents his critique of naturalism, realism, and *verismo*, and his call to recognize the inevitable subjective premise of literature, in the essay 'Soggettivismo e oggettivismo nell'arte narrativa' (1908), reprinted in Luigi Pirandello, *Saggi, poesie, scritti varii*, ed. Manlio Lo Vecchio-Musti, 5th ed. (Milan: Mondadori, 1993) 181–206. Further references to this volume appear in the text (abbr. *SPSV*).

10 Translation modified. Moncrieff translates 'i nostri stessi' as 'ourselves.'

11 See Moses, 'Film Theory' 61; Termine, *Pirandello e la drammaturgia del film* 108–9; and Grignani, 'Quaderni' 12–13. Grignani names Benjamin earlier in her essay, but not when she speaks of an 'inconscio ottico.' Yet she evokes Benjamin's remarks (which I quote below) almost verbatim. Regarding Nestoroff's reaction to her own image, she states: 'The photographic shock consists also in revealing, with the elaboration of space and the technical aids of the close-up and possibly slow motion, a sort of optical unconscious ['inconscio ottico'] different from normal binocular perception and closer, if anything, to the Freudian unconscious'; Gieri also relates Benjamin's unconscious optics to Pirandello, but not to the images noted above, such as Nestoroff's view of herself, or Gubbio's imaginary hidden camera; rather, to parts of the novel in which she sees a 'cinematic' alternation of narrative point of view, as well as Pirandello's general awareness of the 'psychological foundations of the artistic process.' Gieri 37–40.

12 Benjamin, *Selected Writings* 265–6.

13 See Franca Angelini, '"Si gira . . . ": L'ideologia della macchina in Pirandello,' in *Il romanzo di Pirandello*, ed. Enzo Lauretta (Palermo: Palumbo, 1976) 143–60; Fausto De Michele, 'Serafino Gubbio, la vertigine, il fragore e l'effimero ovvero l'opera d'arte nell'epoca della sua riproducibilità tecnica: Luigi Pirandello e Walter Benjamin,' in *Il cinema e Pirandello*, ed. Lauretta, 291–309; Gieri 39–40, 55–8; Grignani, 'Quaderni' 12, 23n8; Maria Antonietta Grignani, 'Il romanzo sul cinema,' in *Il cinema e Pirandello*, ed. Lauretta, 83; Moses, 'Film Theory' 57–63; Liborio Termine, 'La costruzione del sogno e dell'infelicità: Commento alle lettere di Luigi Pirandello a Marta Abba sul cinema,' in Giovanni Verga et al., *Il cinema e la vergogna: Negli scritti di Verga, Bontempelli, Pirandello*, ed. Ira Fabbri, Chiara Simonigh, and Liborio Termine (Turin: Testo & immagine, 1998) 219–20; and Termine, *Pirandello e la drammaturgia del film* 115–20.

14 Benjamin, *Selected Writings* 260.

15 According to Benjamin's note, the source was Léon Pierre-Quint's 'Signification du cinéma,' in *L'Art cinématographique*, vol. 2 (Paris: Librairie

Félix Alcan, 1927) 1–28. Benjamin, *Selected Writings* 276n25. Also noted in Moses, 'Film Theory' 57. Pierre-Quint's essay is reprinted in *L'art ciné-matographique no. 1–8* (New York: Arno Press and the New York Times, 1970). The 1970 edition is a compilation of the original French volumes 1–8, each of which is reprinted with its original pagination.

16 For instance, De Michele asserts: 'Walter Benjamin reads in Paris a trans-lation [of *Si gira*] and is so struck by it that he cites it abundantly in his famous essay *The Work of Art* ... We may thus affirm that Luigi Pirandello, writer and dramatist, "seduced" a philosopher with his first experimental novel ... Walter Benjamin finds some affinities with Pirandellian thought and for this reason takes the notebooks as basis, metaphor, and territory of inquiry for his philosophical reflections.' De Michele 291. It is certainly pos-sible that Benjamin read Pirandello more extensively than he acknowledges in 'The Work of Art.' The lack of pertinent evidence, however, renders this possibility too speculative for a viable thesis on intertextual influence.

17 Benjamin, *Selected Writings* 259–61.

18 See, for instance, Nino Borsellino, '"Si gira ...," una maschera dell'impassibilità,' in *Il cinema e Pirandello*, ed. Grignani 67–8; De Michele 294; Gieri 55–6, 62; and Moses, 'Film Theory' 57–8.

19 Hansen, along with other scholars, rereads the essay and complicates the argument, addressing the 'self-denigrating slant of the Artwork essay.' Furthermore, as noted in chapter 5, Hansen's analysis of the 'optical unconscious' argues for the redemption of the aura in Benjamin's thought. See Hansen, 'Benjamin' 186, 202–24.

20 Benjamin, *Selected Writings* 255.

21 Hansen, 'Benjamin' 186–8. See also chapter 5.

22 On the clash between the two versions of one's self-image see also Vettori 96–7.

23 Benjamin, *Selected Writings* 266.

24 Giuseppe Paradiso, *Pirandello psicoanalitico*, 2nd ed. (Catania: EPC, 1995) 90. On Pirandello and psychoanalysis, see also Robert S. Dombroski, 'Pirandello e Freud: Le dimensioni conoscitive dell'umorismo,' in *Pirandello saggista*, ed. Paola Daniela Giovanelli (Palermo: Palumbo, 1982) 59–67 and Cesare Musatti, *Scritti sul cinema*, ed. Dario F. Romano (Turin: Testo e immagine, 2000) 220–30. According to Dombroski, there is no indication that Pirandello ever read Freud, either before his writing of *L'umorismo* (the final version of which he published in 1920, and which Dombroski compares to Freud's theory of jokes) or during the Fascist era, when psychoanalysis, 'not at all known in Italy, was believed to be a satanic reign or, at least, an amusing joke or pastime.' Dombroski 59.

25 Translation modified. Moncrieff excludes the phrase 'staccato dal quadro' from his translation. He also translates 'con quegli occhi' as 'and my eyes,' and 'i peli delle ciglia' as 'my eyelashes.' The more literal rendering of the phrases as 'with those eyes' and 'the eyelashes' conveys the distance that an astonished Nuti would like to gain from his own image.

26 On Pirandello's usage of the term *quadro* see Sergio Raffaelli, *Il cinema nella lingua di Pirandello* (Rome: Bulzoni, 1993) 86; see also Grignani's note in Luigi Pirandello, *Quaderni di Serafino Gubbio operatore* (Milan: Garzanti, 1999) 210n37.

27 Benjamin, *Selected Writings* 266.

28 Cf. Grignani, 'Il romanzo' 83 and Moses, 'Film Theory' 58. For a brief comparison of Pirandello to Roland Barthes on this matter see Grignani's notes in Pirandello, *Quaderni* 210n38, 211n39.

29 Translation modified. Moncrieff translates 'si presenta a me, a vuoto, dal vuoto di tutta questa vita' as 'he presents himself before me empty, devoid of all the life.'

30 Benjamin, *Selected Writings* 257–8. Although Benjamin does not draw a direct link between the aura of early photography and the optical unconscious (the latter appearing much later in the essay), he does so in an earlier essay, 'Little History of Photography' (1931), where his similar remarks on nineteenth-century photographic portraits, such as those of David Octavius Hill and Karl Dauthendey, though he does not yet apply the term 'aura,' are directly followed by his definition of the optical unconscious. See Walter Benjamin, *The Work of Art in the Age of Its Technological Reproducibility, and Other Writings on Media*, trans. Edmund Jephcott, Rodney Livingstone, Howard Eiland, et al., ed. Michael W. Jennings, Brigid Doherty, and Thomas Y. Levin (Cambridge, MA: Belknap Press of Harvard University Press, 2008) 276–9.

31 Grignani notes the extensive use of the imperfect tense, which serves as the backdrop of remembrance, and the overall late nineteenth-century flavour of the passage, especially in its slow-pace descriptions and frequent effusions of emotion. See Pirandello, *Quaderni* 27n1.

32 For an alternative comparative analysis of Nestoroff's and Nuti's images, with references to both Benjamin's and Barthes' views on the photographic image, see Termine, *Pirandello e la drammaturgia del film* 106–15.

33 Casella, *L'umorismo di Pirandello* 206–7, 264–70.

34 *SPSV* 127; Luigi Pirandello, *On Humor*, trans. and ed. Antonio Illiano and Daniel P. Testa (Chapel Hill: University of North Carolina Press, 1974) 113. Further citations of both the original and the translation (abbr. *Humor*) appear in the text. Paola Casella shows that the figure of the old lady

derives from Pirandello's early work, starting with the character of Signora Baldinotti from the 1897 novella *Le dodici lettere*. Casella, *L'umorismo di Pirandello* 269n63.

35 This is not true of all the literary examples on which Pirandello draws. For instance, he sees Cervantes's Don Quixote and Manzoni's Don Abbondio as humoristic characters because they elicit conflicting responses all at once (*SPSV* 129–30, 139–45; *Humor* 115–16, 125–31).

36 Casella includes Nestoroff in her list of seventeen Pirandellian female characters from 1897 to 1928 who embody the theme of the old lady; Paola Casella, '*L'umorismo* and Female Characters: Between Theory and Fiction,' in Pirandello's *On Humor* (*L'umorismo*), 1908: Centennial Program: Echoes, MLA Convention, Sheraton Hotel, Chicago, 29 Dec. 2007.

37 For instance, one commonly noted stylistic trait that distinguishes the 1910s Italian silent diva from her foreign and/or later counterpart is the excess physical gesture. Noting her operatic and theatrical mode of presentation, Marcia Landy describes her as the 'consummate interpreter of affect through gesture.' Defined by languid poses and slow gestures, her performances relied as heavily on the body as on the face. Marcia Landy, *Stardom Italian Style: Screen Performance and Personality in Italian Cinema* (Bloomington: Indiana University Press, 2008) 21–2. This being one example, the traits unique to the Italian silent diva are innumerable and complex, and have been the focus of many a scholarly study, the most rigorous and provocative of which is Dalle Vacche's *Diva*, cited above. See also Bernardini, *Cinema 1910/1914* 192–211; Bianchi; Brunetta, *Storia* 71–91; and Lisetta Renzi.

38 In her study of Italian *divismo* vis-à-vis the influence of the philosophy of Bergson, Dalle Vacche notes: 'The impassive lens of the camera makes Varia, and everybody else, aware that the individual is never only one person, but always a series of multiple, coexisting possibilities in flux. And it is in this plural and unstable definition of identity that the legacy of Bergson becomes apparent in Pirandello.' Dalle Vacche 56. I also note that Dalle Vacche, in speaking of 'the impassive lens of the camera,' and given that all we know of the characters is what Gubbio tells, whether or not he is literally behind his camera, implies that Gubbio's view of reality is one with the view through his cinematic lens as a cameraman. This identification is an essential aspect of *Si gira* and will be further addressed in the next chapter.

39 Cf. Moses, *Nickel* 22–3. I borrow the term 'heuristic' from Moses, although I interpret the phenomenon differently.

40 I therefore disagree with the scholars who seem to read Gubbio's words literally and to posit that, for Pirandello, the image reveals an essential truth about the character. Moses claims, for instance, that Gubbio's thoughts on the man caught on camera unawares 'propose the cinematic image as a mediating surface that allows the viewer to penetrate beneath appearances and illusions and to come face to face with the true nature of reality', that 'Nestoroff is deeply upset when she faces the images of her actual deep self on screen'; that 'viewers perceive via the film image precisely that realm "beyond the reach of human vision" mentioned in the essay on humor'; Moses, *Nickel* 22–3. Remarks in this line of thought also appear in Guido Aristarco, *L'utopia cinematografica* (Palermo: Sellerio, 1984) 94, 97n10; Grignani, 'Il romanzo' 88; Stefano Milioto, 'A proposito di cinema . . . ,' in *Pirandello e D'Annunzio*, ed. Enzo Lauretta (Palermo: Palumbo, 1989) 241; and Termine, 'La costruzione del sogno' 221. Furthermore, the idea that the image may unveil a primordial truth complements Moses's and other scholars' readings of Gubbio's images in terms of Benjamin's optical unconscious, as discussed above.

41 The translation of the above excerpts from 'Illustratori' is mine.

42 Cf. John Gatt-Rutter, 'Writing Voices: Aesthetic Desublimation and Narrative Authority in Luigi Pirandello's *Quaderni di Serafino Gubbio operatore* and Italo Svevo's *La coscienza di Zeno*,' *Spunti e ricerche* 19 (2004) 54.

43 John Gatt-Rutter rightly draws attention to the actress's first name, 'Varia,' which means 'various,' or changing, relating it to the fact that each character in the novel perceives her differently. I highlight another aspect of her 'variability,' her diverse portrayals, all of which I see as constructed by Gubbio as a humorist. Gatt-Rutter also argues that the real Nestoroff, despite her variability, may at some level be known: 'The psychology of the *femme fatale* remains a mystery only to the extent that its specific origins in her case remain unknown . . . The ego, in the *Quaderni*, may be conflicted, destructive and self-destructive, but it is not in principle unknowable, undecidable.' Gatt-Rutter 54. This is indisputable, in that all characters, as human beings, could undergo psychoanalysis. Yet Pirandello has a reason to leave Nestoroff a mystery. By alluding to Gubbio's control over all we know, he would like us to focus on reality as something that is infinitely recreated by discourse, rather than seek its underlying essence.

44 Grignani notes Gubbio's tendency to formulate hypotheses, rather than convictions, when speaking about others, which allows him to engage in a polemical dialogue with the common opinion about Nestoroff's character. Grignani, 'Quaderni' 15–16.

45 Dalle Vacche provides an insightful reading of this passage with respect to Gubbio's ability, precisely because of his cinematic perspective as a cameraman, to discover a new layer of Nestoroff: 'By realizing that, thanks to the cinema, he is capable of seeing the same object anew and differently, Serafino begins to accept that the diva's sunlit face can be by far more interesting and, paradoxically, more natural than the cliché he has always perceived her through. In other words, it is the copy that has the power to extrapolate the truth hidden in the original, and the mechanical handle is not heartless, but functions as a device for clearing up Serafino's clogged mind and eyes.' Dalle Vacche 59. Although my own reading of the novel questions the notion of a 'truth hidden in the original,' I repeat (see above) that Dalle Vacche's assumption that Gubbio's perception is conditioned by the cinematic lens is of utmost importance and will be further addressed in the next chapter.

7. Cinema as Humour

1 On the 'feminist streak' in Pirandello's stance about cinema as found in his conception of Nestoroff, see Dalle Vacche 58–60. On the complex construction of female characters in Pirandello's plays, both with respect to humour and addressing specifically his work with the actress Marta Abba, see Daniela Bini, *Pirandello and His Muse: The Plays for Marta Abba* (Gainesville: University Press of Florida, 1998). Although Bini does not study *Si gira*, she takes as a model the character of Signora Ponza from *Così è (se vi pare)* (1917), whom she describes in terms that recall the construction of Nestoroff: 'Signora Ponza represents the dissolution of the self and, in modernist terms, the proclamation of being as only a net of relations.' Bini 16.

2 Roland Barthes, *S/Z*, trans. Richard Miller (New York: Hill and Wang, 1974) 4.

3 Noted by Mario Patanè, 'Una certa idea di cinema,' in *La musa inquietante*, ed. Genovese and Gesù vol. 1: 7.

4 Moncrieff translates 'barbetta' as 'beard.' Its more literal rendering as 'goatee' allows for a more direct reference to Pirandello. He also translates 'malizioso' as 'malicious.'

5 Angelini sees an alternative dichotomy in Gubbio's discourse, claiming that it displays two tonalities, one 'reflexive, of comment or vent, in the present, the other dedicated to narration, mostly of the past . . . and bound to sentimentalism, to the humoristic situation but with banal stories.' The first denotes 'the so-called *impassivity*, which is reflexive and

ironic ['riflessiva e ironica'], the second the uncontrollable passion by which all characters are invaded.' Angelini, *Serafino e la tigre* 38–9. While Angelini's claim about the two tonalities is irrefutable, her choice of terms is sometimes perplexing, at least in view of my own reading of humour. For instance, in coupling 'reflexive and ironic,' it is unclear whether she uses the term 'reflexive' in Pirandello's sense of humoristic reflection, and whether she uses 'ironic' in the sense I discuss it above (which is incompatible with humour and in fact defines Gubbio's mode when he bitterly refers to his impassivity as a mechanical hand), or in some other sense. Likewise, when she calls the sentimental storytelling tone 'humoristic,' the extent to which that refers to Pirandellian humour is unclear. Do the stories contradict each other and lead to irresoluteness when juxtaposed (like the versions of Nestoroff's past as proposed by Gubbio the humorist), or are they humoristic *in themselves*, in their inherent dilemmas (like the Cavalena drama)? While these possibilities are valid, Angelini leaves the term 'humoristic' undefined.

6 The translation of the above excerpts from 'Ironia' is mine.

7 Moses, *Nickel* 20–36.

8 Ibid. 21.

9 Ibid. 21.

10 Ibid. 35.

11 Despite its visual precision, this image is not objective. The meaning of any image in Pirandello is a construct of the subject's unique perception. More important, this specific case involves the mirror reflection of the self, which draws the subject in a self-propagating process of self-definition – a process that is probably more active than if the subject looked, for instance, at the mirror reflection of a person standing nearby. Hence the image is not fixed except fleetingly – not only because the body that it reflects is hardly immobile, but also because the subject, who invests in the image as a means to define his/her identity, the latter being always evasive, must constantly re-evaluate the image. I thus see the adherence to a fixed belief, or to the image (to sustain the metaphor), as a tendency, a wish, rather than an accomplished mission.

12 Liborio Termine also finds Gubbio at a step behind Pirandello, but for reasons that appear different from mine: 'Pirandello knows, even better than his character (who in the awareness of new events and possible solutions is always kept a step behind with respect to his author), that nothing can be as trivial as *truth* without substance.' Termine, *Pirandello e la drammaturgia del film* 87. Termine then cites Gubbio's contempt for the film of the tiger, implying that '*truth* without substance' refers to the projected killing of the

animal, which Gubbio condemns as the only real act amidst a fake world. As we will see, Gubbio expresses his disapproval through an exemplary use of rhetorical irony. Termine thus implies that Pirandello's superiority over Gubbio is a matter of a moral-ironic stance vis-à-vis the industry's cruel treatment of the animal. Yet Termine's remark may be closer to my humorist/ironist distinction than it seems at first glance, or at least complementary to it; for Pirandello's superior 'awareness of new events' may also be linked to his superior humorist's disposition, thus his ability to receive modernity's peculiar phenomena with intellectual irresoluteness, whereas Gubbio's ironic stance leads to his decisive rejection of those.

13 'This gentleman who speaks with Serafino the cameraman, given his absolutely useless, or anyhow superfluous, function, may be considered the *alter ego* of Serafino himself, that is (as the physical description also reveals) Pirandello himself, "who had come out of curiosity" – as then again he had really done, so many times – to a film studio, since he was in fact interested in cinema throughout his entire existence.' Patanè 7.

14 Giorgio Barberi-Squarotti, 'La sfida di Serafino Gubbio operatore,' *Ariel* 1.3 (1986) 206.

15 Tessari 321–37, esp. 333.

16 In his seminal study of Pirandello's humour, Adriano Tilgher states: 'To enjoy Life in its infinite nudity and freedom, outside all the forms and constructs in which society, history, and the events of every particular existence have channelled its course, is not possible.' Tilgher 192.

17 Moncrieff translates 'nulla' as 'nullity' and 'non più di qua' as 'no longer as of old.' In modifying the translation, I also restore the emphasis on 'nothingness' (*nulla*) and 'all' (*tutto*), as found in the original. The absence of italics in the Moncrieff translation erases the conceptual distinction between 'nothingness' and '*nothingness*,' which I am about to explain.

18 Commenting on this passage, Grignani notes: 'The relativism regarding the multiplicity of the I is a cornerstone of Pirandellian philosophy and is richly thematized in *Uno, nessuno e centomila*.' Pirandello, *Quaderni* 68n37.

19 Moncrieff mistranslates 'ma odio, neppure' as 'hatred, if anything.' This destroys the humoristic meaning of the sentence, as it gives the impression that Gubbio nurtures a single feeling towards Nestoroff, that is, hatred, rather than oscillate between diverse feelings.

20 A hunter is distressed when he reads in the Sunday paper that his friend, an engineer, fellow of the Geographical Society, was devoured by a wild beast, while in a scientific exploration in Africa. He fails to compare this incident to the fact that he himself, that Sunday morning, shot a snipe,

leader of a flock of birds of passage, thus itself an explorer like his friend, the engineer. A comparison would be logical, states Gubbio, putting us in the position of the hunter, and with 'qualche vantaggio per la belva, perché voi avete ucciso per piacere e senz'alcun rischio per voi d'essere ucciso; mentre la belva, per fame, cioè per bisogno, e col rischio d'essere uccisa dal vostro amico, che certamente era armato. Retorica, è vero?' [a certain advantage to the beast, since you have killed for pleasure and without any risk of your being killed yourself, whereas the beast has killed from hunger, that is to say, from necessity, and with the risk of being killed by your friend, who must certainly have been armed. Rhetoric, you say?] (*TR* 553; *Shoot!* 36). Thus, Gubbio establishes the moral and discursive principles that will later inform his discussion of the tiger.

21 On the media texts contributing to the 'star-image' see Richard Dyer, *Stars* (London: BFI Publishing, 1979) 68–72.

22 Renzi 126–7.

23 In January 1918 Pirandello wrote to Bragaglia: 'Mi pare che una film adatta per la Menichelli si possa trovare nel mio romanzo *Si gira* . . . , la cui protagonista è una russa: la Nestoroff, donna fatale ecc.' [It seems to me that a film suitable for Menichelli may be found in my novel *Si gira*, protagonist of which is a Russian: Nestoroff, femme fatale etc.]. Quoted in Càllari 88; my translation. Consider, for instance, Menichelli's role in Pastrone's *Il fuoco* (1915), an upper-class poet who seduces a poor artist, driving him to madness. She lives in the 'castle of the owls' and often wears a hat that makes her resemble an owl, thus connoting a combination of wisdom, secretiveness, and menace. *Il fuoco* may be viewed at the Cineteca del Museo Nazionale del Cinema in Turin.

24 Drawing on feminist critics such as Jessica Benjamin and Hélène Cixous, Bini allows us to view the dichotomy between woman-image and man-reason in a positive light. Although she focuses on the plays, where female protagonists literally speak much more than Nestoroff ever does, their speech, which is of the liberating kind and beneficial to all, is structurally akin to Nestoroff's enigma, even if the latter thrives in the visual: 'In giving voice to women, Pirandello accomplished the goals of his male characters: the defeat of logical discourse, the unveiling of the fallacy of words. If, in fact, the male *raisonneurs* denounce the trap of language and logic in which human beings are inescapably caught, the female characters, especially in the plays, enact the deconstruction of logic and language by relying on different elements for communication, such as the use of silence, touch, facial expressions, and tonality of voice. It is with the use of this different language that woman enacts the dissolution of the self and honestly accepts

the burden of being at the same time none and one hundred thousand.'
Bini 15.

25 Grignani explains the *superfluo* as 'the practice of thought, prerogative and
condemnation of humankind, which manipulates nature, diverting incessantly an unfulfilled desire.' Pirandello, *Quaderni* 12n21.

26 Tessari does not clearly differentiate Pirandello's voice from Gubbio's:
'Pirandello, in short, for the sake of man, longs for an Edenic and "beautiful"
relationship with the environment as a violent instinctive negation of the
"rational" negativity of this very environment. Yet it is a matter of a dream
resolved in the mythical dimension of the motif of the "beast," because
man – according to the thought of Serafino Gubbio – separated himself from
the paradise of the natural condition by reason of his absurd instinct of the
"superfluo."' Tessari 331–2. According to Vettori, Pirandello views the *superfluo* as 'something which ought to be eliminated, so that human beings can
go back to their basic status as creatures like any other.' Vettori 101.

27 Harrison 197. Harrison also compares Pirandello's idea of an artificial
world as created by the *superfluo* to Nietzsche's idea of utopia, what is
evidently analogous to the *oltre*: 'As it appears in Nietzsche, an ontology
of ceaseless becoming is also an ontology of utopia. Utopia, however, is
a self-ironizing notion. It labels both an aspiration towards an unrealized condition and also the unrealizability of the same object of aspiration ... Every apparent realization of experience is already predicated on
a derealization, or destruction, of some prior state of affairs. Each opera-
tive form must first be derealized for a different realization to come to
pass (itself derealized in turn in a perpetual and restless cycle).' Ibid. 8.
Harrison also questions the very opposition between reality and illusion,
again comparing the two writers: 'In neither Pirandello's nor Nietzsche's
case can "life in the raw" preserve any meaning, no more than the notion
of a face beneath a mask can. Once the true (that is, ideal) world has been
abolished, as the fable runs in Nietzsche's "History of an Error," so has
the apparent world from which the real was once distinguished. What
is left at that moment are no longer two separate worlds but a single one
in which the opposition no longer holds – or an infinite multiplicity of
worlds.' Ibid. 101.

28 Moses discusses Gubbio's style of narration as mimetic of cinematic representation. Moses, *Nickel* 3–19.

29 Grignani sees the women's present misery as a 'reality,' which allows her
to speak of Gubbio's 'clash with reality.' I instead see it as yet another illusory construct. On the one hand, Gubbio's telling is temporally removed
from the purported occurrence, which may thus easily be transformed into

a grotesque drama in contrast with the equally fictionalized ideal past. On the other hand, as I indicate above, even in the very moment of the occurrence, owing to his state of shock, Gubbio may have perceived the occurrence as more grotesque than someone else might have. On another note, Grignani and Moses provide insightful readings of Gubbio's mental state during his return journey, as an example of that 'insanity' that for Pirandello brings one closer, as it were, to reality in its absolute form. Grignani, 'Quaderni' 19–20; Moses, *Nickel* 27–8.

30 Brunetta states: 'The representation of the world of cinema, by now defined perfectly in its laws and operations, is obtained thanks to a point of view *internal* to the reality described (the narrating I, Serafino Gubbio, is a cameraman), the behaviour of which, exactly because of the narrator's special profession, is only meant to be recorded with an objectivity homologous to that of the camera.' Brunetta, *Storia* 105.

31 Moses also notes: 'The cameraman is unable to see reality in a way other than that dictated by the aesthetic peculiarities of his medium, is drawn to the excitement provided by this, yet is also dimly aware of the superficiality of such a view of life.' Moses, *Nickel* 4–5. Other critics also note Gubbio's identification with his cinematic lens. Angelini describes Gubbio as 'lacking in personal characteristics and feelings, passive, absent and finally mute; . . . a gaze.' Angelini, '"Si gira . . . ": L'ideologia della macchina' 143. According to Gieri, 'we are often lured into trying to distinguish between *real* reality and *film* reality, or rather between what Gubbio sees and what the camera sees. The reader is led to realize that ultimately there is no difference at all between these two visions.' Gieri 41. See also Dalle Vacche 56, 59 and Vettori 90–6.

32 P. Adams Sitney relates metonymy to various aspects of *Si gira*. See 'The Autobiography of a Metonymy,' in *Shoot!* trans. Moncrieff, 223–33. Most relevant to my present point is his remark on the *oltre*: 'The remarkable opening sentence poses the epistemological problem that shapes the novel: "I study people in their most ordinary occupations to see if I can succeed in discovering in others what I feel that I myself lack in everything that I do: the certainty that they understand what they are doing." The first of many italicized words in the original – *oltre* in the Italian text – on the next page, reformulates the lack: "There is something more in everything" . . . Metonymy indicates "there is *something more*"' (*Shoot!* 230). I also redirect my reader to the relevant remarks, mentioned above, in Harrison 8, 100–2, 196–8.

33 Giacomo Debenedetti, *Il romanzo del novecento: Quaderni inediti* (Milan: Garzanti, 2001) 256–80.

34 See *TR* 607, 663, 717, 734 and *Shoot!* 90, 144, 196, 213. Moncrieff translates
    'silenzio di cosa' as 'inanimate silence.'
35 Tessari 333.
36 For a reading of Gubbio's silence in terms of his mysticism, also drawing
    on the religious connotations of his name and surname, see Vettori 98–107.

Conclusion

 1 Antonio Costa, 'Dante, D'Annunzio, Pirandello,' in *Sperduto nel buio*, ed.
    Renzi, 64.
 2 For a parallel between D'Annunzio and Maciste along the lines of the
    Nietzschean myth of the superman and the resistance of the physical
    body 'against positivistic, industrial reality,' see Carlo J. Celli, '*Cabiria* as a
    D'Annunzian Document,' *Romance Languages Annual* 9 (1998) 181.

Bibliography

Alovisio, Silvio, and Alberto Barbera, eds. *Cabiria & Cabiria*. Milan: Il castoro, 2006.

Angelini, Franca. *Serafino e la tigre: Pirandello tra scrittura teatro e cinema*. Venice: Marsilio, 1990.

– '"Si gira . . . ": L'ideologia della macchina in Pirandello.' In *Il romanzo di Pirandello*, ed. Enzo Lauretta, 143–60. Palermo: Palumbo, 1976.

Antongini, Tommaso. *D'Annunzio*. Boston: Little, Brown and Co., 1938.

Antonucci, Giovanni. *Cronache del teatro futurista*. Rome: Abete, 1975.

– *Storia del teatro futurista*. Rome: Studium, 2005.

Aristarco, Guido. *L'utopia cinematografica*. Palermo: Sellerio, 1984.

L'art cinématographique no. 1–8. New York: Arno Press and the New York Times, 1970.

'Attacco di aeroplani austriaci.' *L'Italia Futurista* [Florence], 10 Feb. 1917: 3.

'Attività futurista.' *L'Italia Futurista*, 15 Oct. 1916: 2.

Augustine, Saint. *Confessions*. Trans. Henry Chadwick. New York: Oxford University Press, 1998.

Baldi, Guido, Silvia Giusso, Mario Razetti, and Giuseppe Zaccaria. *Dal testo alla storia, dalla storia al testo: Letteratura italiana con pagine di scrittori stranieri, analisi dei testi, critica*. Ed. Gigi Livio. Vol. 3.2.a. Turin: Paravia, 1994.

Barberi-Squarotti, Giorgio. 'La sfida di Serafino Gubbio operatore.' *Ariel* 1.3 (1986) 189–210.

Barilli, Renato. 'Motivi di contemporaneità.' In Granatella 275–87.

Barthes, Roland. *S/Z*. Trans. Richard Miller. New York: Hill and Wang, 1974.

Benjamin, Walter. *Selected Writings*. Vol. 4. Trans. Edmund Jephcott et al. Ed. Howard Eiland and Michael W. Jennings. Cambridge, MA: Belknap Press of Harvard University Press, 2003.

– *The Work of Art in the Age of Its Technological Reproducibility, and Other Writings on Media*. Trans. Edmund Jephcott, Rodney Livingstone, Howard

Eiland, et al. Ed. Michael W. Jennings, Brigid Doherty, and Thomas Y. Levin. Cambridge, MA: Belknap Press of Harvard University Press, 2008.

Berghaus, Günter. *Italian Futurist Theatre, 1909–1944*. Oxford: Clarendon Press, 1998.

Bernardini, Aldo. 'Appunti sul cinema comico muto italiano.' In Cherchi Usai and Iacob 21–35.

– *Cinema muto italiano: Ambiente, spettacoli e spettatori 1896/1904*. Bari: Laterza, 1980.

– *Cinema muto italiano: Industria e organizzazione dello spettacolo 1905/1909*. Bari: Laterza, 1981.

– *Cinema muto italiano: Arte, divismo e mercato 1910/14*. Bari: Laterza, 1982.

– 'I comici del cinema muto.' In Cherchi Usai and Iacob 63–134.

Bertellini, Giorgio. 'Dubbing *L'Arte muta*: Poetic Layerings around Italian Cinema's Transition to Sound.' In *Re-viewing Fascism: Italian Cinema, 1922– 1943*, ed. Jacqueline Reich and Piero Garofalo, 30–82. Bloomington: Indiana University Press, 2002.

Bertetto, Paolo, and Gianni Rondolino, eds. *Cabiria e il suo tempo*. Milan: Il castoro, 1998.

Bertini, Simona. *Marinetti e le 'eroiche serate.'* Novara: Interlinea, 2002.

Bianchi, Pietro. *Francesca Bertini e le dive del cinema muto*. Turin: UTET, 1969.

Bianconi, Luigi. '"Arte muta" e letteratura: Il verismo e il dannunzianesimo.' *Bianco e Nero* 6.2 (1942) 3–17.

– 'D'Annunzio e il cinema.' *Bianco e Nero* 3.11 (1939) 3–57.

Bini, Daniela. *Pirandello and His Muse: The Plays for Marta Abba*. Gainesville: University Press of Florida, 1998.

Binni, Walter. *La poetica del decadentismo italiano*. Florence: G.C. Sansoni, 1936.

Borsellino, Nino. '"Si gira . . . ," una maschera dell'impassibilità.' In Grignani 67–72.

Boschi, Alberto, and Giacomo Manzoli, eds. *Oltre l'autore I*. Special issue of *Fotogenia* 2 (1996) 1–196.

Branigan, Edward. *Point of View in the Cinema: A Theory of Narration and Subjectivity in Classical Film*. New York: Mouton, 1984.

Brunetta, Gian Piero. 'Il clown cinematografico tra salotto liberty e frontiera del West.' In Cherchi Usai and Iacob 11–20.

– 'La conquista dell'impero dei sogni: D'Annunzio e Pirandello.' *Annali d'Italianistica* 6 (1988) 18–37.

– *Storia del cinema italiano I: Il cinema muto 1895–1929*. Rome: Riuniti, 1993.

Bruno, Giuliana. *Streetwalking on a Ruined Map: Cultural Theory and the City Films of Elvira Notari*. Princeton: Princeton University Press, 1993.

Bürger, Peter. *Theory of the Avant-Garde*. Trans. Michael Shaw. Minneapolis: University of Minnesota Press, 1994.

Busiri Vici, Andrea. *Jan Frans Van Bloemen Orizzonte e l'origine del paesaggio romano settecentesco*. Rome: Ugo Bozzi, 1974.

Cabiria. Dir. Giovanni Pastrone. Perf. Italia Almirante Manzini, Bartolomeo Pagano, et al. Itala Film, 1914.

– Restoration Eighteen Frames Inc. Charles Affron, 1990. DVD. KINO, 2000.

– Videocassette. Mondadori Video S. p. A., 1992.

Càllari, Francesco. *Pirandello e il cinema: Con una raccolta completa degli scritti teorici e creativi*. Venice: Marsilio, 1991.

Cangiullo, Francesco. *Le serate futuriste: Romanzo storico vissuto*. 1930. Milan: Ceschina, 1961.

Casella, Paola. '*L'umorismo* and Female Characters: Between Theory and Fiction.' In Pirandello's *On Humor* (*L'umorismo*), 1908: Centennial Program: Echoes. MLA Convention, Sheraton Hotel, Chicago, 29 Dec. 2007.

– *L'umorismo di Pirandello: Ragioni intra- e intertestuali*. Fiesole (Florence): Cadmo, 2002.

Celli, Carlo J. '*Cabiria* as a D'Annunzian Document.' *Romance Languages Annual* 9 (1998) 179–82.

Cherchi Usai, Paolo. '*CABIRIA*, an Incomplete Masterpiece: The Quest for the Original 1914 Version.' *Film History* 2 (1988) 155–65.

Cherchi Usai, Paolo, ed. *Giovanni Pastrone: Gli anni d'oro del cinema a Torino*. Turin: UTET, 1986.

Cherchi Usai, Paolo, and Livio Iacob, eds. *I comici del muto italiano*. Special issue of *Griffithiana* 24/25 (1985) 1–150.

Ciani, Ivanos. *Fotogrammi dannunziani: Materiali per la storia del rapporto D'Annunzio – Cinema*. Pescara: Ediars, 1999.

'Cinematografi.' *Il Nuovo Giornale* [Florence], 2 Jan. 1915: 5

'Cinematografi.' *Il Nuovo Giornale*, 27 Feb. 1915: 2.

'Cinematografi.' *Il Nuovo Giornale*, 12 Apr. 1915: 2.

'Cinematografia futurista al Niccolini pro famiglie richiamati.' *La Nazione* [Florence], 27 Jan. 1917: 3.

Colagreco, Luigi. 'Il cinema negli spettacoli di Leopoldo Fregoli.' *Bianco e Nero* 63.3–4 (2002) 40–67.

Comin, Jacopo. 'Ma l'amor mio non muore.' In *Antologia di Bianco e Nero 1937–1943*, ed. Leonardo Autera, vol. 3.2, 934–59. Rome: Edizioni di Bianco e Nero, 1964.

Costa, Antonio. 'Dante, D'Annunzio, Pirandello.' In Renzi 59–69.

Cottini, Luca. 'La novità di *Maciste alpino*.' *Italian Culture* 27.1 (2009) 43–59.

Craig, Edward Gordon. *On the Art of the Theatre*. Toronto: Heinemann, 1957.

– *Towards a New Theatre: Forty Designs for Stage Scenes with Critical Notes by the Inventor*. Toronto: J.M. Dent & Sons Ltd, 1913.

Cretinetti e la paura degli aereomobili nemici. Dir. André Deed. Perf. André Deed
    et al. Itala Film, 1915.

'Cronaca Fiorentina.' *Il Nuovo Giornale* [Florence], 9 Jan. 1917: 3

'Cronaca Fiorentina.' *Il Nuovo Giornale*, 29 Jan. 1917: 3.

'Cronaca Fiorentina.' *Il Nuovo Giornale*, 22 Feb. 1917: 3.

'Cronaca di Firenze.' *La Nazione* [Florence], 14 Feb. 1917: 3.

'Cronaca di Roma.' *Il Cinema Illustrato* [Rome] 16 June 1917: n.p.

'Cronaca di Roma.' *Il Cinema Illustrato*, 23 June 1917: n.p.

'Cronaca di Roma.' *Il Cinema Illustrato*, 30 June 1917: n.p.

'Cronaca di Roma.' *La Tribuna* [Rome], 15 June 1917: 2.

Dall'Asta, Monica. *Un cinéma musclé: Le surhomme dans le cinéma muet italien
    (1913–1926)*. Trans. Franco Arnò and Charles Tatum, Jr. Crisnée (Belgium):
    Editions Yellow Now, 1992.

Dalle Vacche, Angela. *Diva: Defiance and Passion in Early Italian Cinema*. Austin:
    University of Texas Press, 2008.

D'Annunzio, Gabriele. *The Child of Pleasure*. Trans. Georgina Harding. New
    York: Boni & Liveright, 1925.

– 'Del cinematografo considerato come strumento di liberazione e come arte
    di trasfigurazione.' 1914. In Cherchi Usai 115–22.

– *The Flame of Life*. Trans. Kassandra Vivaria. New York: Howard Fertig, 1990.

– *Nocturne and Five Tales of Love and Death*. Ed. and trans. Raymond
    Rosenthal. Marlboro, VT: The Marlboro Press, 1988.

– *Il piacere (The Pleasure)*. Trans. Virginia S. Caporale. Bloomington: 1st Books
    Library, 2000.

– *Prose di romanzi*. Vol. 1. Ed. Annamaria Andreoli. Milan: Mondadori, 1988.

– *Prose di romanzi*. Vol. 2. Ed. Niva Lorenzini. Milan: Mondadori, 1989.

– 'Le stupende frodi.' 1933. In *Letteratura e cinema*, ed. Gian Piero Brunetta,
    15–17. Bologna: Zanichelli, 1976.

– *Tragedie, sogni e misteri*. Vol. 2. Ed. Egidio Bianchetti. Verona: Mondadori, 1966.

– 'L'uomo che rubò la "Gioconda"' (The Man Who Stole the Gioconda).
    Griffithiana 21.64 (1998) 60–79.

daVinci Nichols, Nina, and Jana O'Keefe Bazzoni. *Pirandello and Film*. Lincoln:
    University of Nebraska Press, 1995.

Debenedetti, Giacomo. *Il romanzo del novecento: Quaderni inediti*. Milan:
    Garzanti, 2001.

Demetz, Peter. *The Air Show at Brescia, 1909*. New York: Farrar, Straus and
    Giroux, 2002.

De Michele, Fausto. 'Serafino Gubbio, la vertigine, il fragore e l'effimero
    ovvero l'opera d'arte nell'epoca della sua riproducibilità tecnica: Luigi
    Pirandello e Walter Benjamin.' In Lauretta, *Il cinema e Pirandello* 291–309.

'Dichiarazione di guerra.' *L'Italia Futurista* [Florence], 8 April 1917: 4.

Dombroski, Robert S. 'Pirandello e Freud: Le dimensioni conoscitive dell'umorismo.' In *Pirandello saggista*, ed. Paola Daniela Giovanelli, 59–67. Palermo: Palumbo, 1982.

Donati-Petténi, G. *D'Annunzio e Wagner*. Florence: Felice Le Monnier, 1923.

Dyer, Richard. *Stars*. London: BFI Publishing, 1979.

E.C.O. 'La prima della film futurista "Uccidiamo il chiaro di luna."' *Il Cinema Illustrato* [Rome], 23 June 1917: n.p.

Eisenstein, Sergei. *The Film Sense*. Trans. and ed. Jay Leyda. New York: Harcourt Brace Jovanovich, 1975.

Eliade, Mircea. *The Forge and the Crucible*. Trans. Stephen Corrin. New York: Harper & Brothers, 1962.

Eliot, T.S. *The Sacred Wood: Essays on Poetry and Criticism*. London: Methuen, 1928.

Elsaesser, Thomas, ed. *Early Cinema: Space, Frame, Narrative*. London: BFI, 1990.

Fagiolo Dell'Arco, Maurizio, ed. *Balla: Ricostruzione futurista dell'universo: Scultura, teatro, cinema, arredamento, abbigliamento, poesia visiva*. Rome: Bulzoni, 1968.

Farassino, Alberto. 'Anatomia del cinema muscolare.' In Farassino and Sanguineti 29–49.

Farassino Alberto, and Tatti Sanguineti, eds. *Gli uomini forti*. Milan: Mazzotta, 1983.

Finocchiaro Chimirri, Giovanna. *D'Annunzio e il cinema: Cabiria*. Catania: C.U.E.C.M., 1986.

Folchetto. 'Tutela e controllo della cinematografia: Mutiamo indirizzo.' *Il Cinema Illustrato* [Rome], 16 June 1917: n.p.

Frajese, Vittorio. *Dal Costanzi all'Opera: Cronologia Degli Spettacoli (1880–1960)*. Vol. 4. Rome: Edizioni Capitolium, 1978.

Fregoli, Leopoldo. *Fregoli raccontato da Fregoli: Le memorie del mago del trasformismo*. Milan: Rizzoli, 1936.

Freud, Sigmund. 'Leonardo da Vinci and a Memory of His Childhood.' In *The Standard Edition of the Complete Psychological Works of Sigmund Freud*, trans. and ed. James Strachey, vol. 11, 57–137. London: Hogarth Press, 1957.

– 'The "Uncanny."' In *Standard Edition of the Works of Freud*, trans. and ed. Strachey, vol. 17, 217–56. London: Hogarth Press, 1955.

Il fuoco. Dir. Giovanni Pastrone. Perf. Pina Menichelli, Febo Mari, et al. Itala Film, 1915.

Gambacorti, Irene. *Storie di cinema e letteratura: Verga, Gozzano, D'Annunzio*. Florence: Società Editrice Fiorentina, 2003.

Gatt-Rutter, John. 'Writing Voices: Aesthetic Desublimation and Narrative
    Authority in Luigi Pirandello's *Quaderni di Serafino Gubbio operatore* and
    Italo Svevo's *La coscienza di Zeno.*' *Spunti e ricerche* 19 (2004) 43–64.
Genovese, Nino, and Sebastiano Gesù, eds. *La musa inquietante di Pirandello: Il
    cinema.* 2 vols. Palermo: Bonanno, 1990.
Gentile, Emilio. 'The Conquest of Modernity: From Modernist Nationalism to
    Fascism.' Trans. Lawrence Rainey. In Rainey and von Hallberg 55–87.
Gieri, Manuela. *Contemporary Italian Filmmaking: Strategies of Subversion.*
    Toronto: University of Toronto Press, 1995.
Ginanni, Maria. 'La prima a Roma della Cinematografia futurista.' *L'Italia
    Futurista* [Florence], 17 June 1917: 1.
Ginna, Arnaldo. 'Note sul film d'avanguardia "*Vita futurista.*"' *Bianco e Nero*
    26.5–6 (1965) 156–8.
– 'Le vicende di un film.' *Il Secolo d'Italia* [Rome], 21 Feb. 1969: 3.
Gio:livo. 'Argomenti minimi di gio:livo: Cinematografia futurista.' *Cine-
    gazzetta* [Rome], 11 Aug. 1917: 6–7.
Giudice, Gaspare. *Luigi Pirandello.* Turin: UTET, 1963.
Gordon, R.S. 'The Italian Futurist Theatre: A Reappraisal.' *Modern Language
    Review* 85.2 (1990) 349–61.
'Gorizia uccide Cecco Beppe.' *L'Italia Futurista* [Florence], 10 Aug. 1916: 3.
Granatella, Laura, ed. *D'Annunzio moderno? 'Forse che sì forse che no.'* Rome:
    Bulzoni, 1990.
'Il grande spettacolo di beneficenza alla Pergola.' *Il Nuovo Giornale* [Florence],
    6 Jan. 1917: 3.
'Il grande successo di Cabiria al R. Teatro de la Pergola.' *Il Nuovo Giornale*, 18
    Jan. 1917: 3.
'La [*sic*] grandi rappresentazioni futuriste di domani al Teatro Niccolini pro
    famiglie richiamati.' *Il Nuovo Giornale*, 27 Jan. 1917: 3.
Grignani, Maria Antonietta. 'Quaderni di Serafino Gubbio operatore:
    Sintassi di un'impassibilità novecentesca.' *Rivista di Studi Pirandelliani* 5.3
    (1985) 7–24.
– 'Il romanzo sul cinema.' In Lauretta, *Il cinema e Pirandello* 75–90.
Grignani, Maria Antonietta, ed. *Il cinema e Pirandello (atti del convegno di Pavia
    8–10 novembre 1990).* Florence: La Nuova Italia Editrice, 1992.
Gunning, Tom. 'An Aesthetic of Astonishment: Early Film and the (In)Credulous
    Spectator.' In *Viewing Positions: Ways of Seeing Film*, ed. Linda Williams,
    114–33. New Brunswick, NJ: Rutgers University Press, 1995.
– 'The Cinema of Attractions: Early Film, Its Spectator and the Avant-Garde.'
    In Elsaesser 56–62.
– *D. W. Griffith and the Origins of American Narrative Film: The Early Years at
    Biograph.* Chicago: University of Illinois Press, 1991.

- 'An Unseen Energy That Swallows Space: The Space in Early Film and Its Relation to American Avant-Garde Film.' In *Film before Griffith*, ed. John L. Fell, 355–65. Berkeley: University of California Press, 1983.

Hansen, Miriam. *Babel and Babylon: Spectatorship in American Silent Film.* Cambridge, MA: Harvard University Press, 1991.

- 'Benjamin, Cinema and Experience: "The Blue Flower in the Land of Technology."' *New German Critique* 40 (1987) 179–224.

Harrison, Thomas. *Essayism: Conrad, Musil and Pirandello*. Baltimore: Johns Hopkins University Press, 1992.

Huyssen, Andreas. *After the Great Divide: Modernism, Mass Culture, Postmodernism*. Bloomington: Indiana University Press, 1986.

Innamorati, Isabella. 'Un "manifesto" fatto d'immagini.' In *Il 'Fronte interno' de L'Italia Futurista (Firenze 1916–18)*, ed. Luciano Caruso, 31–6. Florence: S.P.E.S., 1992.

- 'Marinetti nella cinematografia futurista.' In *Marinetti il futurista*, ed. Carlo V. Menichi, 117–46. Pistoia: Tellini, 1988.

- 'Nuovi documenti d'archivio su "Vita Futurista": Peripezie di una pellicola d'avanguardia.' *Quaderni di Teatro* 9.36 (1987) 47–64.

Kipling, Rudyard. *Collected Verse of Rudyard Kipling*. New York: Doubleday, Page & Co., 1910.

Kirby, Michael. *Futurist Performance*. New York: Dutton, 1971.

Kracauer, Siegfried. *The Mass Ornament: Weimar Essays*. Trans. and ed. Thomas Y. Levin. Cambridge, MA: Harvard University Press, 1995.

Landy, Marcia. *Stardom Italian Style: Screen Performance and Personality in Italian Cinema*. Bloomington: Indiana University Press, 2008.

Lapini, Lia. *Il teatro futurista italiano*. Milan: Mursia, 1977.

Lauretta, Enzo, ed. *Il cinema e Pirandello*. Agrigento: Centro Nazionale Studi Pirandelliani, 2003.

- *Pirandello e il cinema: Atti del convegno internazionale*. Agrigento: Centro Nazionale di Studi Pirandelliani, 1978.

Leone de Castris, Arcangelo. *Storia di Pirandello*. Bari: Laterza, 1962.

Lista, Giovanni. *Cinema e fotografia futurista*. Milan: Skira, 2001.

- *Il cinema futurista*. Recco, Genoa: Le mani, 2010.

- 'Un inedito marinettiano: "Velocità," film futurista.' In Boschi and Manzoli 6–14.

- 'An Unpublished Work by Marinetti: "Speed," Futurist Film.' In Boschi and Manzoli 139–42.

Livio, Gigi. *Il teatro in rivolta: Futurismo, grottesco, Pirandello e pirandellismo*. Milan: Mursia, 1976.

Lorenzini, Niva. 'Itinerario attraverso le fonti del *Forse che sì forse che no*.' In Granatella 165–71.

Maciste. Dir. Romano Luigi Borgnetto and Vincenzo Denizot. Perf. Bartolomeo
     Pagano et al. Itala Film, 1915.
Maciste alpino. Dir. Romano Luigi Borgnetto and Luigi Maggi. Perf. Bartolomeo
     Pagano et al. Itala Film, 1916.
Mallach, Alan. *Pietro Mascagni and His Operas.* Boston: Northeastern University
     Press, 2002.
Marabini Moevs, Maria Teresa. *Gabriele D'Annunzio e le estetiche della fine del
     secolo.* L'Acquila: L.U. Japadre, 1976.
Marcus, Millicent. 'Anton Giulio Bragaglia's *Thaïs,* or, The Death of the *Diva*
     + the Rise of the *Scenoplastica* = The Birth of Futurist Cinema.' *South Central
     Review* 13.2–3 (1996) 63–81.
Marinetti, Filippo Tommaso. *Critical Writings.* Ed. Günter Berghaus. Trans.
     Doug Thompson. New York: Farrar, Straus and Giroux, 2006.
– *Let's Murder the Moonshine: Selected Writings.* Ed. R.W. Flint. Trans. R.W. Flint
     and Arthur A. Coppotelli. Los Angeles: Sun & Moon Press, 1991.
– 'Speed.' In Boschi and Manzoli 143–47.
– 'Velocità.' In Boschi and Manzoli 15–25.
Marinetti, Filippo Tommaso, et al. *Teoria e invenzione futurista.* Ed. Luciano De
     Maria. 3rd ed. Milan: Mondadori, 1996.
Marzot, Giulio. *Il decadentismo italiano.* Bologna: Cappelli, 1970.
Mazzuoli, Enrico. 'Attori e attrici nei film dannunziani.' *Quaderni del Vittoriale*
     4 (1977) 37–44.
Merrit, Russell. 'L'uomo che rubò la "Gioconda": Introduzione,' 'The Man
     Who Stole the Gioconda: Introduction.' *Griffithiana* 21.64 (1998) 50–9.
Milioto, Stefano. 'A proposito di cinema . . . ' In *Pirandello e D'Annunzio,* ed.
     Enzo Lauretta, 233–48. Palermo: Palumbo, 1989.
Moses, Gavriel. 'Film Theory as Literary Genre in Pirandello and the Film-
     Novel.' *Annali d'Italianistica* 6 (1988) 38–68.
– *The Nickel Was for the Movies: Film in the Novel from Pirandello to Puig.* Berkeley:
     University of California Press, 1995.
Musatti, Cesare. *Scritti sul cinema.* Ed. Dario F. Romano. Turin: Testo e imma-
     gine, 2000.
Nesbit, Molly. 'The Rat's Ass.' *October* 56 (1991) 6–20.
O'Rawe, Catherine. *Authorial Echoes: Textuality and Self-Plagiarism in the
     Narrative of Luigi Pirandello.* London: Legenda, 2005.
Palmieri, Eugenio Ferdinando. *Vecchio cinema italiano.* 1940. Vicenza: Neri
     Pozza, 1994.
Paradiso, Giuseppe. *Pirandello psicoanalitico.* 2nd ed. Catania: EPC, 1995.
Patanè, Mario. 'Una certa idea di cinema.' In Genovese and Gesù, vol. 1: 7–9.
Perloff, Marjorie. *The Futurist Moment: Avant-Garde, Avant Guerre, and the
     Language of Rupture.* Chicago: University of Chicago Press, 1986.

Pirandello, Luigi. *On Humor*. Trans. and ed. Antonio Illiano and Daniel P. Testa. Chapel Hill: University of North Carolina Press, 1974.

– *Quaderni di Serafino Gubbio operatore*. Milan: Garzanti, 1999.

– *Saggi, poesie, scritti varii*. Ed. Manlio Lo Vecchio-Musti. 5th ed. Milan: Mondadori, 1993.

– *Shoot!: The Notebooks of Serafino Gubbio, Cinematograph Operator*. Trans. C.K. Scott Moncrieff. 1926. Chicago: University of Chicago Press, 2005.

– *Tutti i romanzi*. Vol. 2. Ed. Giovanni Macchia. Milan: Mondadori, 1973.

'Il più bizzarro spettacolo pro "famiglie dei richiamati" Domenica 28 Gennaio.' *Il Nuovo Giornale* [Florence], 22 Jan. 1917: 3.

Poe, Edgar Allan. *Selected Tales: With an Introduction by Kenneth Graham*. Ed. Douglas Grant. London: Oxford University Press, 1967.

Poggioli, Renato. *The Theory of the Avant-Garde*. Cambridge, MA: Harvard University Press, 1968.

Praz, Mario. *The Romantic Agony*. Trans. Angus Davidson. New York: Meridian Books, 1967.

'Il primo esperimento di "cinematografia futurista" al Teatro Niccolini.' *Il Nuovo Giornale* [Florence], 25 Jan. 1917: 3.

Proust, Marcel. *Le temps retrouvé*. 1927. *À la recherche du temps perdu III*, 689–1048. Ed. Pierre Clarac and André Ferré. Bruges: Librairie Gallimard, 1954.

Raffaelli, Sergio. *Il cinema nella lingua di Pirandello*. Rome: Bulzoni, 1993.

– 'Il D'Annunzio prosatore nelle didascalie dei suoi film.' *Quaderni del Vittoriale* 4 (1977) 45–53.

Rainey, Lawrence. 'The Creation of the Avant-Garde: F. T. Marinetti and Ezra Pound.' In Rainey and von Hallberg 195–219.

Rainey, Lawrence, and Robert von Hallberg, eds. *Marinetti and the Italian Futurists*. Special issue of *Modernism / Modernity* 1.3 (1994) 1–302.

'Le rappresentazioni futuriste al Niccolini.' *Il Nuovo Giornale* [Florence], 29 Jan. 1917: 3.

Read, John. *The Alchemist in Life, Literature and Art*. New York: Thomas Nelson and Sons, 1947.

Renzi, Lisetta. 'Grandezza e morte della "femme fatale."' In Renzi 121–30.

Renzi, Renzo, ed. *Sperduto nel buio: Il cinema muto italiano e il suo tempo (1905–1930)*. Bologna: Cappelli, 1991.

Roncoroni, Federico. 'L'ultimo romanzo.' In Granatella 197–218.

Rondolino, Gianni. 'Gli impacchi taumaturgici dei miti di celluloide.' In *Gabriele D'Annunzio: Grandezza e delirio nell'industria dello spettacolo: Atti del Convegno Internazionale, Torino, 21–23 marzo 1988*, Centro Regionale Universitario per il Teatro del Piemonte, 213–28. Genoa: Costa & Nolan, 1989.

Rood, Arnold, ed. *Gordon Craig on Movement and Dance*. By Edward Gordon Craig. London: Doance Books, 1977.

Salaris, Claudia. *Marinetti: Arte e vita futurista*. Rome: Riuniti, 1997.
– 'Marketing Modernism: Marinetti as Publisher.' Trans. Lawrence Rainey. In Rainey and von Hallberg 109–27.
Salinari, Carlo. *Miti e coscienza del decadentismo italiano: D'Annunzio, Pascoli, Fogazzaro e Pirandello*. Milan: Feltrinelli, 1986.
Sassoon, Donald. *Becoming Mona Lisa: The Making of a Global Icon*. New York: Harcourt, 2001.
Schnapp, Jeffrey T. 'Propeller Talk.' In Rainey and von Hallberg 153–78.
Seigel, Jerold. *The Private Worlds of Marcel Duchamp*. Berkeley: University of California Press, 1995.
Sherrard, Phillip. 'Cavafy's Sensual City: A Question.' *The Mind and Art of C. P. Cavafy: Essays on His Life and Work*, 94–9. Athens: Denise Harvey & Co., 1983.
Sitney, P. Adams. 'The Autobiography of a Metonymy.' In Luigi Pirandello, *Shoot!: The Notebooks of Serafino Gubbio, Cinematograph Operator*, trans. C.K. Scott Moncrieff, 1926. Chicago: University of Chicago Press, 2005. 223–33.
Smith, William, ed. *A Dictionary of Greek and Roman Biography and Mythology*. Vol. 3. London: John Murray, 1880.
Somigli, Luca. *Legitimizing the Artist: Manifesto Writing and European Modernism, 1885–1915*. Toronto: University of Toronto Press, 2003.
Spackman, Barbara. *Decadent Genealogies: The Rhetoric of Sickness from Baudelaire to D'Annunzio*. Ithaca: Cornell University Press, 1989.
'Gli spettacoli futuristi al Niccolini pro famiglie dei richiamati.' *La Nazione* [Florence], 29 Jan. 1917: 3.
Stone, Jennifer. 'Cineastes' Texts.' *Yearbook of the British Pirandello Society* 3 (1983) 45–66.
Strauven, Wanda. *Marinetti e il cinema: Tra attrazione e sperimentazione*. Pasian di Prato: Campanotto, 2006.
Syrimis, Michael. 'Decadent Repetitions, Technological Variations, in Gabriele D'Annunzio's *Forse che sì forse che no*.' *Romance Notes* 45.2 (2005) 141–50.
– 'Film, Spectators, and War in Italian Futurism.' In *Italian Cultural Studies 2001: Selected Essays*, ed. Anthony Julian Tamburri et al., 168–85. Boca Raton, FL: Bordighera Press, 2004.
– 'The Humoristic Lens in Pirandello's *Si gira*.' *Journal of the Pirandello Society of America* 21 (2008) 45–63.
– 'Mona Lisa's Gaze: D'Annunzio, Cinema, and the "Aura."' *Quaderni d'Italianistica* 27.1 (2006) 69–88.
Taylor, F. Sherwood. *The Alchemists: Founders of Modern Chemistry*. New York: Henry Schuman, 1949.

'Teatri di questa sera.' *Il Giornale d'Italia* [Rome], 14 June 1917: 3.

'Teatri di Roma.' *Il Travaso delle Idee* [Rome], 17 June 1917: n.p.

Teatro dell'Opera, ed. *Dal Costanzi al Teatro dell'Opera, 1880–1968*. Rome: ATENA, 1969.

Termine, Liborio. 'La costruzione del sogno e dell'infelicità: Commento alle lettere di Luigi Pirandello a Marta Abba sul cinema.' In Giovanni Verga et al., *Il cinema e la vergogna: Negli scritti di Verga, Bontempelli, Pirandello*, ed. Ira Fabbri, Chiara Simonigh, and Liborio Termine, 215–60. Turin: Testo & immagine, 1998.

– *Pirandello e la drammaturgia del film*. Turin: Fiornovelli, 1997.

Tessari, Roberto. *Il mito della macchina: Letteratura e industria nel primo Novecento italiano*. Milan: Mursia, 1973.

Tilgher, Adriano. *Studi sul teatro contemporaneo*. 3rd ed. Rome: Libreria di Scienze e Lettere, 1928.

Vaccari, Walter. *Vita e tumulti di F. T. Marinetti*. Milan: Omnia, 1959.

Valentini, Valentina. *Un fanciullo delicato e forte: Il cinema di Gabriele D'Annunzio*. Rome: Biblioteca del Vascello, 1995.

Valesio, Paolo. *Gabriele D'Annunzio: The Dark Flame*. Trans. Marilyn Migiel. New Haven: Yale University Press, 1992.

Vaughan, Dai. 'Let There Be Lumière.' In Elsaesser 63–7.

Verdone, Mario. *Cinema e letteratura del futurismo*. Rome: Centro Sperimentale di Cinematografia, Edizioni di Bianco e Nero, 1968.

– 'I film di D'Annunzio e da D'Annunzio.' *Quaderni del Vittoriale* 4 (1977) 13–27.

– 'Gabriele D'Annunzio nel cinema italiano.' *Bianco e Nero* 24.7–8 (1963) 1–21.

– *Il movimento futurista*. Rome: Lucarini, 1986.

Verdone, Mario, ed. *Manifesti futuristi e scritti teorici di Arnaldo Ginna e Bruno Corra*. Ravenna: Longo Editore, 1984.

Verdone, Mario, and Günter Berghaus. '"Vita futurista" and Early Futurist Cinema.' In *International Futurism in Arts and Literature*, ed. Günter Berghaus, 398–421. New York: Walter de Gruyter, 2000.

Vettori, Alessandro. 'Serafino Gubbio's Candid Camera.' *MLN* 113.1 (1998) 79–107.

'Vita futurista.' *La Nazione* [Florence], 15 May 1916: 6.

Wohl, Robert. *A Passion for Wings: Aviation and the Western Imagination 1908–1918*. New Haven: Yale University Press, 1994.

Woodhouse, John. *Gabriele D'Annunzio: Defiant Archangel*. Oxford: Clarendon Press, 1998.

Index